AF580943

# JUST BE

Jamie Klusacek

tiny wonder
PUBLISHING

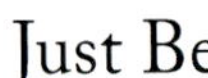




Published in 2020 by Tiny Wonder Publishing
Printed in the United States
First Printing, 2020

ISBN: 978-1-7361181-0-8 Paperback
ISBN: 978-1-7361181-2-2 Hardcover
ISBN: 978-1-7361181-1-5 eBook
Library of Congress Control Number: 2020922950

Cover and Interior Design: Milan Klusacek
Cover Photo: Matheus Bertelli

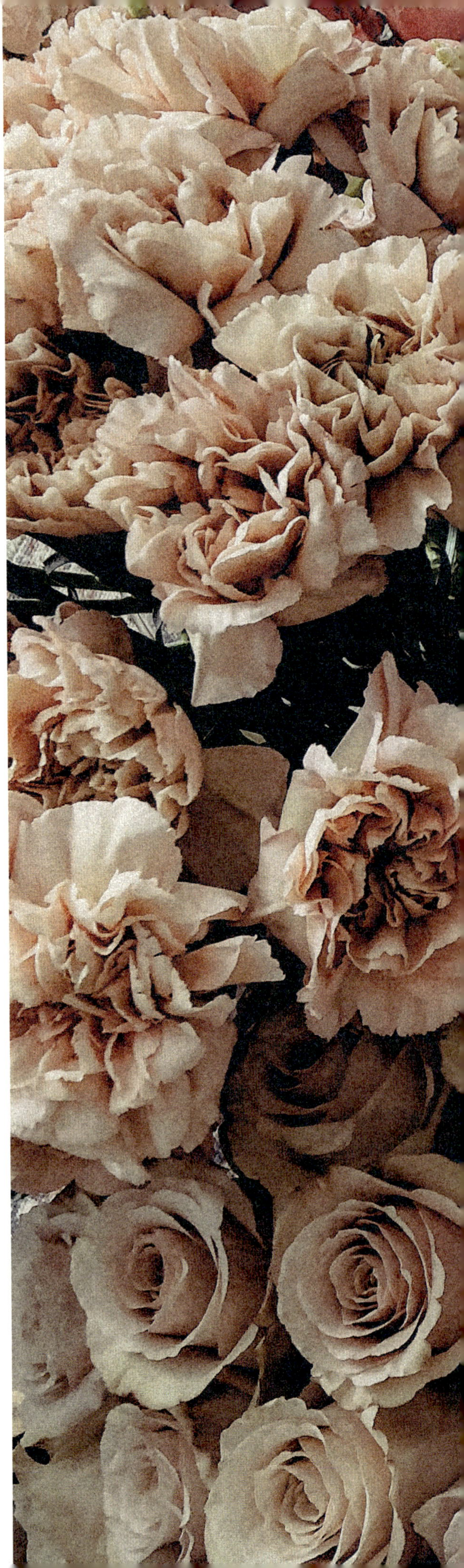

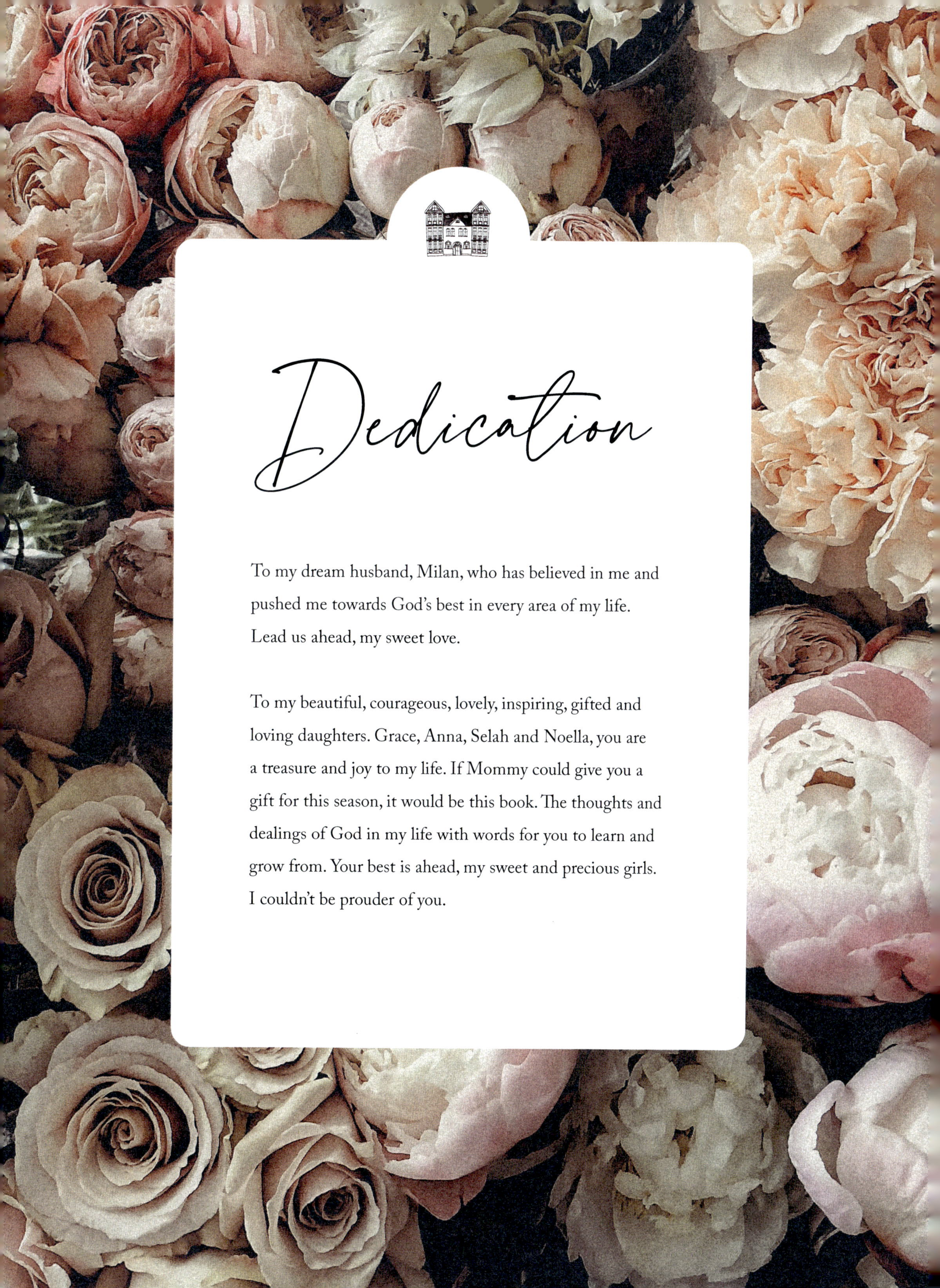

# Dedication

To my dream husband, Milan, who has believed in me and pushed me towards God's best in every area of my life. Lead us ahead, my sweet love.

To my beautiful, courageous, lovely, inspiring, gifted and loving daughters. Grace, Anna, Selah and Noella, you are a treasure and joy to my life. If Mommy could give you a gift for this season, it would be this book. The thoughts and dealings of God in my life with words for you to learn and grow from. Your best is ahead, my sweet and precious girls. I couldn't be prouder of you.

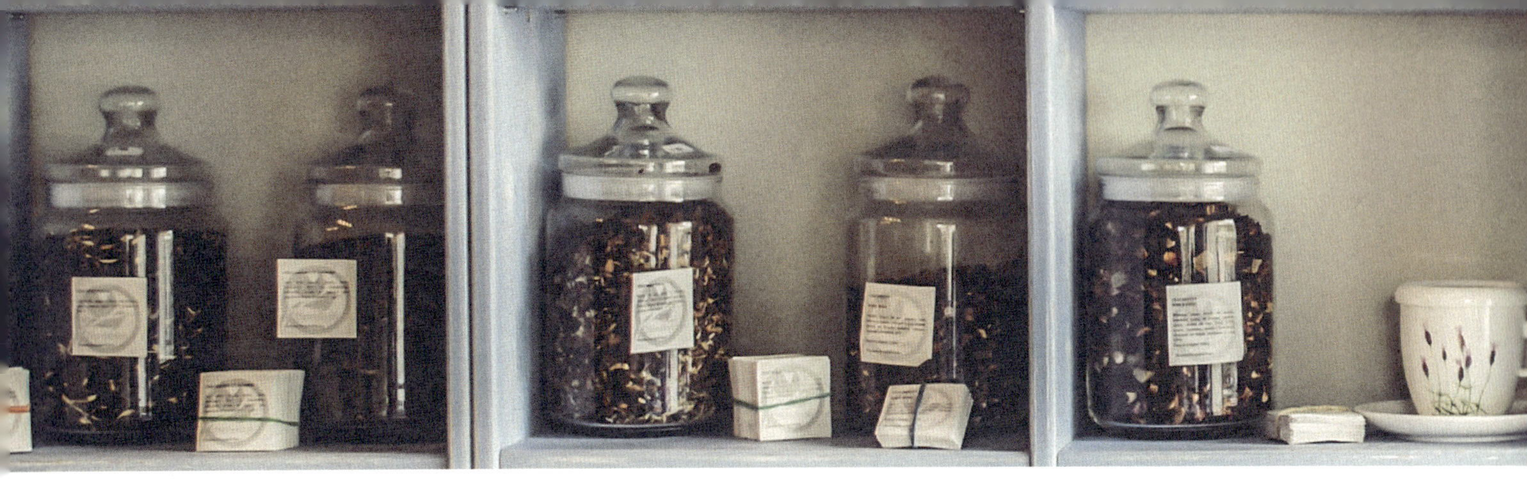

# TABLE OF CONTENTS

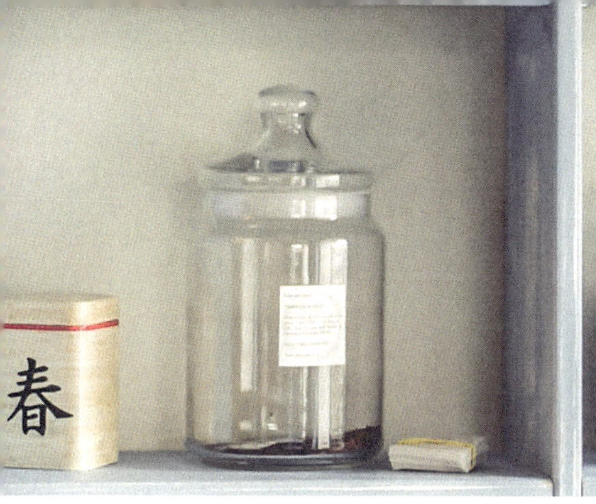
春
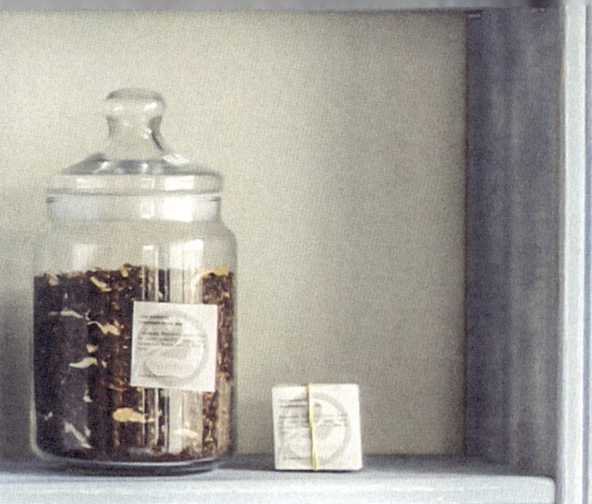
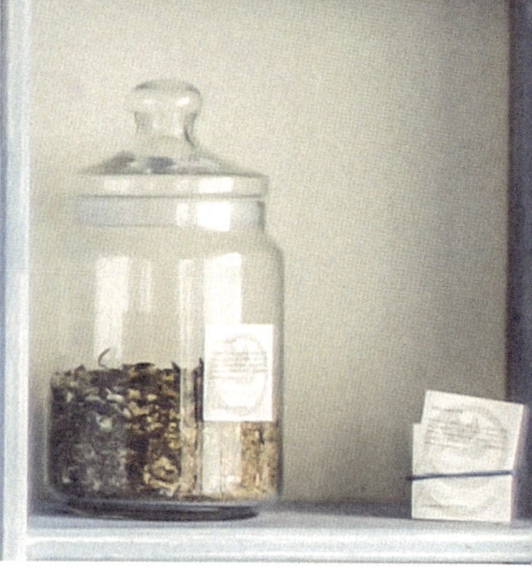

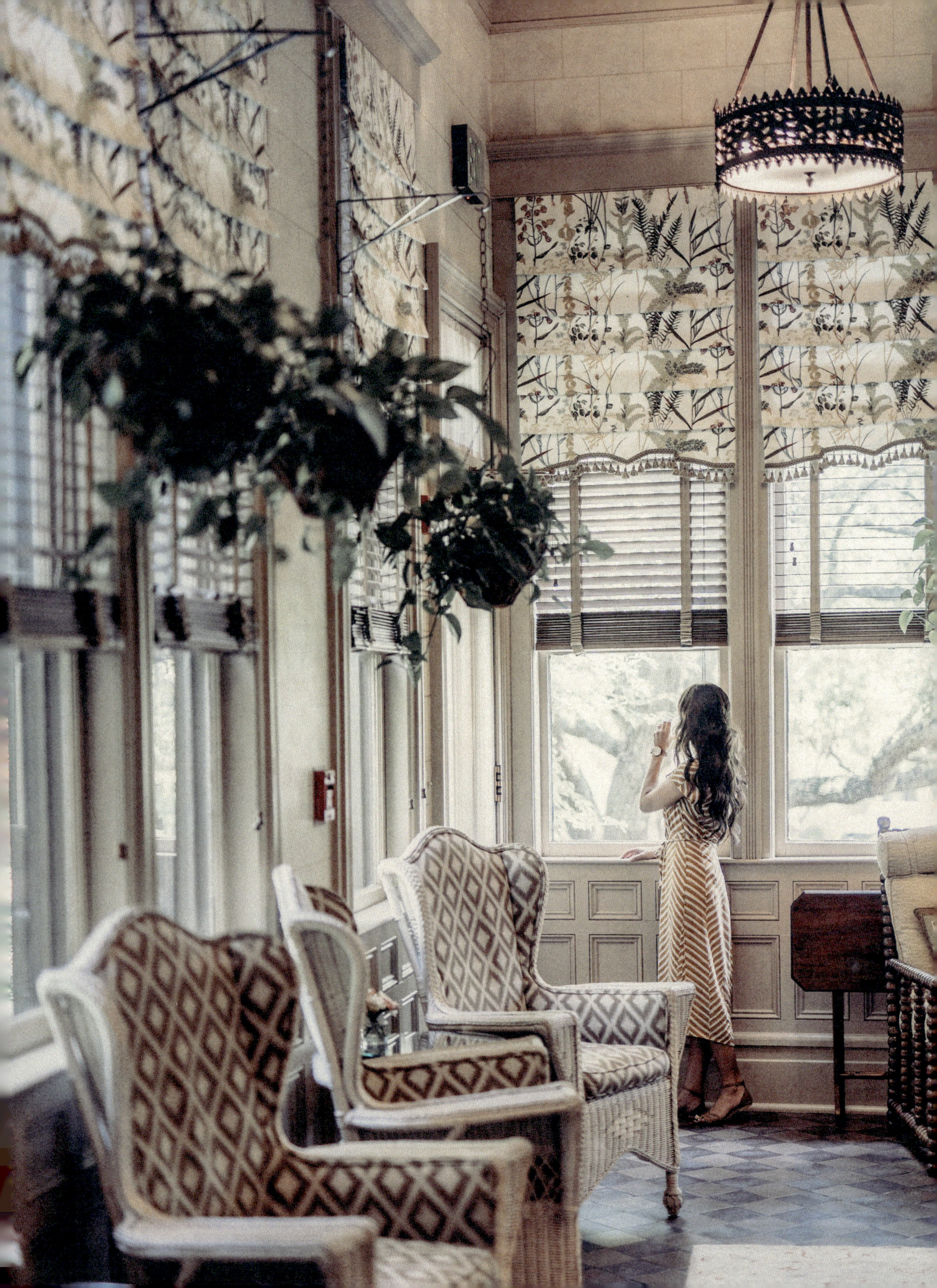

# Before you read this book

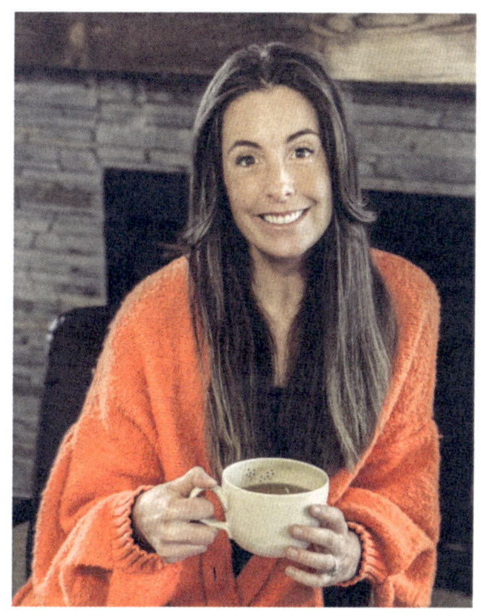

Make your favorite cup of tea and read the book of Ruth. It's only four chapters. Trust me, it will be worth it! Use it as a foundation for your understanding as you read this book.

Get a set of really cool non-bleeding colorful markers to highlight and underline your way throughout the pages. Pigma Micron markers are my favorite non-bleeding brand! You can get a set on Amazon or in person at Hobby Lobby.

Be prepared for God to speak to your heart. Get a journal or take notes in the margins. If you're the journaling type, Designworks Ink journals are currently my favorite. If you like to write in your books, we've intentionally created room for you to scribble your way through the pages! Draw pictures, take notes or simply highlight what God is speaking to your heart. Enjoy!

-Jamie

CHAPTER ONE

# JUST BE *Unfiltered*

AN HONEST LOOK AT ME

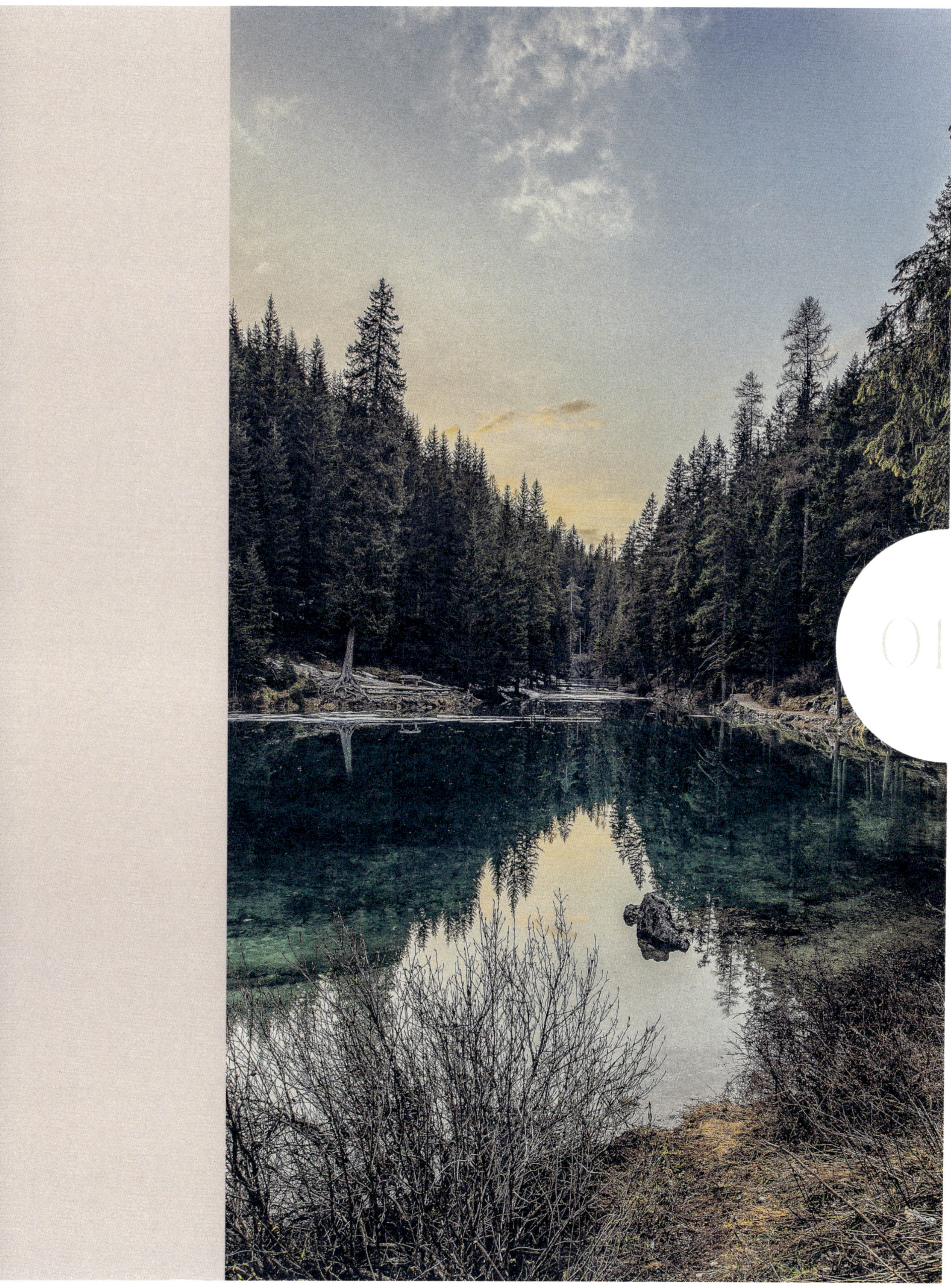

01

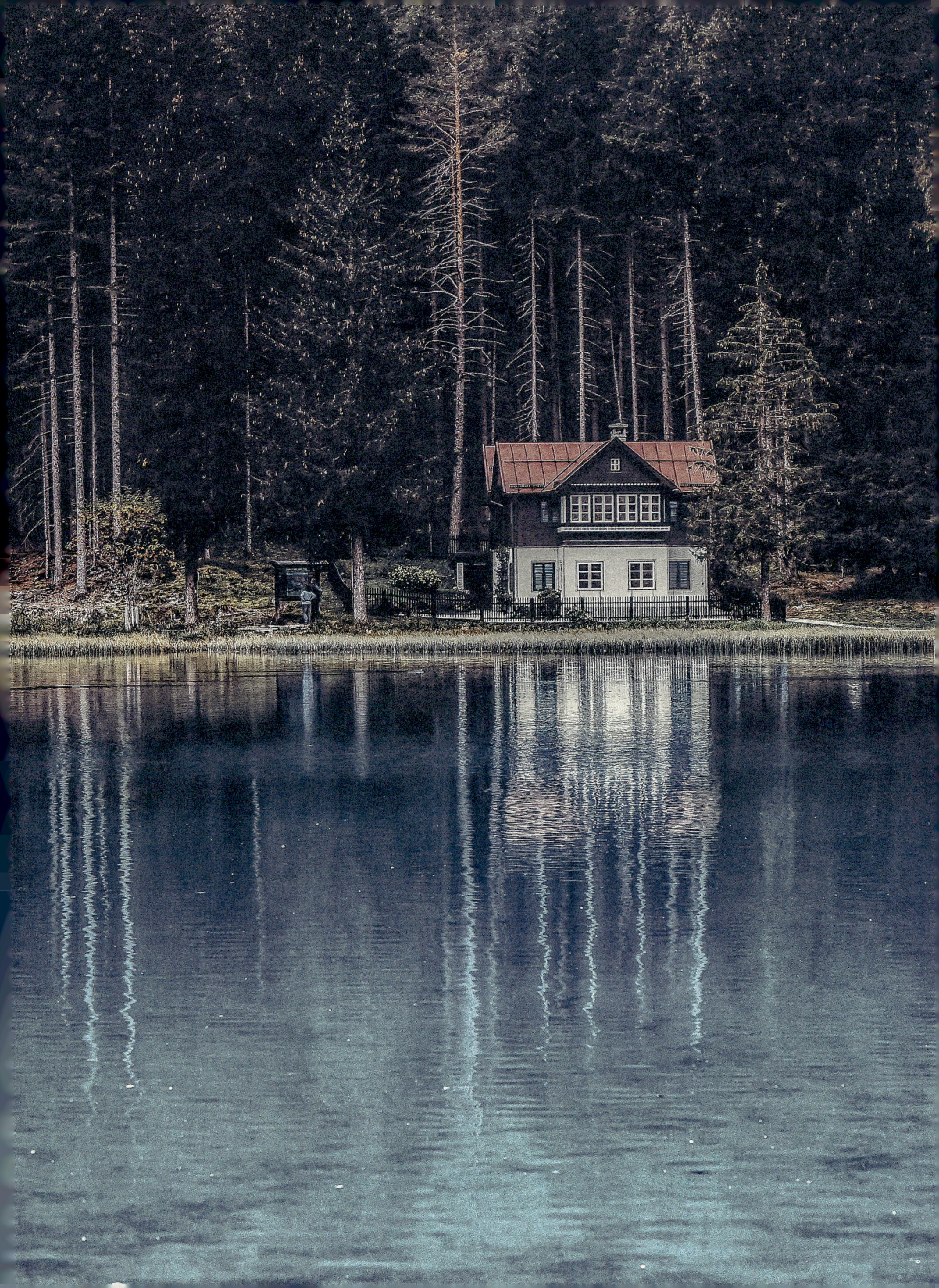

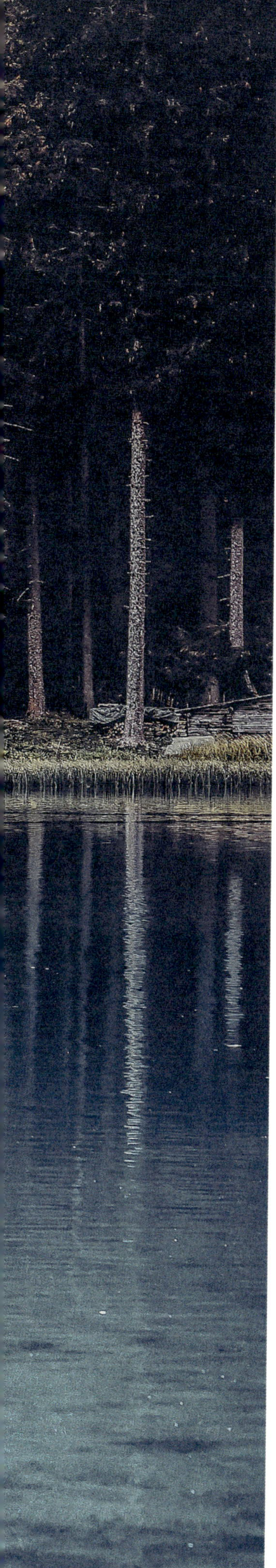

You timidly tiptoe your way across my front lawn as if unwilling to disturb a single blade of grass highlighted by patches of brilliantly white snow. I love you already. Hair gently touches your face as the wind blows tiny tendrils across your beautiful forehead. You clutch your bag with both arms in anticipation or perhaps preparation for what is ahead. I see an uncertainty in your eyes as I watch you discreetly from my expansive front window. What are you hoping happens in our time together, I wonder? Is your heart as expectant as mine? Do you know, as I do, what lavish life lies beyond our discussions today? You make your way noiselessly to my front door and pause a moment before gently pressing the doorbell. I can't believe you're actually here, in my home! I take a minute to compose my excitement and then open wide the front door. I greet you with the biggest smile I can muster.

*"Welcome, my sweet friend,"* I say as I hug you tightly. You feel like a little marshmallow in your precious winter coat. *"I'm glad you could finally make it,"* I add soothingly.

*"Me, too,"* you respond quietly. *"Me, too."*

You take off your coat and lay it on the cherry red Pottery Barn sofa in my front sitting room. The cool winter breeze is gone, but a memory. In its place, warmth from the crackling fireplace envelops us, beckoning us onward into the family room. You are home. Our eyes lock on each other for a moment. No more words are spoken, only an unwavering knowingness that the miraculous is going to happen in our lives today—if we let it. And so our day together begins.

Can I start out by telling you that I don't have it all figured out? I am now forty, which in human years sounds ancient. An apology to my older readers out there, but my fifteen-year-old self just takes over sometimes. I can remember the dialogue in my head when I saw a forty-year-old at the age of fifteen, and "spring chicken" wasn't the first phrase that came to mind—maybe more like old, spent or wrinkled. In all honesty, "prune" also may have been a descriptive word.

I have four beautifully gorgeous daughters, an amazingly brilliant husband, and still at times I feel like my life is nowhere near where I thought it would be. In many ways, that's a good thing, a great thing, a God thing. But in other ways I wonder if I'm doing enough.

On the mom side of things, am I connecting with my kids? Am I teaching them about God and what it looks like to have a relationship with Him? Do they really know how loved and valued they are, not just by a mama and papa who love them, but by a Heavenly Father who loves them more than they could ever know? Am I speaking words of life into their lives and leaning into their purpose? Am I really fulfilling my mom and wife duties, or at least fulfilling what I think they should be?

Take family mealtime for example. Is it healthy for my children to have cereal for dinner five nights in a row? I mean, let's be real. Maybe I will try to feed them some more well-balanced meals in the future. Life happens and when I'm not on my A-game, things begin to unravel—and that's just the mom side.

Then there's the wife side. My husband is amazing, I've gotta say. He is a living example of the concept that you can get better with age. He's more attractive and in shape now at forty-two than he was at thirty. God has blessed me! He works with excellence on many different fronts. He's a game-changer in the best sense of the word. Because I notice his hard work and I love him so much, I feel a responsibility there too. Am I leaning into our marriage the way God is asking me to? Am I taking care of him? Am I encouraging him enough? Have I made dinner for him this past week and packed his lunches, or is he starving on the side of 16th Street in downtown Denver because I've been slacking? Yes, we live in Denver, one of the top destination cities in the United States. It feels like it's buzzing here with all the people coming and going. And that in and of itself can add a new set of pressures, or rather, expectations. Just being real here.

"I BELIEVE THIS BOOK IS GOING TO BE FREEING FOR YOU AND FOR ME."

Then there is the personal dream side of things, the ministry dreams, and God-sized dreams rolling around in my heart. Coupled with that come questions like, am I serving in church enough? Am I serving too much? Am I encouraging, uplifting and building people's lives? Am I developing team members the way that I should? Am I truly mining for the gifts and talents that God has given to those around me and pushing them towards their destiny in God? Am I personally growing into the person that God created me to be or am I somehow missing His best for me? Am I really doing this for God, or for some sense of accomplishment and acceptance from people? How do I even know if I am hitting the mark? Am I sure that I am hearing His voice, or was that just a personal desire in my heart? Is it a great idea for me, or just a great principle for someone else? Bottom line, am I fulfilling God's purpose for my life?

If you've ever asked yourself any of these questions, welcome to the club! The crazy thing is, the same questions I ask myself now, I also asked myself in different forms when I was an eighteen-year-old about to enter college, or at age twenty-five when I was trying to make career decisions. It's the same aching feeling—that desire to discover and fulfill God's best for my life in this world.

"IT'S WHO YOU ARE AND WHAT YOU ARE BECOMING THAT COUNTS BEFORE GOD."

In all honesty, I'm not sure that desire will ever go away. I can say, though, through a series of yeses to God in each season, you can and will grow stronger in the journey. I am nowhere near where I was five or ten years ago. A newfound faith, purpose and contentment holds on to me stronger than it ever has. And this is the place I write to you from now. You can reach a place in your faith where the questions of the unknown no longer control your thoughts, actions and perceptions. Instead, they vanish in the vastness of who God is and His control over your life.

I believe this book is going to be freeing for you and for me. Like diving into a cool mountain lake buck-naked with no one watching. Yes, I said naked in my first chapter. I'm not sure if that's the correct thing to do, but it is what it is. Body-flubber-fear completely gone. No glaring eyes judging us. Feeling the fresh water kiss our skin with no restraints and nothing covering us that wasn't meant to be there. And then, when we finally emerge from the water, we open our eyes wide to see the most beautiful scenery we could ever imagine. Calm. Serene. No shame. No worries. No weights.

### *Just me, being me.*

So here's the heart of this book: it's not your occupation or station in life that defines you, it's ***who you are*** and ***what you are becoming*** that counts before God. It's staying true to who God made YOU to be and allowing Him to shape you on the inside, no matter what the season. Our circumstances will change, opportunities will come and go, but if we can manage to *Just Be* no matter where we are, no

"GOD HAS INVESTED ENTIRELY TOO MUCH IN YOU FOR YOU TO BE COMFORTABLE IN ANYTHING LESS THAN YOU WERE CREATED TO BE."

-T.D. Jakes

matter what comes our way—to *Just Be* the person on the inside that God wants us to be—the game will change, freedom will come, and EVERY promise of God will fall into place.

This book is about ***character***. It's about breathing deeply. It's about release and trust and enjoying the God who made you for this journey called life. And for those Type A personalities, just chill. This isn't a list of "must-do's" that you need to accomplish this month. That would totally negate the purpose of this book. Rather, it is about the character traits God is working in me in every season, over time. Though my outward is far from perfect, God is wanting to work on me inwardly. It's in those moments that He makes me stop and remember what my life is truly about.

I hope this helps you on the path before you. I'm so excited to start this journey with you. Now breathe deeply, friend. Take another breath, relax, and trust God.  Let's make some memories!

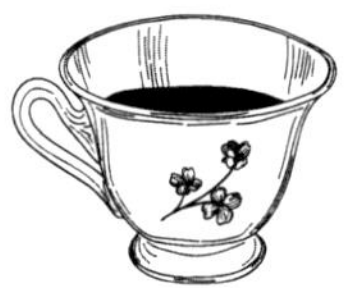

BOOK RECOMMENDATION

## Identity *by T.D. Jakes*

Discover who you were meant to be in the light of scripture. For me, T.D. Jakes is one of the most compelling, inspirational, father-like communicators of our time.

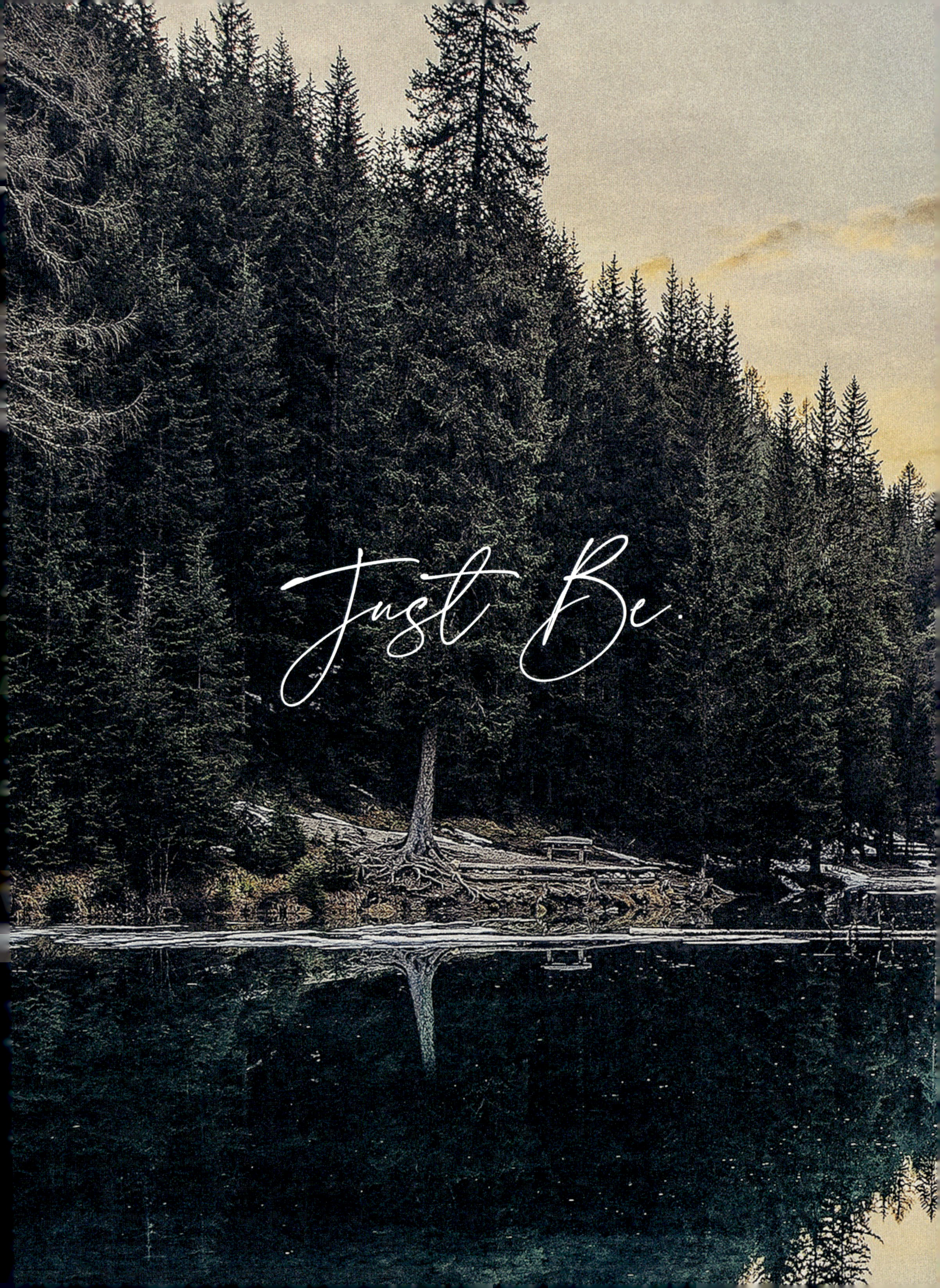
Just Be.

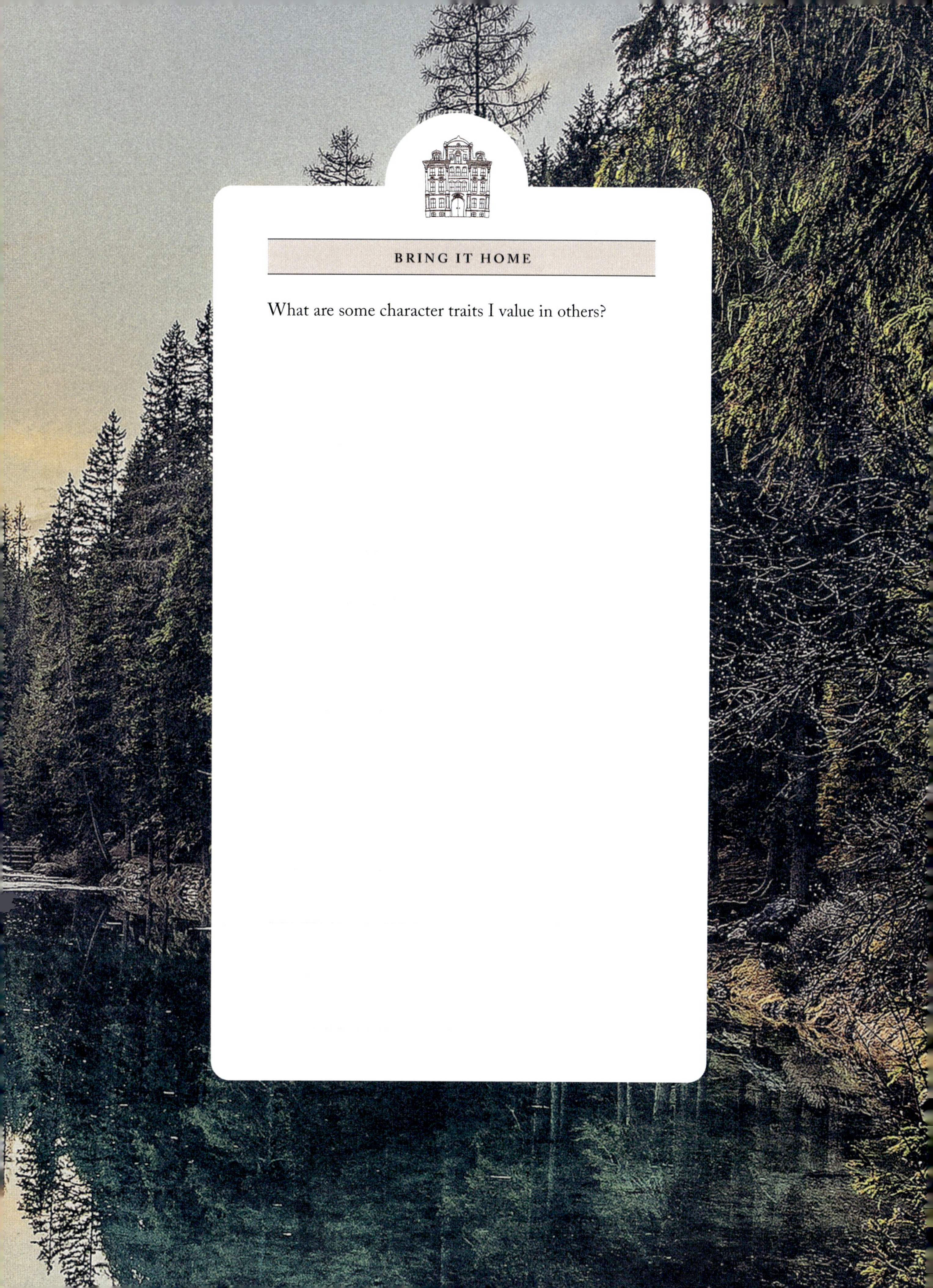

## BRING IT HOME

What are some character traits I value in others?

CHAPTER TWO

# JUST BE

# *A Blank Page*

GOD IS WRITING A BESTSELLER

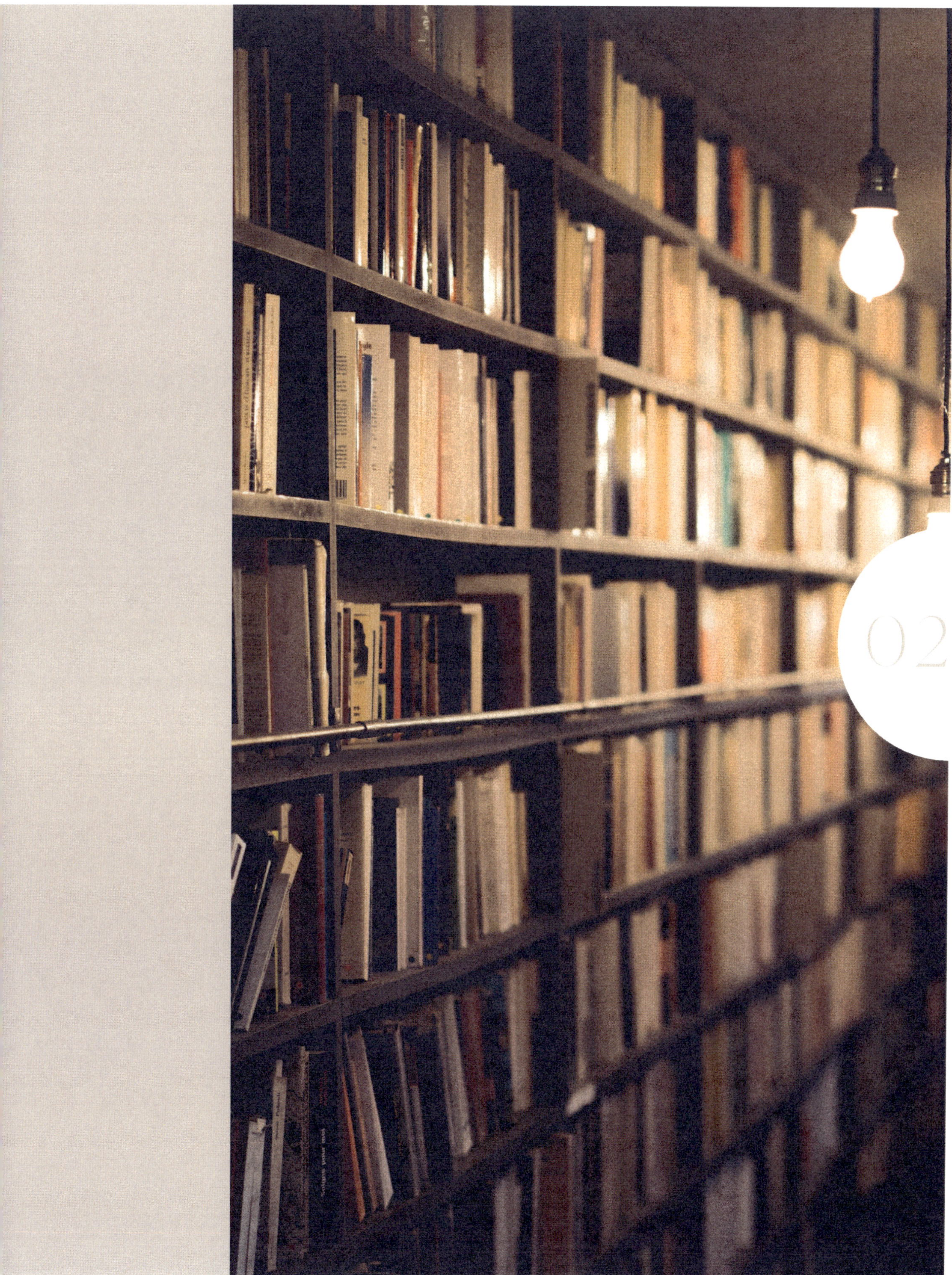

02

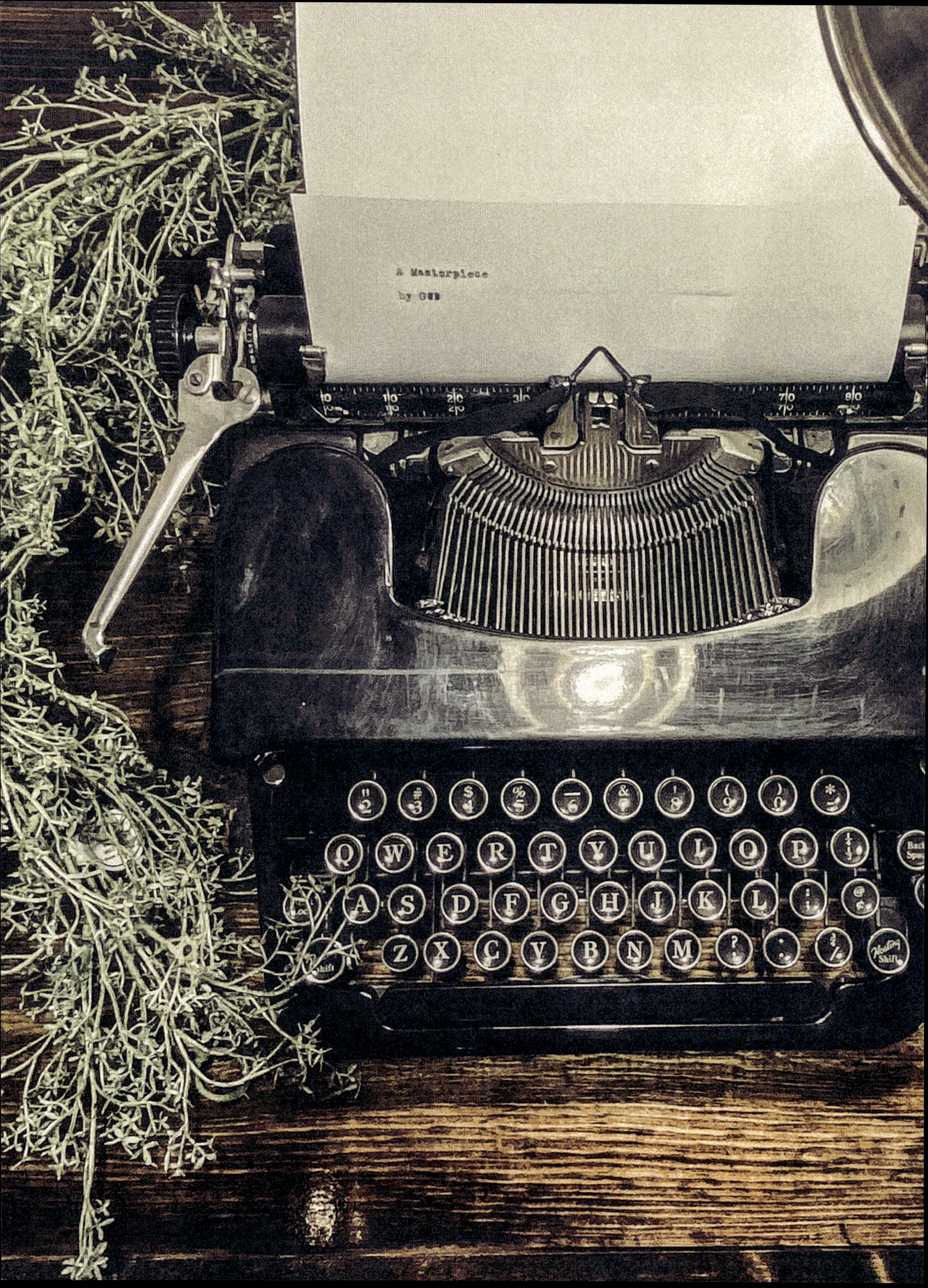
A Masterpiece
by

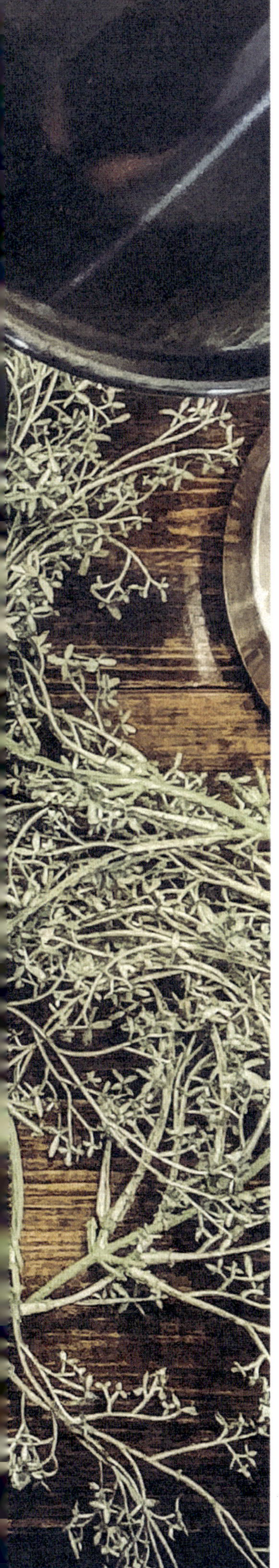

*Other* people's lives inspire me. One person's life can be full of so many lessons that you can use to benefit your own. A life is like a novel. When the one writing it is an experienced, exceptional, inspiring author, it usually has the potential to become a bestseller. An exceptional author understands his or her skill in writing. They take time to develop it and know what the world is needing through their book.[1] Better yet, they discover what will move and change the hearts of their reader. Whether through actual history or fictional stories, they touch the reader and for a brief moment in time the reader rests in the author's hands. Their hopes and dreams bare before him. The author sets a stage, which in turn determines the message that will be taught through their story. Then, when you read a novel by an author you've grown to love—one who inspires you and brings the pages or script to life—you can't help but wait in anticipation for the next book or script to be released. With each bestseller, the author becomes more well known. Their reputation precedes them.

This is why I'm dead-set on letting the greatest Author of all-time write the story of my life. In my quest to know Him, I've studied His words. I've become one of those beautifully, over-the-top-crazed-fans. I feel like I need a t-shirt made with His face on it and mine cut and pasted in next to Him, to wear around the neighborhood.[2] I've seen the books He's created in the past—each story in the Bible and the manuscripts He is currently working on—and I am fully convinced there is no better Author to write the story of my life than the One who made it all begin, God Himself.

Because I have known this Author for a good portion of my life and studied many of His countless works, I know His script can and will be the best possible script for my life. I've seen Him work and move. I've seen Him orchestrate miracles for those He loves. I've seen Him take the deepest tragedy and weave life and hope into the story to create an ending that far surpasses what had been lost. The more you get to know

"

THIS IS WHY I'M DEAD-SET ON LETTING THE GREATEST AUTHOR OF ALL-TIME WRITE THE STORY OF MY LIFE."

Him, the more you'll realize He will do the same for you.

You see, world-class authors have the big picture in mind. They understand how their hearts beat for the characters even before they come into existence. Before the ink saturates each blank page, a plan is formed, a destiny in mind. It's more about who the characters will become in their story, not so much the small details that surround them. Where they go to school, what family they were raised in, their occupation—these are all minor details. Who they are becoming on the inside is the big picture. Taking someone of insignificance and obscurity and transforming them into someone who has boot-shaking courage, honor, bravery and selflessness—that is big picture. The details surrounding them only serve as stepping stones to shape their character along the way, preparing them for the divine moments ahead where they must choose to do what is right.

God gives us a glimpse of His plan for His masterpiece in this: if you allow Him to work on the inside, in whatever way He chooses, He will get you there on the outside! If you just breathe, just be the woman or man of character and integrity that God designed you to be—day to day—God will fight your battles. He will give you wisdom when you need it for each decision you make—details. He will part the Red Sea. He will heal. He will restore. God will open the right doors—all details. God will direct your path and NO DECISION you could make will unbolt you from your CREATOR—because God works all things together for good in His stories.[3] His master script for your story will come to pass because He is sovereign, and in the secret places you are offering your life to Him as a blank page. Allow Him to shape you into the person of character and integrity He has destined for you to be behind the scenes.

So, let your life be a blank page in the hands of history's greatest Author. He is the most well-known Author of all time, by far. Stop imagining your future, stop dwelling on the past. With a heart of complete and utter abandoned surrender, offer your life to God wholly, fully. Then watch, eyes wide open with wonder at the God of the universe orchestrating a masterpiece on your behalf, for the fame of His name.

If you've started writing your own story, get out your eraser and erase everything you've written thus far. Or better yet, file it away in the circular file. Trust me, God's story for your life will far surpass

"I'M A LITTLE PENCIL IN THE HAND OF A WRITING GOD, WHO IS SENDING A LOVE LETTER TO THE WORLD."

-Mother Teresa

anything you could ever write. Why not just give Him a blank page to begin with? Let His ink hit the page of your life with an intentional fervency like you've never experienced before. May you sense His love and passionate desire for you with every pen stroke. May the destiny which lies within each page of your life be felt through every chapter.

You are a blank page on its way to becoming a masterpiece.

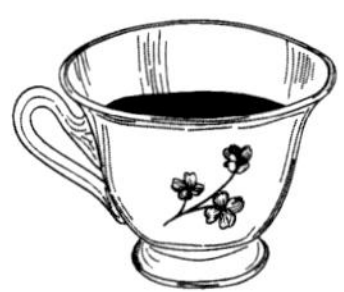

BOOK RECOMMENDATION

## Against the Tide *by Elizabeth Camden*

Elizabeth Camden writes and crafts her romantic historical fiction with detail and word choice that is beautifully intriguing. She has been an academic librarian for a good portion of her life.

JUST BREATHE

*God will fight your battles*

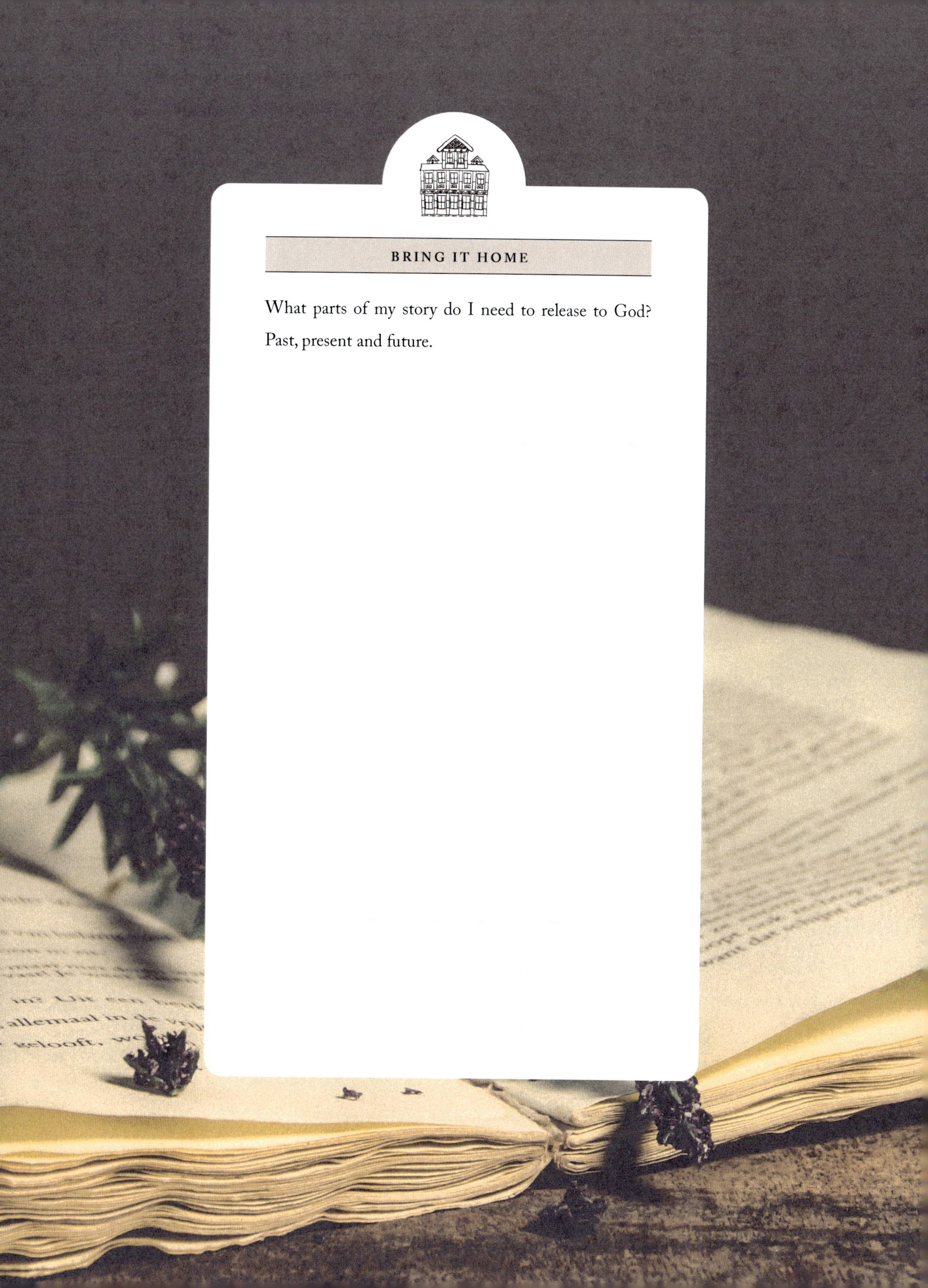

## BRING IT HOME

What parts of my story do I need to release to God? Past, present and future.

CHAPTER THREE

# JUST BE *With Him*

A MATCH MADE IN HEAVEN, LITERALLY

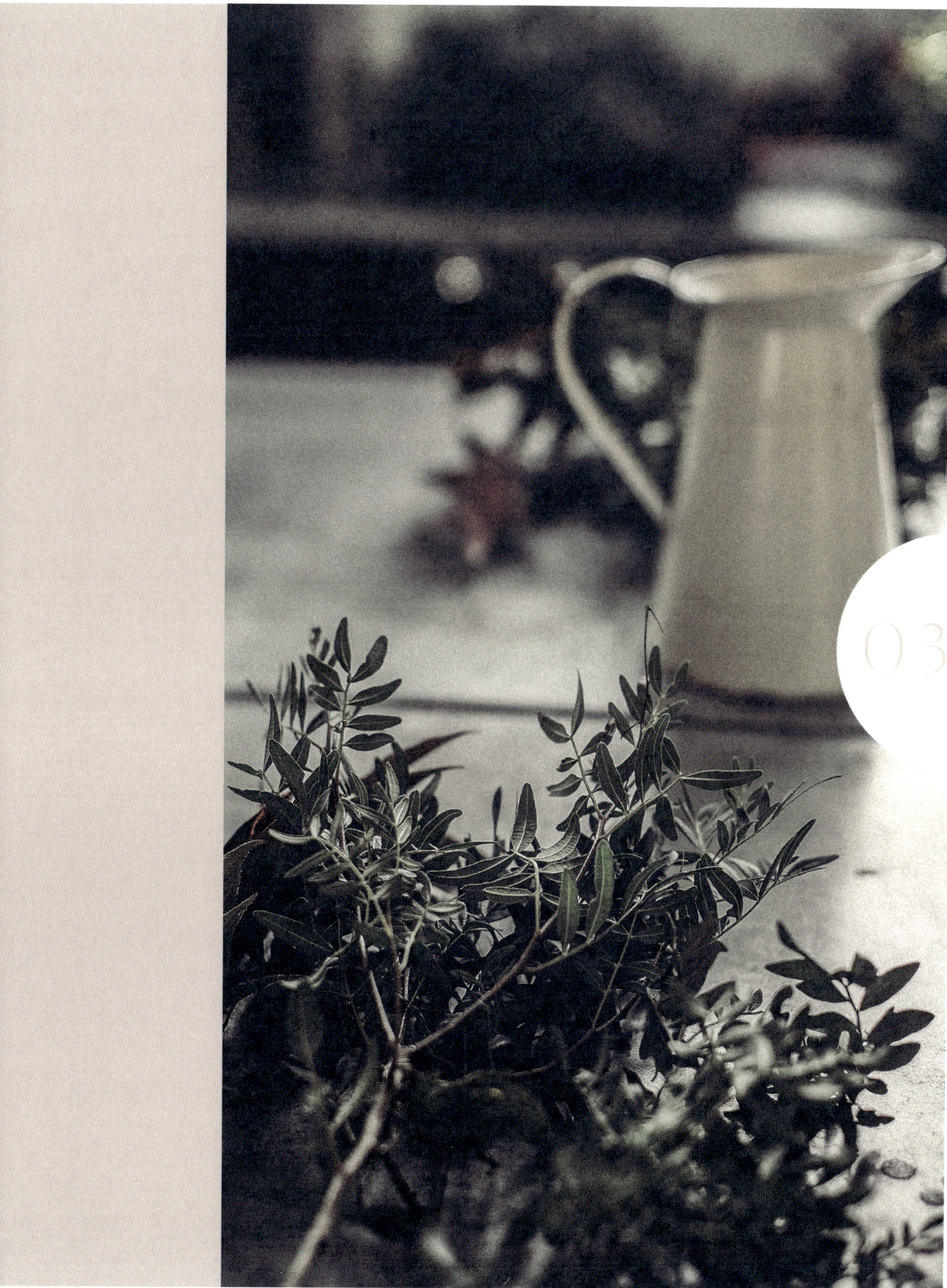

03

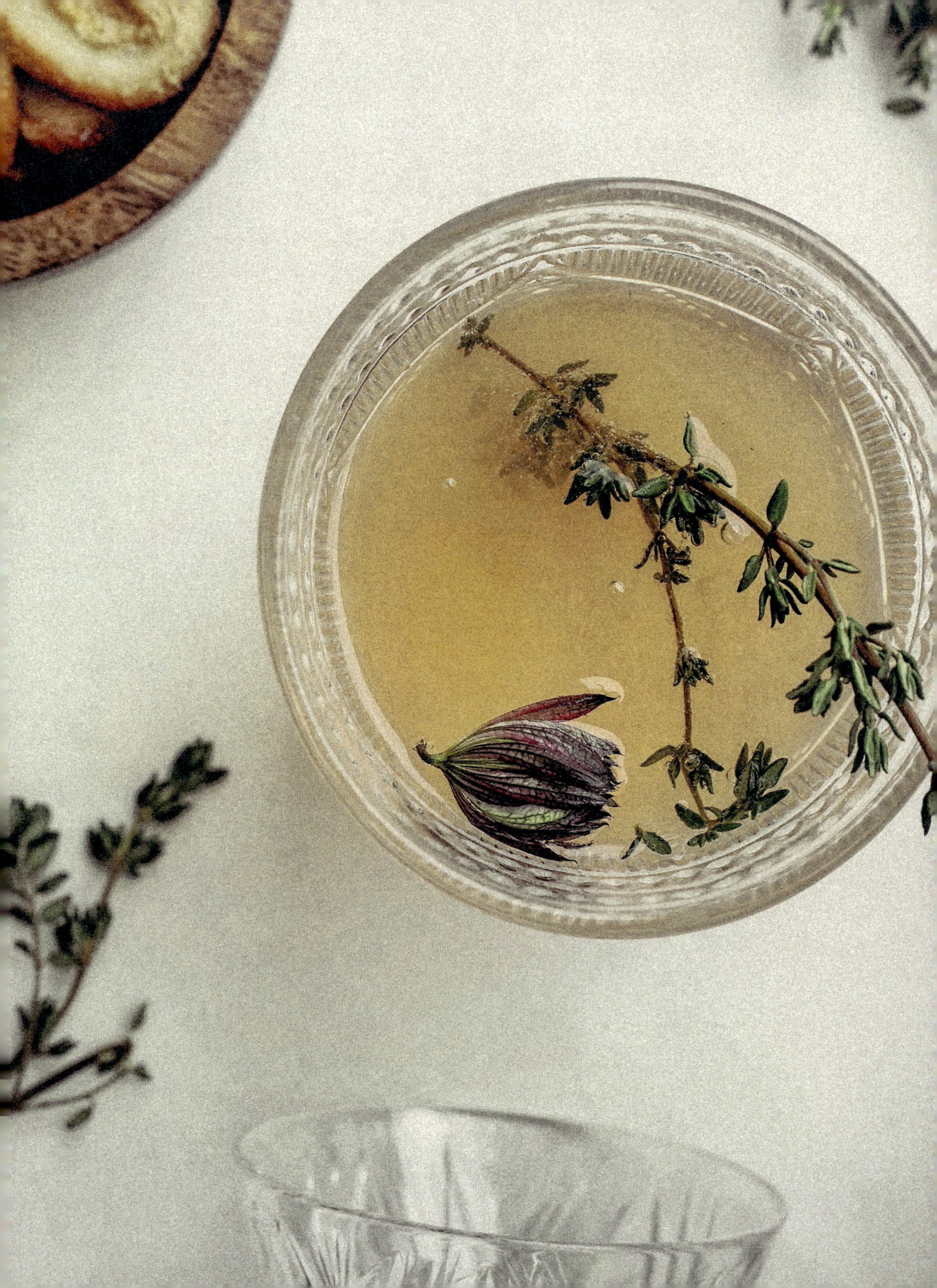

One of my favorite movies growing up was *A Little Princess* directed by Alfonso Cuarón. It's a movie based off of the classic novel by Frances Hodgson Burnett published in 1905. The movie made its debut in 1995 and inserted itself straight into my high school years, when renting VHS tapes from the local video store was a weekly ritual.

Living in a small town, we didn't have a plethora of video stores to rent from. Holly Video and the local library encompassed all of our video rental options. I remember hearing the little brass bell ring each time I entered, announcing my arrival. Sometimes I wished that bell wasn't there. I'd much rather sneak in and take my time searching for the perfect picture film without having watchful eyes on me. I would begin browsing the rows of VHS tapes like a treasure hunter, searching for the film I would choose to rent. I had to make sure it was appropriate for my two younger sisters, of course, or there would be no way in God's green earth my mother would allow me to watch it. Enter *A Little Princess*.[4]

I was usually drawn to old love stories, those with Doris Day, Gene Kelly, Clark Gable, or Debbie Reynolds, but somehow *A Little Princess* sparked my interest. After watching it, I was deeply moved. Having recently encountered God at the age of fourteen, it became a personal internal picture of my encounter with Jesus.

It is the story of a young girl, Sara, who lives with her father in Africa on the cusp of World War I. She loves her father very much, but when her father is bound to fight in the war, she gets sent off to a boarding school for safety. Not long after Sara's arrival she receives a letter that her father is missing in action. Many presumed he was dead. She went from being a student at the school to a servant. She was ill-treated and misunderstood. Through a course of events throughout the movie, she discovers her father is alive and much nearer than she had realized. What she doesn't know is that he has suffered amnesia from the war and cannot remember who she is. She manages to escape from the boarding school with authorities in hot pursuit, and lands in the very home where her father is residing. The moment when they meet again, face to face, is palpable as she pleads with him, *"Papa, Papa, it's me Sara,"* but he simply can't remember her.

I can imagine her desperation, knowing that she had no one else in the world to turn to but him, and amid all her weeping and wailing he still could not remember her. All the years, all the memories, all the hopes and dreams forgotten. Just as the authorities begin to drag Sara away, her father stands to his feet and yells out her name. *"Sara!"* At that very moment, he remembered. They run into each other's arms, their faces drenched in tears, and embrace. Sara is home, finally home, in the arms of her father, fully restored. Wow, I'm tearing up even now as I'm writing this. Just go watch the movie and you'll understand.

## Beautiful Face to Beautiful Face

I think I'd like to have a face-to-face conversation with you. I would bring you to my house and make you a hot cup of peppermint tea, in one of my favorite mugs, with just the right amount of honey and a touch of whole milk on the side as creamer. We would sit in my living room, hot tea in hands, and overlook what we like to call "Mount Klu," which in reality is a small, unusable hill directly behind our house. It just sounds so much better calling it Mount Klu, don't you think? More regal. *Turning the mundane into something magnificent.*

We'd wrap ourselves in cozy warm blankets, because of course it would be wintertime, and we would just talk. I would sit and pour out my heart to you, bathing you in words that God has spoken over your life. Because wouldn't you know it, every daughter wants to know and re-know that she is beautiful and loved, special and invaluable in the eyes of her Father. Just like Sara's father's passionate reaction when he finally remembered who Sara was, God is filled with passion and love for you every time your name comes to His mind. This is our Creator. This is the God our hearts know and long for.

> "EVERY DAUGHTER WANTS TO KNOW AND RE-KNOW THAT SHE IS BEAUTIFUL AND LOVED, SPECIAL AND INVALUABLE IN THE EYES OF HER FATHER."

My hand on your hand. I'm gently squeezing it now as if to reassure you that I am here. I open my mouth and with all the genuine love I can muster from the depths of my heart, I proceed to tell you ...

*"God wants a deep, fulfilling relationship with you. It's at the core of*

*your purpose. It's what you were created for. It all starts here. Your Father loves you deeply. To Him, you are beautiful. You are chosen. God notices you, here and now in this moment. In Him your future is bright and beautiful and full of hope, because your Father is on your side. He is working behind the scenes for your good. Nothing is wasted. You haven't made too many mistakes to negate the will of God for your life. He hasn't passed you by to look for another. He is actively pursuing you. You aren't too young. You aren't too old either. You are perfectly placed in the plan of God. You are right where He wants you. Your Father has His eyes on YOU."*

I proceed to slip you a beautiful piece of paper lined with promises that God has for your life and quietly whisper to you, *"He's only just begun with you."*

Something stirs in my heart when I think of the fact that God, the God of the universe, has you and me on His mind. It's easy to think as life passes by that God isn't noticing you anymore. After all, there are many times in my life where I have looked back and maybe forgotten about God, so why would He remember me? I feel unworthy, and I must confess, I get things wrong ... often.

> YOU HAVEN'T MADE TOO MANY MISTAKES TO NEGATE THE WILL OF GOD FOR YOUR LIFE. YOU ARE PERFECTLY PLACED IN THE PLAN OF GOD."

I wonder, if God really does care about me, why would He let bad things happen in my life? Doesn't He see what I'm going through? I'm sure you've asked yourself the same questions before. I cannot begin to understand the reasoning of God, but I do know He promises all things to work together for good.[5] I don't know your story, but I can be brutally honest about mine. He hasn't forgotten you, just like He hasn't forgotten me. Your Father has His eyes on you, because that is who He is, a God who relentlessly loves His children. We were made for a relationship with Him. No matter what wounds you carry—even the deep ones you wonder about and wish God wouldn't have allowed—God is still using those things for a greater purpose than you could ever imagine.

The more you know Him, the more you realize He is a good God and Father. Getting to know your Creator is, and always will be, at the foundation of your purpose. He is the One thing that can serve as a link to everything in your life. Every season, relationship, problem and blessing—He is the string that weaves them all together. He is the One who has the answer to every question you could ever ask or think. He is the only thing that can and will truly satisfy your life. A relationship with Him is the ultimate purpose for you and me. If we achieve everything else we could ever dream of, but leave this one aspect out, we will have missed the core of our purpose.

*He is our Match Made in Heaven.*

*The one perfect counterpart to our beautiful souls.*

*Without Him at our center, we are missing the One who completes us.*

Start with the Bible as proof. As you begin to study Scripture, you will see the importance of a relationship with God. The characters I love the most are the ones who simply and honestly love God desperately, regardless of all their inadequacies, deficiencies and shortcomings. Despite the despairing situations these characters find themselves in, God remains a God of hope, friendship and redemption characterized by saving power.[6] When it comes to our lives, He always has an ultimate purpose in mind. He knows the end from the beginning. The ways He seems to work all things together for good in the lives of those who know and love Him amazes me.

When I talk about knowing God, it's not just about knowing who God is in the Bible, it's about knowing how that translates to your life, your day to day. I'm talking about really knowing Him, like you would your spouse or children. I know more than just a description of my children, I know their quirks, their loves, the creases on their brows. When I close my eyes, I can see each child in my mind's eye. I can see their smiles, the beautiful coloring of their sparkling eyes and their precious faces. I can see the freckles on Noella's nose and the gorgeous grin on Selah Faye's face, missing tooth and all! I can see inside too—their hearts, their spirits, the special people God has created them to be. If I imagine hard enough, I can feel their little bodies next to mine snuggling me on a cold winter morning.

***When I think of my children, my mind fills with memories of the past and hopes for the future …***

This is the way God thinks of you. And this is the way God wants you to know Him. He wants

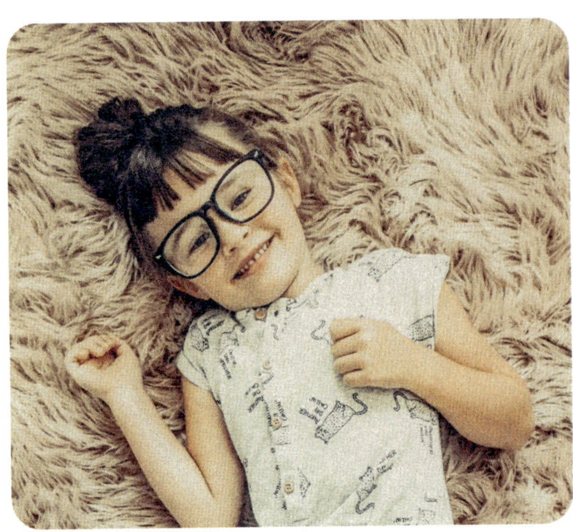

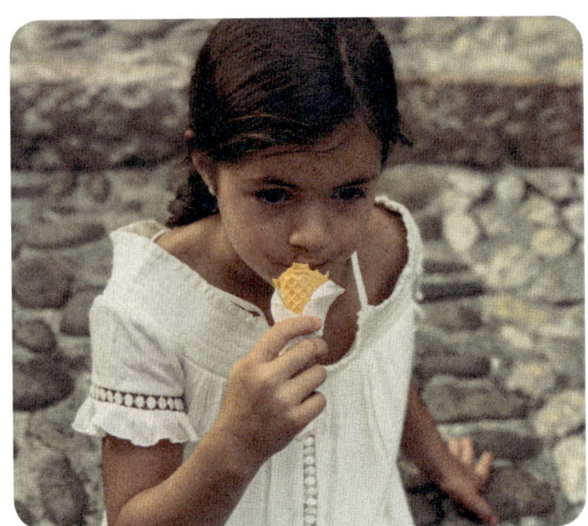

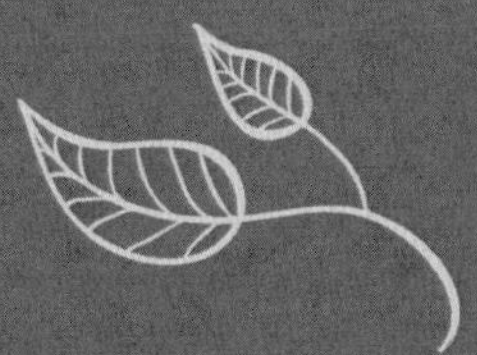

"GOD LOVES EACH OF US AS IF THERE WERE ONLY ONE OF US."

-Saint Augustine

> "GETTING TO KNOW YOUR CREATOR AND FATHER IS THE MOST IMPORTANT STEP IN JUST BEING."

your life to be filled with memories of Him. A life of learning to hear His voice. Memories of Someone who is so precious to you that when you close your eyes, you can imagine Him right next to your side. You can sense His presence. You know exactly how His voice sounds, so at the very instance He speaks, you can pinpoint the direction He wants you to walk in. You know the contours of His face and the moment He gently touches your heart. You feel His arms around you and see the love in His eyes. You know the unseen, too: His character, His heart, and the deep love He has for you and others. A lifetime spent knowing the One who intimately knows you.

Getting to know your Creator and Father is the most important step in *Just Being.* It's something we must cultivate in the daily rhythms of who we are. A lifetime of exploring the many facets of who God is. Opening His Word and digging for the treasure and promise within. Opening our hearts wide to receive daily what He wants to give. It's at the center of who we are. It's freedom. It's joy. It's peace. Cultivating a love for God starts here: Spend time reading the love letter He's given you, called the Bible. Take time talking to Him like you would a friend.

As you learn more about God, you also begin to not just imagine, but stand firmly on who God created you to be. The study of the Word of God is essential in the life of any believer. Many times, we look to people to define our identity, but the only one who can truly define us is the One who created us.

When we dig down deep into the Word of God, it's like we are reading what the Creator truly designed for our lives. We become discoverers of the truth. No more guesswork. We can replace our meager attempts of discovery with the sureness of the truth of God. The word begins to renew our minds, just as He promised, giving us a clear picture of who He is and who we are.[7] The Word of God can replace the lies that we believe about our identity. We rediscover our true intent. At our core, we are all destined to be in relationship with God, love Him deeply, love others deeply, and bring glory to Him alone. Literally, the Word of God has transforming power.

If I go too long without spending significant time with God, I succumb to my alter ego—which includes, but is not limited to, impatience in the school drive line. Yelling at the kids for no reason.

Blaming my weaknesses on others. Doubting my purpose. Running from difficult situations. Looking to others for my sense of worth, security and belonging. Saying yes to everything even if I don't have the time or energy to do it. Devouring too many donuts on Sunday mornings, and crying—a lot. The cycle just goes on and on ... it's not pretty. But when I'm rooted in God, I know who I am and whose I am.

I am a daughter of the King.[8] I am called and chosen and specifically crafted for this season. I have wisdom from on high and strength to face any battle.[9] I have provision from God for every promise He has given me.[10] I am perfectly loved. I am more than able. I am kind and generous. I am a light to this world for Him.[11] I am not as cranky and irritable. I am positive and encouraging because I stand in the hope of who God has proven Himself to be. I am held. I am a warrior. I am His. This is who you are.

I love how Sara, in *A Little Princess*, just wanted to be with her father. It was less about what her father could do for her and more about just being with him. When's the last time you really spent time with God just because? The timing is perfect, now. Grab your Bible and start somewhere. Old Testament or New. Underline all the verses that mean something to you and speak to your heart. Then ask God, what are You trying to speak to me today and how can I *Just Be* with You? It's life changing. Keep a journal of the precious revelations He is speaking to you through His word. Trust me, a relationship with Him is more than worth it. It's the best investment of your time you could ever make.

## Extra: A sneak-peek into my time with Jesus

Before I disclose what my time with God actually looks like, let me tell you what my ideal morning would look like with Jesus: sitting with hot tea in hand. Fireplace blazing. Cozy blankets. Quiet. Instrumental music or worship playing faintly in the background. Colored pencils and markers. Bible. Journal. Books. Jesus. All distractions gone so I can focus only on Him.

Here's a more accurate picture of what the past fourteen years have looked like: When I first started having children, I was not happy with the fact that I couldn't have my personal "quiet" time with God, and that's an understatement. It seemed everywhere I turned there was a child needing something. A diaper to change, a kid to feed, a toy to find. And with four girls, they were always crying about something because their feelings were hurt. Lord help me, I had four little "me's" running around the house. After months of letting my disappointment fester, I decided to do something about it. I couldn't wake up at 4:00 a.m. every morning to spend time with God, I was just too tired. Instead I decided I was going to spend time with Him during the day, distractions and all, even though my circumstances weren't ideal. I would set a timer on the microwave for thirty minutes of prayer. I sat the kids down and told them that Mommy was going to spend time with Jesus and they couldn't ask me any questions until the timer went off. Surprisingly, it worked. They weren't non-existent, but they were quieter. It just became a part of my day, and inadvertently a way to teach them in the process. I'll never forget the day when I turned around and saw my two older children following me around the house with their blankets, fingers folded sweetly together, walking prayer circles behind me as I prayed. It was in that moment that I realized, even my imperfect, non-ideal time with God was making a difference in the lives of those I held most dear. I know, I cried.

All this is to say: you can make time. It might not be ideal, but in God's eyes it's the pursuit that matters. Friend, you have grace for this season so find a way to connect with Him. I laugh with Him. I cry with Him a lot. I go to Him for wisdom and counsel. I pray His Word over my life, my children, my husband and friends. I tell Him the deepest ugliest things in my heart, and you know what? He loves me just the same. He already knew what was in there before I even said it, so I might as well tell Him. I ask Him to speak to me throughout the day and as I read His Word. I spend time writing about what I've learned in the Bible and about life. My journal is like a series of love letters to God, like the ones I used to give my husband Milan in high school—because back in the day, before we had texting, we used to have to write on paper to communicate, or talk face to face. BAM. There's something deep in that!

Take a breath and just begin to be with Him. Unlike people, God will never turn His back on you. You don't need to worry if He will return the feelings, He will. He's already got His eyes on you and once He sees you pursuing Him, it's all over. It's in the bag. There's a freedom in knowing He's already chosen you and you don't need to do anything to earn it.

Just being with Him daily will drastically change the course of your life for the better ... you'll start experiencing the love you've always longed for ... I promise.

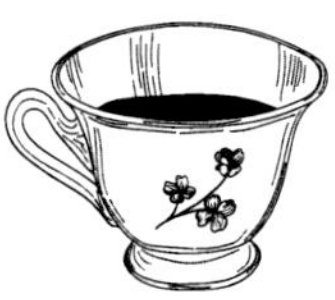

BOOK RECOMMENDATION

## Whisper *by Mark Batterson*

This book is about hearing the voice of God in your day-to-day life. Crafted unlike any other, you can tell the author is an avid reader and researcher by the detailed connections he makes throughout his work.

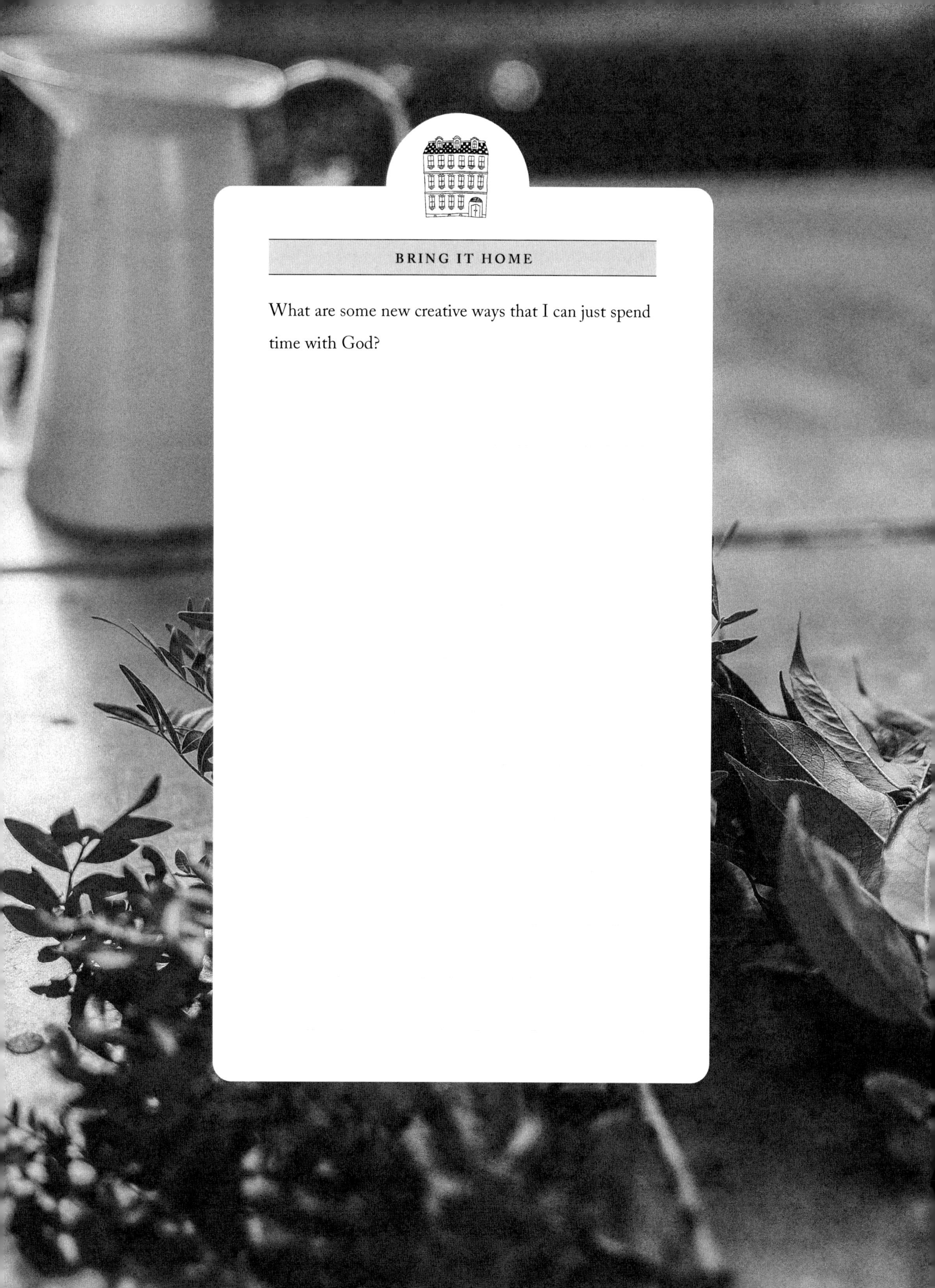

## BRING IT HOME

What are some new creative ways that I can just spend time with God?

CHAPTER FOUR

# JUST BE

## *A Work in Progress*

IN YOU, THEN THROUGH YOU

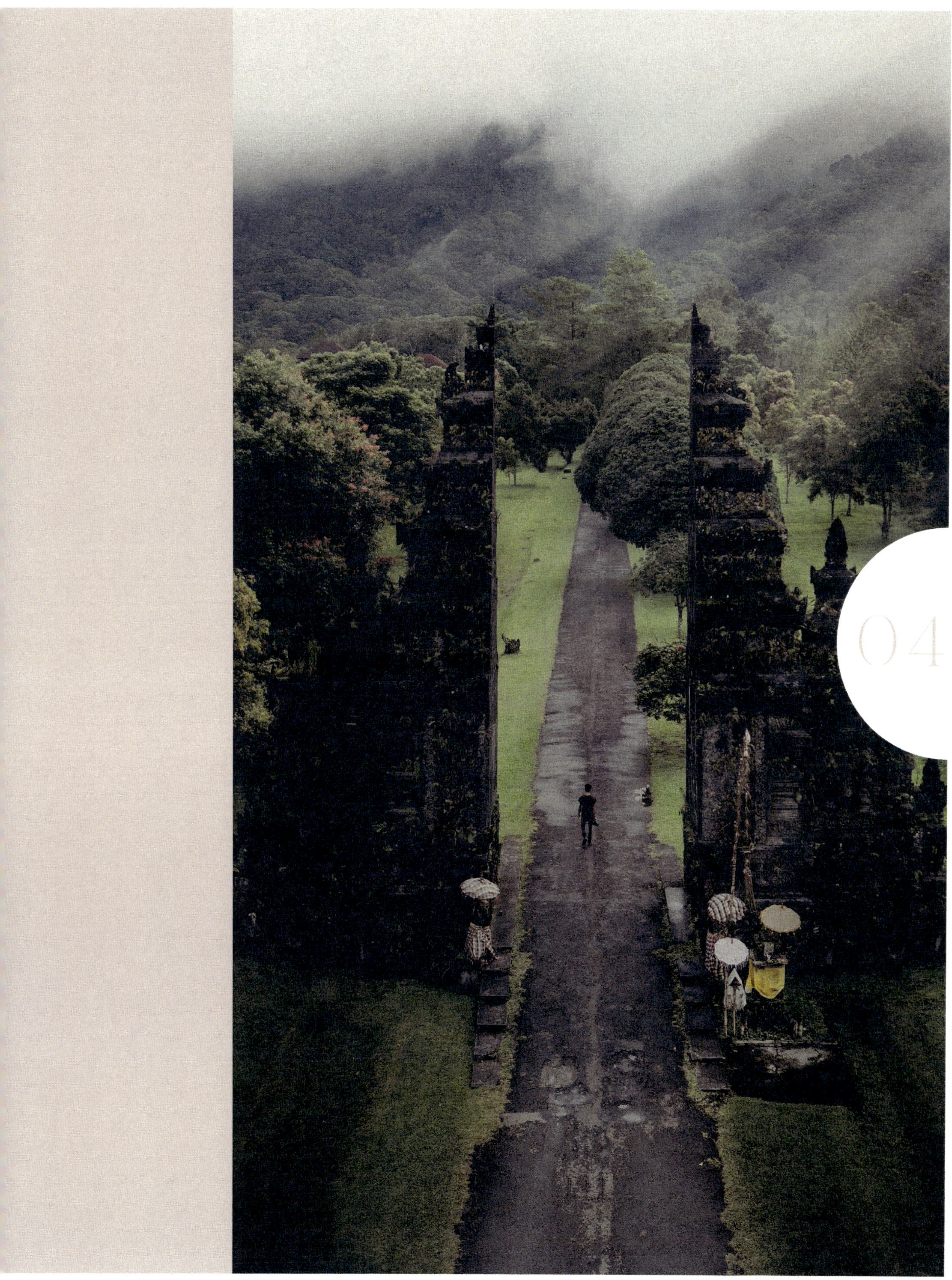

04

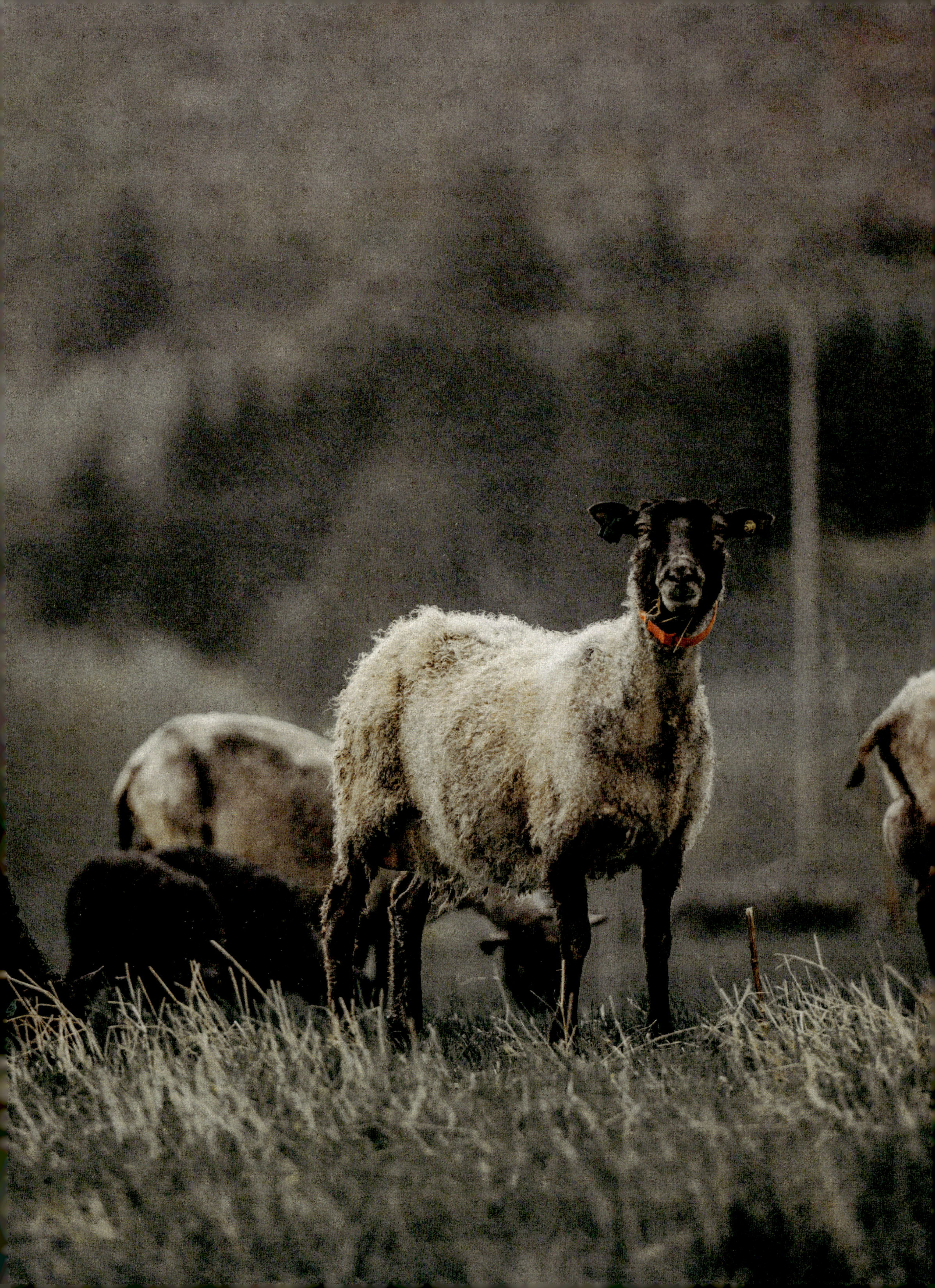

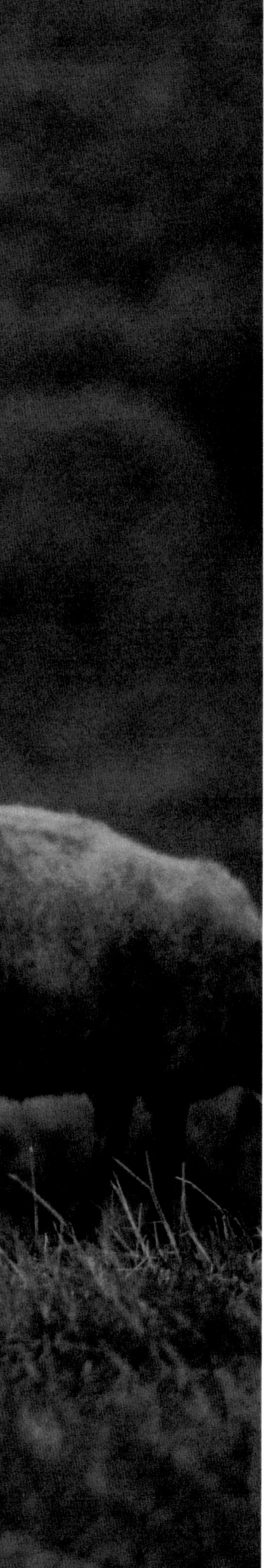

"Are *you hungry?"* I ask. You reply with a nod, which signals my descent to the kitchen once again. I have pre-made my favorite banana bread, a recipe passed down from my mother.[12] I heat the bread in our microwave for thirty seconds, cut off two slices and serve it to you on one of my favorite colorful plates. I place a little cup of milk on the side to pour over the top of each slice, which makes the bread extra yummy.

You take a bite. I try to measure your reaction. You look pleased, so I proceed to take my first bite, reveling in the goodness I have just placed in my mouth. I realize once again how much I love food. Lord help me ... it looks as if you love it too. We giggle in delight. I pause to think about how I'm going to bridge the gap into our discussion.

*"Do you know what I think?"* I say in a manner not actually requesting an answer. *"I think God cares more about our character than our accomplishments."*

And so our story begins.

There once was a man. He was quite handsome in appearance, the kind of man who would turn your head and make you glance twice. I don't know personally what he looked like, but I imagine he had a smile that would light up a room every time he walked in. His eyes sparkled like the clearest blue skies, but met you as deep wells of water you could get lost in. Captivating and kind. Thick, dark hair, perhaps a bit shaggy and untamed that spoke not of his lack of grooming, but rather his carefree spirit and confidence in who he was created to be.[13] His personal demeanor exuded strength and when you were in his presence you genuinely felt cared for. Whether young or old, beggar or king, there was a genuine love and concern for people that permeated his speech and action.

He was personable and confident, an expert musician and creative. He was so skilled, in fact, that kings and countrymen alike would call upon him for his services to minister to them in music at their darkest hour. Yet, he was humble. He chose to serve in the most menial ways. Whether delivering meals to the hungry, sleeping in the fields, or watching over another man's flocks, he was willing. He cared neither for status or fame, for he knew no matter what position he held, his worth was found in his Creator. He learned to love the things that God loved at a young age. He had been chosen by God when he was just a boy, but loved and sought God even before he was anointed as leader.

Perhaps it was his upbringing or his lack of status in life that caused a genuine love for God and love for people to follow him throughout his lifetime. A shepherd boy who no one really gave notice to, but would one day turn into a warrior and the greatest king a nation had ever known. Meet David, son of Jesse, King of Israel. A man after God's own heart.

When I read about David, it makes my heart smile in delight and ache at the same time. God calls David a man after His own heart, yet David's story is laced with years of heartache, failures and setbacks. Maybe my heart aches because deep down I was hoping to read about a perfect character. But only God is perfect. We all make mistakes, lives laced with triumphs and failures. It is true that God did many miracles for David throughout his lifetime. His anointing as king, the slaying of Goliath, his marriage to the king's daughter Michal, and His reign over Israel are just some of the highlights. But what about his years in the wilderness, fearing for his life? Or the heartache that followed him after he sinned with Bathsheba? The death of his sons and the potential usurping of his reign—was God found in these moments too?

Sometimes we can't control what happens to us, but we can be assured that God is desiring to shape our character through the good and the bad, the beautiful and the ugly. God is after character. Shaping us to be the people He has called us to be. And yes, we can't control everything, but we can ask God to shape our character and help us to respond well. At our core, I believe this: *God will not fulfill His promise for us at the expense of what He is doing in us. Who we are becoming means more to Him than what we could ever do for Him. If we can JUST BE the person God wants us to be on the inside, I think no matter where we find ourselves, our purpose will find us.*

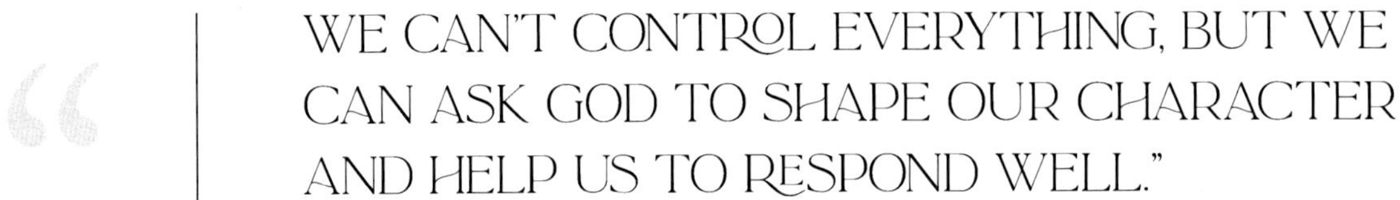


I cannot begin to understand all of God's ways. He allows us to make decisions that we must pay the consequences for, yet at the same time, He sovereignly knows those decisions ahead of time and

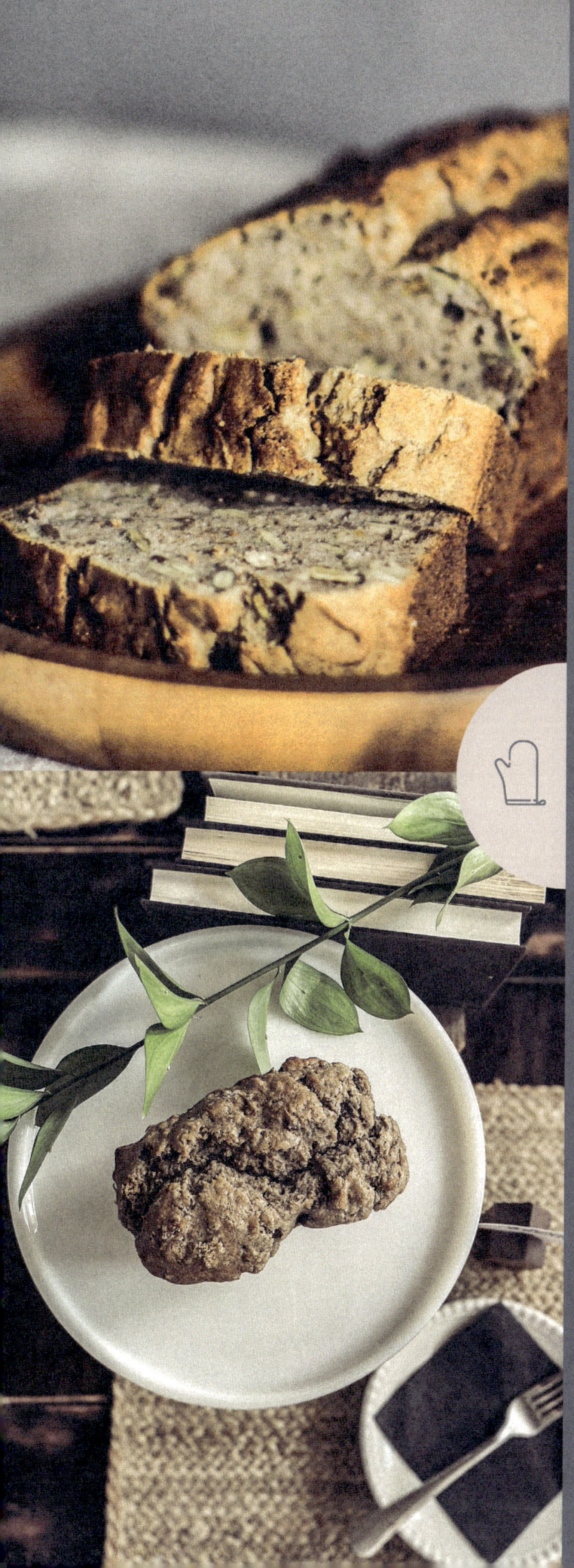

# *Mom's* BANANA BREAD RECIPE

3 ripe bananas

½ cup oil (whatever kind you choose)

½ cup brown sugar (packed)

2 eggs

1 tablespoon vanilla extract

½ cup applesauce (not necessary)

2 cups flour

2 teaspoons baking powder

1 teaspoon cinnamon

Dash salt

Chocolate chips (I add these)

Mix the wet ingredients. Add the dry ingredients. Bake in a pan of your choosing for 45 to 60 minutes at 325 degrees.

chooses to work them together for good if we turn to Him. No matter how many times David royally messed up, he always turned to God in repentance. The key wasn't found in living a perfect life, but rather, surrender to God. God would not fulfill His promise at the expense of David not becoming, on the inside, who God had created him to be. The key is character.

So many times, we are striving endlessly to be all the things that God has created us to be. We want to know and discover our purpose for this season, but we forget that our character is molded on the journey, not upon the arrival of our destination. In this very moment, we are right smack-dab in the center of God's purpose for our lives. Everything that surrounds us is pointing to our purpose and molding our character. Every family member and relationship, every heartache and every victory are lined with an underlying purpose. God's sovereign hand in all of it, asking us to allow Him to mold our character.

Each season, each instance, is marked with purpose. And, while I appreciate our aspirations to help others and change this world, it should never be at the expense of missing this current season and identifying it as being drenched with purpose. Our character is being molded, and character is what God is after in the story of our lives. Instead of focusing on the doing, let's lean into being ...*Just Be.*

I think God was trying to teach David to value what God cares about. He was trying to mold David's character. I think God knew, if David could learn to value the things that touch the heart of God, then in the end, whether David was a shepherd boy or a fugitive, God would bring the promise of kingship to him. It was all about character.

Today, ask God to help you be the man or woman of character God has called you to be. From the most insignificant decision to the life-altering ones. From who you are in the light of day, to who you are in the shadows. From your workplace, to your home. Allow God to shape your character in it all. You are a work in progress.

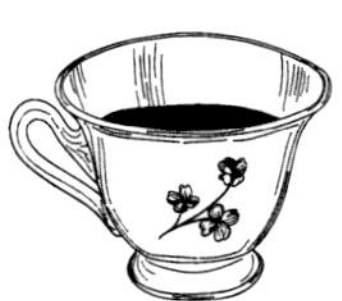

**BOOK RECOMMENDATION**

### Scouting the Divine *by Margaret Feinberg*

This book helped me understand the intimate relationship between a shepherd and their sheep, which in turn reminds me of David in his early years. Beautifully written.

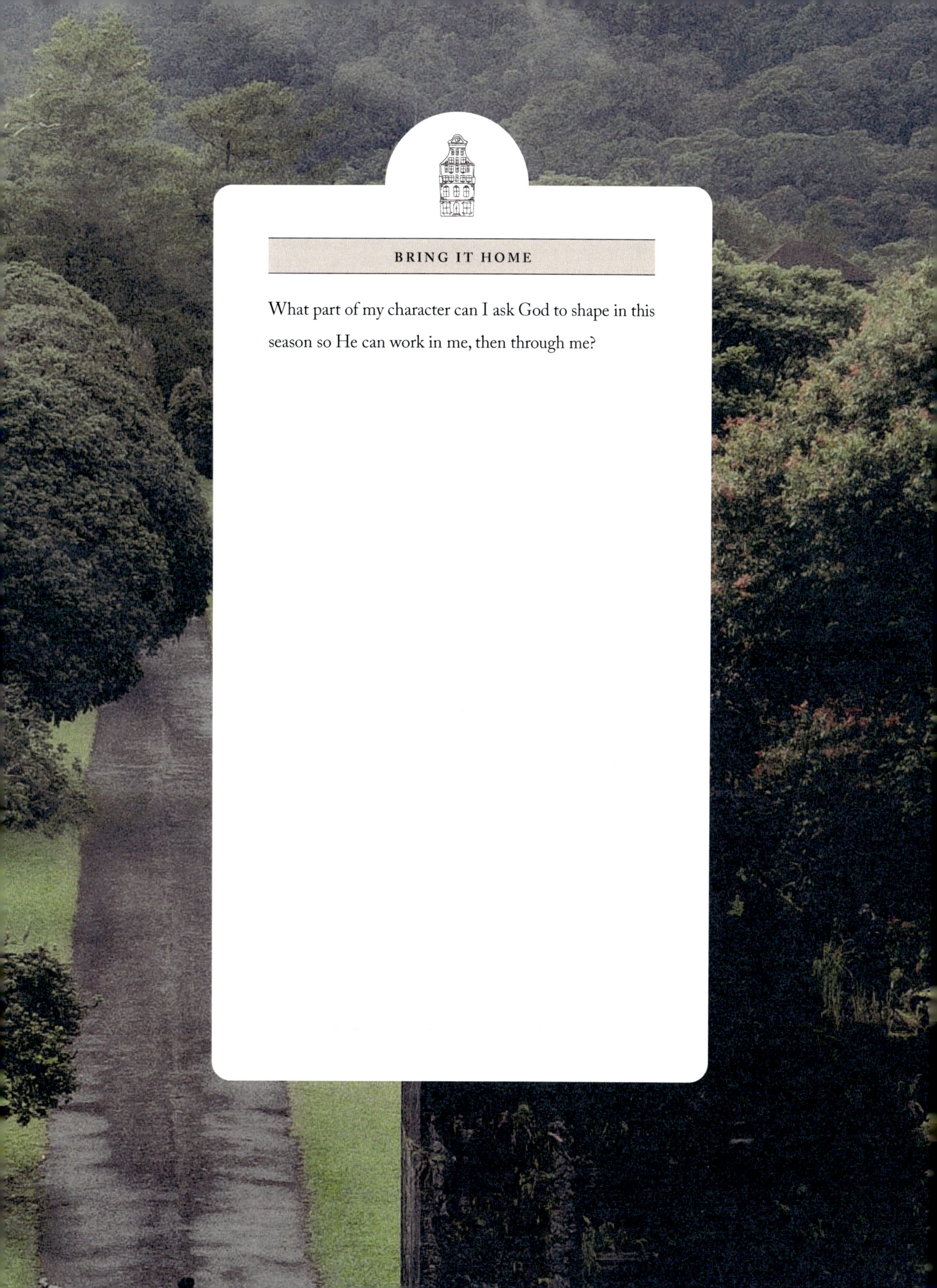

BRING IT HOME

What part of my character can I ask God to shape in this season so He can work in me, then through me?

CHAPTER FIVE

# JUST BE

## Defined by Your Creator

---

YOU ARE A UNIQUE CREATION

---

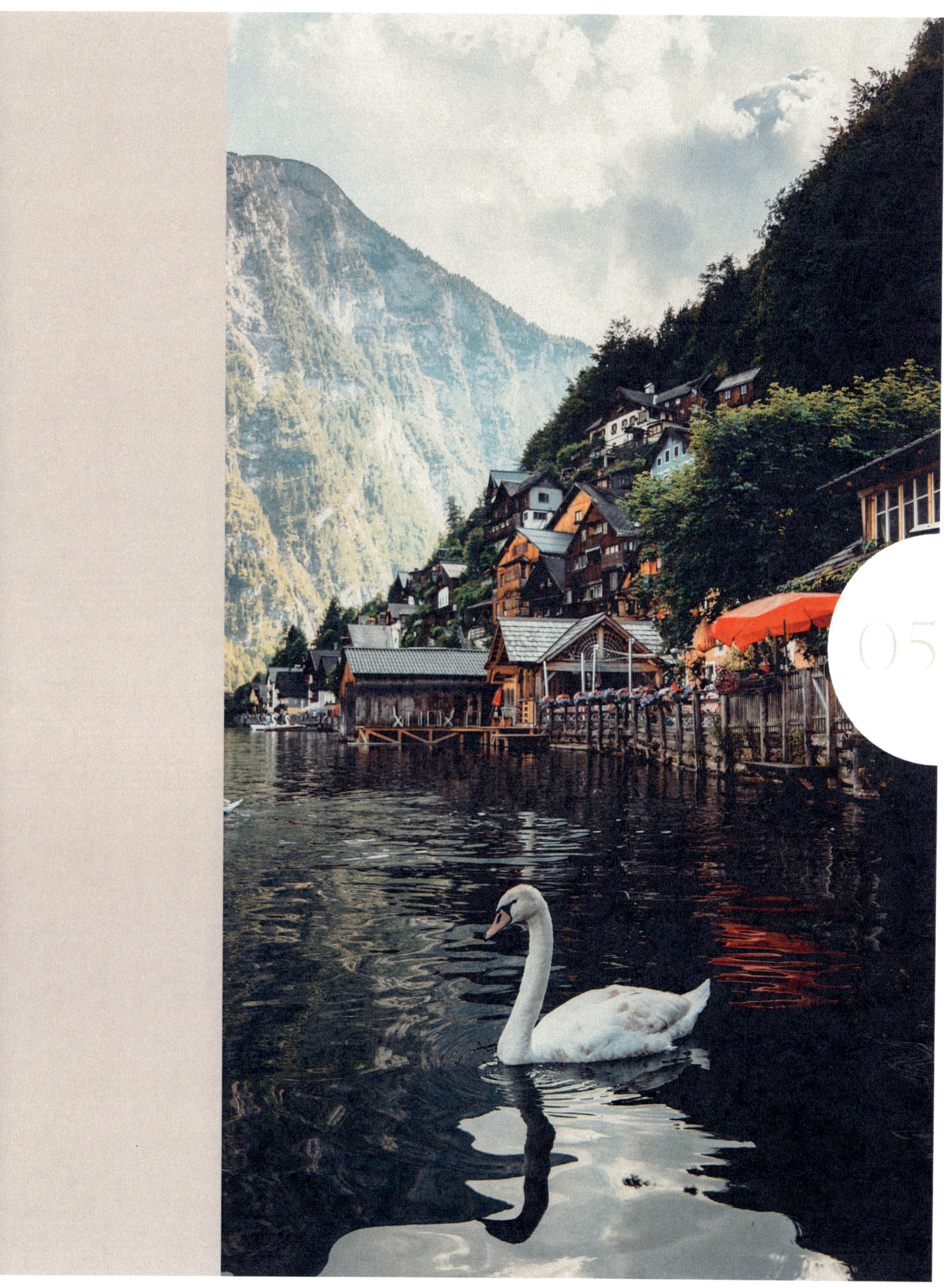

05

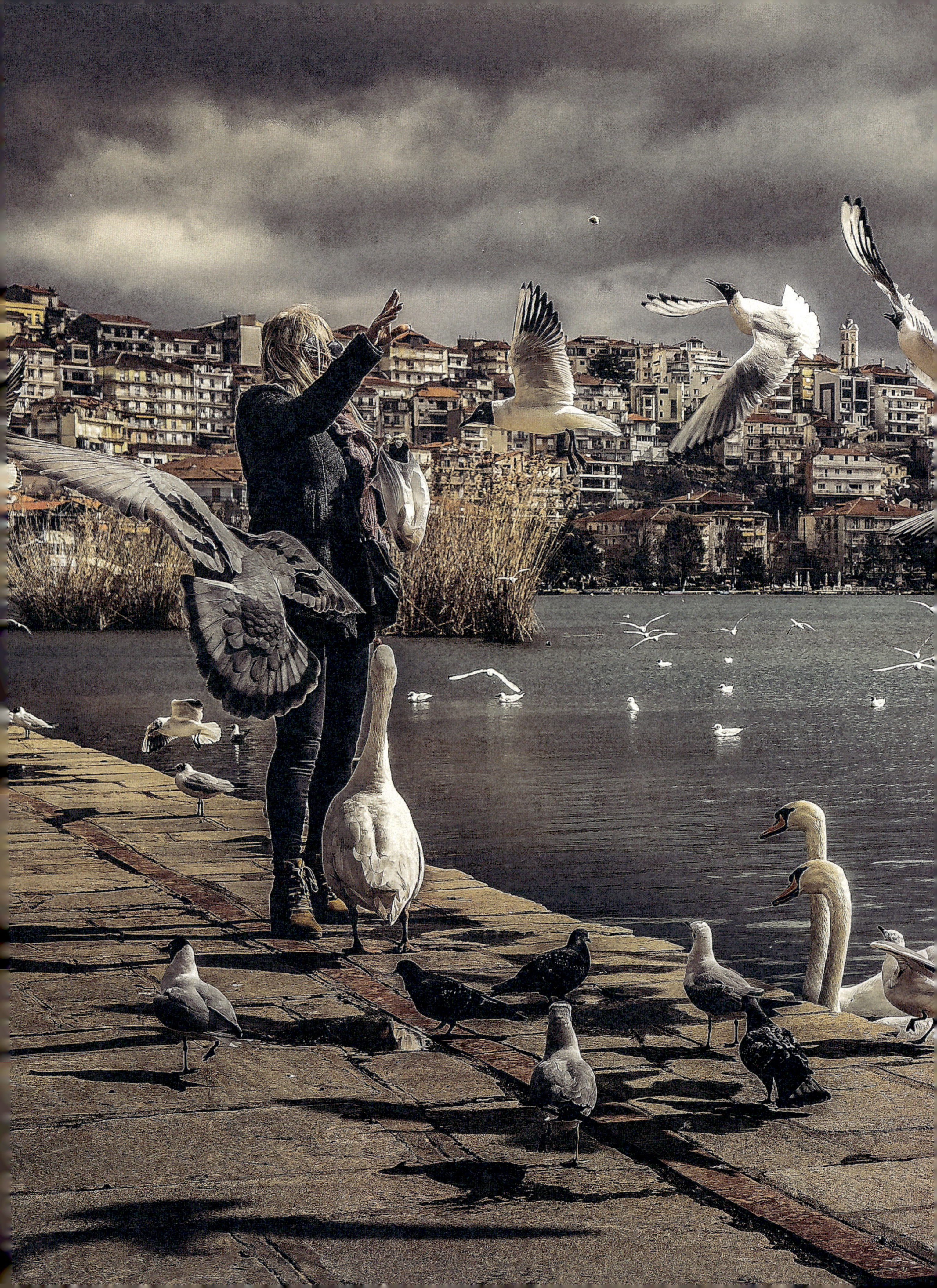

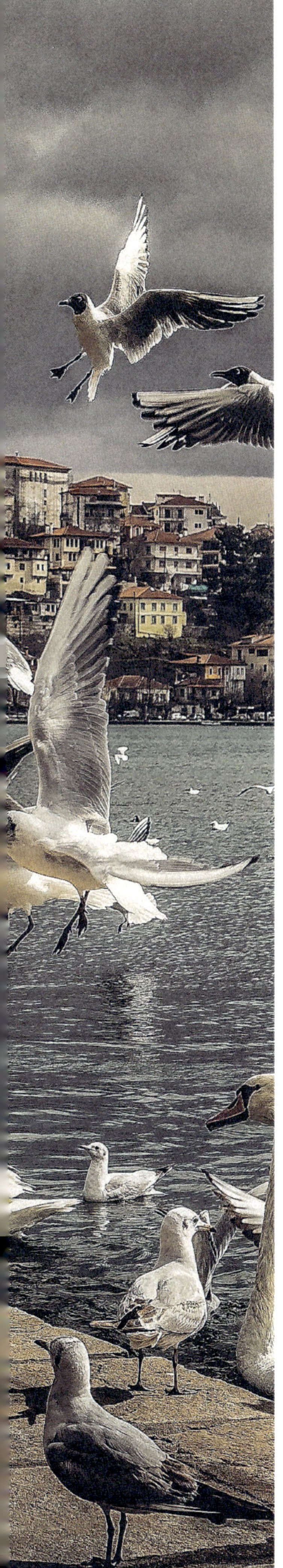

*"It was lovely summer weather in the country, and the golden corn, the green oats, and the haystacks piled up in the meadows looked beautiful ... In a sunny spot stood a pleasant old farm-house close by a deep river, and from the house down to the water side grew great burdock leaves, so high, that under the tallest of them a little child could stand upright.*

*The spot was as wild as the centre of a thick wood. In this snug retreat sat a duck on her nest, watching for her young brood to hatch; she was beginning to get tired of her task, for the little ones were a long time coming out of their shells ... At length one shell cracked, and then another, and from each egg came a living creature that lifted its head and cried, 'Peep, peep...'*

*'One egg is not hatched, yet,' said the duck, 'it will not break. But just look at all the others, are they not the prettiest little ducklings you ever saw?' At last the large egg broke, and a young one crept forth crying, 'Peep, peep.' It was very large and ugly. The poor duckling, who had crept out of his shell last of all, and looked so ugly, was bitten and pushed and made fun of, not only by the duck[s] but by all the poultry ... he was quite miserable because he was so ugly and laughed at by the whole farmyard. So it went on from day to day till it got worse and worse. The poor duckling was driven about by everyone; even his brothers and sisters were unkind to him, and would say, 'Ah, you ugly creature, I wish the cat would get you,' and his mother said she wished he had never been born. The ducks pecked him, the chickens beat him, and the girl who fed the poultry kicked him with her feet. So at last he ran away, frightening the little birds in the hedge as he flew over the palings ... It would be very sad, were I to relate all the misery and privations which the poor little duckling endured during the hard winter; but when it had passed, he found himself lying one morning in the moor, amongst the rushes. He felt the warm sun shining and heard the lark singing, and saw that all around was beautiful spring. Then the young bird felt that his wings were strong, as he flapped them against his sides and rose high into the air. Everything looked beautiful, in the freshness of early spring. From a thicket close by came three beautiful white swans, rustling their feathers, and swimming lightly over the smooth water.*

*'I will fly to those royal birds,' he exclaimed, 'and they will kill me, because I am so ugly, and dare to approach them; but it doesn't matter; better be killed by them than pecked by the ducks, beaten by the hens, pushed about by the maiden who feeds the poultry, or starved with hunger in the winter.' Then he flew to the water and swam towards the beautiful swans. The moment they espied the stranger, they rushed to meet him with outstretched wings. 'Kill me,' said the poor bird; and he bent his head down to the surface of the water and awaited death. But what did he see in the clear stream below? His own image; no longer a dark, gray bird, ugly and disagreeable to look at, but a graceful and beautiful swan. To be born in a duck's nest, in a farmyard, is of no consequence to a bird, if it is hatched from a swan's egg. He now felt glad at having suffered sorrow and trouble, because it enabled him to enjoy so much better all the pleasures and happiness around him … He had been persecuted and despised for his ugliness, and now he heard them say he was the most beautiful of all the birds. Even the elder-tree bent down its bows into the water before him, and the sun shone warm and bright. Then he rustled his feathers, curved his slender neck, and cried joyfully, from the depths of his heart, 'I never dreamed of such happiness as this, while I was an ugly duckling.'"*[14]

Each one of us is created uniquely different. Like the ugly duckling, sometimes we look at ourselves, look at others, and then back at ourselves and say, "God, what in the world were you thinking when you created me?" But if we are patient and obedient to God's process, one day in the future we will see our reflection clearly, thankful for the person God has crafted us to be. As just a wee duckling, everywhere the duck turned his companions were reminding him of his ugliness. They damaged him, not just by their words, but by their harsh treatment. When he was fully matured it was hard for him to shake off those memories imprinted on his mind of days gone by. The words of others had wrongly defined who he was and what he would one day become. And yet, with time, the ugly duckling did indeed turn into something beautiful. A beautiful swan. At full maturity, everyone saw a swan. The other swans, the children, even all of creation acknowledged his beauty. But because he experienced years of being told otherwise, he couldn't believe it. It wasn't until he stood face to face with his own reflection that he saw how beautiful he had become. Because he had not seen the change God was doing in him along the journey, he still viewed himself as what he once

"BECAUSE HE HAD NOT SEEN THE CHANGE GOD WAS DOING IN HIM ALONG THE JOURNEY, HE STILL VIEWED HIMSELF AS WHAT HE ONCE USED TO BE: AN UGLY DUCKLING."

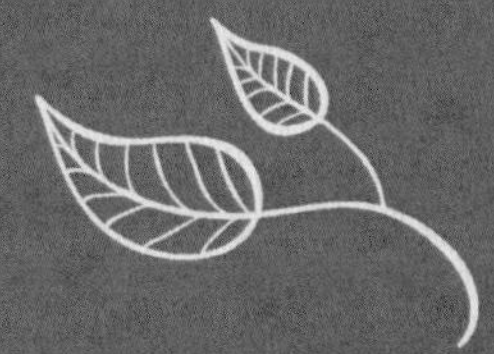

GOD DOESN'T LOVE US BECAUSE OF OUR WORTH, WE ARE OF WORTH BECAUSE GOD LOVES US."

-Martin Luther

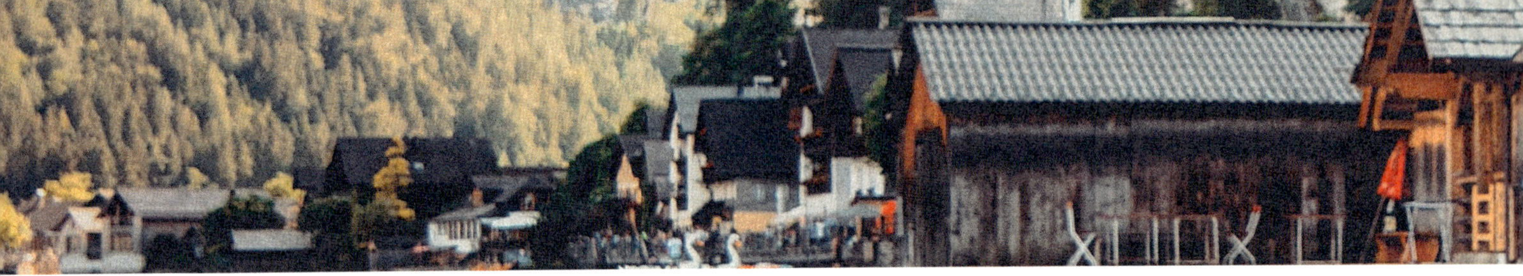

used to be: an ugly duckling. Little did he know that through the journey, he had been transforming. You see, the duckling was transformed during the journey, not in an instant. In his meager beginnings, where others saw a mess, God saw potential.

The same is true for you and I. Aren't you glad that God can transform what others label as ugly or messy into something beautiful? God knew exactly what He was doing when He created you. You are being transformed into a beautifully magnificent creation. You may not be fully there just yet, but your destiny is bright and beautiful and full of life. God is shaping you into a man or woman of supernatural strength, courage and purpose to reflect His glory. It begins on the inside, of course, but the inner beauty eventually radiates to others, impacting the lives around you. I believe the ugly duckling could have walked proudly even through his seasons of ugliness, if only he knew that he would one day become a swan. He needed someone in his present to prophecy into his future. Someone who could see the seasons ahead and speak aloud to his beautiful identity found in the unique creation God destined him to be. To speak purpose over his unknown, awkward years, assuring him that his current season was a part of a divine plan. And so God is speaking. God is speaking to you even now, assuring you that you are a magnificent creation. Until we stare at our own reflection, looking through the mirror of God's Word, hearing HIS voice, we will never truly discover who we are. We need to be defined by our Creator alone. That way, it doesn't matter what seasons we walk through, we know in the end God will transform us into something beautiful. What a shame it would have been if that little duckling had never glanced into the water to see the beautiful creation that he had become. He would have simply remained acting, thinking and believing that he was—and forever would remain—an ugly duckling.

> "THE DUCKLING WAS TRANSFORMED DURING THE JOURNEY, NOT IN AN INSTANT."

No matter where we find ourselves on our journey, every season holds a choice. We choose who we are going to let define us. It is in our hands. So, who are you allowing to define you? Whose voice are you listening to? Are you operating out of what you once were or what others have told you in the past? Or are you staring in the deep reflection of God's Word?

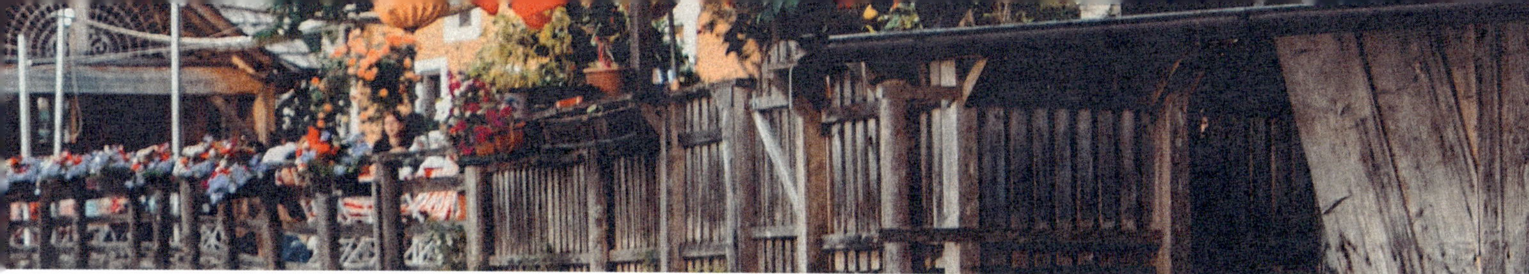

## Here's what others might say:

- She'll never amount to much.
- Look at the family she's come from, nothing good could come from that.
- She's not very pretty.
- He's unloved.
- She's made too many mistakes.
- She's worthless.
- He's not talented or gifted enough.
- She's a terrible mom.
- She'll always live bound and struggling.
- Her future is grim.

My prayer is that the moment these taunting words cross the threshold of your mind, may a full-force rushing wind of God's spirit step in—reminding you of who you truly are, of whose you truly are.

## Here's what God's words are for you today:

- You are valuable. Uniquely crafted from before time. *Psalm 139:13-16*
- You are God's child. It doesn't matter what your past looks like, or even your natural family, you are a child of the Most High God. His heir. *Galatians 3:26, 4:7*
- You are beautiful. You are a crown of beauty in the hand of your God. *Isaiah 62:3-5*
- You are fully loved, accepted and valued. God loves you so deeply that He gave His life for you. *1 John 3:1 and John 3:16*
- God will use all things in your life for His glory. Whether bad or good, past or present, God can and will take all things and use them for good as you lay them in His hands. *Romans 8:28*
- You are worthy. Not because of what you've done, but because of Christ. You are the apple of God's eye. He cherishes and loves you. *Psalm 17:8 and Isaiah 1:18*

- You are gifted and talented because the most high God lives in you. All the creativity from the Creator lives in you. You have full access. All you've got to do is ask. *1 Corinthians 3:16-17 and Jeremiah 33:3*
- You are fully equipped! He's given you everything you need for a life of godliness. He will teach you how to become a great mother, friend, daughter, spouse, father—everything is at His disposal. *1 Peter 1:3*
- You are, and will live, free. God paid the price for full freedom in Him, not partial freedom. *John 8:36*
- You have a beautiful future ahead. God promises to give you a future filled with hope and promise. *Jeremiah 29:11*

Know today that you are not ugly, forsaken or unworthy. You are found, loved and known by Him for a great purpose. You are beautiful and perfectly chosen. You may not see it now, but this is your reality. Stop believing the lies within. Start believing the truth of God. Let go of what once was. Embrace what is. Pursue what will be and remember: "To be born in a duck's nest, in a farmyard, is of no consequence to a bird, if it is hatched from a swan's egg."[15]

> TO BE BORN IN A DUCK'S NEST, IN A FARMYARD, IS OF NO CONSEQUENCE TO A BIRD, IF IT IS HATCHED FROM A SWAN'S EGG."

Maybe you can't see it, but you need to know today that you are surrounded by swans in the faith. There are people on this end of the story who are praying for you and see with God-given perspective the beautiful creation that you will become. They are ready to prophecy into your future. They are shouting at you, speaking words of life, encouragement, love and divine purpose. They see beyond your present into what you are becoming. Embrace these words right here, right now. Don't allow your years of feeling less than keep you blinded to the beautiful creation you are becoming. God is speaking promise and direction over and over again to you, reassuring you of who you are and what He has called you to be through His Word. It's time to take the veil off and truly see. It's time to ask God to help you see, and remember who He has created you to be.

When you discover who God has defined you to be, a new sense of courage rises within. You get a

God-given confidence instilled deep down. It doesn't come from selfishness or pride, but rather in the unwavering reality of who you are in God. Your identity is strong. Your beliefs cannot be shaken. No matter how many chickens, hens or people call you otherwise, when you look in the mirror you know who you will become—and it is not an ugly duckling. It's a destined-to-be-one-of-God's-most-beautiful-creations type of being.

> "KNOW TODAY THAT YOU ARE NOT UGLY, FORSAKEN OR UNWORTHY. YOU ARE FOUND, LOVED AND KNOWN BY HIM FOR A GREAT PURPOSE."

At the foundation of knowing and living out your purpose, you've got to know in confidence who God created YOU to be. To be defined by your Creator. After all, if you don't know who you are, how in the world will you ever be able to *Just Be* you? You will constantly be changing if it's not rooted in the right thing. Every obstacle and difficulty will cause you to question your God-given identity, tempting you to waiver in your faith and jump ship every time the going gets hard. But when your identity is secure in Him, you can stand courageous and grounded. Though seasons will change, your true self remains the same. You stand strong, immovable, safe in the Father's hands.

Let God alone define you.

**BOOK RECOMMENDATION**

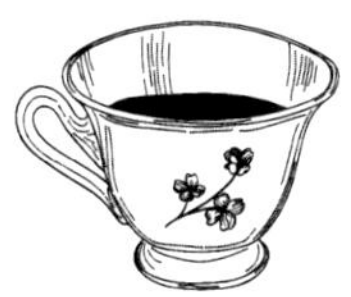

## I Declare *by Joel Osteen*

Be reminded of who God is and who He created you to be. This book is comprised of short daily readings for 31 days of the month. I like to write my journey with God throughout the pages along with the miracles I've seen Him do.

LET
GOD
ALONE
DEFINE
YOU.

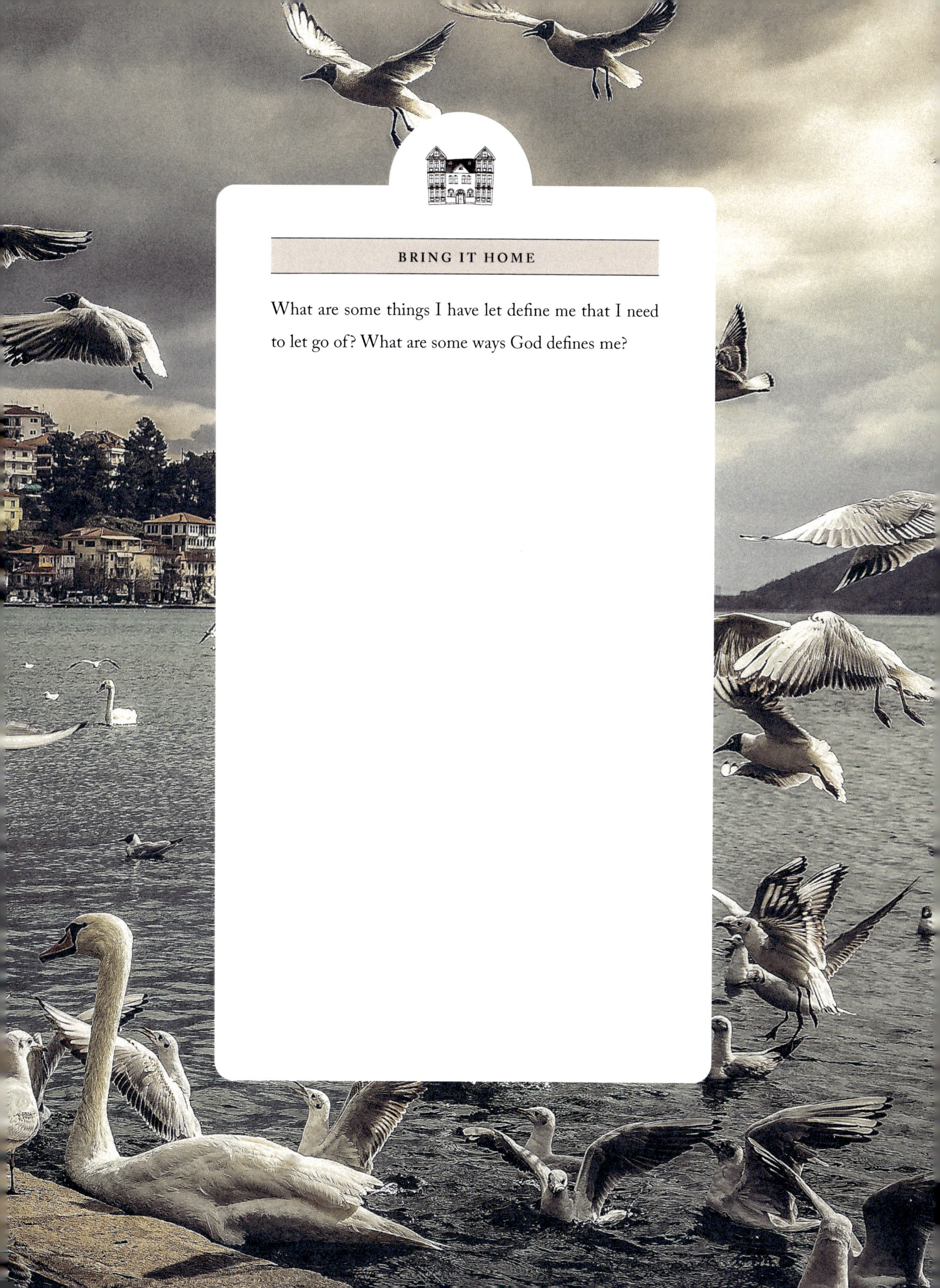

## BRING IT HOME

What are some things I have let define me that I need to let go of? What are some ways God defines me?

CHAPTER SIX

# JUST BE *Reminded*

PRECIOUS GIFTS OF PROMISE

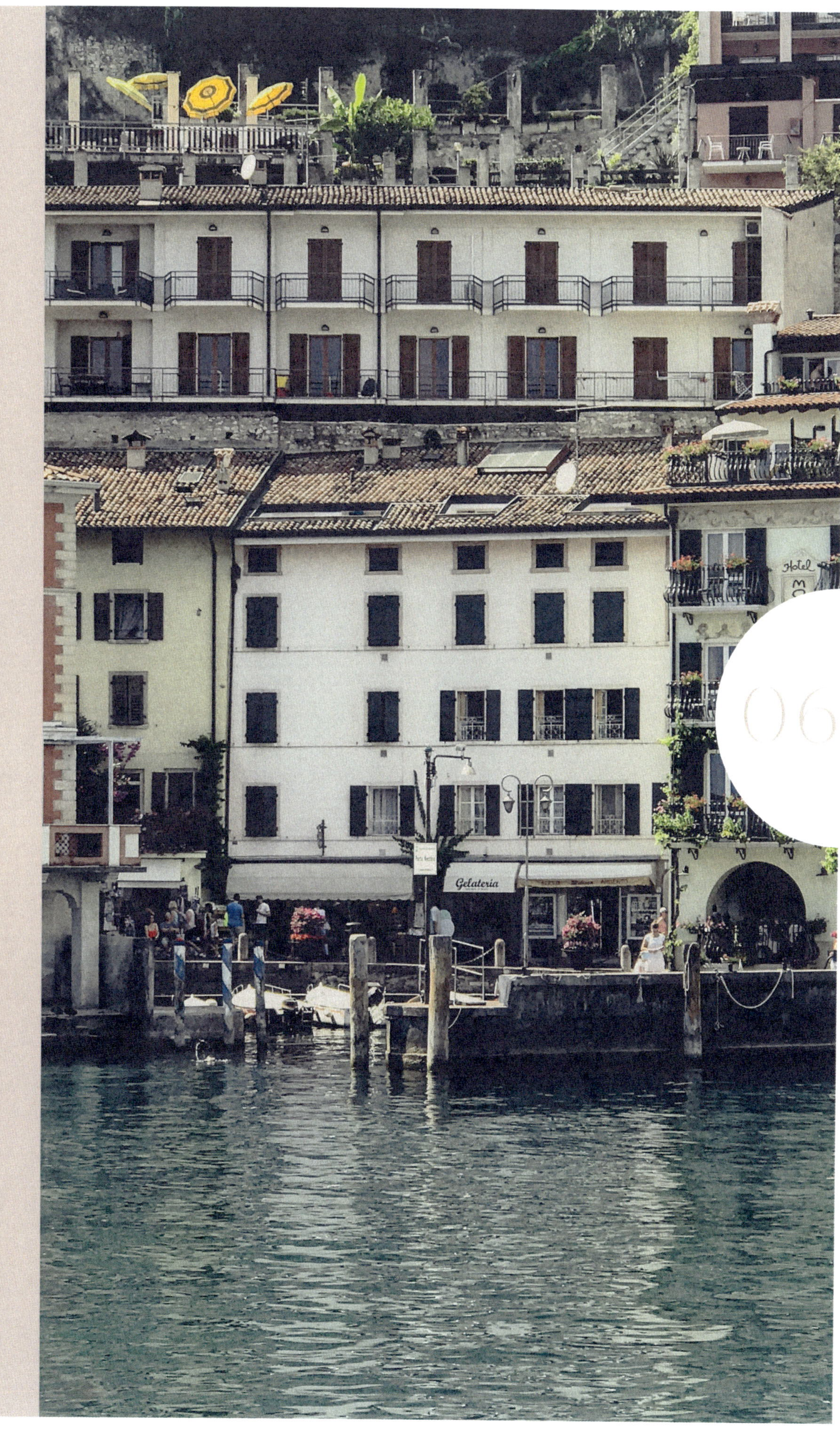


06

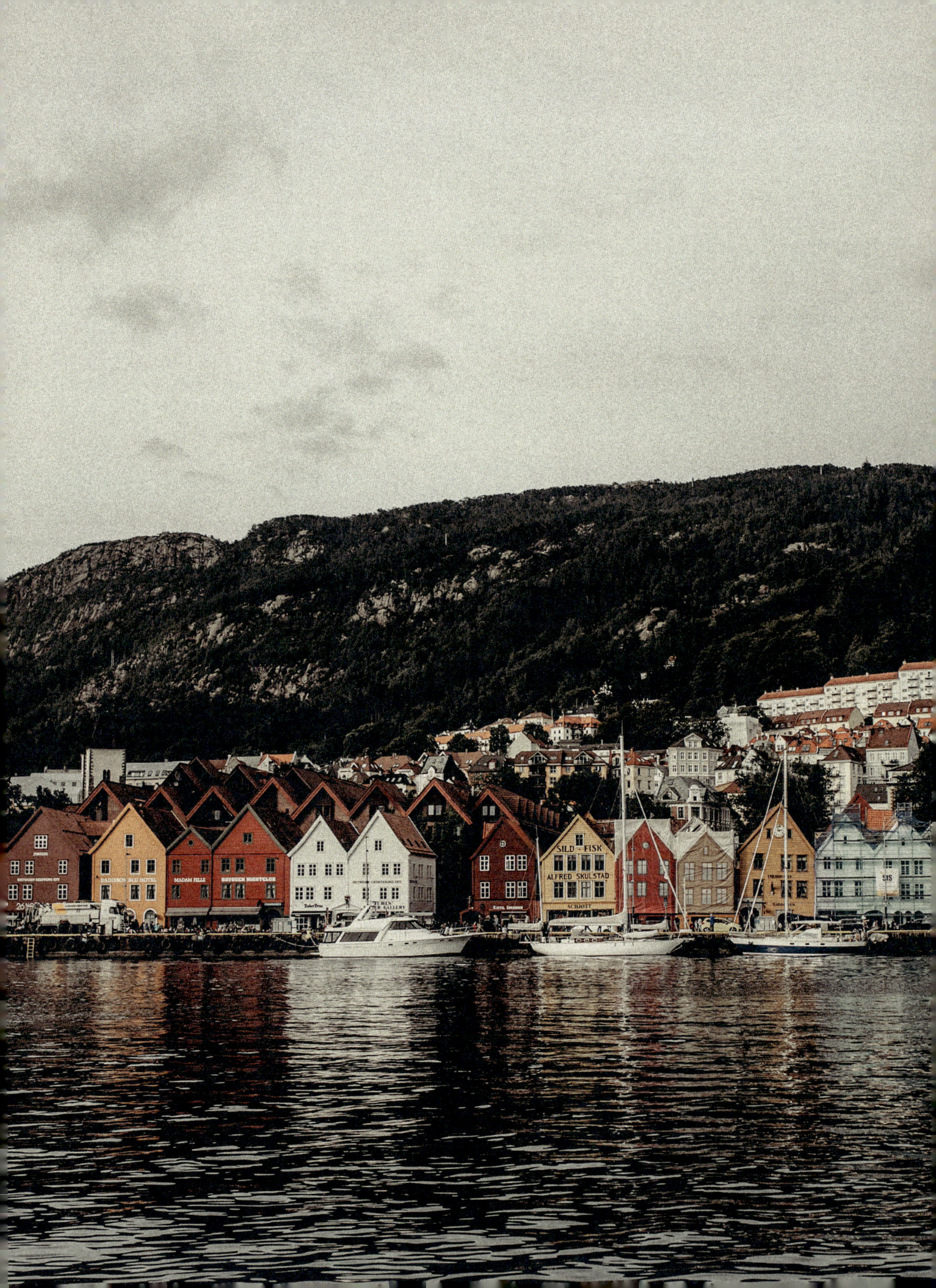
RADISSON BLU HOTEL
MADAM FELLE
BRYGGEN NIGHTCLUB
SILD-FISK
ALFRED SKULSTAD

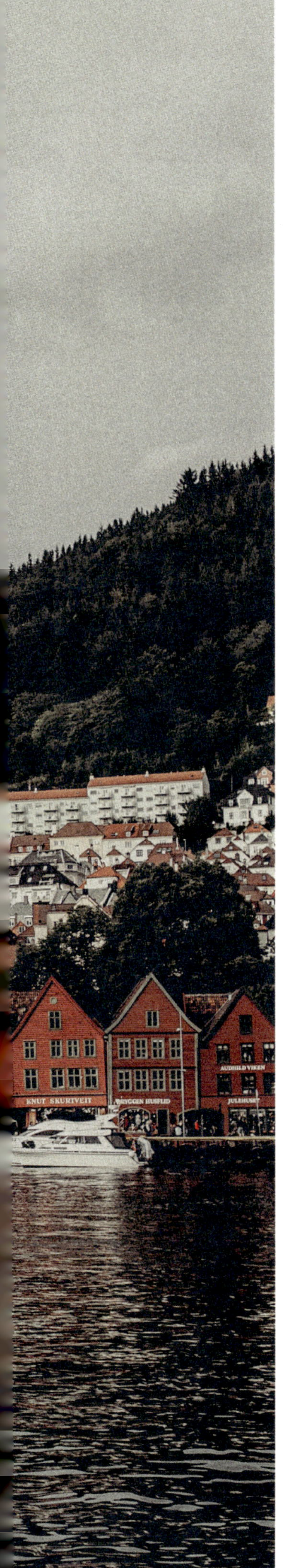

"Do *you need your cup of tea warmed up? I like mine extra hot. I can put it in the microwave for a minute or so and it will be perfect!"* I take the tea from your hands and head to the kitchen.

I rejoin you on the sofa, with a hot cup of tea placed in your hands and listen to your heart as you begin to pour out your thoughts and feelings towards God. One solitary tear streams down my face. As I look at you I sense the love the Father has towards you and my heart wants to burst.

There's a box of lotion-infused Kleenex on my coffee table, I place a couple sheets in your hand and squeeze your hand lovingly in mine. The more we talk about God, the unique masterpiece He is creating and His love for us, the lighter we feel. Glistening hope envelops us. We pause for a moment. We gaze out the window as the sun casts its rays across the field. The tall grass and willowy trees gently sway as the breeze kisses their leaves. A wave of peace and God's presence sweep through the room. God is near.

You open the piece of paper I placed in your hands moments ago. There's a beautiful flower design on the outside, representing the fresh work God is about to do in your life. You flip it over and see four written promises for your life from the Word of God. This is a portion of the promise-filled pages God is writing for you.

*"Can I be honest with you? God grabbed ahold of my heart when I was fourteen and I still need to be reminded of the promises of God. I'm forty years old! As I get to know Him more, I'm reminded of how He thinks about me. And let me tell you, He only has the BEST in mind,"* I say lovingly to you. So, mother to daughter, sister to sister, or friend to friend, I have a few things written on the journal of my heart from God to you. As you seek God today, may you be reminded.

## The Master Architect

The first promise I would give you is Jeremiah 29:11. It's a life verse for me. From the moment I read this verse years ago, I highlighted it,

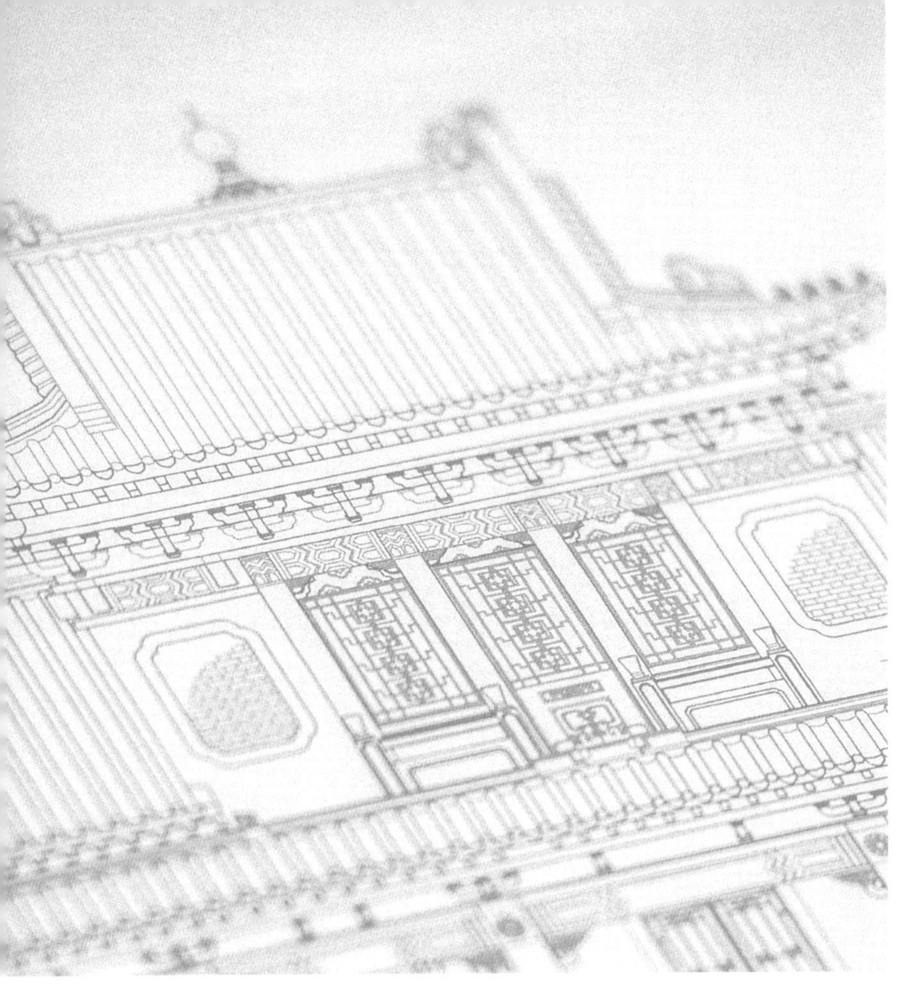

circled it, colored it and wrote it in my journal. I copied it on papers, wrote it on my school folders and I'm pretty sure it's hanging inside my kitchen cabinet right now. Every time I use or put away a dish, there it is to remind me, and that happens often!

Here's the verse: *"For I know the plans I have for you—this is the Lord's declaration—plans for your well-being, not for disaster, to give you a future and a hope."*[16] God has a plan. I pray that this verse sinks deep into your heart. I pray it is a verse you can stand on in the years to come. I pray that walls crumble in your heart and mind as you embrace this truth. I pray you have the ability to take God at His word.

He has a plan for YOU. It's not just a thought, it's a plan. A plan is defined by Merriam-Webster as *"a method of achieving an end; a detailed formulation of a program of action; to have in mind; to have a specific intention."* It's as if God is the chief architect of your life. Have you ever seen an architectural drawing? It does not resemble my six-year-old's drawing of a house with curved walls and undistinguishable attributes.

God's drawing is detailed and thorough. It's specific and beautiful. It's complete as-is without us adding or taking away from it, and each aspect is necessary. It's not just any plan; it's a plan for your good and not for evil, to give you the future you hope for. God is weaving every situation, every person, every circumstance together to accomplish His plan for your life.

Be reminded that God's plans for your life are good and not evil. Many times, we try to separate the different parts of His plan for our lives away from their whole. We want to scrap the things we don't like and add things we do, but God is saying, "Every part is needed and will work toward the hope that I have for you." Be reminded today that as you accept His plan, He will work it into the future you hope for.

## A Broadway Musical

The second promise is found in Jeremiah 32:37-40 and says: *"What's more, I'll make a covenant with them that will last forever, a covenant to stick with them no matter what, and work for their good."*[17] God is working for your good. You must realize that no matter what you've seen with your eyes in your past or what you are predicting for your future, you can trust that He is working for your GOOD. Your present is marked with His goodness. Trust that even if you can't see Him moving, He is.

Anyone who knows me will quickly discover how much I love music. It stems from a deep love for olden day musicals. When I was younger my mom used to rent us every musical she could think of. They were clean and appropriate for all ages, usually. I remember being a kid and watching Doris Day in Calamity Jane and dreaming of singing, dancing and shooting a gun like her![18] Just being real. She was a modern-day Wonder Woman who could sing and dance. A kick-butt woman with vocal power. I loved it. So when I gave my heart to the Lord, that love just carried over. Singing and writing songs for the Creator of the Universe (who is my dad, by the way) couldn't be a better gig. Though it's never actually been a gig, instead it's just something I have loved to do. I always had a desire to write and produce a musical in the Christian sphere, and as crazy as that may sound, I actually got to![19] Side note: no dream is too crazy for God.

When it comes to God working for your good, think of it like a Broadway musical. There are so many aspects that go into making a production successful. The script and actors. The stage design. The music and fifty-piece orchestra. The sound and the lights. Need I say more?

If we aren't familiar with the production, we have no way of knowing, as an audience, what could possibly come next. But behind the scenes, things are moving. The right people are lining up for what comes next. The stage design and lighting crew are getting ready to move pieces out for the next phase of the performance. It's all working together for an ultimate purpose, and ultimate good. That's exactly how God works behind the scenes in your life.

You may not see it now, but God is lining up the right people, the right situations, the right pieces in your life behind the scenes for the next season you are about to walk in.

## Take me by the hand, Papa

I remember when my dad first taught me to ride a bike. I was so scared. To me, falling off my bike felt like falling off a two-story building. The injuries could be endless. Scraped knees. Scraped elbows. A broken nose. A leg getting cut off. You name it, I imagined it. What curbed my fear was that my dad

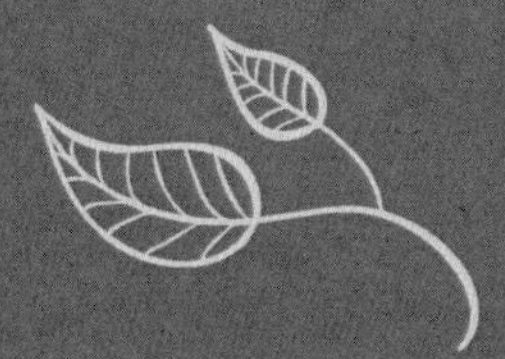

"WHAT WE CHASE SHAPES OUR RACE, SO DON'T SIMPLY LET YOUR HEART BE YOUR GUIDE"

-Ruth Chou Simmons

was right there. He promised not to let go of that bike. I knew with the promise of his presence and his hand on me that I would be ok. He wouldn't let me fall. He was so patient. Time and time again, I rode down the driveway and into the cul-de-sac. Every time I looked back he was there running behind me, his hand on my bike, assuring my success. Until one time, he wasn't there and I was riding all by myself. He knew when he needed to be close to help me and he knew when I was ready to soar—yet he was there in it all, always.

For promise number three, be reminded that God is the same way. In Jeremiah He says, *"I take their hands and lead them, lead them to fresh flowing brooks, lead them along smooth, uncluttered paths."*[20] Let God be your guide. Realize that you may not need to know all the answers, but that God will take you by the hand and lead you to the places He wants you to be. He will take YOUR hand. He is near. He is close. He will not leave you unattended to fend for yourself. He is your personal guide.

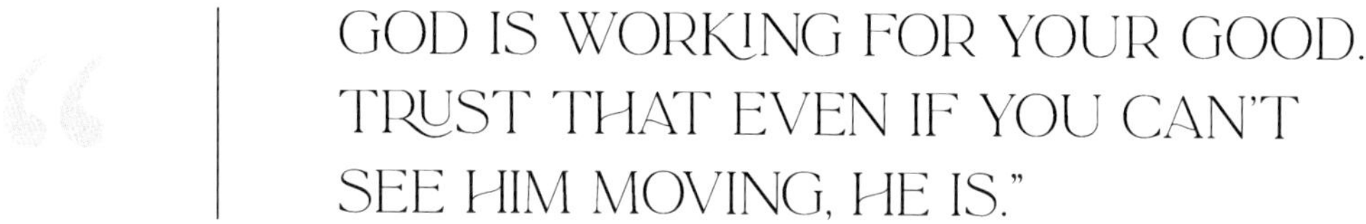


In order for a guide to be effective, he or she must be close. When I guide my children, I am next to them. I not only help them find the correct way, but many times when I grab their hands it's for more than just direction. It's as if I'm saying, stay close. I am reassuring them that I am there ... Mommy's got you. I am protecting them. I am pulling them up if they are teetering on rocky ground. I am there to bring assurance because they have never walked this way before. Either way, Mommy is there. And if the journey becomes too difficult, I don't hesitate to pick them up and carry them safely to their destination.

I like to think God is the same with us. He is reassuring us of His nearness as He takes our hand. He is directing us, protecting us and carrying us when needed.

## Just give me a call

Last, but not least, be reminded of Jeremiah 33:3: *"Call to me and I will answer you. I'll tell you marvelous and wondrous things that you could never figure out on your own."*[21] God has the answers you need. He is your counselor.

Have you ever had an important phone call with someone? You know, a call you have been anxiously awaiting to have with anticipation. You even find yourself counting down the days beforehand. The day of, you're ready a couple minutes early. You round up the kids, put on a long movie, and make sure they have enough snacks to feed an army. You set out ten glasses of water, just in case your kids forgot how to get water on their own. You wrap them in blankets, but dress them in tank tops. You have to cover all your bases: blankets if they get too cold and tank tops if they are too hot, that way there is no excuse as to why they need to disturb you.

You quickly tuck the dogs away in the laundry room with their dog bed, assuring yourself that there will be no barking during this call. Every fan is on in every bathroom and you turn the noise makers on for good measure. No distractions. You find a quiet place, shut the door and now you're left alone, just you and your phone.

You watch the minutes tick by awaiting the call. You get that nervous feeling stirring in your stomach and even though they can't see you face to face, you feel like they will be able to stare you down through your device. You wait. And wait. Finally, you text them, wondering if they remembered your call ... no answer. After fifteen minutes, you are resigned to the fact that they aren't calling, they've forgotten about you.

God always shows up for us. He is awaiting your call, but unlike us, He's not going to leave if we don't show up after fifteen minutes. He hasn't forgotten about you. In fact, He has arranged everything in His schedule just to meet with you. Knowing your Creator, partially, is knowing that He is waiting to hear from you and answer you. Realize in this moment that God is here, waiting for you to call on Him and trust Him in new ways, with a fresh revelation of who He is. You just need to show up. He promises He will answer. He has an answer to every need, question and problem already mapped out, and His answer is greater than anything we could ever figure out on our own. Remind yourself of the promises of God today. Breathe again and *Just Be* reminded … His love for you is sure, His promises are endless.

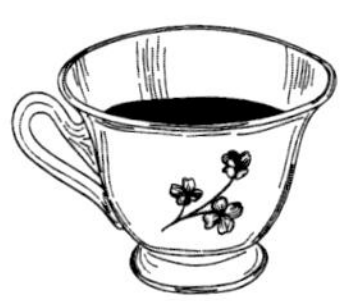

BOOK RECOMMENDATION

## Gracelaced *by Ruth Chou Simmons*

As an artist, author and inspirational speaker, Ruth has the canny ability to partner her strengths in this book. It's a beautifully crafted inspirational read about finding God in our day-to-day life.

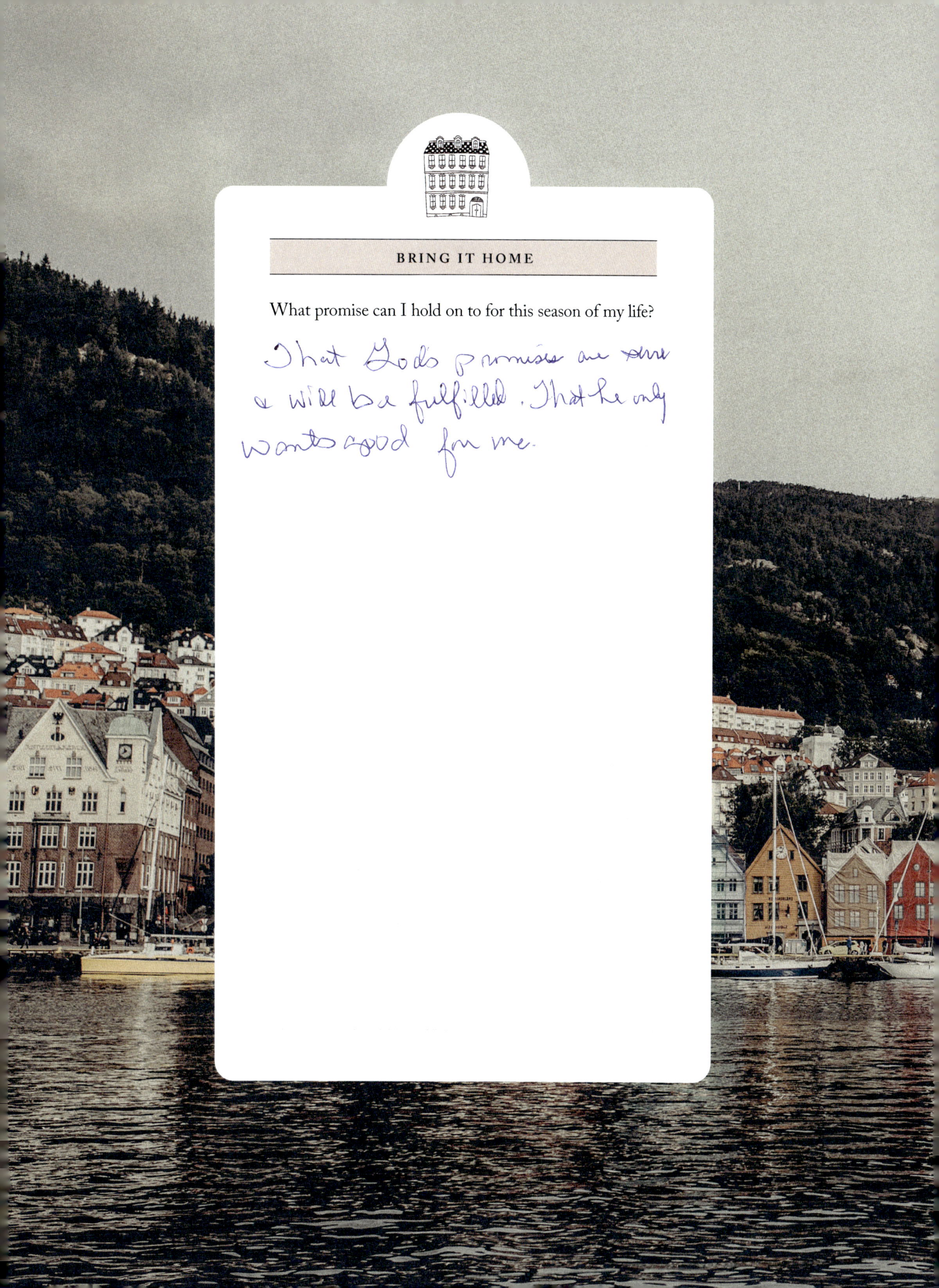

## BRING IT HOME

What promise can I hold on to for this season of my life?

That God's promises are sure & will be fulfilled. That he only wants good for me.

CHAPTER SEVEN

# JUST BE *Aware*

THE NEARNESS OF GOD IN EVERYDAY MOMENTS

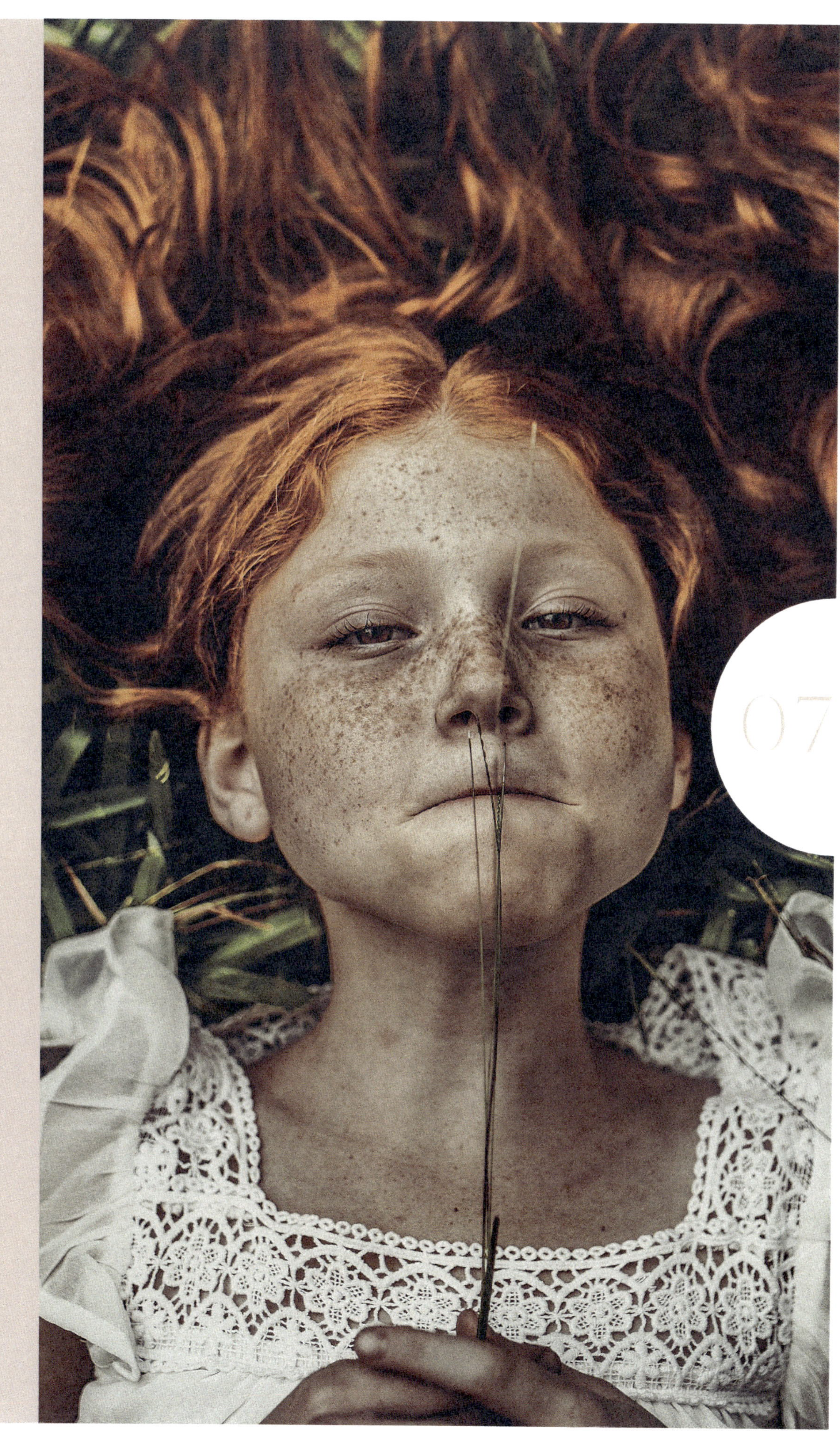

07

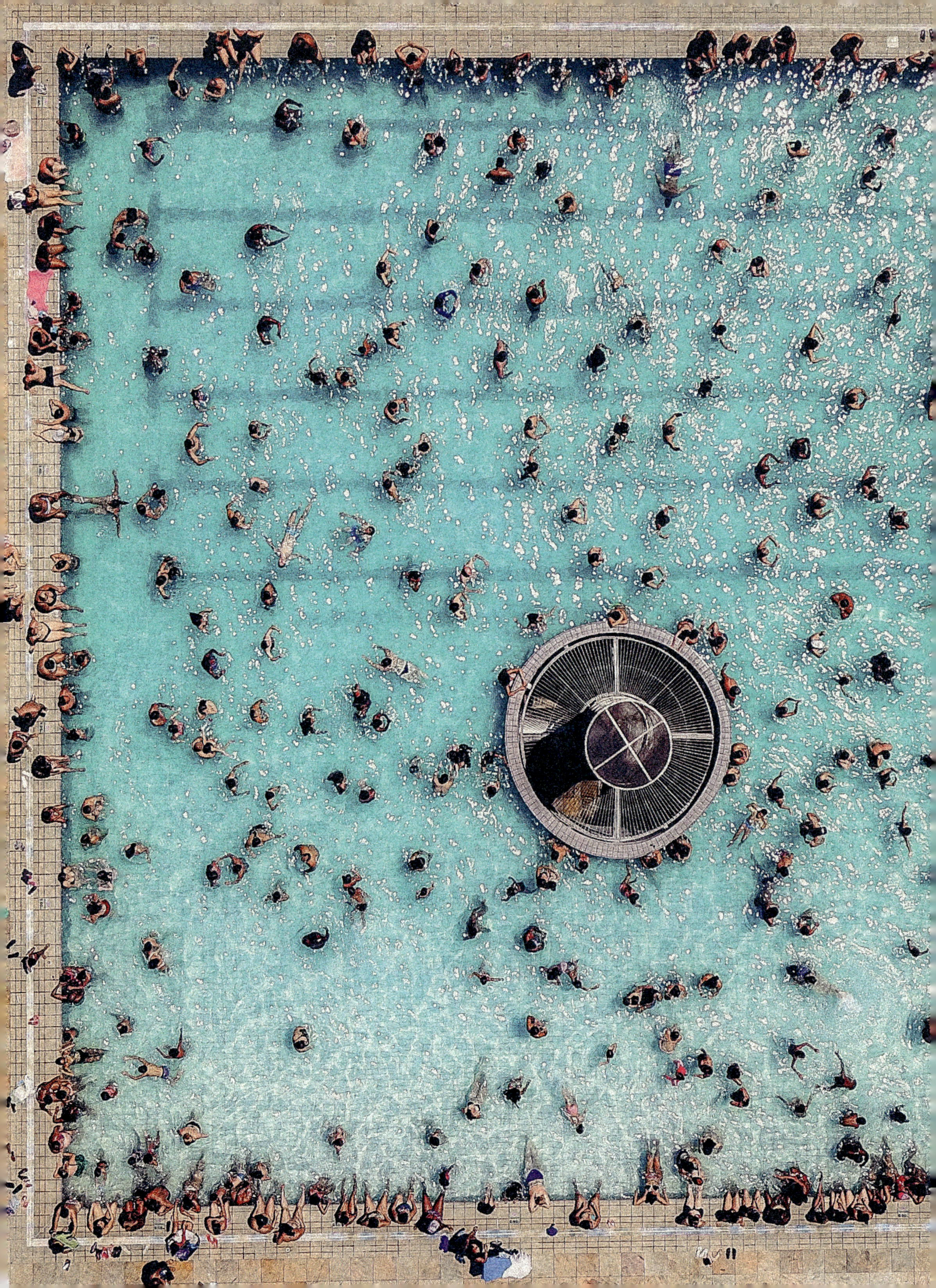

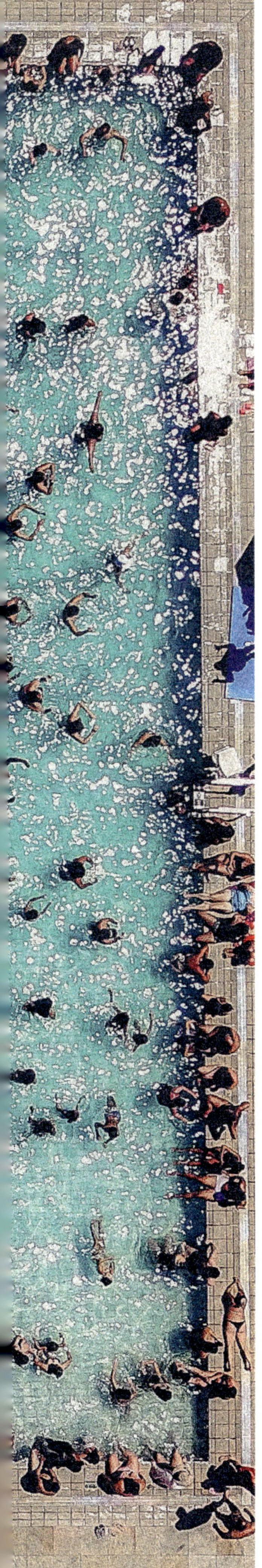

*"God took hold of my heart when I was fourteen,"* I continue, *"I have never been the same since that day ... There have been ups and downs, but through it all, He constantly reminds me that He is always there."*

I begin to think of the goodness of God and how He sought after my life at such a young age, when He knew I needed Him most. My mind races at the fact that since that heavenly moment, His pursuit of me has never stopped, only intensified with each year that has passed. My eyes gaze downward as I am fully aware of His love for me, overwhelmed by Him, and I sense the tears welling up in my eyes. I try to blink, hoping they will quickly fade away, but it only gives them permission to tumble down my cheeks. I look up and I see you are crying too ...

I sniffle slightly and try to lighten the mood by recalling stories of my life that re-emphasize the goodness of God throughout it. My mind is drawn back to my childhood days. The long, hot, beautiful days of summer ... we begin to talk of days gone by.

Growing up with all girls in my family left limited pool game options. After all, one could only play *The Little Mermaid* for so long before we all got tired. We didn't have mermaid tails back then so we tried our hardest to keep our little legs together, swim our hearts out, and sing with the sweetest voices we could muster. Needless to say, all my sisters wanted to be Ariel.

Being the oldest, however, I took on the weighty responsibility of choosing each character, and I was usually cast as Ariel, go figure. When cootie-licious boys or precious friends came to the pool, we usually resorted to playing Marco Polo. I especially didn't like to be "it" during this game because that meant I had to swim around the pool with my eyes squeezed shut yelling out "Marco," praying that I would eventually catch someone. I have to admit, there were times when I was "it" so long I had to peek, which is the one thing I wasn't supposed to do!

At moments in my walk with God, I feel like I'm in a game of Marco Polo. I'm in a large pool surrounded by a plethora of people. My eyes

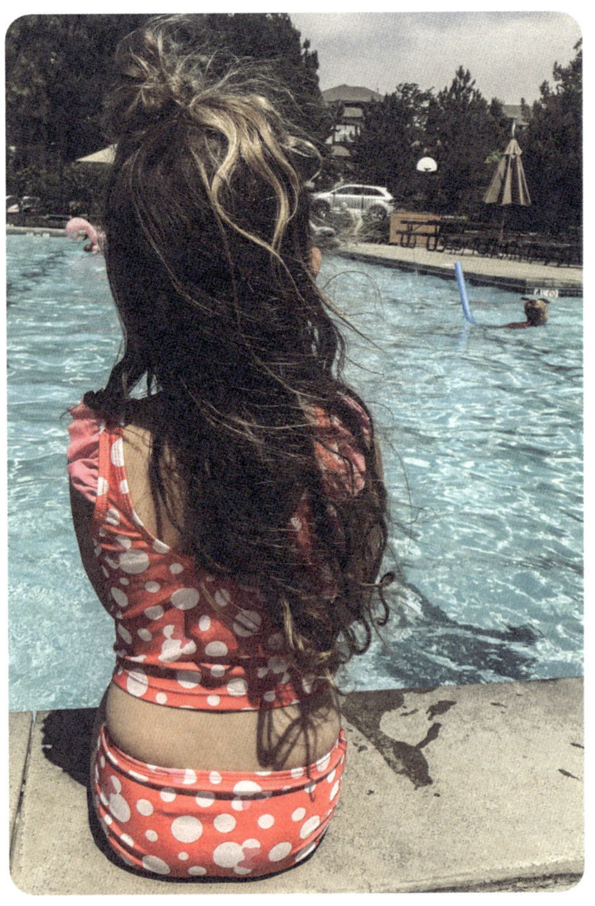

are shut tightly and I'm yelling out "Marco!" (aka "Jesus") all the while trying to distinguish the voice of God from the others yelling back "Polo!"

Sometimes I can hear Him so clearly. I'm in the shallow end and He is right there next to me. His voice is unmistakable and even with my eyes closed I know it is Him. I reach out and touch Him. I open my eyes and there He is, smiling down at me.

Other times I can barely hear Him through the noise of others around me. I'm trying my best to swim toward Him, but the multitude of voices around me prove to be very distracting. I feel tired, but this I know: if I keep yelling out, I'll find my way back to Him. He won't let me stay "it" for too long. Oftentimes I don't even need to find my way to Him because when I open my eyes to peek at where He is, I notice He's been right there by my side all along. He is always there. In the discouraging silence, when God seems so distant and all we desire is to hear His voice—those are the moments when He is near. Nearness, as if you can feel the warmth of His breath caress your soul and you honestly believe if you were to open your eyes in that moment you would see that He is standing right beside you.

I can't often see God in the moment, though I am actively asking Him to give me eyes to see Him in the here and now—an acute awareness of His presence and what He is doing in the world around me. Although we may not see His every move or understand His every decision, if we trust that He has the BEST in mind for us, we can have peace knowing that He is nearer than we think.

The promises found in the last chapter are promises that I have posted around my house for the moments when I doubt. In my cupboards, on my mirrors, on the walls in our living room, on my prayer board, on the antique buffet I got for twenty-five dollars on Craigslist …

*The promises of God line my home to remind me,*

*everywhere I look,*

*that His eyes are on me and He is nearer than I think.*

*In fact, at any moment God could burst in with a miracle.*

*Our lives as children of God are marked for unexpected miracles*

*and drenched with the nearness of God.*

## When in doubt, remember this ...

When I'm tempted to doubt the promises God has spoken over my life, doubt His goodness for me, doubt His nearness in my life, I remember this: *Just Being* means I must rest in His love for me, His promise assured, His nearness undoubted. Whether I understand Him or not matters little; I choose to trust. I choose to rest in His love. Whether I feel Him near or not, I choose to remember He is there.

Choosing is just that; it's a choice. It's a decision that doesn't negate my feelings—because let me tell you, they are still alive, well and roaring—yet in the middle of them I can choose to believe God is working for me and He is with me. Look at what the word of God says: *"Can a woman forget her nursing child, or lack compassion for the child of her womb? Even if these forget, yet I will not forget you. Look, I have inscribed you on the palms of my hands."*[22] How could He ever forget me if my name is inscribed on the palms of His hands? I can't help but think the inscription looks a little bit like nail holes. Precisely, beautifully scarred nail holes. And within that hole is written, on the inner lining, my name: Jamie Kay Klusacek. Every time I remember His hands, I'm reminded of His love for me.

*"I have loved you with an everlasting love; therefore, I have continued to extend faithful love to you."*[23] He loves YOU with an everlasting love that cannot be shaken. And the nearer we get to Him, the more we see He loves us and created us just as we are. Our quirks, our perceived imperfections, our desires, our hopes, our dreams all rest safely in His hands. We begin to embrace who we are. No longer are we striving to be someone else. We let go of our pursuits to cultivate talents God clearly has not called us to have—and we rest in the arms of the Father whose love will NEVER fail or falter.

I can *Just Be*. A freckle-faced, taller-than-most-girls, not-perfect, still-wears-a-retainer, makeup-less dreamer, wanna-be writer and composer, bless-the-world, promise-carrier, wife, mother of four,

"OUR LIVES AS CHILDREN OF GOD ARE MARKED FOR UNEXPECTED MIRACLES AND DRENCHED WITH THE NEARNESS OF GOD."

deeply-cherished-princess-of-God who realizes that she is the one true love of her Father, just as she is. And with Him by my side anything is possible.[24]

You are the one true love of our Father. Just the way you are. Perceived faults, failures and all. He is not repelled by you, He is drawn to you in every way you could possibly imagine. He is the only One who will ever truly love you and fulfill the deepest longings of your heart. We try to find it in accomplishments, striving to do and be what we deem as significant, but that only leads to disappointment. We try to find our value in relationships, but there is only one relationship that can fill our souls—a relationship with Jesus. NOTHING and NO ONE can ever replace the love God has for our lives. There's no better time than the present. In each new moment we can discover a greater love, a greater nearness, a greater compassion, a greater purpose from Him than we have ever thought possible. God can accelerate the years that may have been wasted and cultivate a nearness to Him within you that you never dreamed possible. You are deeply loved. He is with you.

*Just Be* reminded again. Start creating rhythms in your life that remind you of the beautifully present, tender nearness of God.

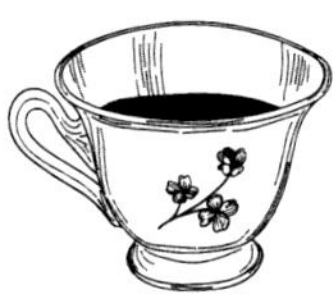

**BOOK RECOMMENDATION**

## Jesus Calling *by Sarah Young*

Sarah served as a missionary for many years. This compelling devotional documents her desire to listen for and discern the voice of God in her everyday moments.

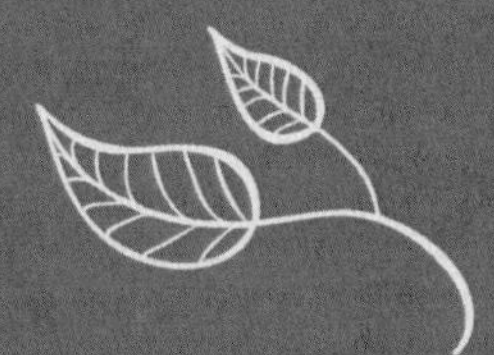

"WE MUST KNOW THE ONE WHO WILL ALWAYS FULLY EMBRACE US AND NEVER HOLD BACK."

- Lysa TerKeurst

# FRECKLE-FACED FEMALE CONFESSIONS

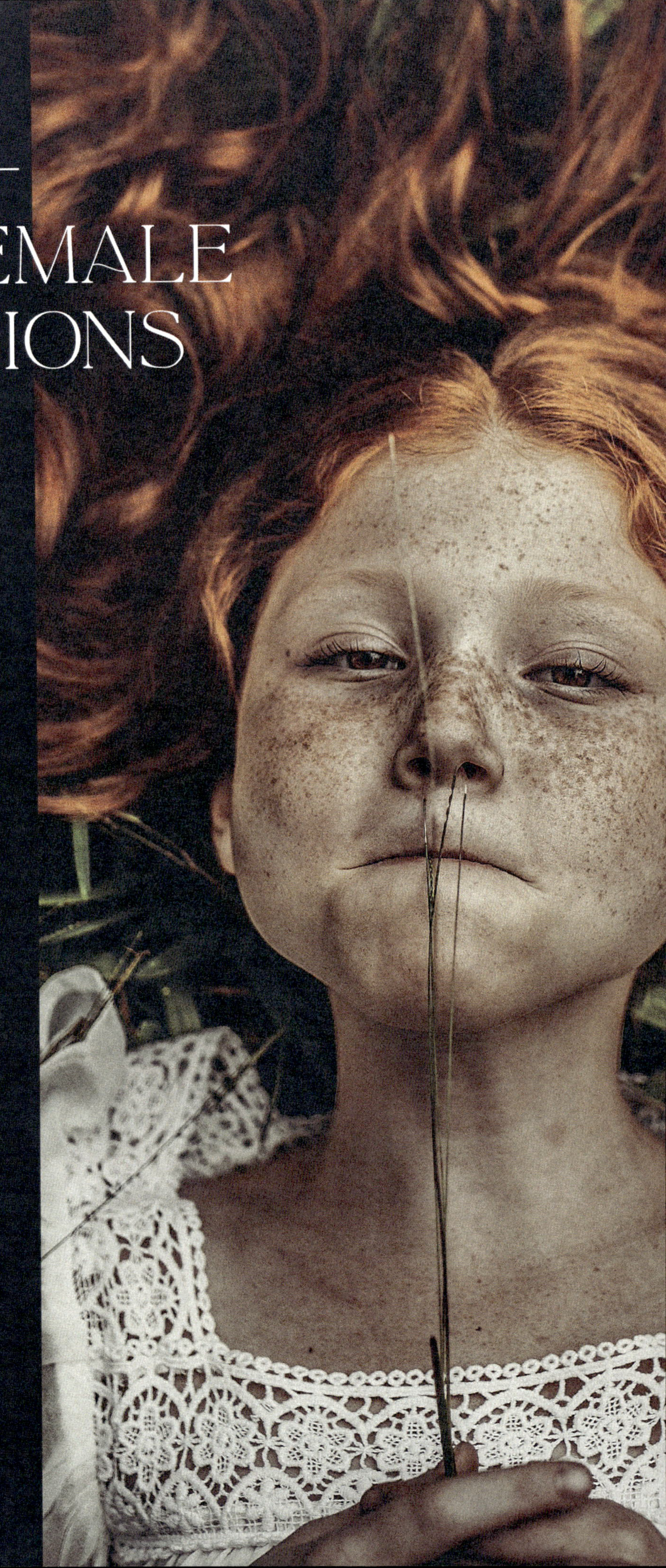

"I can *Just Be*. A freckle-faced, taller-than-most-girls, not-perfect, still-wears-a-retainer, makeup-less dreamer, wanna-be writer and composer, bless-the-world, promise-carrier, wife, mother of four, deeply-cherished-princess-of-God who realizes that she is the one true love of her Father, just as she is. And with Him by my side anything is possible."

-Jamie

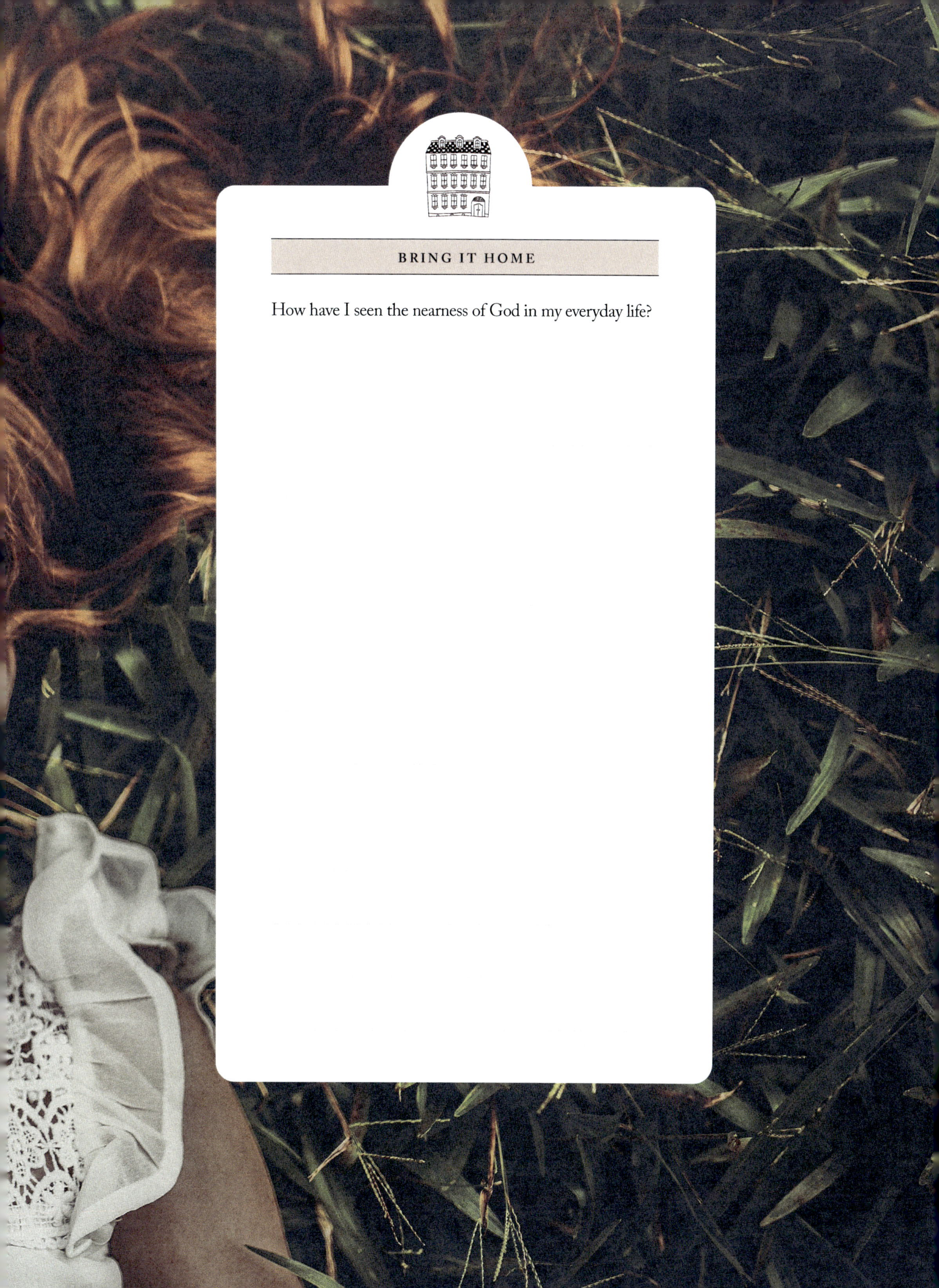

BRING IT HOME

How have I seen the nearness of God in my everyday life?

CHAPTER EIGHT

# JUST BE *Content*

LIVING LIFE IN THE SHADOWS

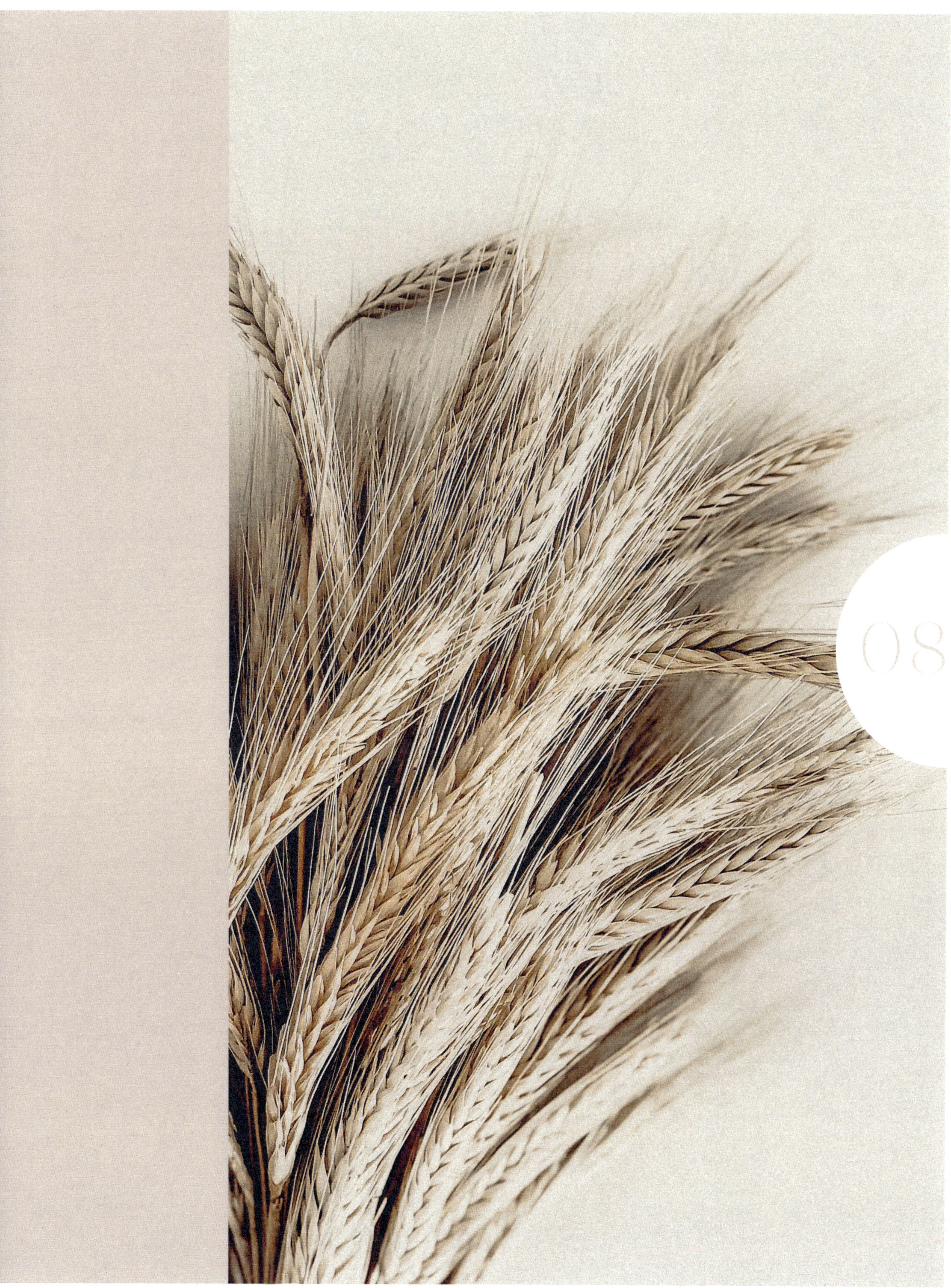

08

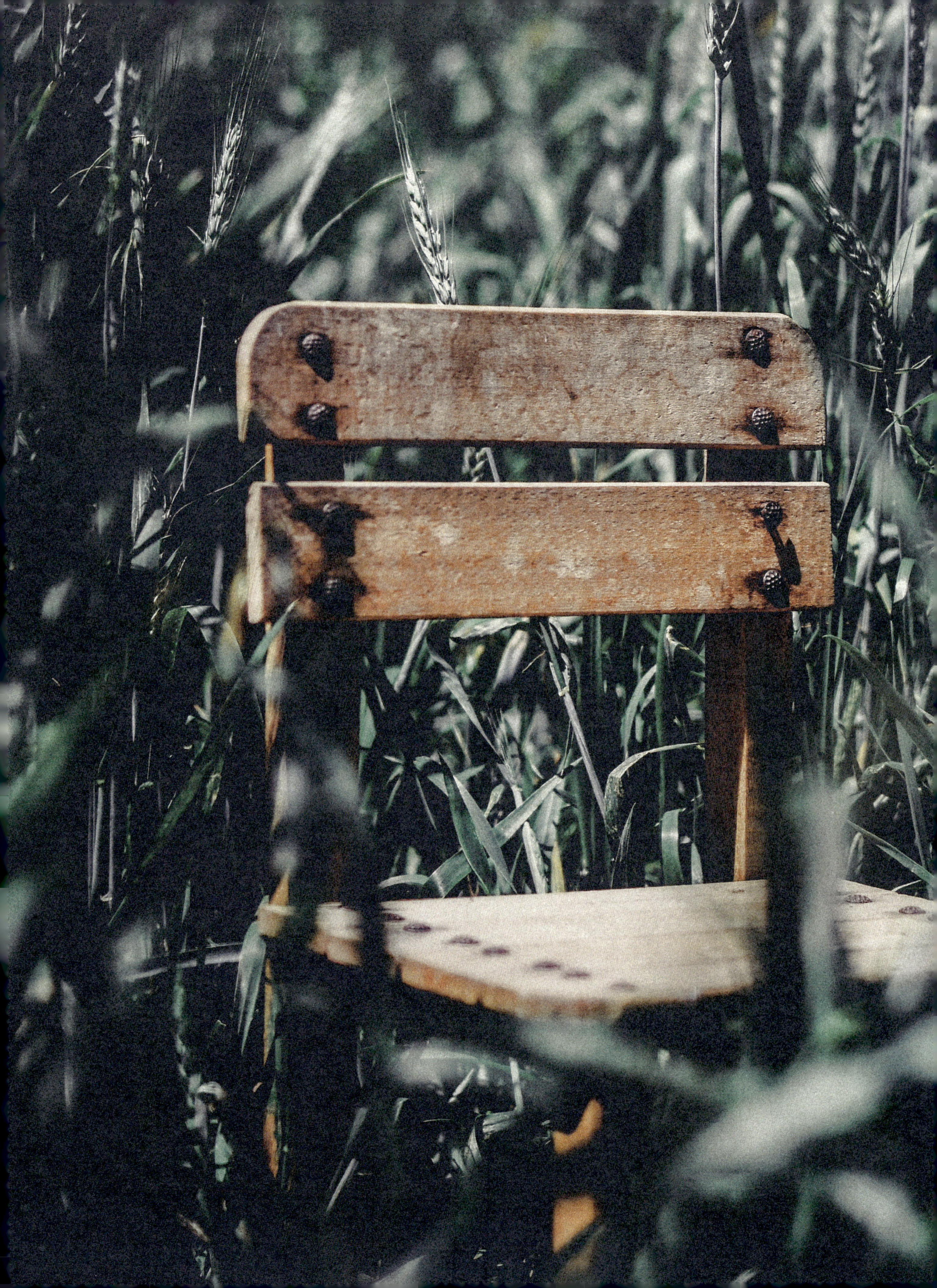

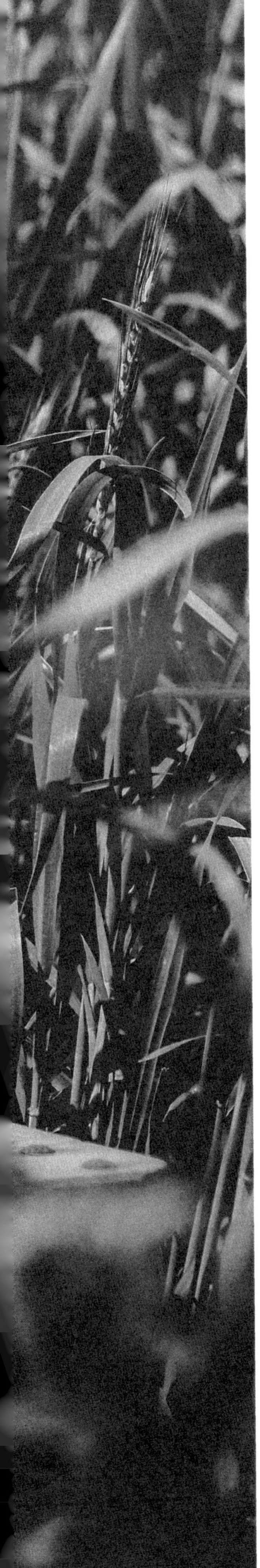

*"Boaz answered her 'Everything you have done for your mother-in-law since your husband's death has been fully reported to me: how you have left your father and mother and your native land, and how you came to a people that you didn't previously know* [This is your testimony, the things you've done when you thought no one was watching]. *May the Lord reward you for what you have done, and may you receive a full reward from the Lord God of Israel, under whose wings you have come for refuge.'"*[25] *-Ruth 2:11-12*

Open your Bible and read the Book of Ruth. I promise it will be worth the effort and only deepen the awareness of your purpose as we talk about it in the pages to come. There are three main characters, or heroes in the faith, that we are going to study together: Naomi, Ruth and Boaz. All of the characters in this story play a significant role in God's plan. All are very different. From this book, I'm going to tackle a few of the things God has been speaking to me about *Just Being* who God has created me to be in the secret places of my heart. They are concepts, even characteristics, that I have seen woven in the fabric of every great story the Author of my life has ever told. My prayer is that God deposits even greater truths to your heart as you read the next section of this book. Your best years are ahead of you. God will accomplish His plan in you and through you. We are on this purpose-finding journey together.

## In the shadows is where purpose is defined and developed

I don't know what dreams and aspirations Ruth had. I'm not sure what secret desires laced the seasons of her heart. What I do know is that she was a woman, and if she was in any way like me, she had longings and desires. She probably had a scrapbook of pictures detailing what her life would become. The Bible doesn't go into great detail about Ruth's life prior to her marriage to Naomi's son, Mahlon. Many rabbis maintain that Ruth was one of the daughters of King Eglon of Moab, and that

Orpah was actually her sister. Ruth was, potentially, the daughter of a king. Imagine that.

Now, the Moabites and Israelites were not on the best terms. God had warned His people not to dwell or intermarry with people of a foreign land because they could draw them away from the One true God to serve other foreign gods. Still, Elimelech and his wife Naomi ventured out to dwell with the Moabites.

When Naomi and her husband, Elimelech, settled in Moab from Bethlehem with their two sons, little did the sisters know what would lie ahead. I'm sure at this point Ruth and Orpah had heard of the Israelites. They had heard of the wondrous true God rumored among the nations. And now they were to be married into this awe-inspiring, fearful nation. After ten years of marriage had come and gone, both Orpah's and Ruth's husbands died. I'm certain during those years each sister learned of Yahweh, the God of the Hebrews. They had heard time and time again of His great deliverance, His justice, His love. They were left with a choice: stay with their widowed mother-in-law and venture back to Judah, or return to the home of their father, the king.

I think many times we read scripture with the ending in mind. Forget about Ruth's ending for a moment, and try to imagine this decision from her perspective. She had one of two choices to make. Within option one lies an open door (P.S. not all open doors are God-doors) to return to her home—and not just any home, but potentially, the home of a king. She once again would have the status of being the king's daughter and all the luxuries that came with it. She would be significant in the land once again. As the king's daughter, she was virtually assured to be remarried. Who wouldn't want to marry the daughter of a king? Children, grandchildren, great grandchildren filled the portrait of this path. It may have assured her of a future filled with hope. A future that she had potentially dreamed of. Not only that, but it was familiar and comfortable, in the only way "home" could be. There was safety there. She had every right to choose this path.

The other choice was filled with uncertainty. It involved, but was not limited to, following a mother-in-law who had no means to provide for herself. In fact, by making this choice Ruth was essentially devoting her life to provide for Naomi, with no return-on-investment except gratitude. She would be living her life selflessly for another. Ruth would be venturing into a land of people who were not inclined to accept her. She was from an enemy nation. In addition, the Israelites were instructed not to marry "her kind," so the potential of Ruth ever getting married and having children was slim to none. She may never be a mother. And what about when Naomi passes away? Ruth would then be left with no one. She could remain unknown for the rest of her life, but in the process, she would have the chance to help someone who was most dear to her. What would she do? The choice was hers to make.

It's not as easy when put in this perspective, is it? One path seems tangled with problems, the other with provision. One path assured her a life of honor, back in the king's palace, the other a life in the shadows of a nation who despised her. More often than not, this is how our lives unfold.

In front of us lies a path that, in all our calculations, leads us straight to everything we've dreamed. It encompasses our past, present and future, meshing it into one ball of exquisite dreams being fulfilled. Meanwhile, the other path seems as if it will only lead us into the shadows, unloved, unknown, undervalued—a perpetual sacrifice. But things aren't always what they seem. Many times, they can be exactly the opposite. Only God can see the end from the beginning and no matter how hard we try to imagine what may come from the decisions we make, the only thing we are assured of is the reward of obedience.

The path of the shadows is a place where character is built, strength is given, purpose is formed and contentment is nurtured. God says He will bless the righteous and surround them with favor as with a shield.[26] Ruth has a tough decision to make, but every sacrificial step of obedience she took in the shadows was paving the way for her destiny to be fulfilled. The foundation to carry the weight of your purpose is built in shadows of daily obedience. This is where heroes are developed. The path of selfless sacrifice was the choice she made, and many times, this is the choice that leads us to the promise God has for our lives.

There is a disease that is plaguing our generations and its name is *more*. It rages through our ranks breeding discontent and discouragement. It turns what is lovely into what is contemptible. It makes the pure less than adequate. When we arrive at our fulfillment of purpose, it breathes down our necks and whispers in our ears, "It's not enough." It cripples our feet, binds our hands and darkens our minds. It causes the rich in life to become poor in spirit. It whispers promises it doesn't intend to keep and leads us running in circles, never quite good enough. It is masked with false kindness toward others, secretly trying to benefit itself. It is a plague that I am ready to be rid of.

Ruth could have chosen the path of what seemed like *more*, but in the end it would have left her lacking. She chose instead to make her mark, not defined by her comfort or status, but by bettering the life of someone else through simple kindness and service. She died

"THE FOUNDATION TO CARRY THE WEIGHT OF YOUR PURPOSE IS BUILT IN SHADOWS OF DAILY OBEDIENCE."

"TALENTS ARE BEST NURTURED IN SOLITUDE; CHARACTER IS BEST FORMED IN THE STORMY BILLOWS OF THE WORLD."

–Johann Wolfgang von Goethe

to her desires in order to help someone else live.

Embracing the path of the shadows does not mean you are unimportant, but rather you know what is most important. You are content with the season you're in. In God's eyes, you are enough. You are loved. You are the daughter of the King and always will be. Ruth chose to follow and care for Naomi, and she had to make sacrifices in the days to come because of that choice.

Though there may be times of difficulty and sacrifice, you must trust you are in the hands of the One who created you. You know Whose you are. Instead of trying to work out every detail of your life, focus more on who you are becoming. Wait expectantly in the shadows for the moments of fulfilled promise to come your way, but until then, continue to walk in daily obedience and just be the person God is asking you to be. When that promise does come, it won't change or define you; you already know who you are. Whether in the palace, the field or the wilderness, you are being who God created you to be.

If you're in a place where you feel as if you are in the shadows, have hope—God is working some deep things in you and your time of promise will come. You may feel looked over and passed by, but trust that God has a purpose for exactly where you are. He is building your character for an ultimate purpose. Be faithful while you're in this season. Allow God to work contentment in the depths of your soul. Don't jump ship. Ruth had the opportunity to jump ship. She made the choice to stay with Naomi and when Naomi told her to go home, Ruth stood firm. She was passionate when she told Naomi,

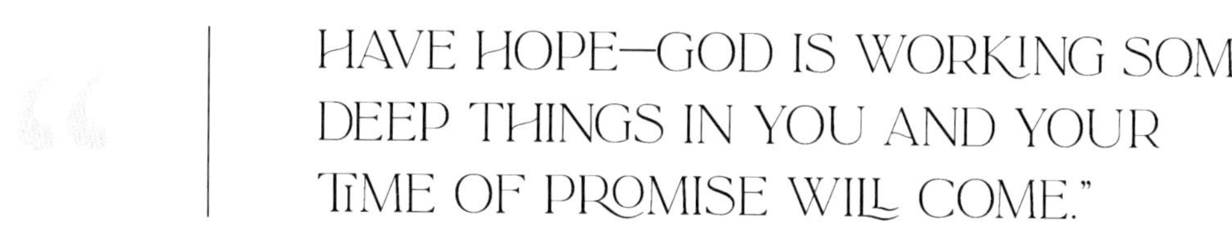


*"May the Lord punish me, and do so severely, if anything but death separates you and me."*[27] She had made up her mind and she would not turn back.

You may have made the initial decision to choose God's way and it isn't what you planned. You're in the shadows and now you're wanting to run home. Don't do it. Stay put. Allow God to work in you the character He needs to take you to where He wants you to go. It may be five years, ten years or twenty-five years, but trust that God will get you to where you need to be. Stay rooted and grounded in the season God has you in and allow Him to mold your character. Stay there until He tells you otherwise. I often pray, "God, don't take me to a place or position where my character isn't strong enough to sustain me—Your name means so much more to me than that." Your character means more than your accomplishments ever will.

I find it interesting that when Ruth actually meets Boaz, the man who would one day marry her, it wasn't her beauty that gave her favor in His eyes. It wasn't her father's house or that she was the daughter of a king. It wasn't how thin she was or her feminine strength. It wasn't her skillfulness, talent or giftings. What turned this man's heart towards Ruth was the testimony of who she was. Her sacrifice. Her love and care for Naomi. It wasn't her Instagram account or how many followers she had. None of that mattered in the scope of her destiny. Her character is what opened the door to her promise. The same is true for you. Your character will open the door of promise in your life, so be content in your placement. *"For godliness with contentment is great gain. For we brought nothing into the world, and we can take nothing out."*[28]

**Added Bonus:** For those of you still wondering if following God in the shadows will really pay off, consider this. In my studies, I have discovered that many of the Jewish rabbis believe that Orpah was the great-grandmother of Goliath, and Ruth was the great-grandmother of David. David and Goliath. Isn't that crazy! They both chose different paths, but only God knew where each path would lead. Studying the scripture is fascinating and faith building.[29]

BOOK RECOMMENDATION

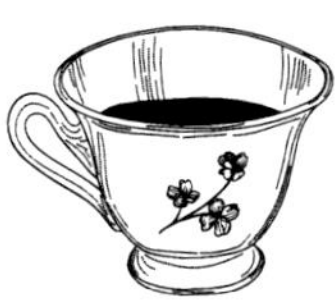

## Anonymous *by Alicia Britt Chole*

This is a book focusing on character developed in unseen moments. Learn the lessons you need in the shadows, embrace it and come out a better you.

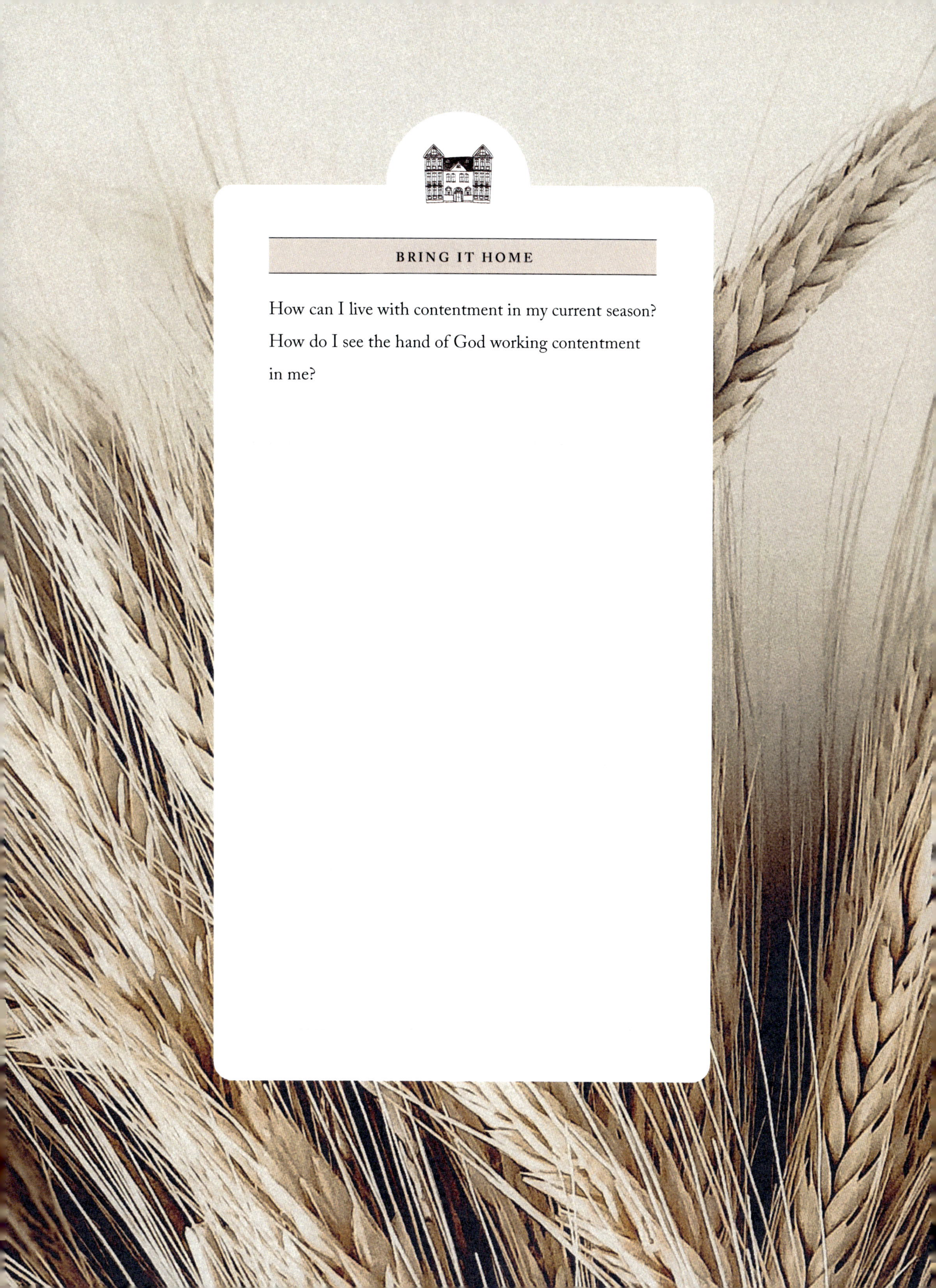

## BRING IT HOME

How can I live with contentment in my current season? How do I see the hand of God working contentment in me?

CHAPTER NINE

# JUST BE *Present*

THERE'S BEAUTY IN YOUR EVERYDAY

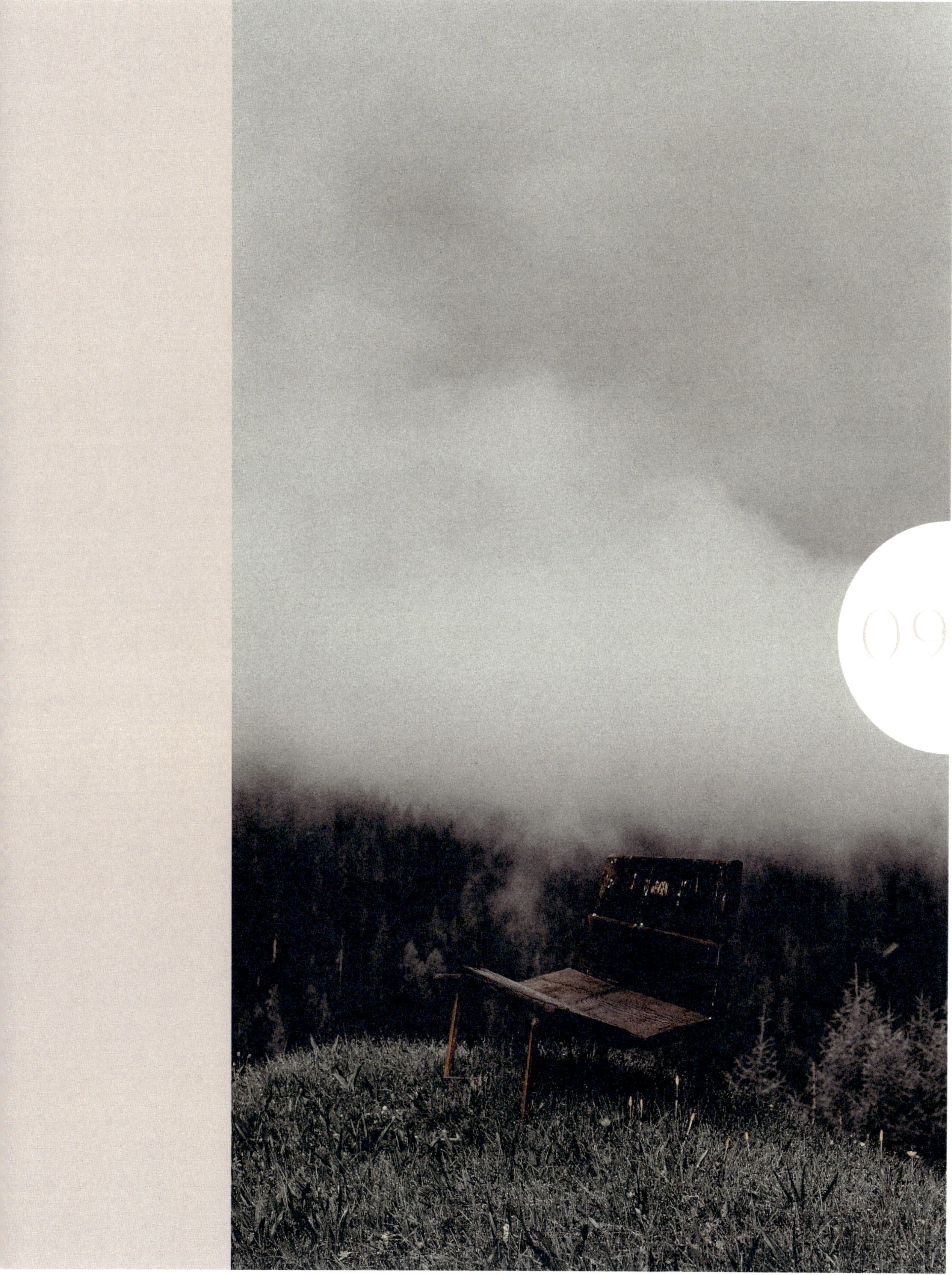

09

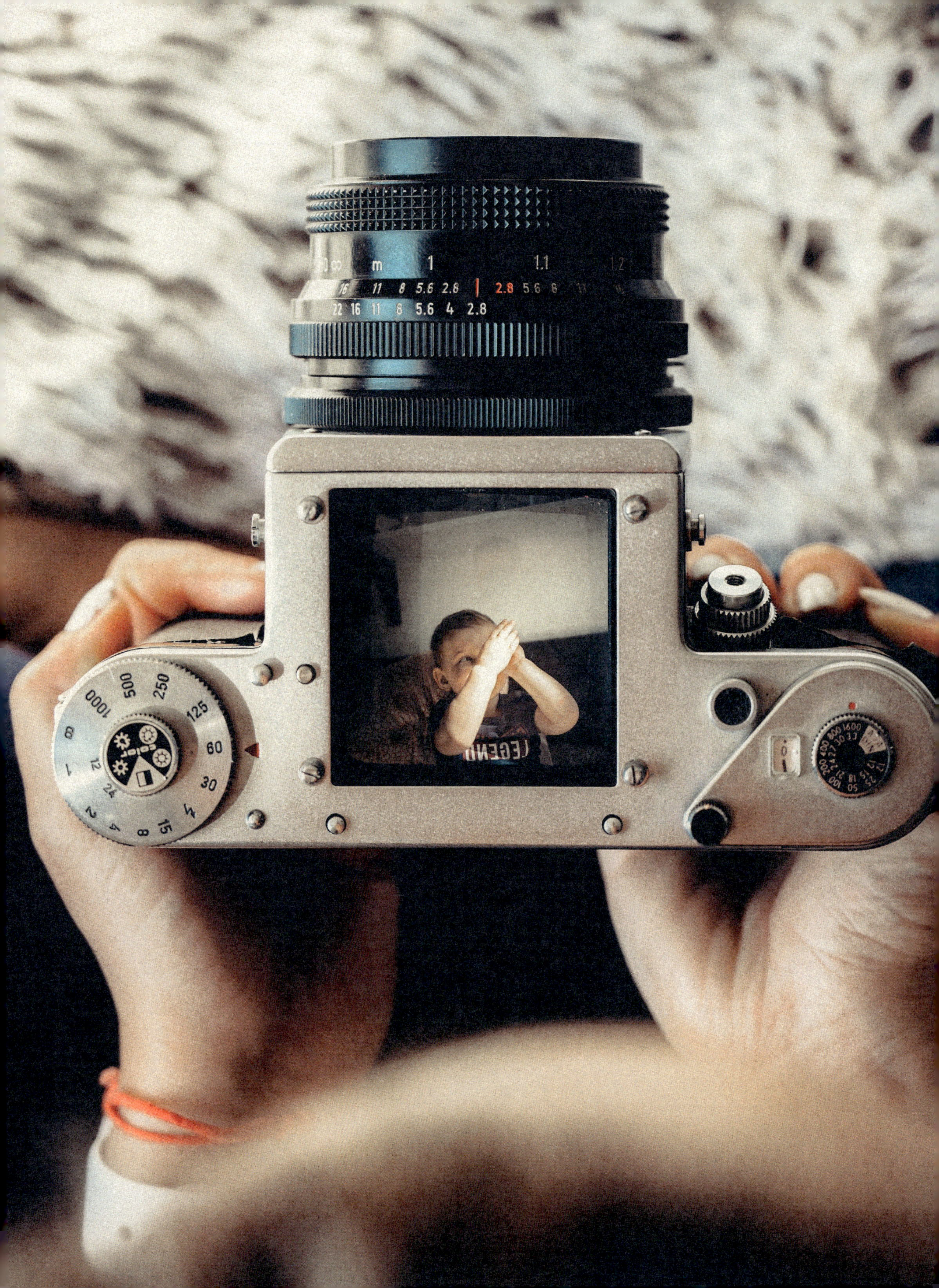

m 1 1.1 1.2
22 16 11 8 5.6 4 2.8
1000 500 250 125 60 30 15 8 4 2

*"When Ruth went back to work again, Boaz ordered his young men, 'Let her gather grain right among the sheaves without stopping her. And pull out some heads of barley from the bundles and drop them on purpose for her. Let her pick them up, and don't give her a hard time!'"*[30] *-Ruth 2:15-16*

I'm sitting right now overlooking the Rocky Mountains in a cabin perched on a hill—secluded and peaceful. It's June, but there is still snow on the tippy tops of the range. All my four children are running around the cabin. Giggling like glitter scattered across the room, leaving little sparkles on everything it touches. A gentle rain is descending from the heavens, depositing a darker hue of color on each facet of the scenery. The trees look greener. The mountains look a deep royal blue. Rain, despite the gloominess that comes with it, is beautiful and is ever needed for growth. The sun is beautiful too, but as much as I love it, when the rain comes something shifts in my soul. It's as if the rain gives me permission to pause and breathe again.

I've been learning to enjoy the everydayness of life. It's something God has been working in me after I experienced a longer-than-wanted season where my life was marked with stress and worry. I used to live for special events, words from others, approval, affirmation, confirmation and out-of-the-box words from God. Then a divine shift happened in my spirit and I realized that EVERY DAY is filled with precious gifts from God and if I don't choose to live in the present I may miss the simple things God wants to deposit into my life. Don't get me wrong, the big promises are wonderful, but I'm learning to enjoy the handfuls on purpose that God gives me daily just as much.

I'm learning to enjoy it all. Little blessings that I used to miss. My eyes being opened, my heart listening to the beautiful words of promise woven around me. Whispers from heaven echoing throughout my day to day, found in the rhythms of rest as well as big moments. The everydayness of life. Sunday morning set up for a portable church. Nighttime novel reading. A cup of

"IT'S UP TO US
TO CHOOSE
CONTENTMENT AND
THANKFULNESS
NOW - AND TO
STOP IMAGINING
THAT WE HAVE TO
HAVE EVERYTHING
PERFECT BEFORE
WE'LL BE HAPPY."

-Joanna Gaines

coffee with a lifelong friend. Group song writing. Friday book writing. Loose leaf hot tea in my favorite mug. Opening my heart to people who barely know my name. Spending time with those who know every detail of my soul. My children rain-dancing through the sprinklers. Uncontrollable laughter at the dinner table. Revealing secret places of my heart to God. Living open. Honest. Vulnerable to the right people. Friends who have become family. Bike rides around the neighborhood. Becoming a dream-pusher. Discovering treasures hidden in others. A competitive game of cornhole. Bedroom love notes on my nightstand from beautiful munchkins. Snuggling on the sofa with my husband. Eating Takis on the drive home from the school carpool line. Morning runs with the two pups. Comfy slippers. My favorite sweatshirt. Classical music. Time with Jesus. All team huddles. Playing sweet melodies on the piano. My bright yellow backpack. My keychain rings that remind me of God's promise. The list could go on forever.

It's as if my mind has been blown, my eyes open to see the precious treasures that lay all around me. Everything I thought I knew is no longer relevant because there's a God who is infinitely greater than what I can imagine on my own. I make it a consistent prayer: God help me to be present in my day to day and acknowledge the beautiful blessings You have placed in my life along the journey. Give me eyes to see. I love this quote I read from Christine Caine this week: "You know you're growing when you value the process as much as the destination." I'd add to that another facet of truth: "You know you're growing when you learn to value and enjoy the process as much as the destination."

Although Ruth may not have been doing what she dreamed about doing, God was leaving handfuls on purpose every day for her to find. Now, this didn't mean that Ruth could just sit back and be lazy. She still got up each morning readying herself for the heat of the day and the labor ahead, but she was on the lookout for God's blessings. Imagine if she would have walked into that field with a bad attitude. Grumbling and complaining about what she didn't have. Comparing herself to the other workers and how good their lives were. Longing to go back to her father's home where her life was much easier. Wasting her time on things she wasn't supposed to be doing because she was discontent with where God had placed her. With that kind of attitude, she could have missed the handfuls on purpose that God was trying to leave her. Her focus would have been on other things and not the task at hand. She very well could have missed the miracle God was trying to leave her. Her time would come. God would fulfill her dreams, above and beyond what she could dream. Until that time, she had to embrace the season she was in and look for the handfuls on purpose God was leaving in her everyday life.

How many times do we try to sidestep the season God has for us in order to get to what we want faster than God wants to take us? We look at the lives of others and become discontent. We miss the beautiful blessings that are before us because our focus has become fractured. Our discontent dampens our joy. We hone in on what we don't have or what we need to have in order to make us happy. This is not the way God intends us to live. He wants us to live with joy and contentment in our present.

A clean house. For years it was hard for me to sit with Jesus without being stressed out. There was always something else to clean. Cupboards to organize. Floors to wash. Dishes to do. Laundry to fold. Toilets to clean. The list is never ending. When I would sit with God and try to focus, instead I would see with my eyes everything that needed to be done. I would tell myself, "If I could just clean that thing then I could relax and enjoy my time with God." The problem was, there was always more to do. By responding like this I would miss the precious moments, the promises and provision God had for me daily.

A couple of things helped me do a divine shift in my perspective to be present.

**1. Realize there will always be more to do.** The to-do lists will never be done. I was chasing the illusion of peace and tranquility by accomplishing tasks, but true peace is only found in Jesus. There is always more to do, something that could be better, or another need to meet. Find peace in the midst of the messiness.

**2. Relinquish your superpowers.** Give yourself permission to be a sidekick. Granted, the best darn sidekick in sidekick's history. You were never meant to be a superhero, only God can hold that role. That means you don't need to do everything. In fact, God hasn't created you to do everything. Maybe in your lifetime you'll be able to do a few sidekick responsibilities extremely well and be a master in your field. Decide ahead of time what those things are for this season, develop them, then give the rest to God.

**3. Decide what will add the most value to you today and do that.** If I can't do the extra stuff in a day, it's okay. He'll provide. He will leave handfuls on purpose in every area of my life. I trust Him to help me decide what to do and when to do it. Leave margin in your day. God moves in the margin.

*God, give us hearts to be fully present today. Grant us the eyes to see the handfuls on purpose You are leaving to bless us in the everydayness of life.*

BOOK RECOMMENDATION

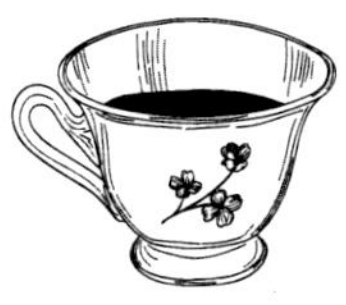

## Homebody *by Joanna Gaines*

Learn to create an environment that is clean, inspirational, relaxing, welcoming and feels like home. I place things in my home that remind me of God's blessings every day.

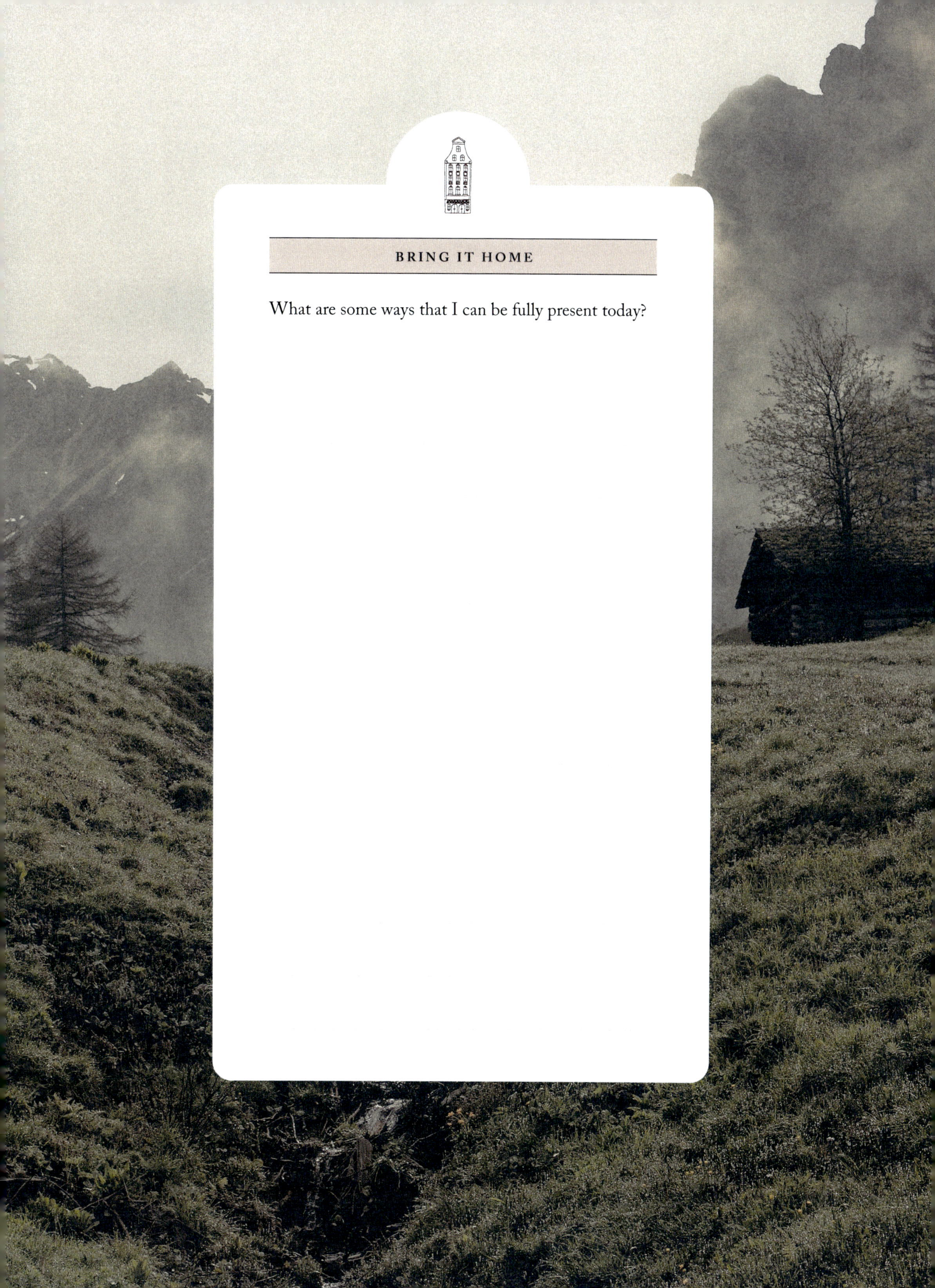

BRING IT HOME

What are some ways that I can be fully present today?

CHAPTER TEN

# JUST BE *Obedient*

KNOWING AND DOING THE WILL OF GOD

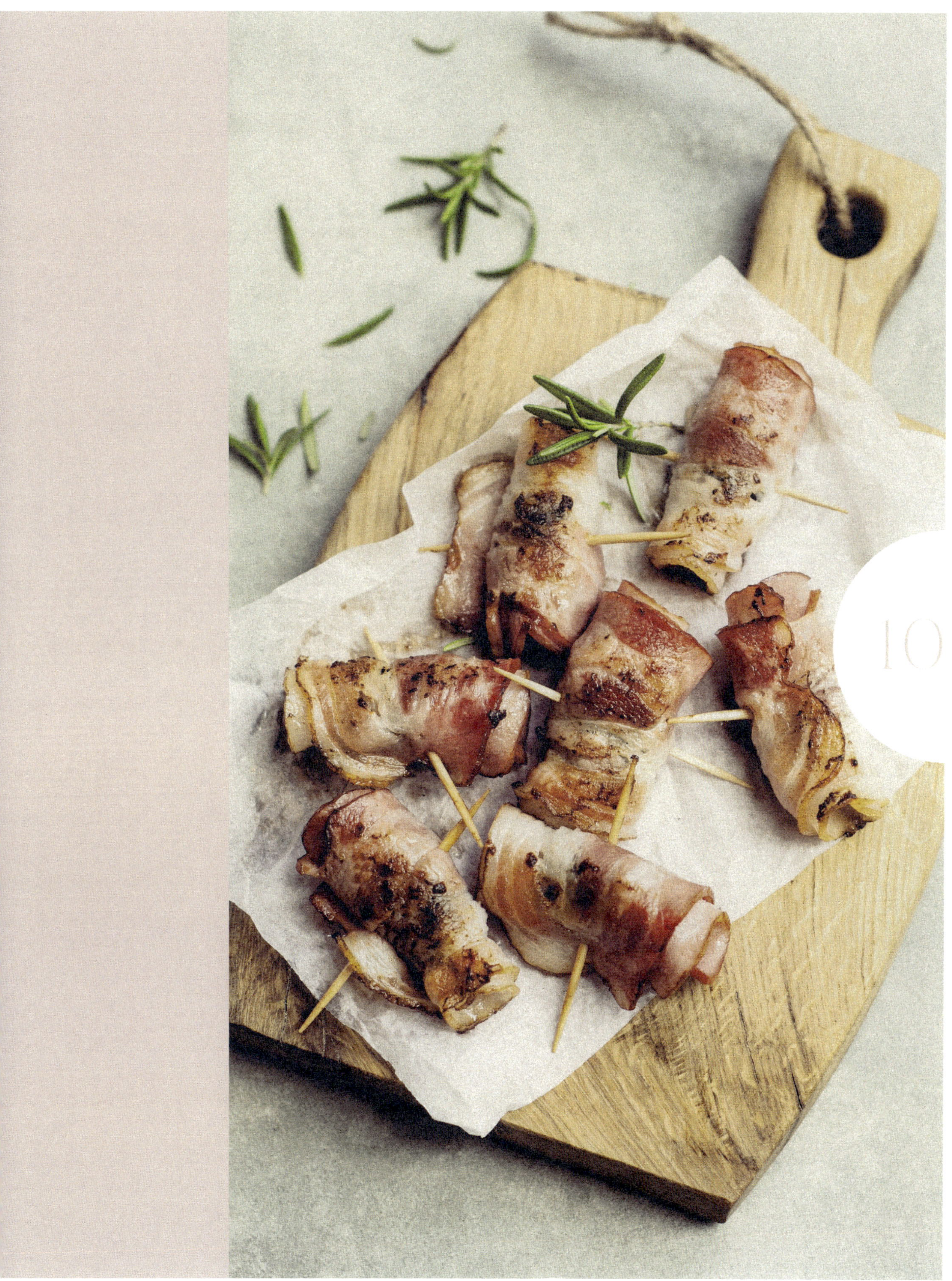

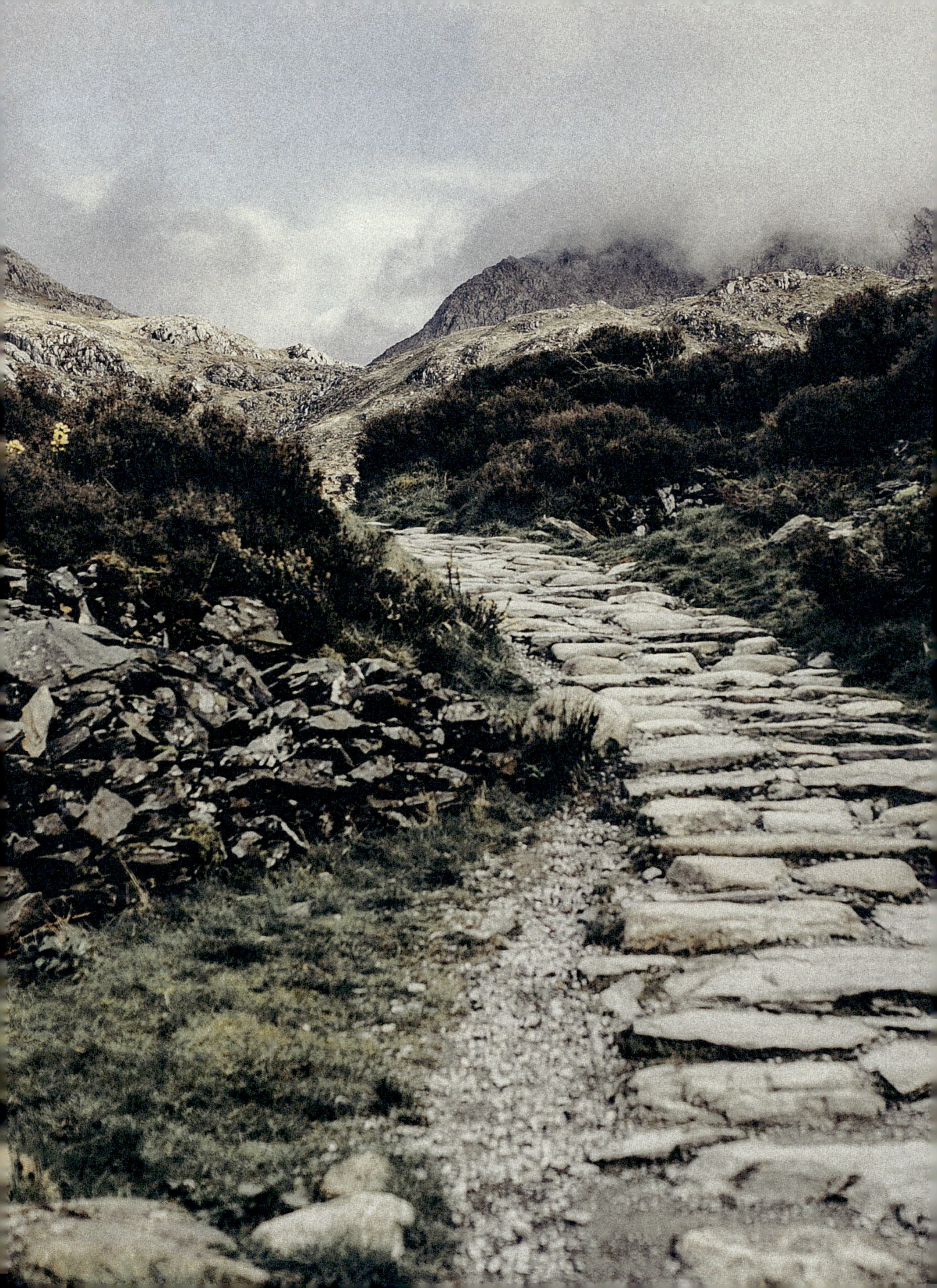

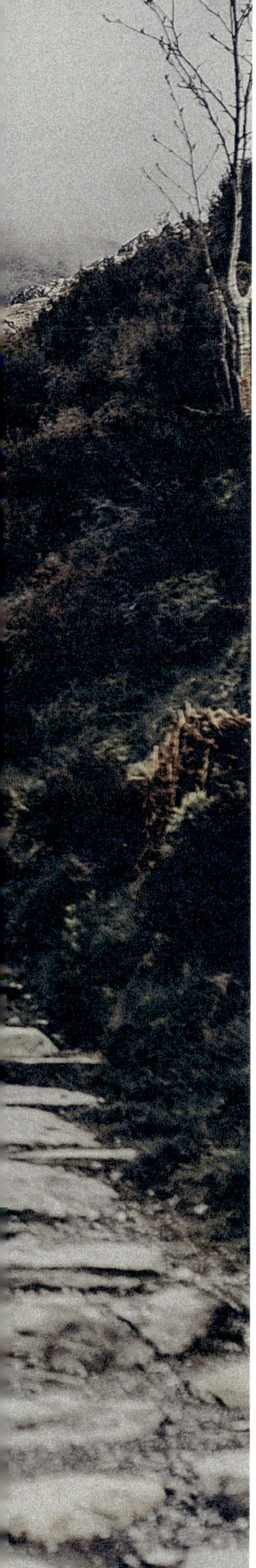

*"I cling to your decrees; Lord, do not put me to shame. I pursue the way of your commands, for you broaden my understanding."*[31]
*-Psalm 119:31-32*

When my husband had to leave his job in full-time ministry, I didn't see the hand of God. In all honesty, I just cried and cried asking God why. I didn't want to step out of the church world. It wasn't in my plan and definitely not something I had ever considered. Looking back, I probably responded like a child who got a tiny band-aid ripped off her arm, but acted like someone just hacked her arm off.

Our dream had been to be in full-time ministry together forever, but in following the direction of God for our lives we found ourselves in an unexpected place surrounded by the unknown. I knew I had to trust God, but what if God leads you to a place that's not a part of your dream? Key word being "your" dream. Despite my circumstances, I felt His peace and trusted Him fully, but I didn't understand. Isn't that where we find ourselves many times, crying before God saying, "God, I trust Your plan, but I don't understand Your process."

He spoke to me after a few weeks filled with monsoons of tears and snotty-faced prayers, which I might add, was my feeble attempt to change His mind on the matter. Then one day I was reading Acts 10 about Peter's life. For those of you who don't know, Peter was one of Jesus' twelve disciples. He walked with God, talked with God and ate with Jesus for three years. If anyone knew who God was, it was Peter. At one point in his story, God asked Peter to do something that he wasn't comfortable doing. God dropped a huge sheet full of animals on a rooftop and then God asked Peter to rise and eat.[32]

Peter responded to God, "*No way Lord, I've never eaten anything that was unclean, I'm not going to start now.*" (That's a Jamie paraphrase.) You see, Peter had never before eaten anything that was considered unclean in the Jewish law. Yet, now God was dropping down a sheet full of those very unclean animals. God's response to Peter was simple and direct. *"What God has made clean, do not call impure."*[33] Peter obeyed and did as the Lord asked.

Sort of reminds me of my kids when they tell me they won't eat their vegetables at dinner. My response is typically something like, *"You better get your butt on that chair and don't get up until you've eaten every brussel sprout on that plate."* I think God is just a little nicer than me.

It was at that moment, reading about Peter's experience, that I felt God speak to my heart. *"Jamie, you need to stop praying about this and just do it. You keep calling this unclean, but I am calling it clean. This is part of your purpose."* I stopped praying about it and received it as the hand of God in my life for this season. I began studying the passage and realized that God used this very instance as a catalyst for Peter to bring the Gospel to the Gentiles. Out of one simple act of obedience, one change in perspective, a nation was offered a relationship with God. Thousands of years later, I am still reaping the reward of Peter's obedience. Could God do the same with my life through obedience?

You may not understand what God is asking of you in this season. You may not even want it, but our obedience to Him is a milestone telling God that we trust Him in the process. It wasn't until years later that I looked back and saw the hand of God weaving through every facet of that job decision. We knew it was Him. Our church needed to focus on one hire, our pastor, and we fully agreed with that. My husband stepped into his "non-church" job and the favor of God exploded in his life. Relationally he grew. Creatively he grew. Doors of opportunity and favor surrounded him. He got a chance to run in creative lanes with people who were the best in the world. And all his training and prepping made him even better for what he brought to God's people. My perspective shifted. I'm not sure it would have had I not been forced to follow God down the path He was calling us to. I realized that it's not your occupation that defines you, it's who God has called and created you to be. So, no matter where your foot lands, you can be God's vessel in that place. It was a divine revelation for me.

> "OUR OBEDIENCE TO HIM IS A MILESTONE TELLING GOD THAT WE TRUST HIM IN THE PROCESS."

Luckily God gave me just what I needed at that moment. He didn't reveal the full picture because He knew I would have totally freaked out. There was a miracle found in that moment, in that season, but I would have missed it if I didn't respond in obedience. You see, there are two types of obedience: delayed obedience and first-time obedience. When I tell my kids to clean their rooms and

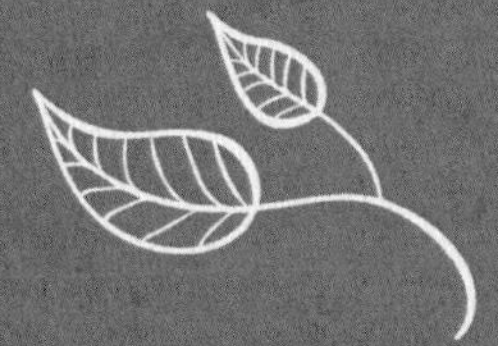

"THERE IS MORE COURAGE IN US THAN DANGER AHEAD OF US. YOU ARE STRONG ENOUGH FOR THE BATTLES AHEAD."

-Erwin McManus

> "CULTIVATE A LIFE THAT CAN JUST BE OBEDIENT WITH FIRST-TIME OBEDIENCE."

they act like they didn't hear me, drag their feet and find anything and everything that needs to be done in the house before they clean their rooms, that's delayed obedience. When they hear my voice and jump up from their soft spot on the sofa to do what I ask, when I ask it, that's first-time obedience. I can't tell you how many times in my life I have literally said to them, *"Mommy wants first-time obedience,"* and every time I do, I feel the spirit of God echo in my heart and spirit. *God wants the same from me.*

Side note here: Does anyone else ever refer to themself in the third person when talking to their children? LOL. My husband and kids just graciously pointed out that I refer to myself as "Mommy" when I talk to them. My response was to emphatically deny it, until two minutes later I found myself talking in the third person again—I burst out laughing.

Don't delay your obedience to God. Cultivate a life that can *Just Be* obedient with first-time obedience. Whether God is asking you in this season to be quiet and rest in Him, or charge the front lines with all the strength you can muster—be obedient. Whether He is asking you to remain firmly planted or walk with uncertainty towards a land yet unknown—be obedient. Whether He is asking you to be a vegetarian, or like me, be figuratively willing to eat pigs in a blanket—be obedient. You can't see the big, awe-inspiring picture for your life, but God does. You don't know the end of the masterpiece He is creating, but He does. Don't delay your obedience one more day. The results of an obedient life will be beyond what you can imagine.

May our response to God always be first-time obedience.

BOOK RECOMMENDATION

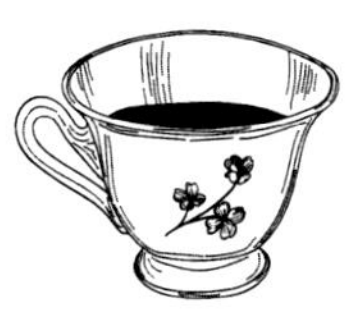

## The Last Arrow *by Erwin McManus*

There's no time to waste. We've all been given one life to live, so live it well. Whether you're an entrepreneur, creative, business leader or mom of ten, this book is sure to inspire you to live at the best level you can.

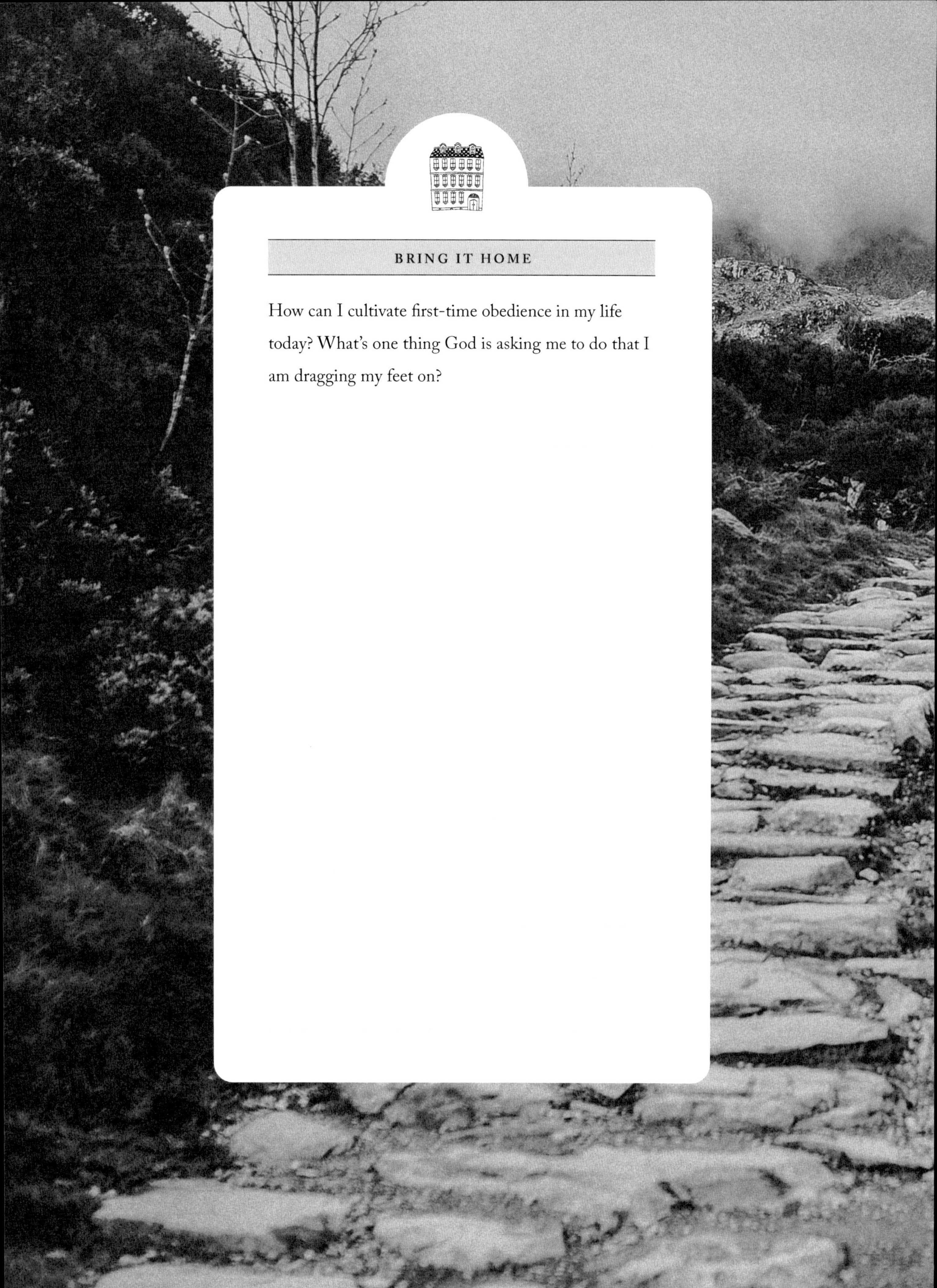

BRING IT HOME

How can I cultivate first-time obedience in my life today? What's one thing God is asking me to do that I am dragging my feet on?

CHAPTER ELEVEN

# JUST BE *Willing*

LETTING GOD USE WHAT'S IN YOUR HAND

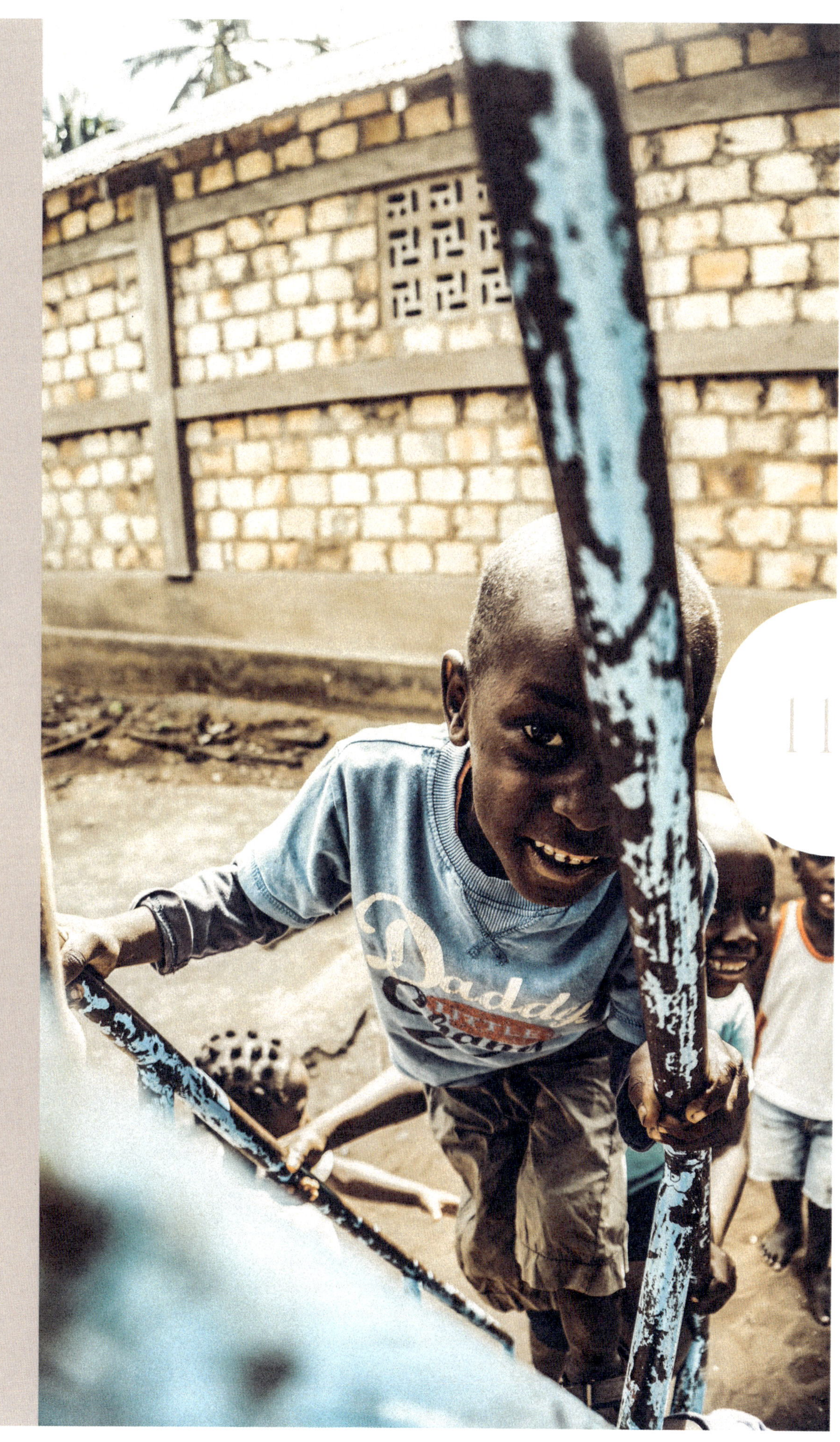


11

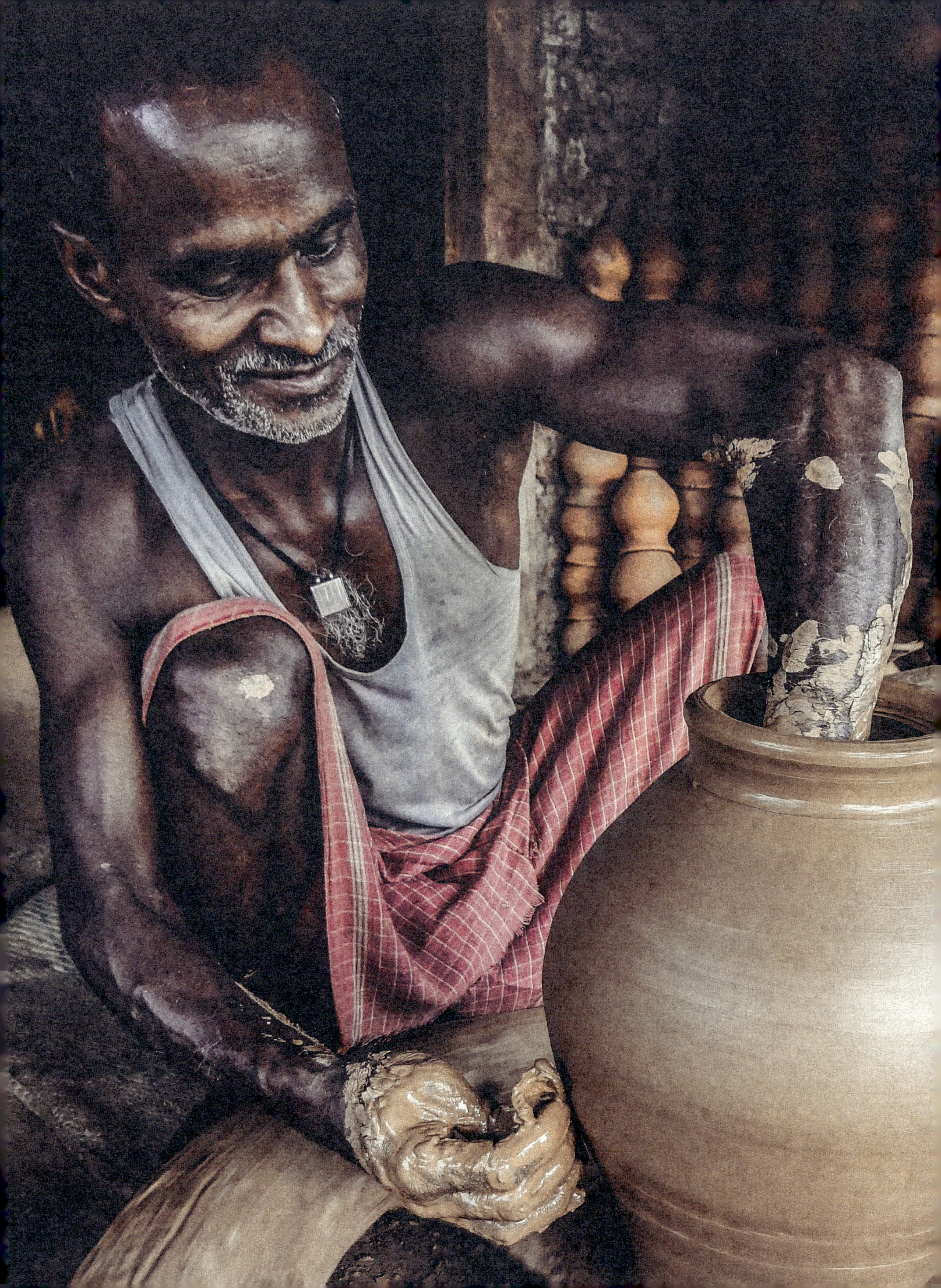

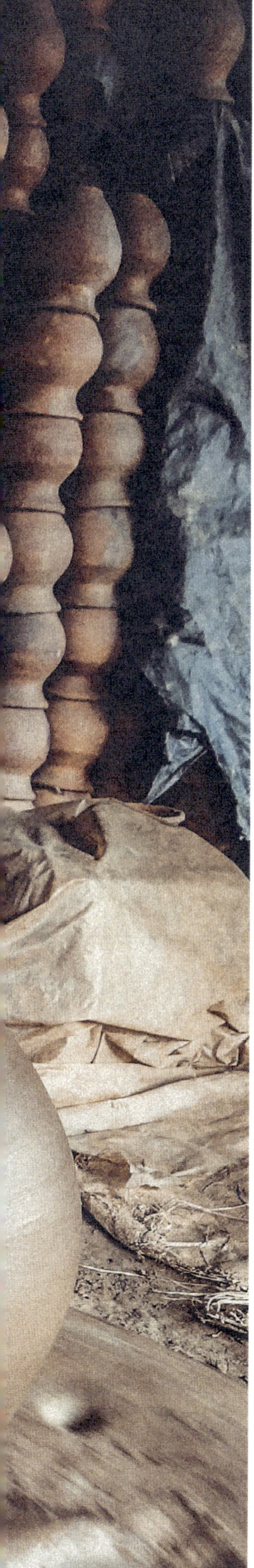

*"One day Ruth the Moabite said to Naomi, 'Let me go out into the harvest fields to pick up the stalks of grain left behind by anyone who is kind enough to let me do it.' Naomi replied, 'All right, my daughter, go ahead.' So Ruth went out to gather grain behind the harvesters. And as it happened, she found herself working in a field that belonged to Boaz, the relative of her father-in-law, Elimelech."*[34] *-Ruth 2:2-3*

I don't have a voice that can melt butter. I know, I know, you need to speak positively about yourself, but can I say you also need to be honest? I'm not saying that I don't impact people through my voice or my heart for worship and writing songs. I'm just saying that I've embraced who I am. I will never be like Michael Bublé, and not just because I'm a female. Although I'd be lying if I didn't admit that at times I've prayed to God in a divine-holy-awe-inspiring-moment to give me a rich, deep, move-wherever-I-want-it-to kind of voice that would bring tears to the multitudes when I sang. Yeah, that just sounds pretty conceited when I say it out loud.

I don't know what it is with me and music, but it stirs me deep in my soul. Have you ever heard someone sing that gives you goosebumps and warms the inner depths of your being simultaneously? Or listened to a song that moved you so much emotionally, it brought you to tears? That's the way I'd like to be used by God. But many times it's not the things that others see that God puts His finger on to use in me; more times than not, it's the seemingly insignificant things.

When it comes to fulfilling your purpose and *Just Being*, God starts with the small, seemingly insignificant things as a pathway to lead us to our promise. Ask yourself what's in your hand, and then *Just Be* willing. What have you currently been given that God could use? Let me tell you, it's rarely our winsome smile and magnetic personality that God is looking for (although He may use that too). Usually, it's the barely noticeable, unobvious things that God puts His finger on and says, "I want to use that!" So, what is in your hand?

In the case of Moses, God used the staff that was in his hands to perform miracles in front of Pharaoh. His staff was something insignificant that God used on the pathway to the promised land. God used Moses's rod all throughout their journey as a tool to perform miracles. His shepherding staff represented a piece of who Moses was. For forty years, he had been a shepherd. I'm positive many times he used that staff to comfort sheep. To correct sheep. To personally lean on when the job got difficult and to assist himself in reaching new heights. It was a piece of him. I find it interesting that God took something that was very much a part of who Moses was to help usher him into his future. He once was shepherding sheep, but now he would be shepherding hundreds of thousands of people to God's promised land. Maybe even in that, God used valuable lessons from Moses's forty years with the sheep to help him better shepherd God's people. The staff was more than a tool, it was a reminder of where Moses had been and where he was going. It was in his hand and God used it.

In 2 Kings 4 a miracle of provision took place for a widow and her two sons. She was on the brink of losing everything she had: her home, her children, all that was dear to her. When the prophet Elijah came her way to visit, he could sense that something was troubling her. She explained to him her strenuous circumstances. There was no way out in her mind. The first thing the prophet asked was, *"What can I do for you? Tell me, what do you have in the house?"*[35] All she had was a small jar of oil, but God multiplied it. There was a miracle waiting to happen in her house. All she needed to do was be willing to give what she had.

> "THERE WAS A MIRACLE WAITING TO HAPPEN IN HER HOUSE. ALL SHE NEEDED TO DO WAS BE WILLING TO GIVE WHAT SHE HAD."

In the new testament, Jesus fed 5,000 people with a boy's seemingly insignificant lunch. In John 6 the Bible says, "*When Jesus looked up and noticed a huge crowd coming toward him, he asked Philip, 'Where will we buy bread so that these people can eat?' He asked this to test him, for he himself knew what he was going to do. Philip answered him, 'Two hundred denarii worth of bread wouldn't be enough for each of them to have a little.' One of his disciples, Andrew, Simon Peter's brother, said to him, 'There's a boy here who has five barley loaves and two fish - but what are they for so many?'*"[36] You know how the story ends. Jesus took the meager lunch the boy had and multiplied it to feed 5,000 people, with twelve baskets left over to boot! God can use anything to perform a miracle.

In the book of Ruth, God performed a miracle by simply using what she had. In this case, it was literally her hands and feet coupled with her willingness to work the labor intensive fields. Her willingness provided the pathway for her miracle. It was in the very field where she went to work that she found Boaz. He was the man who would usher provision into her life. So, what's in your hand? Kindness, compassion, finances, friendship, or a certain skill set perhaps? God has wired the inside of you in a specific way. He's brought you in and out of seasons, each of which leaves you with a different toolset to offer up to God. It's time to use what's in your hand.

## A shepherd's staff, really?

Sometimes, before we can use what's in our hand we need to identify and be aware of the needs around us. If we don't have a need for God to move, why would He? If there is no purpose to the promise God has given us, why would He need to fulfill it in our lives? Using what is in your hand can start simply and honestly with identifying a need. A need can vary based on the specific season you are in. In the case of Moses, he desperately needed a sign to convince the people that God had truly sent him. He couldn't go on his journey without it. He needed God's help to fulfill the destiny before him. God took his staff, transformed it and performed miracles through it.

In the case of the widow, she needed to survive. She needed money. Her husband had died and the creditor was on his way to collect her two children and make them his slaves. I am so glad that when we go into debt these days, our children are not used as collateral! Could you imagine? She needed money, but she had nothing in the house but a small jar of oil. Nothing. Everything else had been taken. God isn't choosy when it comes to how He will perform miracles in our lives. Sometimes all we have left is next to nothing. He'll take it and use it to do a miracle in your life if you just release it to Him. God took her oil, multiplied it and performed miracles through it.

In the case of the 5,000 people, well, they were just hungry. They wanted to hear the words of Jesus and they needed healing, but they also needed food to eat. The little boy didn't have enough, but what he did have, he gave to meet the need. Jesus took it, multiplied it and performed miracles through it.

Ruth and Naomi had a need too, and it was called survival. They had no jobs or occupation, but they needed to eat. What was Ruth going to do? There was a need and she filled it. Bottom line. She didn't debate about it or wonder if it lined up with her calling; she did what needed to be done. She woke up, went outside, and wandered through the fields collecting leftover grain for her and Naomi to eat. That's it. Why do we think that we need to do something spectacular for God to move? We base our obedience on whether or not the deed is deemed grandiose enough for us to do it. We want the divine, jaw-dropping miracle to happen when more times than not, God is just asking us to do what is needed

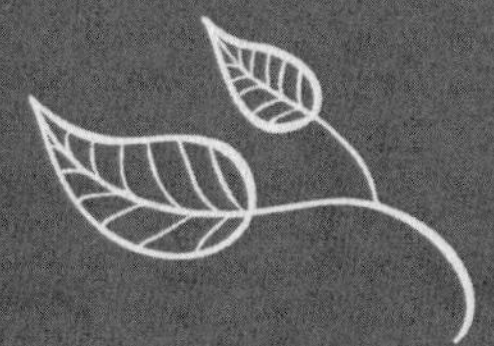

"LIFE IS ABOUT LETTING GOD USE YOU FOR HIS PURPOSES, NOT USING HIM FOR YOUR OWN PURPOSE."

-Erwin McManus

in our current season.

I've met many people who sidetrack the will of God for their lives because they weren't willing to get the job done right where they were. They jump from job to job, discontent and never truly satisfied. They struggle with the fact that what they are doing isn't what they are gifted or called to do. Imagine if Ruth saw the need but turned her back because it wasn't in her calling. What if she decided that hard labor was beneath her? The outcome of the story could have been very different. Ruth came from the household of a king, yet she was willing to collect scraps from a field that she did not own. She saw a need and was willing to fulfill it.

When I was in Mozambique, I was confronted with need on an entirely different level than I had

RUTH CAME FROM THE HOUSEHOLD OF A KING, YET SHE WAS WILLING TO COLLECT SCRAPS FROM A FIELD THAT SHE DID NOT OWN."

ever experienced. I was a junior in college at that time. My friend and I had decided to pack our bags and head to Africa for six weeks. We stayed with some missionary friends in Harare, Zimbabwe. During the course of those six weeks we traveled to local schools, did puppet shows (when that was still cool), human videos, and taught children about God. It was amazing, until we went to Mozambique for a week. Mozambique had recently gone through a civil war. The country was war torn and poor. Poor is not the correct word to use; destitute would be a more accurate description. I think everyone should go on a mission trip to a third-world country at some point in their lives because it changes you. I was changed in Mozambique. My heart tore into a trillion pieces. The needs were so great I didn't know where to begin. I would cry on my pillow every night and pray to God, "What can I do with such a great need?" Every day we would see children starving. Families living with more mouths than they could feed in little stick forts with dirt floors. Many did not have shoes. Their tattered clothes barely protected their skin from the fierce sun. Yet with all their lack, it didn't seep into their spirit. They were some of the happiest, untethered people I have ever met. We decided in that moment that though we could not provide for every need, we could make a difference in a handful of lives. We preached the gospel every day. We loved them deeply. Laughed with them. Prayed for them. Cried with them. Played with them. Squeezed them tightly in our arms—and for two of the most glorious weeks of our lives,

> "When we actually stop long enough to open our eyes to the world around us, we will see a tsunami of needs at our doorstep."

we left a piece of our hearts on the beautiful plains of Mozambique. I left most of my clothes there for the people to keep. I went home and collected clothes from my classmates in college and shipped them back to Meg and Timu, our contacts there. You see, I initially wanted to retreat when I saw the need. I was overwhelmed and almost paralyzed. But God helped me give what I had, and through that process my life was changed. A willingness arose in my heart to give what I had, what God had gifted to me in that moment, for His glory.

Obviously, we cannot meet every need. When we actually stop long enough to open our eyes to the world around us, we will see a tsunami of needs at our doorstep. Many times, it can be daunting. God doesn't ask us to meet every need, but He asks us to do our part. What's a current need in this season that you can meet in someone else's life? Are you willing to step out in obedience and meet that need with what God has placed in your hand?

Sometimes I want what I feel gifted to do to supersede all other things in my life. I want to use my purpose as a get-out-of-jail-free card from meeting the needs of others. But what if cultivating a willing heart to use what God has given you will only add value to your purpose and serves as a catalyst to get you to your destiny? Talent should never replace character. Character should be the driving force behind the decisions we make. A willing heart before God is of great value. It gives us eyes to see beyond ourselves and inspires us to leave this world a better place. When character is our driving force, God will undoubtedly lead us in the path of our calling. *Just Be* willing to use what's in your hand along the way.

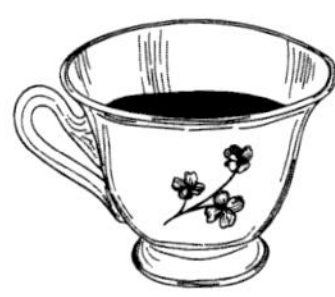

**BOOK RECOMMENDATION**

## Made to Last *by Vanessa Murray*

This is a compilation of handmade products by artists that span the globe. Proof that God can use the uniqueness of what's in your hand.

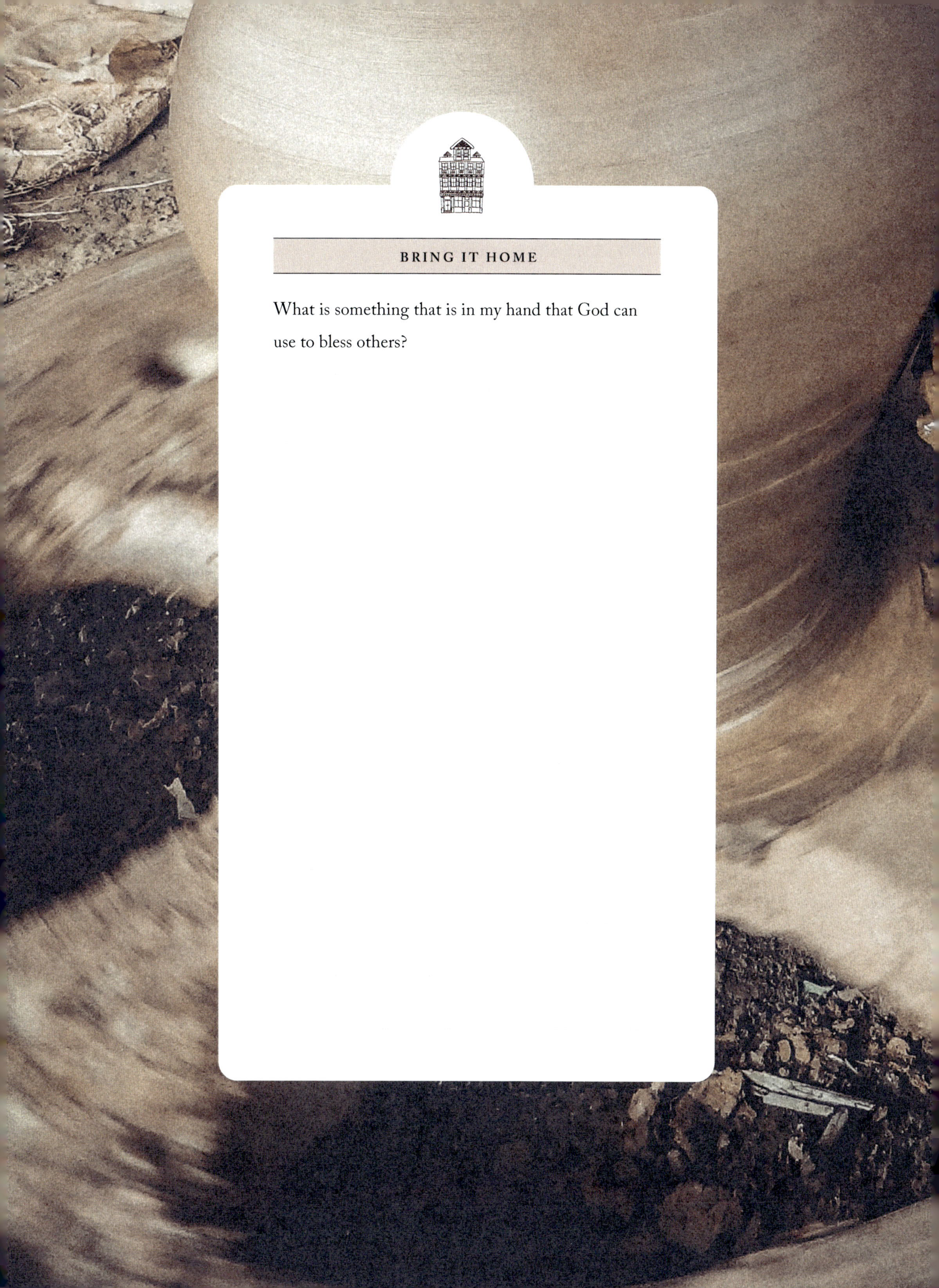

## BRING IT HOME

What is something that is in my hand that God can use to bless others?

CHAPTER TWELVE

# JUST BE *Consistent*

RUNNING YOUR RACE WITH FULL BUY-IN

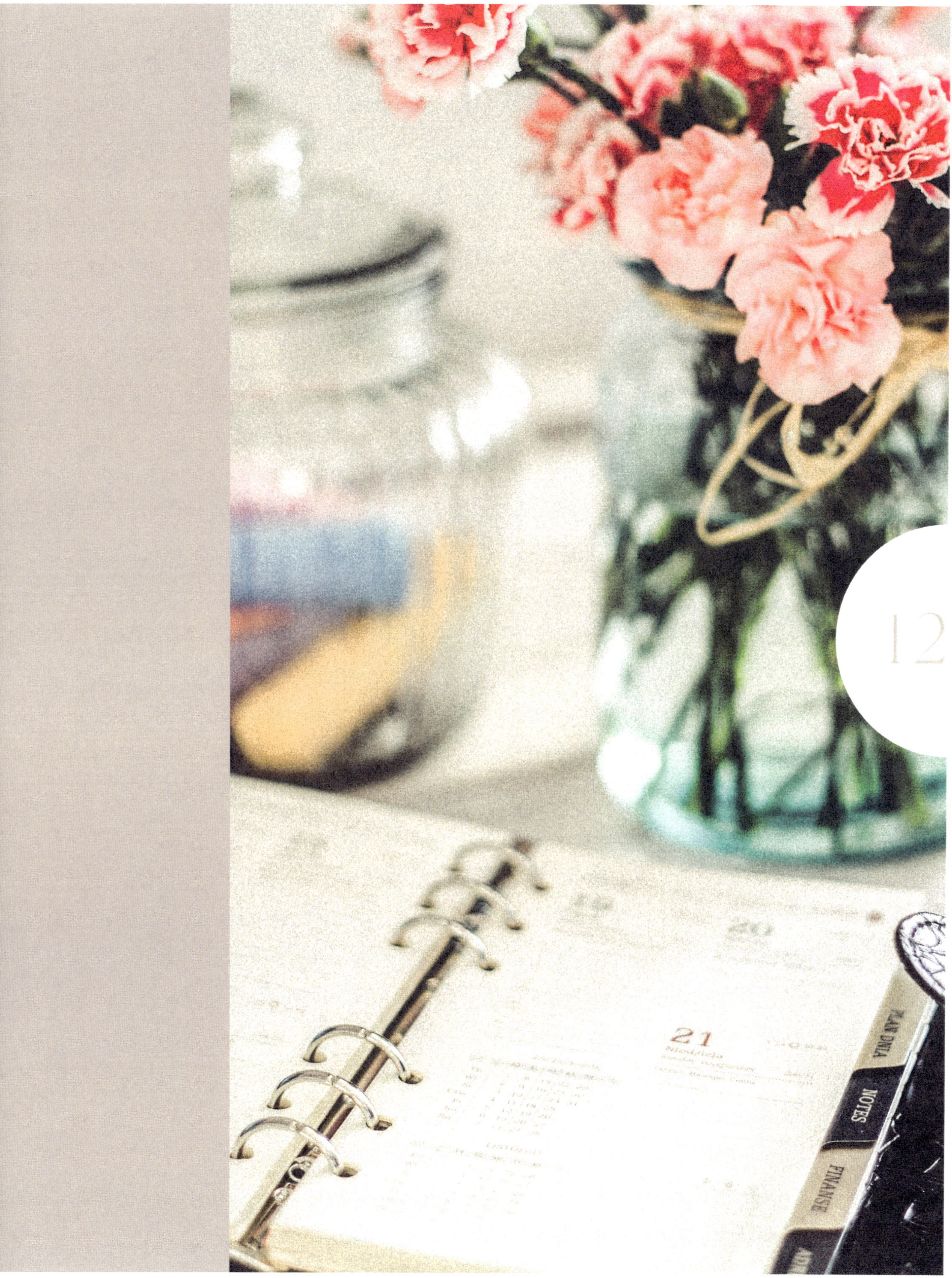


# 12

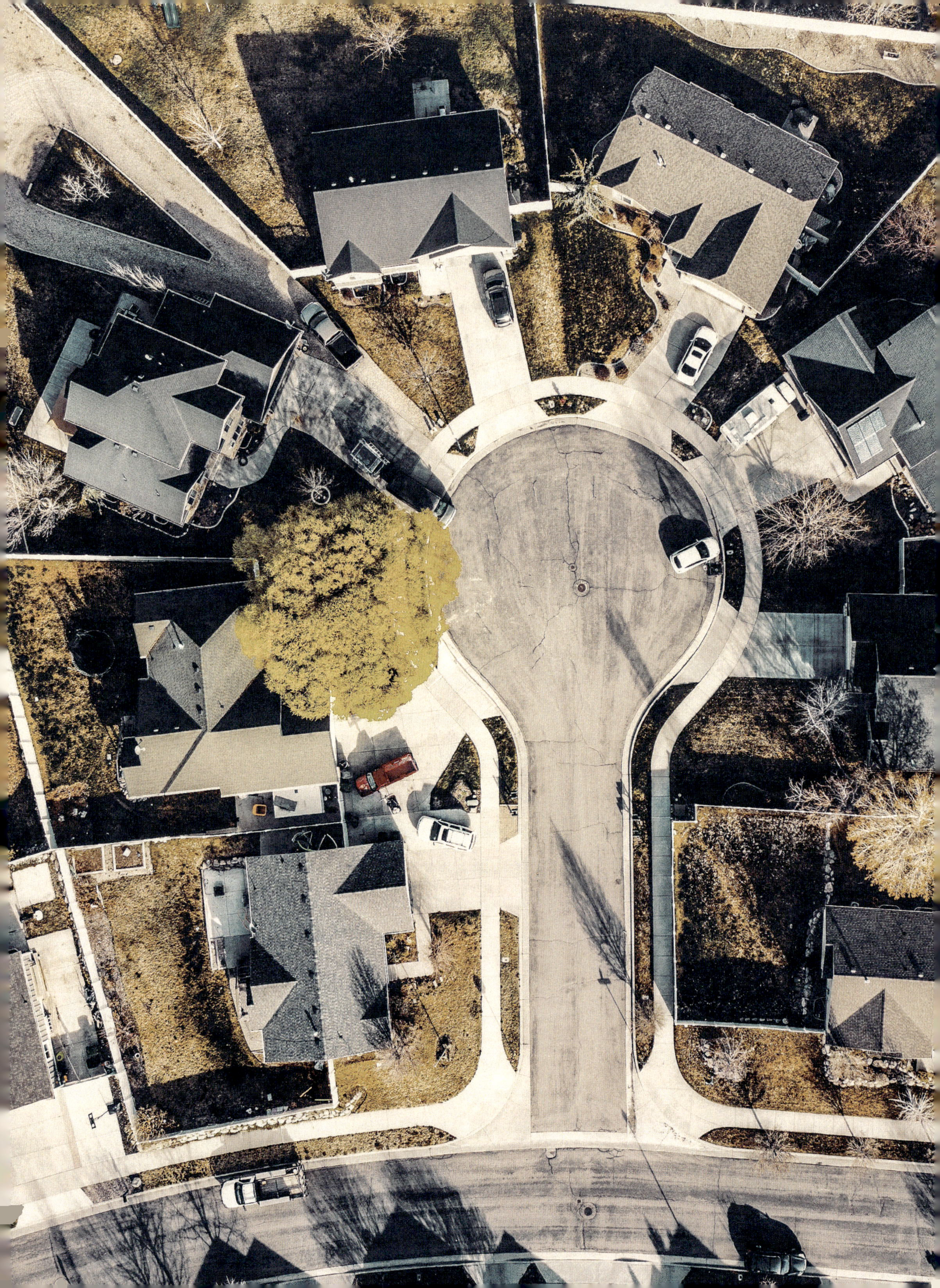

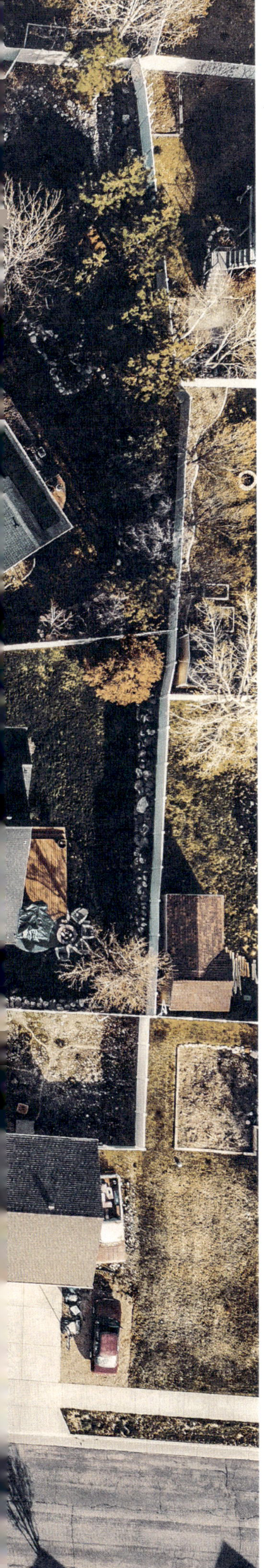

*"Ruth stayed close to Boaz's female servants and gathered grain until the barley and the wheat harvests were finished. And she lived with her mother in law."*[37] *-Ruth 2:23*

I love to read books from authors that inspire me. Those who repeatedly remind me that God not only loves me but cares about every delicate detail of my life. Books that I close filled with hope. Now these authors don't replace my relationship with God or nullify His voice in my life, but rather, they accompany what He is currently doing in me. A word of wisdom: with any author, preacher, friend, co-worker, or person you allow into your life, you've got to take what they say and who they are, line it up with the Word of God personally, then eat the meat and leave the bones. If all you ate was a steady diet of podcast preachers and authors but never sought God for your own life, an imperative piece of you would be missing. God has designed us to be in relationship with Him, which means hearing His voice personally through His Word.

We are all created differently, and I am someone who can be overly critical of myself at times. My temperament benefits from a good, frequent dose of a preacher named Joel Osteen. He has a refreshing way of encouraging me to believe God and His best, despite what I see with my eyes. The first time I met him was at a book signing with his wife, Victoria. I think my face went a full shade of ruby red when I asked for a picture with him. Mind you, this was the kind of red that no filter can correct—you know the kind. My poor, sweet husband was so kind about it all too, he knows how I get. In all fairness, my face always goes ripe tomato red when I'm around someone I truly admire. It happened with Darlene Zschech, Natalie Grant, Jared and Megan Anderson, Kari Jobe, and Clark Beckham—even though I'm at least a full decade Beckham's senior. Yes, I could be his mother, but that doesn't negate the fact that his voice sounds like homemade melted icing on a fresh warm-out-of-the-oven cinnamon roll! In fact, when I met Clark, I purposefully didn't place myself in the picture. I had already lived and learned my red-faced lessons. Instead, I made all my friends wrap their arms tightly around him for a pic. Thank God those friends deeply love me, and thoroughly harassed me about it later, I might add.

All that to say, when I first started running, I needed a little encouragement in my life. I wasn't someone you'd look at and be immediately defined as a runner. When I think about runners, I definitely have a specific picture that is conjured up in mind. Usually they are thin, lanky, toned in the right places and not aerodynamically challenged. I'd describe myself as lanky for sure, but more like a had-four-kids-C-section-varicose-veined type of lanky.

When I finally decided I was going to get back in shape, I was filled with excitement. I went out and bought some new running clothes, as if they would somehow transform me into a well-trained athlete. I was pumped when I opened my front door to run around my subdivision. This was going to be awesome! I started off running a whopping 0.3 miles and I swear it nearly killed me. I was gasping for breath as I jogged around the block and I could barely make it that far. And when I say "jog," I use that term loosely. I think my mother could have walked faster than me. It was almost like I was running in place.

I needed something to boost me into the runner I was meant to be. Insert Joel Osteen. If anyone could give me some good faith-building advice on running, it was him. Joel would often encourage people throughout his books and podcasts to speak in faith. I thought maybe, just maybe, this was the exact thing that would push my running career over the top. I started making declarations to myself out loud every time I ran. "I am a natural-born runner," I'd say as I huffed and puffed along my 0.3 mile course. I would even tell others, as my husband can attest. He would laugh at me as I charged forward jogging a fourteen-minute mile. When it felt hard, I'd press through, telling myself that I was a natural-born runner. Still to this day, when I run and get exhausted, I find my brain doing some preaching and declaring, "You're a natural-born runner, Jamie Kay."

For all my self-talk, though, running never got easier. I would run for a bit, then it would get hard and I'd stop. I would run long distances once in a while. I even ran the Crim, which was a ten-mile run in downtown Flint, Michigan. But I was never fully consistent. In all honesty, I never enjoyed it and I found it difficult, no matter how much self-talk I mustered up! But then something changed.

After decades of wanting to be a runner, literally, something shifted. I was post child number four and ready for a change. I was looking to do something I could afford that would get me in shape and get my mind off the exhaustion I was feeling in every other area of my life. Plus, I needed some alone time as well as something that didn't cause me to have to pack up all the kids and travel. I love gyms, but it wasn't ideal for this season. I needed something I could just do anywhere and running seemed to

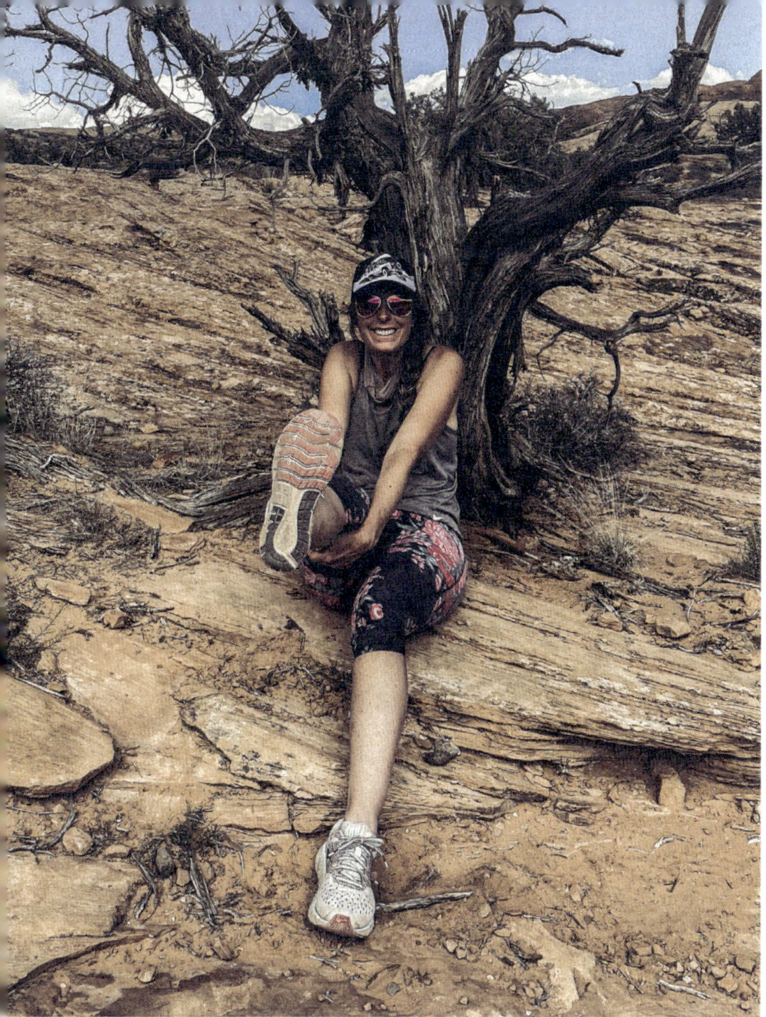

be the solution.

Please don't laugh too hard at what I'm about to disclose. In fact, everyone I currently love has already come to terms with what I'm about to tell you. The solution to my problem wasn't just running. You see, I had a two-year-old. The idea of pushing her 35-pound body around the mountain slopes of Colorado did not leave me leaping for joy, but neither could I leave her home alone. So, I decided it would be best to run around my cul-de-sac. Yes, that little circle area surrounded by five homes in my subdivision. My plan was to open the front window, unlock the front door, put a show on for her and if she needed anything she could just step outside and yell to Mommy. Great plan, right? At first, I thought about what the neighbors would think (and yes, I did get many questions from them), but once I explained the reason behind what I was doing, instead of looking at me like I just grew a third eye, they encouraged me in my running journey. I used my Map My Run app to determine how many times around the cul-de-sac was one mile—thirteen times if you're wondering—and then I set out to just do it.

I would run three times a week to start, two miles each time. From there I thought maybe I could push myself. On Mondays and Wednesdays I'd run the allotted two miles. Then on Fridays I would push myself to add one mile, every two weeks. Slowly but surely, I was getting stronger. When I reached the eight to ten-mile mark consistently I noticed that running two miles was easier than it had ever been. In fact, to go out and run two miles was actually fun and undaunting. I was learning to love running.

The most I've ever run in my cul-de-sac is fifteen miles. That's 195 times around the cul-de-sac! Potentially weird I know, but think of all the benefits the neighbors receive including, but not limited to, a part-time neighborhood watch employee looking out for their home three days a week in the darkly lit dawn mornings. I listened to my Bible App on loud speaker during my Friday long runs, so no one would ever dare come near me for fear of the wrath of God. Added bonus, the neighbors could listen too. Then I would use the last two miles of every long run to pray.

"YOU'RE NOT MISSING OUT. YOU'RE NOT FALLING BEHIND. YOU'RE RIGHT WHERE GOD WANTS YOU."

-Joel Osteen

Before I knew it, my long Friday runs were something I looked forward to every week. I was learning wells of wisdom by listening to the Bible for extended periods of time. I would hear full, complete stories of the Bible instead of bits and pieces. It was as if God was running next to me and just speaking. Well, I guess He literally was since He was on speakerphone in my Bible App! I was partnering my reading with prayer and all together it was changing my perspective little by little. I was turning into a runner and my heart was being transformed at the same time. It was what I had always dreamed, but it didn't happen until I became consistent and stretched my "status quo" expectations that things changed. It's the same in our journey with God.

I love this verse in Ephesians 4. It has been a life motto for me for the last six years. I pray it weekly for my life and over the lives of those I love. It says this:

*"In light of all this, here's what I want you to do. While I'm locked up here, a prisoner for the Master, I want you to get out there and walk—better yet, run!—on the road God called you to travel. I don't want any of you sitting around on your hands. I don't want anyone strolling off, down some path that goes nowhere. And mark that you do this with humility and discipline—not in fits and starts, but steadily, pouring yourselves out for each other in acts of love, alert at noticing differences and quick at mending fences."*[38]

When it comes to our walk with God we have got to know what road He has called us to travel. Ask Him. Seek it out. Get wisdom from others who are passionate about God. But then, in humility and discipline and steadiness, we have to put one foot in front of the other and begin to walk that road. Become consistent in the calling He's placed on your life. We want God to move in and to use our lives. We want to step into the fullness of what He has called and destined us to be. But it's never just a step, it needs to be a walk.

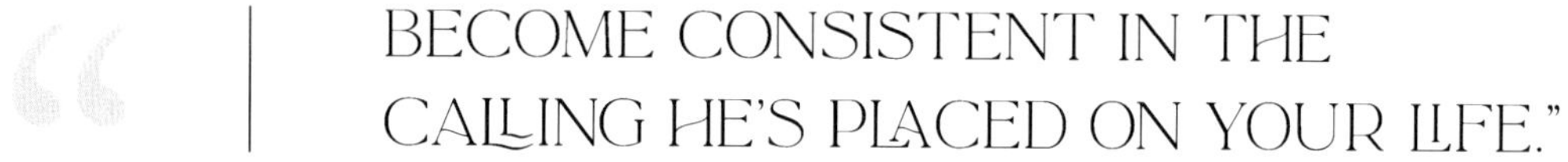


For decades, I knew what I wanted and needed, but I was never consistent in my application. I wanted to be a runner, but I was never willing to make the consistent cost. When my desperation level exceeded my discomfort, change began to take place. I was shaky at first. I didn't know what I was doing. I could barely breathe. But I stuck with it because I knew it was what I wanted, what I needed. It was the same in my walk with God. I didn't know how to seek Him at first. I didn't know how to talk to Him. I felt clumsy and inadequate, but as I remained consistent, I grew to know

> "WHEN MY DESPERATION LEVEL EXCEEDED MY DISCOMFORT, CHANGE BEGAN TO TAKE PLACE."

and love Him. Many of us wait for magical moments in God to shift us into hyper-drive in our relationship with Him. The fact is sometimes there are those magical moments, but more often than not consistency breeds craving in our lives. It was consistency that changed my perspective. Consistency fueled my love for Him. If you want a great relationship with Him then go get it, my friend. He's waiting for you.

It's the same with our purpose. Imagine if Ruth would have decided on day one that working in the field was too hard? If she would have turned around, she could have missed her miracle. The Bible says that Ruth worked consistently in that field. She stayed through the barley and wheat harvest seasons, laboring, gathering. We may not think about it, but that was months of hard work. She didn't quit and her miracle came. Sometimes God does a miracle in a moment, but more often than not He asks us to consistently walk with Him on the path to our purpose and then the miracle happens.

What is it that you need to be consistent with today, friend? Maybe you've started something. Stopped it. Started it. Stopped it. God is asking you now to be consistent with it. Whether it's your walk with Him, a relationship in your life, your character, or a purpose He's birthed in you, know this—kingdom timing is what matters. In our day and age it seems as if you can become a one-hit-wonder overnight, but God's not into that game. Anything worth value takes time. Function on His timetable. If you take consistent steps of obedience, whether you feel like it or not, He can prepare you for your miracle AND give you the character needed to sustain it. Consistency starts today.

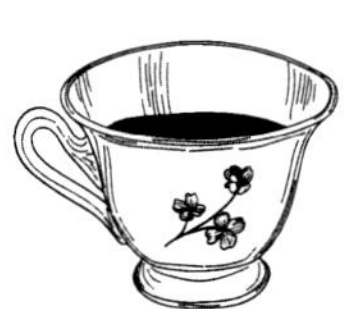

**BOOK RECOMMENDATION**

## Principle of the Path *by Andy Stanley*

This is a great book about putting consistent action toward the dreams, goals and desires you have in your life. Map out a pathway to the purpose you were created for. Great read for those entering their college years.

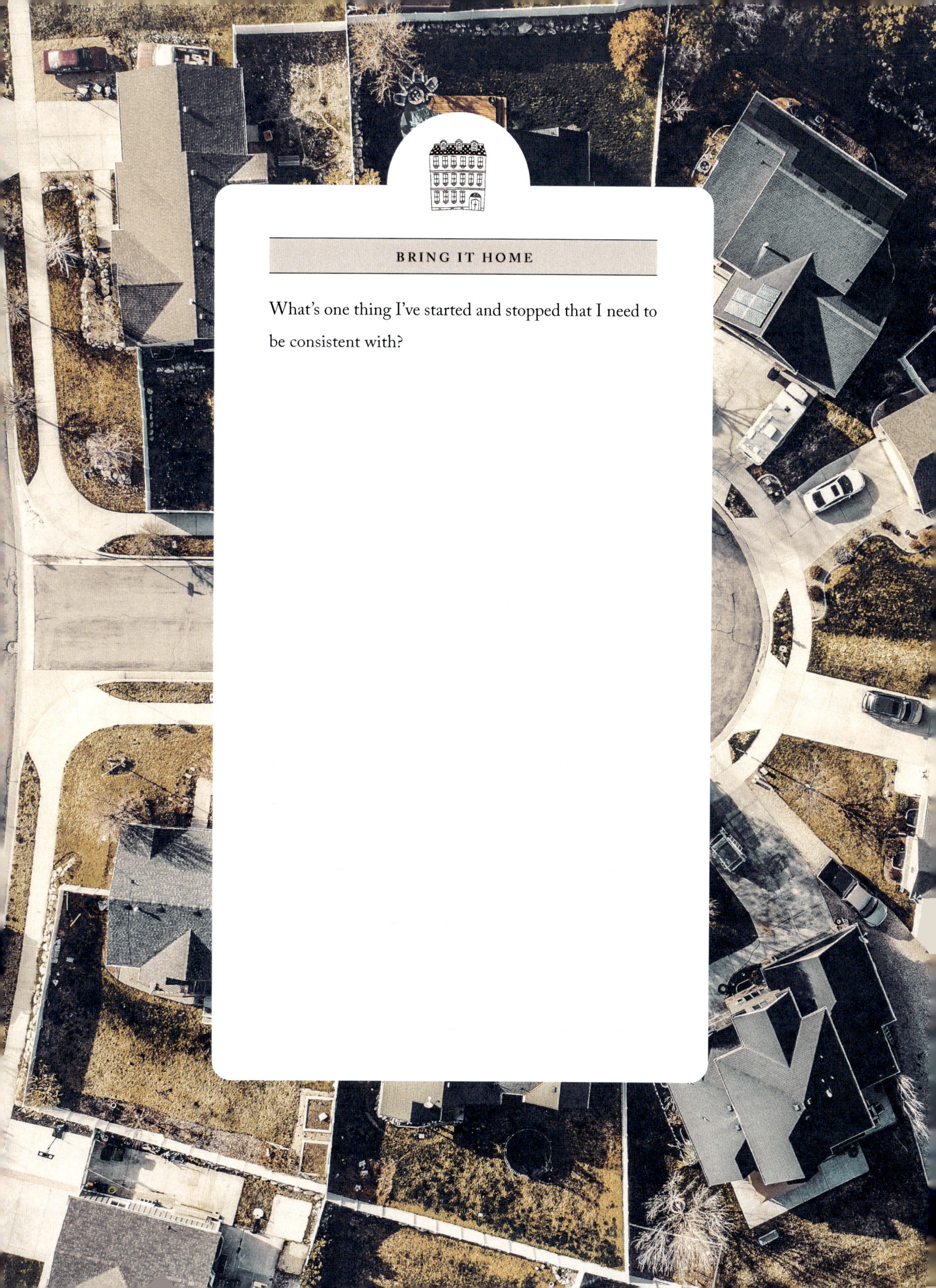

BRING IT HOME

What's one thing I've started and stopped that I need to be consistent with?

CHAPTER THIRTEEN

# JUST BE *Trustworthy*

WALKING WITH GOD UNDER PRESSURE

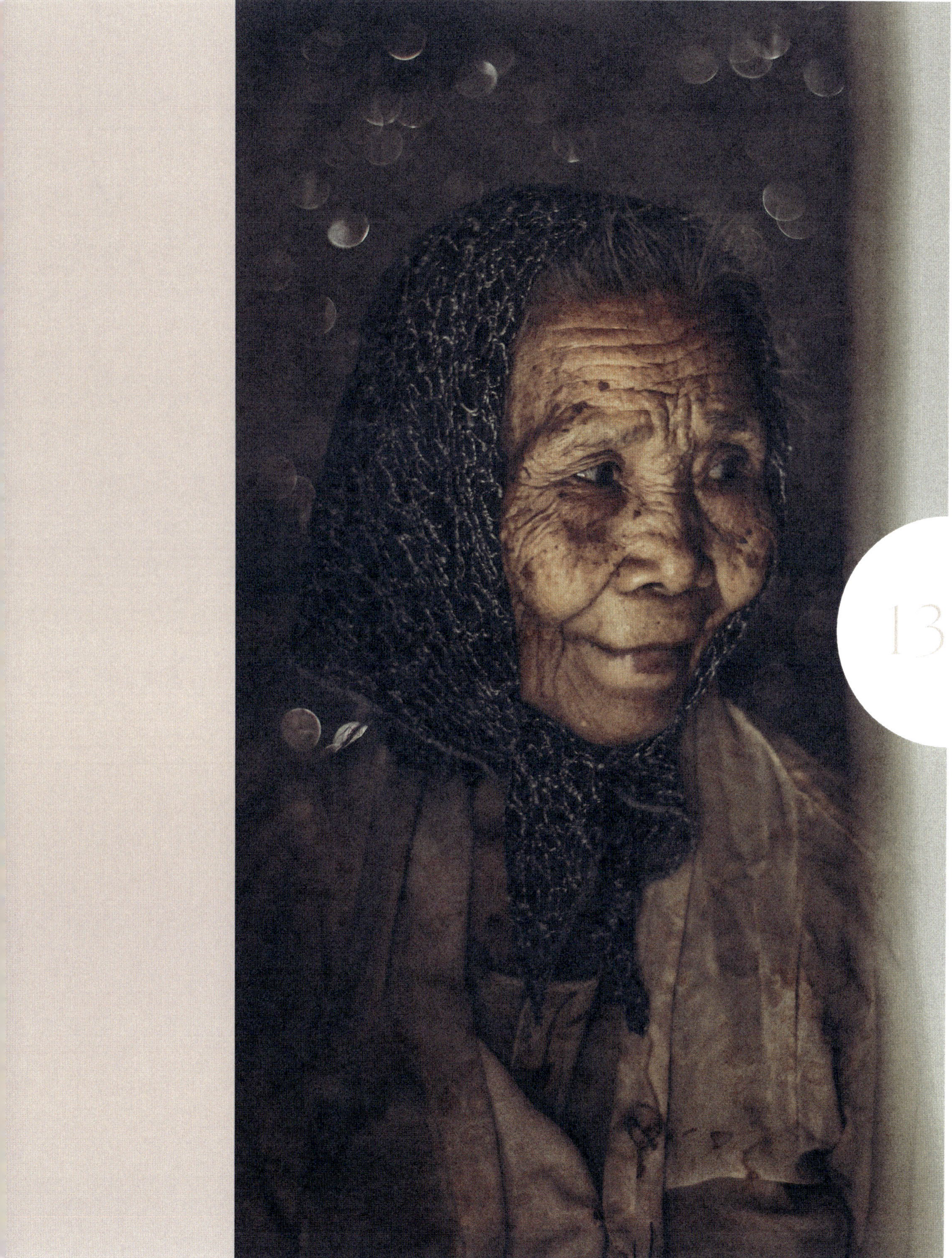

13

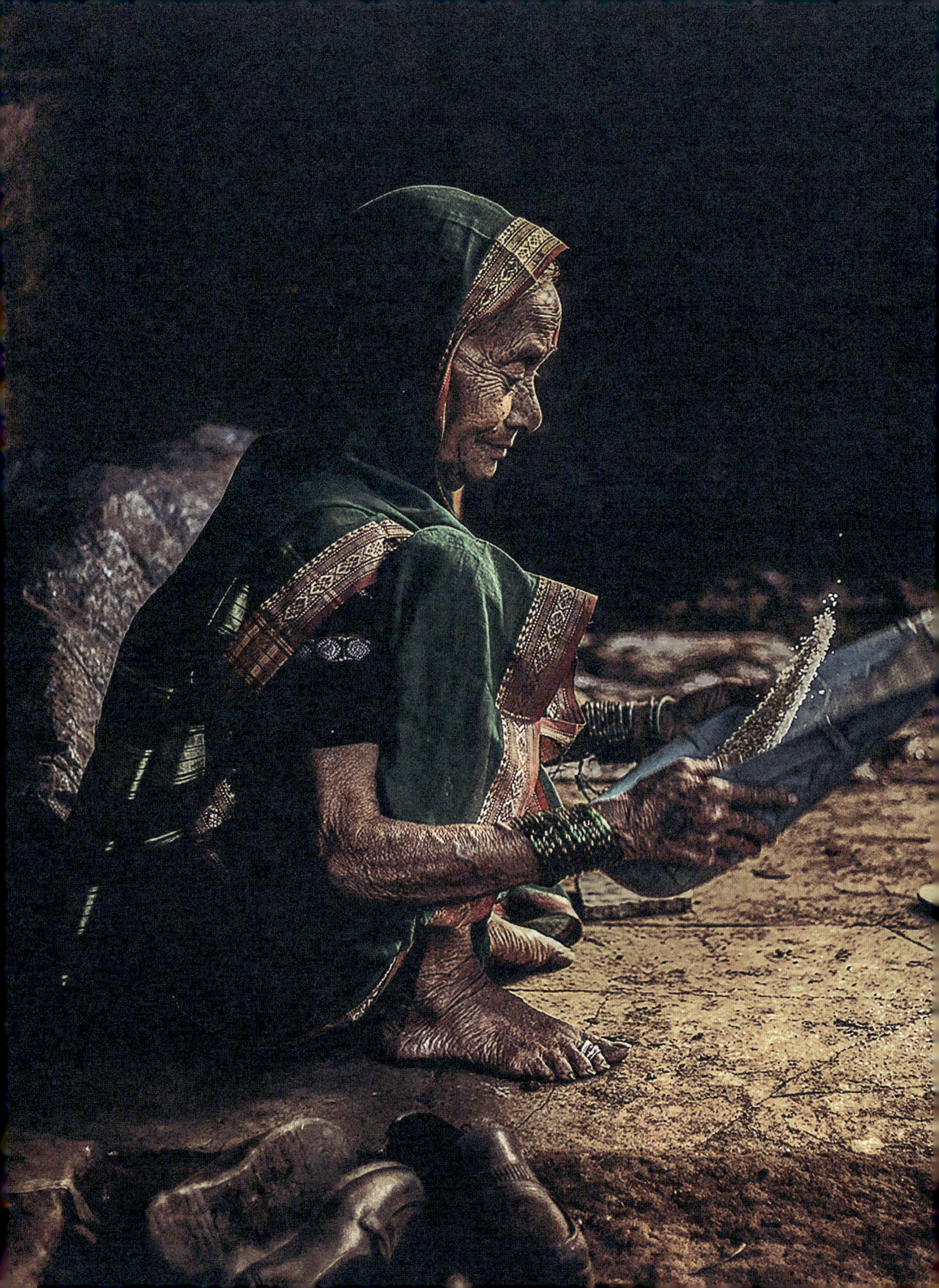

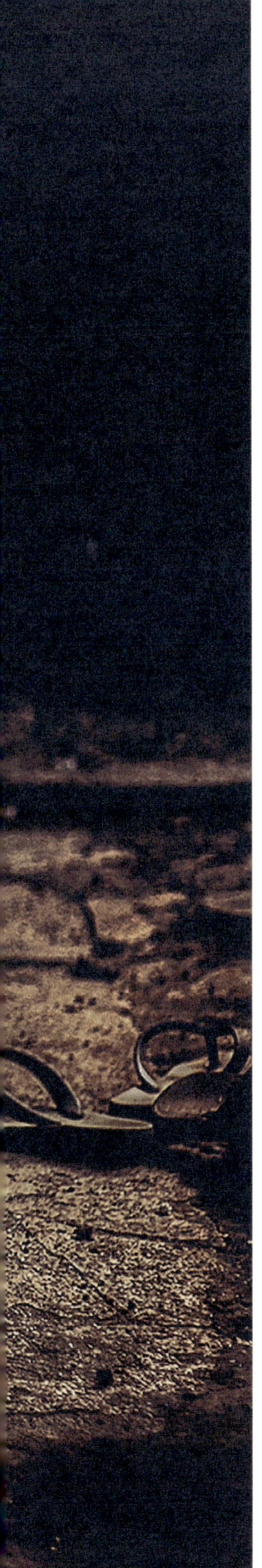

*"In the days when the judges ruled in Israel, a severe famine came upon the land. So a man from Bethlehem in Judah left his home and went to live in the country of Moab, taking his wife and two sons with him. The man's name was Elimelech, and his wife was Naomi."*[39] *-Ruth 1:1-2*

We're over halfway through our time together. You've wrapped yourself in my favorite floral blanket, the one that I paid an exorbitant amount for due to its softness. There's a twinkle in your eye and I notice the right side of your lips curling up in a secretive smile. I'm surmising that you must still be contemplating the fact that I ran 150 times around my cul-de-sac in one day. It does sound crazy when I say it out loud like that. As if reading my thoughts, you begin to giggle and I burst out with a full-fledged belly laugh—not too hard, though, or I might pee my pants! That's what happens after you birth four children. I silently ask God to direct our next conversation, trusting God no matter what the season.

Naomi. Imagine growing up as a little girl and hearing the stories of God's deliverance: water stopping dead in its tracks, city walls crumbling, victories won against all odds with the only possible explanation being an all-powerful, supernatural God fighting on your behalf. If there was one thing known, or rumored at the very least, it was the fact that God fought for His people. Not only did He fight for them, but He provided for them and took care of them too. They were special.

When the Israelites were in Egypt, God used Moses as a voice for deliverance. Four hundred years of slavery ended in a matter of weeks. God used signs and wonders and released His people from Pharaoh's hand of bondage. God provided deliverance in the midst of their slavery. He didn't just provide for their needs, though; He sent them away with everything their hearts could desire. Their children and all their belongings, down to the last cow, pig and pet goat. Nothing was left behind. God even gave them things they didn't ask for or need. Moses tells the people in Exodus to ask the Egyptians for silver and gold items and for clothing. The Bible says in Exodus 12:36, *"And the Lord gave the people such favor with the Egyptians that they gave them what they requested. In this way, they plundered the Egyptians."*[40] God provided above and beyond for them, even in their years of captivity.

For those of you wondering if God will provide for you and those you love in this season, the answer is a resounding yes! Never mind the fact that they turned around and made the unexpected blessing God gave them into an idol in the wilderness (the golden calf). Meditate on the fact that God's blessings for a certain season aren't meant to be idols, but rather provision for the next. Know what to use your blessings for.

He provided for them on their journey to the promise, because God is just that big. In the wanderings of the wilderness, their clothes didn't wear and their shoes didn't tear. They were never left hungry, even after their rebellious behavior. God gave them food to eat via quail and manna. God provided water for them to drink in a climate that sees, on average, less than two inches of rainfall per year.[41] They literally saw the fire of God directing them. It warmed them at night when desert conditions got into the low fifties Fahrenheit. And He gave them a cloud by day to give them shade from the hot sun with temperatures that could exceed the hundred-degree mark. God didn't just take care of them in the promised land, God took care of them on every aspect of the journey. Even when they were rebellious and angered God, He continued to provide ways for them to be restored into a right relationship with Him.

We see God's provision again in the promised land. God's presence went before them. He worked miracles in splitting the Jordan River for them to step into their promise on dry land, and not one was left behind. He gave them a leader, Joshua, to help spearhead the conquest of the land. He gave him strategies and fought for them and with them. What an amazing testimony of the goodness and provision of God.

Naomi and Elimelech knew God was a God of supernatural provision, but there was a drought in the land. A famine had come in the very land God promised to their forefathers. This wasn't just a scarce season, this was life or death.

Do you ever find yourself right in the middle of what God has asked you to do and where He has called you to be, but everywhere you turn you see lack? In those moments I'm tempted to cry out, "God, where are you? I thought this would be easy! Where's your provision?" That's usually right before I'm tempted to up and run. I'm sure Naomi and Elimelech started imagining the worst. What would happen to their children if they stayed? They had heard that the land of Moab was doing just fine, so maybe they should pack up and move there even though it wasn't what God had promised them. We will never know what would have happened if they stayed in Judah, but we can surmise a couple of truths from their predicament.

## Your promise will undergo pressure

God never promises that we won't have difficulty, He only promises that He will give us the strength to make it through that difficulty. He doesn't promise that we won't be tempted to up and run; in fact we probably will. We could be right smack dab in the middle of God's promise for our lives and still be tempted to up and run! Why, you ask? Because we are human and for some reason the grass always seems to look greener in our neighbor's lawn. 1 Corinthians 10:13 says that God won't allow us to be tempted beyond what we can bear. Pressure will come. Trials will cause you to question the promise God has given you, but in those moments, we have an opportunity to stand in faith and trust God. Trust that the same God who has provided for His people for centuries past will provide for you as well. You see, each trial and each moment of pressure is an opportunity for a miracle in your life. It's an opportunity for you to allow your trust in an ever-present, ever-providing, ever-loving God to become that much stronger.

> "EACH TRIAL AND EACH MOMENT OF PRESSURE IS AN OPPORTUNITY FOR A MIRACLE IN YOUR LIFE."

What would happen if God raised up a generation of individuals who stood firmly on the promises God had given them? What if they rested confidently in their season despite the drawbacks of what they saw with their eyes? What if they waited patiently for the miracle God wanted to do for them and through them? Nobody said this would be easy. Rest assured that your promise will be put under pressure. But if God has called you, He can and will sustain you. The question is, do you trust Him?

## Turn back to the promise

Maybe Naomi didn't have a choice in the matter, but when the choice was in her hands she decided to return. She knew where her promise was. She heard that God was providing for His people in Judah. She left her promise ten years earlier trying to find provision somewhere else. She went to the land of Moab full and returned utterly empty. The very place she went to save her family was the place where her family died prematurely. The very thing she feared would happen in the land of promise

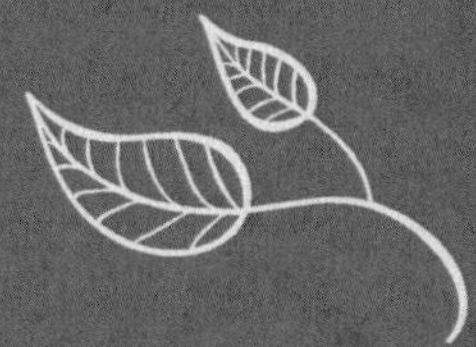

"GOD IS CONSTANTLY ON THE MOVE. I CANNOT STAY WHERE I AM AND FOLLOW GOD AT THE SAME TIME; RESPONDING REQUIRES MOVEMENT."

-Margaret Feinberg

happened to her in the land of Moab. Meanwhile, God was providing for His people back in Judah. Never let fear control your fate. Never make life-altering decisions based on fear. The death of Naomi's husband and sons caused a desperation to arise in her life. If her sons and husband had not died, maybe she would have never returned. But something needed to die in her life to get her desperate enough to return to her promise.

What needs to die in your life to get you back to the place that God has called you to be? I'm not talking about people literally dying here, but it's a valid principle we can learn from. Maybe it's friendships that have taken you so far from trusting God you don't even know where you've ended up. Whatever it is, don't wait for God to bring you to a destitute place before you realize you need to turn back to your land of promise and once again trust Him completely. Maybe you could just walk away now. Maybe it's time that you did like Naomi did and turn back. Maybe it's time you return to your land of promise.

## Oops, I did it again, but God can still make it beautiful

With all barriers down, in a place of hopelessness, Naomi returns to God. I imagine, she's not happy about what she's been through or even where she's going. It's a good thing God loves us past these moments. In fact, He welcomes us with open arms. She blamed God for her past. It's funny how our disappointments can begin to mar our view of God. When she arrives back to Bethlehem, she tells her peers, don't call me Naomi anymore, call me Mara, which means bitter, because God has dealt bitterly with me. Let me say that I believe God appreciates these moments of honesty. You know the moments where you don't look like the picture-perfect, put-together image of beauty. Instead you question God and His goodness in your life. You may even wonder if you will ever be able to trust Him again. Sweet, precious friend, you can and you will trust God again. Trust God with the deepest parts of your heart and life and He will ALWAYS provide above and beyond what you need.

Many times after these desperate moments, He makes us eat our words and opens our eyes to see just how wrong we were about Him. Little did Naomi know that within a matter of months her friends would be saying these words over her life: *"Praise be to the Lord, who this day has not left you without a guardian-redeemer. May he become famous throughout Israel! He will renew your life and sustain you in your old age. For your daughter-in-law, who loves you and who is better to you than seven sons, has given him birth."*[42] I love some things here. They make me want to jump out of my seat and dance around the house in unfettered excitement. First I see that Naomi's friends tell her that God will renew her life. God used something, or rather someone, from her very discouraging and depressing past to speak life into her

> "EVEN IN THE BAD, UNLOVELY SEASONS MARRED WITH IMPERFECTION, GOD CAN MINE OUT BEAUTIFUL THINGS TO LEAD YOU TO YOUR PROMISE."

future. Oh God, may I be the type of friend that speaks life into those I love. Who speaks hope into the discouraging moments of those around me. Who sees from a heavenly perspective the good that God can and will do. A person who refuses to accept any names given that are anything less than God's best for that person. A friend who calls my friends by the names given to them by God. You see, God had brought Ruth right smack dab into Naomi's present and uses her to bless Naomi's future. He works ALL THINGS together for good to those who love Him and are called according to His purpose.[43] This means that even in the bad, unlovely seasons marred with imperfection, God can mine out beautiful things to lead you to your promise. Trust Him. For Naomi, God brought Ruth. God renewed Naomi's life. To renew means to "make like new: restore to freshness, vigor or perfection; to restore into existence; to begin again."[44] After all that she had lost, God breathed in new hope. He gave her a fresh start. He was taking care of her, giving her reason to trust again.

In the end, I'd like to believe that God brought Naomi to Moab simply to pick up Ruth. It was like He wanted Ruth to be a part of His promise, even though she was born outside of it. Whatever the thought, I know this: you can trust Him in every season.

---

**BOOK RECOMMENDATION**

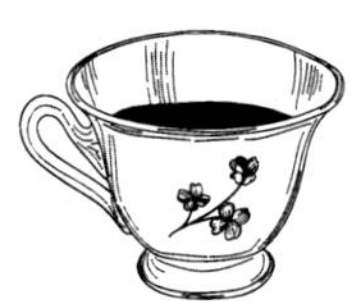

## Joy *by Margaret Feinberg*

This book is about Margaret's journey through her diagnosis and treatment of cancer. She decided in the middle of her fight to choose joy amidst the pain and heartache. Raw. Real. Beautiful.

---

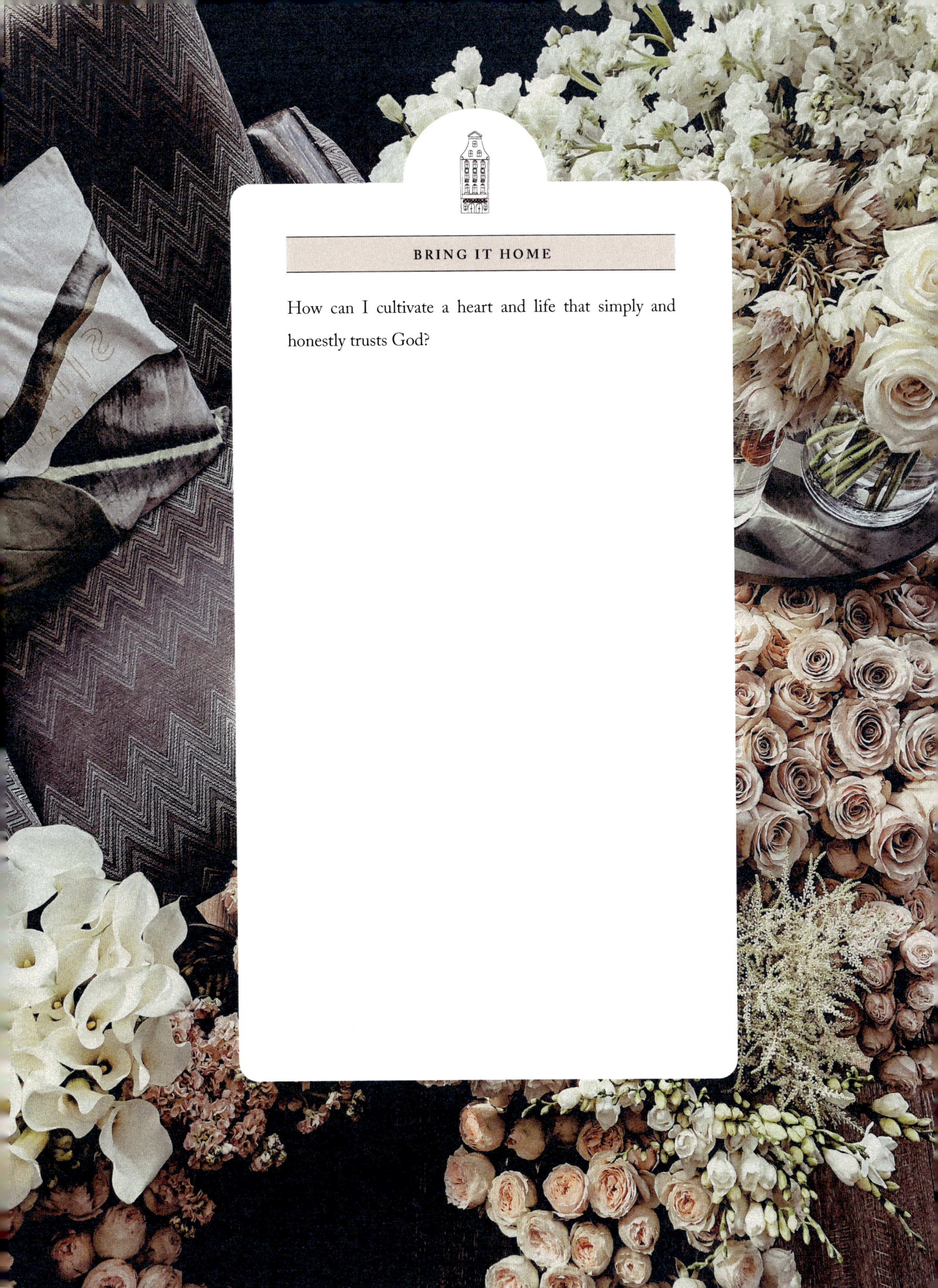

BRING IT HOME

How can I cultivate a heart and life that simply and honestly trusts God?

CHAPTER FOURTEEN

# JUST BE *Kind*

A LITTLE KINDNESS CAN MAKE THE LARGEST DIFFERENCE

KING'S ARMS
Coffee House & Tea S
Pure Veggie Food
domū
coffee house

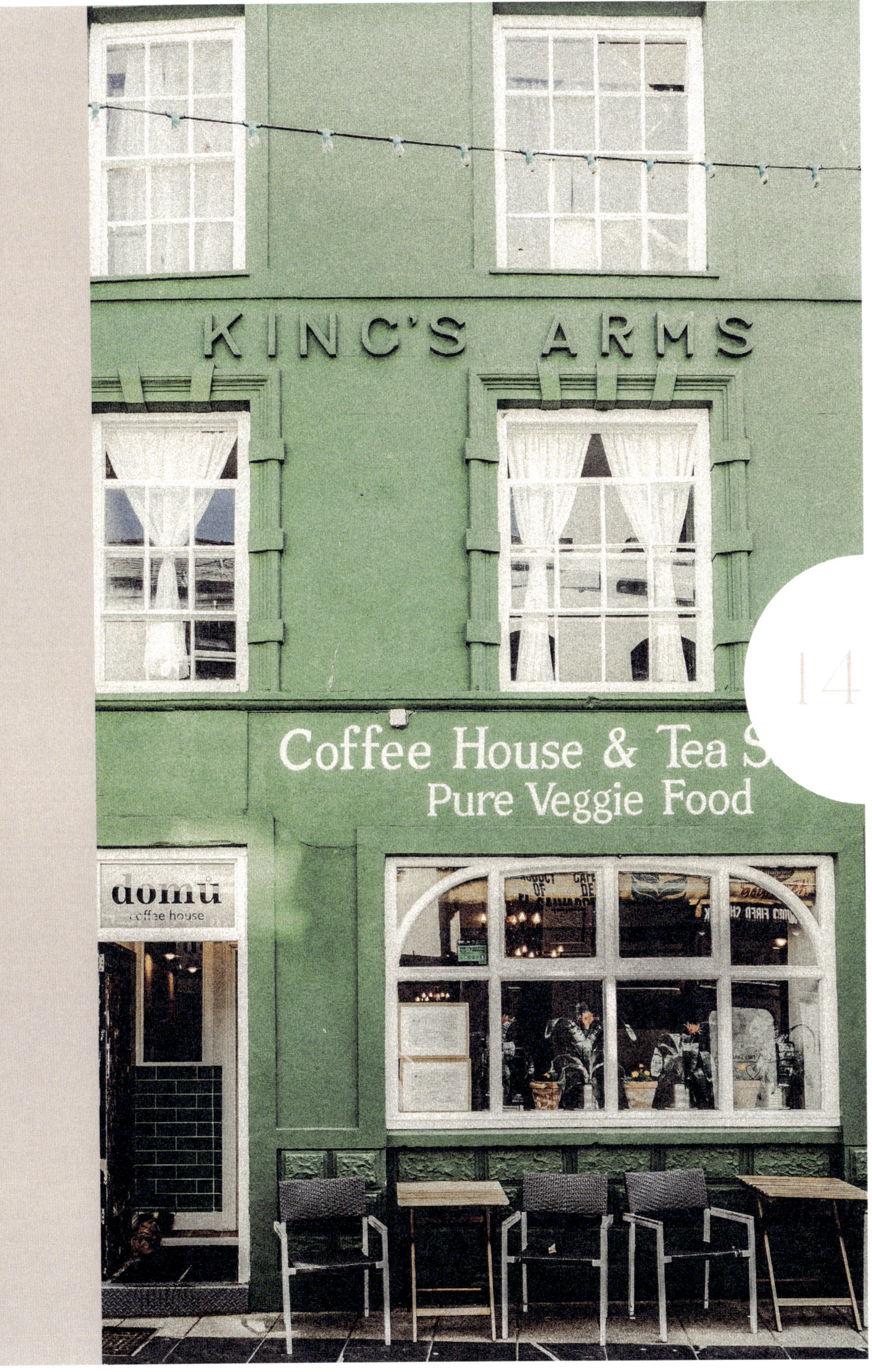

14

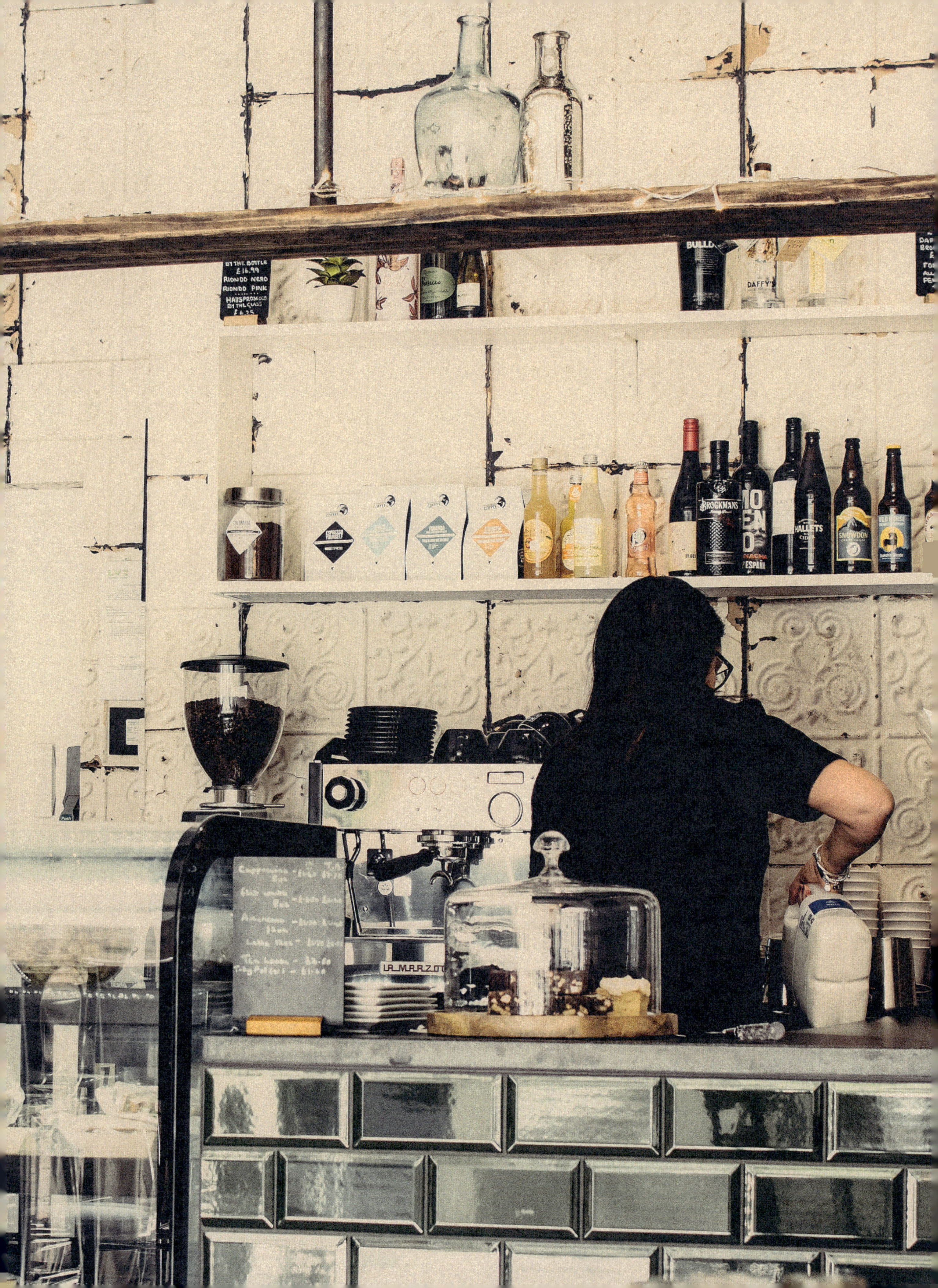
BY THE BOTTLE
£16.99
RIONDO NERO
RIONDO PINK
BY THE GLASS
BROCKMANS
ESPAÑA
HALLETS
SNOWDON
DAFFY'S

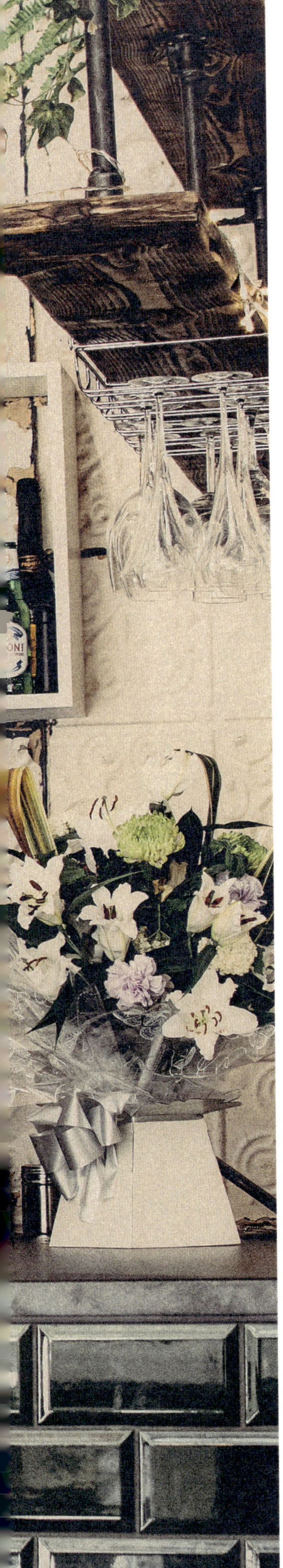

*"I hope to continue to please you, sir,' she replied. 'You have comforted me by speaking so kindly to me, even though I am not one of your workers.' At mealtime Boaz called to her, 'Come over here, and help yourself to some food. You can dip your bread in the sour wine.' So she sat with his harvesters, and Boaz gave her some roasted grain to eat. She ate all she wanted and still had some left over ... So Ruth gathered barley there all day, and when she beat out the grain that evening, it filled an entire basket ... 'Where did you gather all this grain today?' Naomi asked. 'Where did you work? May the Lord bless the one who helped you!'"*[45] *-Ruth 2:13-19*

A little kindness changes everything. I wonder if Boaz knew when he laid eyes on Ruth that someday she would be his wife. I can imagine her in that field the first time he saw her. Dressed in nothing fashionable but practical for a hard day of work ahead. Long tendrils of dark hair escaping from the head covering she wore, her brow glistening as the sunlight hit her face from the heat of the day. Hands gentle, but marred by hard labor. Eyes marked with determination. Weary, but persistent. Resolved to do her part. Her beauty went beyond physical and was woven deep into the fibers of who she was on the inside. Such beauty was hard to find. She was a hard worker. She was kind and honorable, yet she was unmarried, uncared for and striving to do what was necessary to survive.

At least that's how I imagine she was. If it were me in that field, the description may have varied slightly and sounded a little more like this: Oversized Walmart running shorts with paint stains made in no intentional order graced her figure. A full-covering loose tank top sagged down her torso drenched with sweat from the hot day. Armpit sweat rings added a darker hue of color to each of her sides. A navy colored Patagonia ballcap crowned her head, also drenched in sweat, looking as if it were decades old. Her hair hung in a long braid through the back of her hat and down her back, looking as if it hadn't been combed in weeks. Her face was beautiful, but exhausted. Her hands were torn and aching. Her nose covered in freckles. Her entire demeanor looked as if she was about to pass out! Worn running shoes graced her feet with soles that were clearly detached from the shoe itself. Well-loved perhaps? Maybe. She tried to "look" as if she knew what she was doing, but clearly, she didn't. Besides her highly impractical outfit, the woman looked as if she hadn't harvested a grain of wheat in her life, because she hadn't and she had NO IDEA what she was doing. But there was a determination in her eyes that couldn't be mistaken. Deep down inside, she was willing to do what was necessary to survive. Sound a bit more realistic? For me, yes!

## Who is that?

The Bible tells us that Boaz noticed Ruth. This tells me that even though Boaz was a wealthy landowner, and in old Jewish manuscripts named "the prince of the people," he still knew those within his care.[46] He knew his people. Their faces. Their workmanship. Their lives. So, he knew the moment someone new came into view. He took the time to notice.

Many times, I'm too busy to notice new things around me. Too busy to take time out and admire the little differences all around me in the people God has placed in my path. But not Boaz. He noticed Ruth. He asked his harvesters about Ruth's life, and in return he heard the testimony of who she was and what she had done for Naomi. Ruth, driven by her love for Naomi, stepped up and took the weight and responsibility that should have rested on a son's shoulders onto herself. Her kindness had been a game-changer in his mind, and now he offered his kindness in return. Not only did he pull her aside and allow her to eat with his laborers, but he spoke kindly to her. He asked her to stay in his field so that he could provide and protect her from any harm that may have resulted in another field.

I don't know if he knew when he offered her food and grain what the end result would be. Isn't that the case for many of us? The moment we choose kindness, we may not see the full picture. We just know that it is the right thing to do, so we do it. Months later, Ruth would lay at his feet and he would redeem her. The kindness you show others will never return to you void. Kindness, however, is a choice and there will always be a cost involved. The more you choose kindness the easier it becomes the next time, until eventually it's a habit you form and a character quality you possess. At times you must let kindness interrupt your day, your schedule, your plans and your life, otherwise you'll miss it.

## Can I get a gift card, please?

Here's how choosing kindness often interrupts my day. I'm sitting in a coffee house right now writing and just spending time with Jesus. This is much cherished and coveted time, I might add. With four children—and my mother and sister and her two kids here in town, staying at our house—this has been some longed-for quiet time. Don't get me wrong, I love my family and am so honored when they stay with us, but sometimes I just need a moment to breathe. This is my moment, and I've been looking forward to this day all week!

My imagination at this coffee house switches into overdrive. I imagine Jesus right there with me, speaking, sitting and conversing as if He were physically there. I try to listen intently for His voice. I was very careful to pack all five of my devotionals that I'm reading as well as my Bible and journal. I also inserted my five non-bleeding markers into my ragged leather satchel. I made sure my noise-canceling headphones were packed so that I could listen to classical music on Spotify.[47] Those are my writing tunes. I can't listen to any songs with words in them because I will inadvertently start singing the lyrics and get distracted from the task at hand. Today's tasks: Jesus time and writing. I usually pack my blue light-protecting spectacles (although I forgot them today) and wrap a warm blanket around me. I like to bring the blanket in with me and wrap it around my neck. In reality, the blanket is more like a large scarf. My hair is wet and all rolled up in a bun on top of my head. Friday is my "Jamie" day, so it starts with a run and Jesus. That's why my hair is wet, because I just got washed, dropped the kids off at school and here I am. I don't know why, it's as if every time I'm with Him, I'm overcome by Him. I can't explain it. I often travel to different coffee houses to read and write. It helps me stay inspired and I find myself expectant as I write. Sometimes just a change in location provides all the inspiration I need, and Jesus of course.

"AT TIMES YOU MUST LET KINDNESS INTERRUPT YOUR DAY, YOUR SCHEDULE, YOUR PLANS AND YOUR LIFE, OTHERWISE YOU'LL MISS IT."

So today, my friends, is a good day. In the midst of my journal writing and Jesus readings, an elderly man walks into the coffee house. Probably in his eighties. He has a dark complexion like extra bold coffee with a hefty amount of hazelnut creamer added, and light blue eyes. Those eyes like tranquil pools of the bluest little robin's eggs I've ever seen. Deep, beautiful wrinkles line his face. He walked in slowly, taking in his surroundings. There is a happiness about him. I couldn't help but notice his Navy hat and tattered Navy uniform that served as a reminder of decades past when he served our country. Slowly, proudly, he strides to the counter to place his coffee order. Do you ever notice how proud those who serve our country can be? Proud in a fantastic, mesmerizing, awe-inspiring

"LET NO ONE EVER COME TO YOU WITHOUT LEAVING BETTER AND HAPPIER. BE THE LIVING EXPRESSION OF GOD'S KINDNESS: KINDNESS IN YOUR FACE, KINDNESS IN YOUR EYES, KINDNESS IN YOUR SMILE."

-Mother Teresa

way. They don't hide it, they aren't ashamed. I think that's how God wants us to approach His kingdom.

My heart begins to overflow with love for this man and what he's given to gain our freedom, but my mind is telling me to stay put. After all, this is my time with God, this is what I've been waiting for all week. I desperately need this time so I don't turn into Oscar the Grouch when I pick up my kids in two hours and return home! Plus, I don't want to miss a word of what God is speaking to me. What if I go over there to talk to him and I lose the cherished time that was meant to be spent with God? What if my schedule then gets thrown all out of whack and I don't get to spend time writing today? But what if God wants to speak to me and through me by letting an honored veteran step into my life unannounced and unexpected, breaking through my schedule and plan? Instead of sitting with God, I could walk with God and be His hands and feet of love and care to someone I don't even know. God often has a way about Him that's unrelenting. I tried to go on with my time with God, but I couldn't shake the feeling that I had to thank this man for serving our country and buy him a gift card. The next time he comes to this coffee house, even if I'm not there, his drink and his breakfast is on me.

I set my Bible down and I marched over to the counter to buy a ten-dollar gift card. I then waltzed casually to the table where he was eating his pastry and drinking his hot coffee. "Excuse me, sir," I said. "I just have to thank you for serving our country and I wanted breakfast to be on me next time you come here." A smile lit his face from ear to ear. The beautiful wrinkles grew in size and depth and his hazy blue eyes sparkled as he whispered thank you.

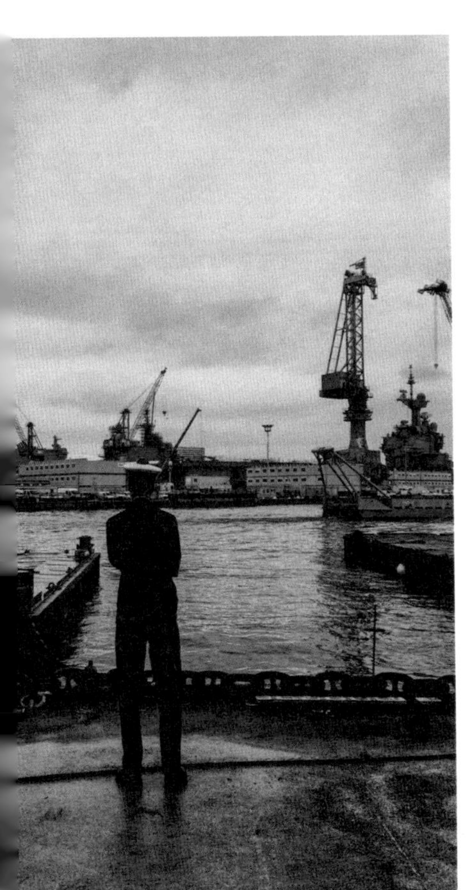

I'm tearing up even now, again, as I write this. I could have missed that moment, too busy with me to notice the others surrounding me. There's a beautiful woman sitting to my left, in her forties, maybe I could tell her she's pretty today. There's another woman here, and I have handbag envy. She's got the cutest handbag with her! It's extremely large and trendy at the same time. Maybe I could tell her how much I love her bag. Moments like these surround us all. God, give me eyes to see it and a heart and life to respond to it. I know it could be awkward. It's definitely a cost I've had to calculate. But I'd rather risk being awkward than forgo an opportunity to bless someone else with kindness. The littlest of moments can change the largest life.

Did Boaz know that day that Ruth would be his wife someday? Probably not, but his simple act of kindness led the way for a future he couldn't have possibly dreamed of. He saw a woman in need. He heard her story. He was moved with compassion. It interrupted his daily duties and responsibilities, but he was okay with that. He saw an opportunity to show kindness and he took it, and then God did a miracle. That's the way it works with God. You don't know today what fruit your actions might produce tomorrow.

Boaz didn't just notice Ruth, he went above and beyond. He let her sit at his table and treated her like she was one of his own. Then as he left, he went behind her back and told his servants to watch over her, protect her, and leave her "handfuls on purpose." Extra grain to alleviate some of the work that was before her. She wasn't Boaz's responsibility at that point. She was just a woman in need, but Boaz saw this opportunity to show her kindness and jumped all over it.

This is the way God works in our lives. He goes above and beyond what we see to work His goodness in our lives. The Bible says that God can do exceedingly, abundantly, above all that we ask or think.[48] That's a God who doesn't just do the minimum for His children; He goes all out, overflowing, over-the-top for His own. I think this is the way God wants us to be with others. Lives characterized by over-the-top kindness towards others.

So how do we know when to speak up and act in kindness, and when to be silent? I think we always choose kindness. If God brings it to your attention, making you aware, choose kindness. God has placed people in your life that you can breathe life into. There is purpose in those people that He can use you to mine out. Don't miss your opportunity to be kind to others. As you do, you will find God will go above and beyond on your behalf, providing everything you could ever need. We think if we pour out too much that we will be left wanting. God's kingdom doesn't work that way. As we pour out to others, God will always pour back into us.

Just be kind today in ways that matter.

**BOOK RECOMMENDATION**

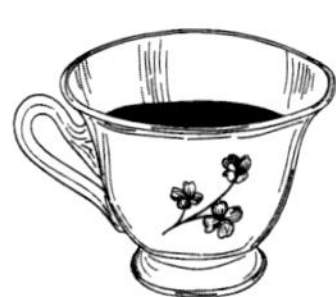

## Giving It All Away *by David Green*

This is the story of Hobby Lobby and how it became what it is today. Such an interesting read. I loved understanding the philosophy behind one of the greatest stores of this time.

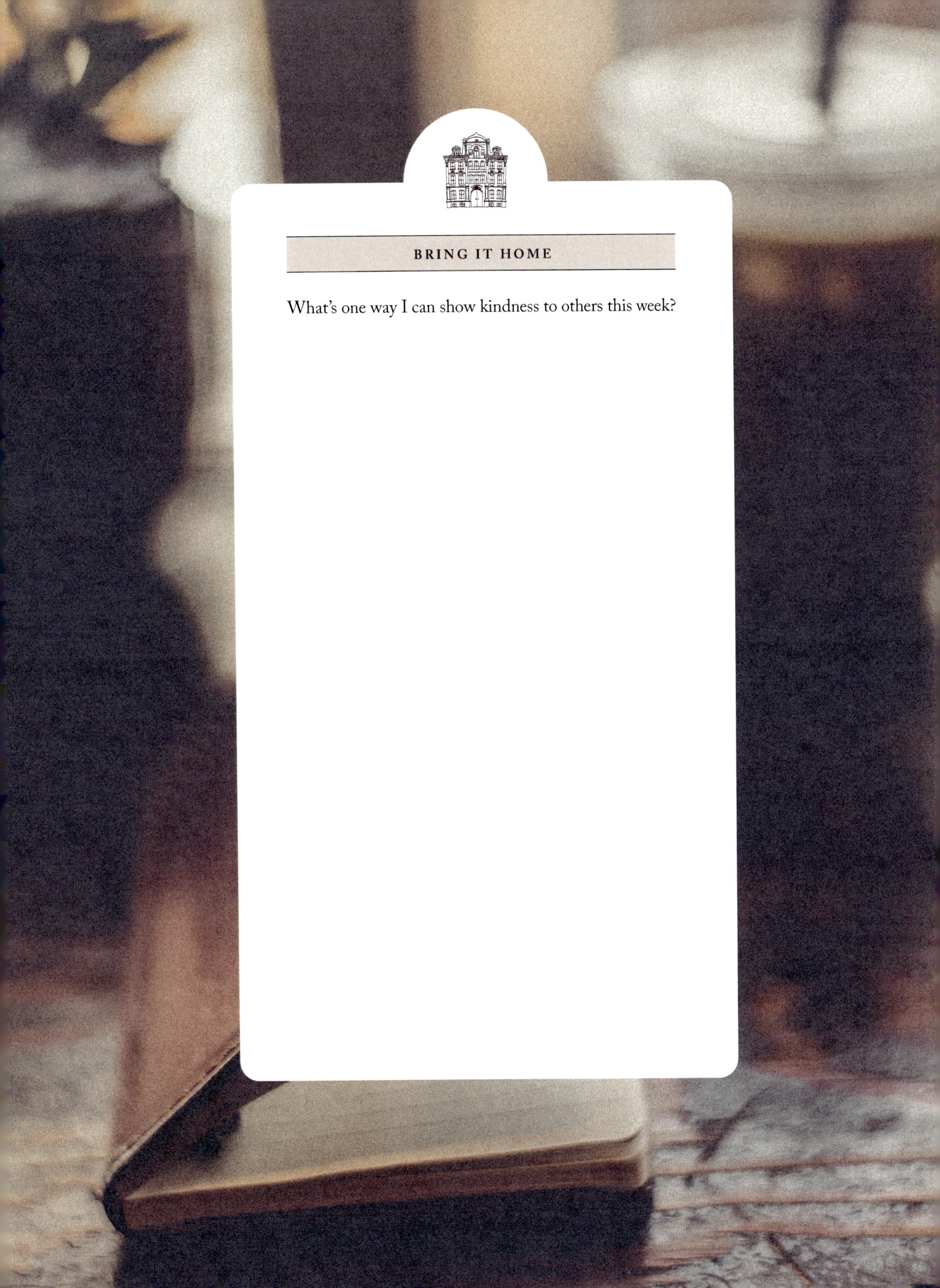

## BRING IT HOME

What's one way I can show kindness to others this week?

CHAPTER FIFTEEN

# JUST BE *Loving*

SHARE THE LOVE OF GOD WITH THOSE AROUND YOU

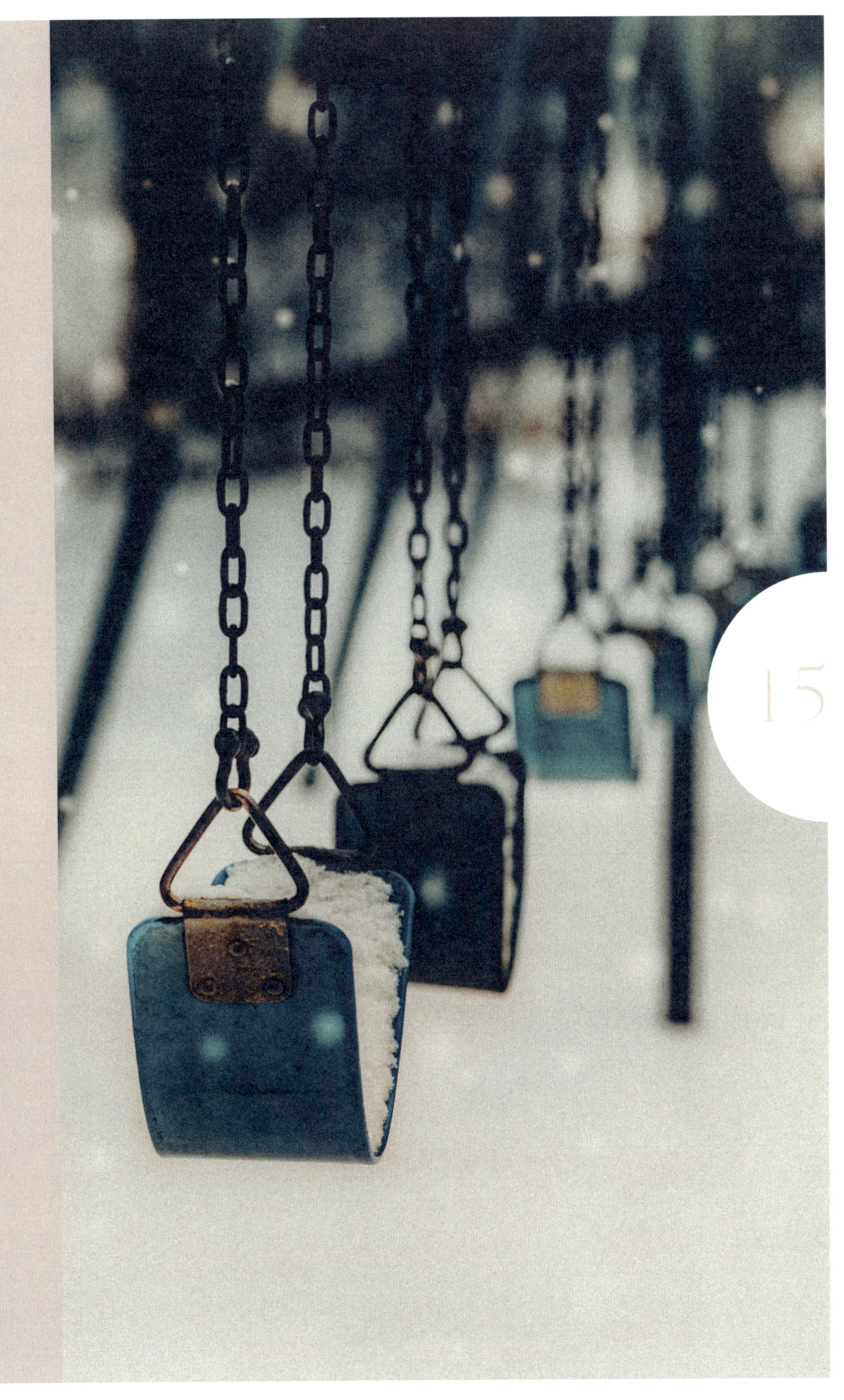

# 15

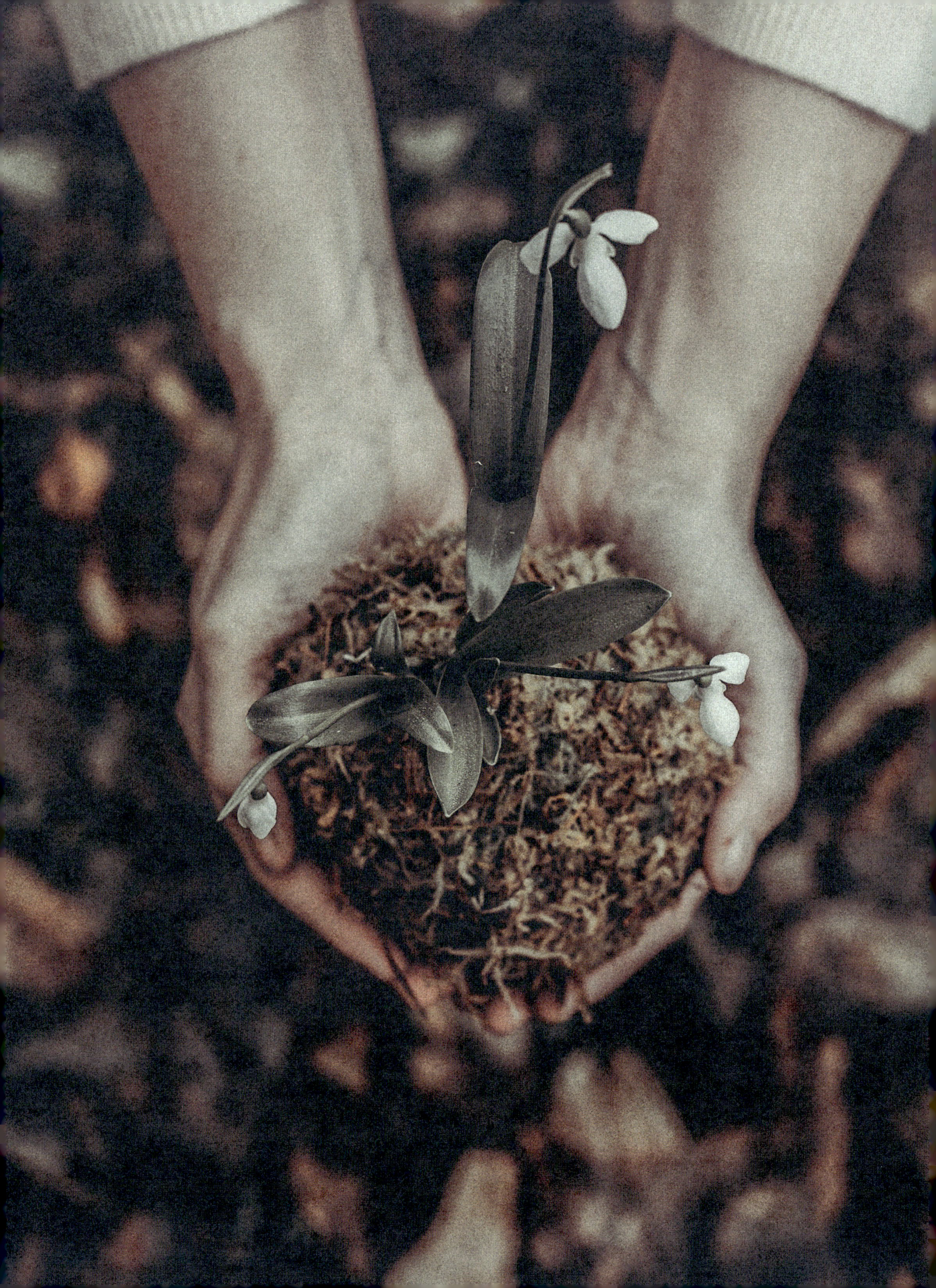

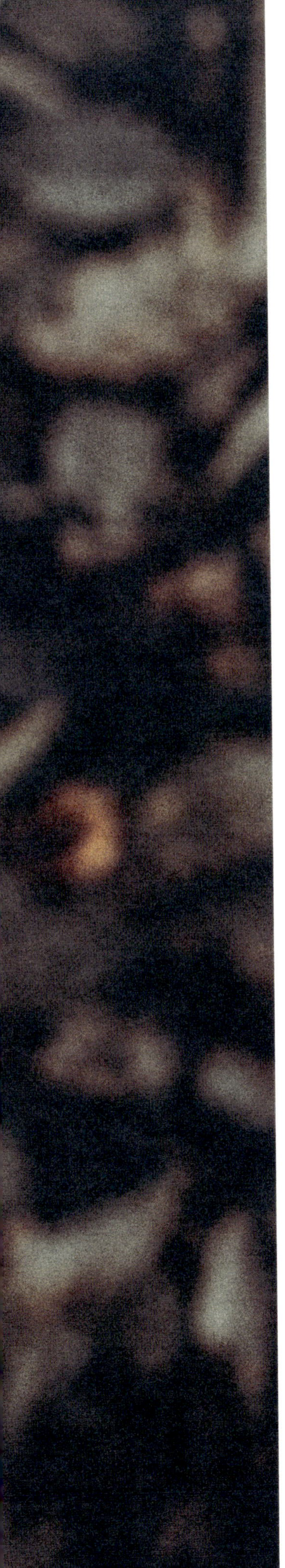

"*For* *God so loved the world in this way: He gave his one and only Son, so that everyone who believes in him will not perish but have eternal life."*[49]

*-John 3:16*

Does anyone miss their elementary school days like I do? It was in those precious years that my one main goal was to play with my friends as much as I could. Learning was important of course, but recess was the highlight of my school days. Playing with my friends was the ultimate for me. It was characterized by the years when I was short enough to actually fit on the jungle gym—before I grew to 5'10" in high school. Days when I could twirl around the gymnastic beam with ease and make it lightning fast across the monkey bars without blistered hands and pulled muscles in my shoulders (Yes, I did just try tackling monkey bars this past month and both of those things occurred). I'll never forget the year I moved into middle school, aka the awkward years. Despite being made fun of for having beaver teeth, the thing I resented most was the lack of recess and being separated from my church friends.

In elementary school, I had one best friend who would play with me every day. We walked to and from school in the wind, ice, rain and snow, uphill both ways to school and home. She loved God like I did and was a gift from God to me in that season. One day at recess my friend and I decided we were going to ask a group of girls if we could be their friends. We really wanted to be a part of their cool group. You see they were the "popular" girls who ruled the roost in fifth grade. So I scraped up enough courage and decided to talk to them. I can remember the day as if it were yesterday. I was longing for deeper friendships on the inside and I wanted to be an amazing friend. I would try hard and love well. When we finally got up enough nerve to ask the girls if we could be their friends, they calmly said they had to discuss it with each other before they made a decision. Didn't they realize the gravity of this situation for me? They would give us an answer in the morning, which seemed like an eternity. My heart waited in bated anticipation. I could barely sleep that night. I tossed and turned, imagining that I may actually have a group of girls to play with where I felt like I belonged. Tomorrow could be the day where everything in my world changed. The stars would align and the universe would beam down on me with favor, or at least I hoped that would happen.

We tentatively made our way to school the next morning awaiting their answer. I'll never forget the girl who came and told me that they had discussed my proposal and decided that I couldn't be their friend. To make matters worse, they decided to accept my friend, and not me! They invited her to come play with them, leaving me all alone. So I was left in solitude with my shame, embarrassment, a frizzy fake perm, zebra stirrup leggings and the feeling that I wasn't enough. A part of my heart broke that day and I wondered if stepping out with others was actually worth the risk of disappointment. To my best friend's credit, she decided she didn't want to be a part of their group if I wasn't there. We continued to be thick as thieves throughout all of high school. It was a blessing in disguise. Little did I know that God was protecting me and setting me up for the greatest love and acceptance I could ever have known.

When I experienced the love of God at age fourteen, my life was never the same. Before that encounter, all I wanted, all I lived for, was the approval of others. It was my number one desire. In my grades, in sports, in friendships and with family, I needed approval. Perhaps I was simply looking for belonging and for people to accept and love me. I can remember heading into summer camp telling God that I was going to have a singular focus on Him this time through. The last year I went, I was infatuated with boys, so needless to say I spent most of my time pursuing them. That year was different. If God was real and personal I wanted to know it. I'll never forget the night I first encountered Him for as long as I live. I can't remember the message or much of anything else, I only remember that God spoke to me. He was so near. I had heard His voice for the first time whispering to my soul, *"Jamie, I love you just the way you are. No one is ever going to love you the way I do."* My heart melted. In an instant, my life was changed. Funny how a moment with God can do that. Turns out, all I wanted was to be loved and God loved me just the way I was. With Him, nothing else mattered. What others labeled as unlovable and awkward, God labeled as perfectly lovely. He knew

"WHAT OTHERS LABELED AS UNLOVABLE AND AWKWARD, GOD LABELED AS PERFECTLY LOVELY."

what I needed. I finally had a place to belong, and it was the only place I wanted to be: with Him.

The love of God will always choose you. You are His number one pick. Once we grasp a realization of how deep the Father's love is for us, it only helps us cultivate a deeper love for others. And part of loving others well is knowing what they need. God knew me so well, He knew exactly what I needed. God knows us all so well. He knew no matter how hard we tried, we would still fall short. In the end, we would need a Savior. Enter Jesus. God saw our need, and He provided for that need. In addition to that, He is always searching out ways to meet our needs personally, so that we can intimately experience His love. Just like He knew what I needed as a teenager, He knows what you and I need in this season of life.

In God's explanation of His plan for redemption, He starts out by talking about love. True love is one of the most powerful aspects of God's character. He tells us in scripture that all His commandments hang on the principles of loving God and loving others.[50] If we want to give our attention to what's most important, our focus should undoubtedly be love. So how do we do that, you might ask? First, accept and experience His love. Once you are overflowing with that awareness, you can pour out in a greater way to others. The Bible says to love your neighbor as you love yourself.[51] I heard a Joyce Meyers podcast where she said something along the lines of this: we miserably fail to love others because we've never learned to love ourselves. Do you know that God loves you just the way you are? There is no one else in this world that is like you. You are His unique creation. Until we learn to love the person God has created us to be, receiving His love without reservations or objections, we will never be able to love others well. Secondly, when it comes to loving others, like God, find out what they need. Love them the way they need to be loved, not the way you want to love them, or even the way you receive love. My friend in elementary school made a choice, it was a choice of love. She could have been popular but instead she chose friendship, and me. That was what I needed. That was love.

When Naomi needed a companion, Ruth stepped in. Ruth and Naomi needed food for survival, and Boaz provided grain. Ruth needed a redeemer, and Boaz stepped in with provision. It would have been ridiculous if Ruth was in desperate need for food and Boaz stepped in and gave her an adorable puppy. As soft and cuddly as that would have been, it would be one more mouth for her and Naomi to feed. God pours out His love on us by seeing the need we have, before we even realize it. He then steps in and provides for that need in ways that we actually need Him to.

I have a friend who at this very moment is going through a really hard time with her family, mostly due to health issues. It seems as if everywhere she turns, she is getting one negative doctor's report after another. We could cry in a corner together, weeping and wondering why God would allow this in her

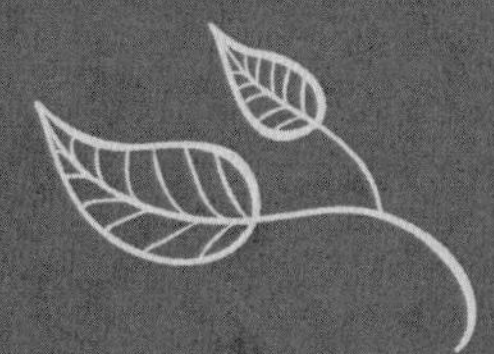

"WE CAN CURE PHYSICAL DISEASE WITH MEDICINE, BUT THE ONLY CURE FOR LONELINESS, DESPAIR, AND HOPELESSNESS IS LOVE."

-Mother Teresa

life, but I know that is not what she needs right now. True love looks at the situation and asks God for a solution. There are times for laughing and times for tears, but what she needs right now is a faith-filled, life-giving friend. Someone who will speak promises of healing over her life and family, when all she can see is death and darkness surrounding her. I adamantly refuse to feed the fears lurking in the shadows. Instead, I am feeding her faith. Faith in a God who is more than able to do a miracle. Her life is marked for miracles. Her time of mourning will lead to hope in God. Her family is marked for miracles. Whether it is a note left on her door, an inspirational magnet, or a text of encouragement, so help me, faith will prevail. Faith is not the denial of bad things happening, but it's the knowledge that through it all we are still deeply loved by God. This is how I can love her through this season. Your life, my friend, is marked for miracles too. I'm not sure where you are right now, but maybe you needed to hear this faith-filled declaration for your own life: God is more than able.

Sometimes it's not easy to assess a person's need and figure out how God can help us love them. Many times, I have to dig a little deeper to find out what a friend really needs. Perhaps their need isn't even a perceived need, but it's found in relation to their passions, dreams and desires. Ask them questions, get to know them and see how God can use you to push them a little closer to their destiny. That is true love.

When's the last time you went out of your way to show love to someone else? Love could look like a hot cup of tea with a friend, or a slice of your mom's homemade banana bread around a table of meaningful conversation. A friendly promised-filled text to a neighbor. A hot meal to a new mother. A beautifully wrapped package of cookies left on the doorstep of a friend. A warm hug on a cold day. Or behind the scene prayer for that loved one. Let loving others not be something you do, but define who you are. Side note: remember, you cannot give what you have not received.

Take time to receive the love of God today.

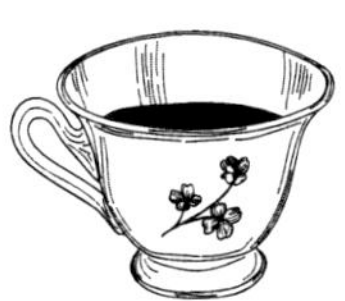

**BOOK RECOMMENDATION**

## They Smell like Sheep *by Lynn Anderson*

Awkward name for a book, but it contains great leadership principles around the fact that in order for you to lead people well, you need to be relationally invested in them. Good read for non-profits.

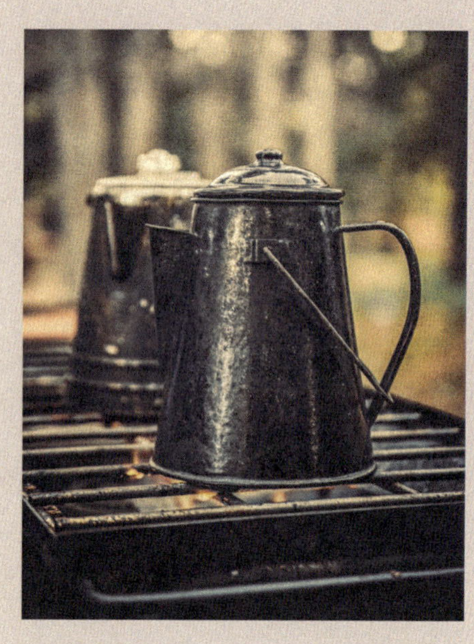

"

LOVE COULD LOOK LIKE A HOT CUP OF TEA WITH A FRIEND, OR A SLICE OF YOUR MOM'S HOMEMADE BANANA BREAD AROUND A TABLE OF MEANINGFUL CONVERSATION."

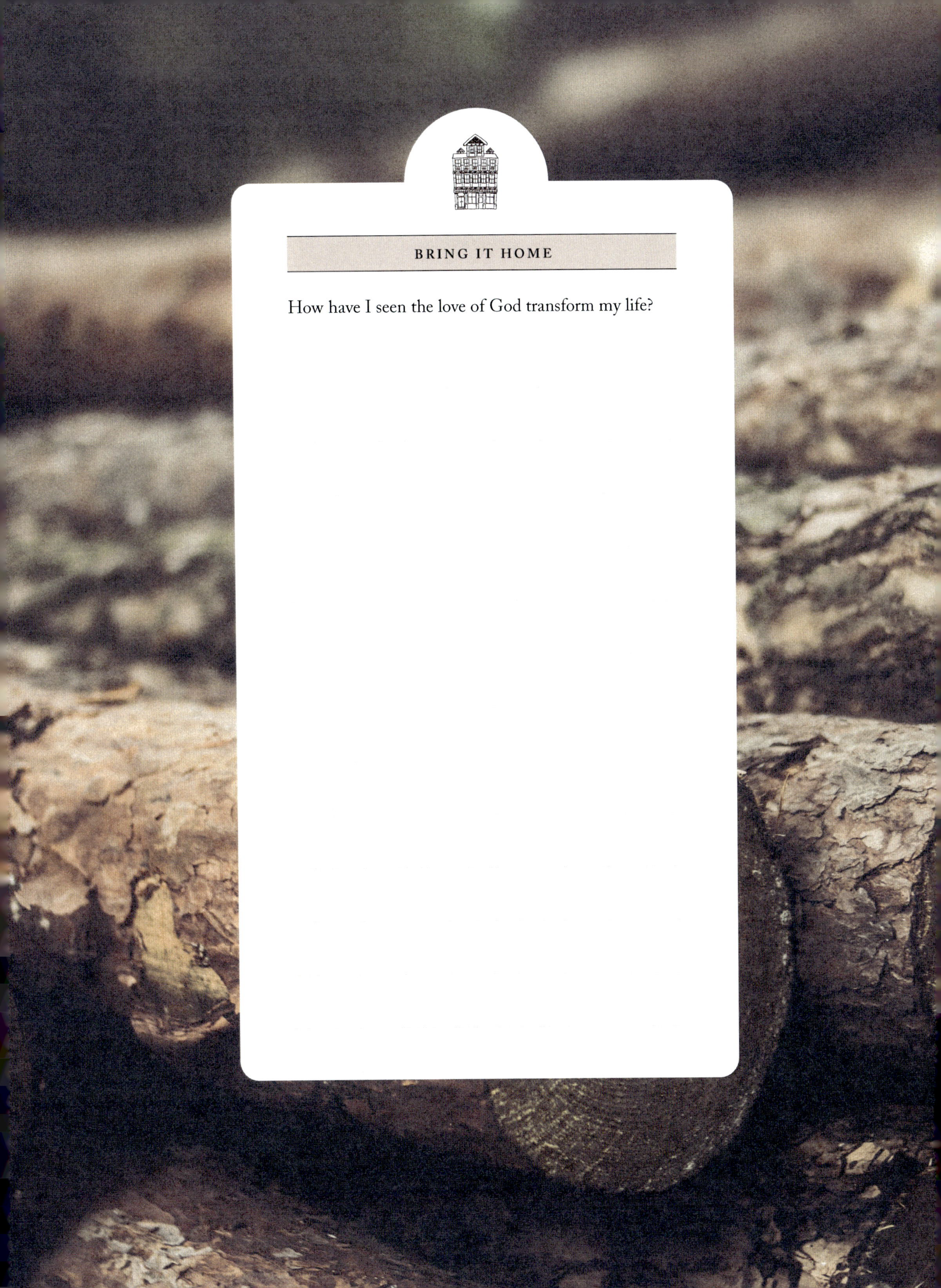

BRING IT HOME

How have I seen the love of God transform my life?

CHAPTER SIXTEEN

# JUST BE *Generous*

BEING LOVED DEEPLY LEADS TO GENEROSITY

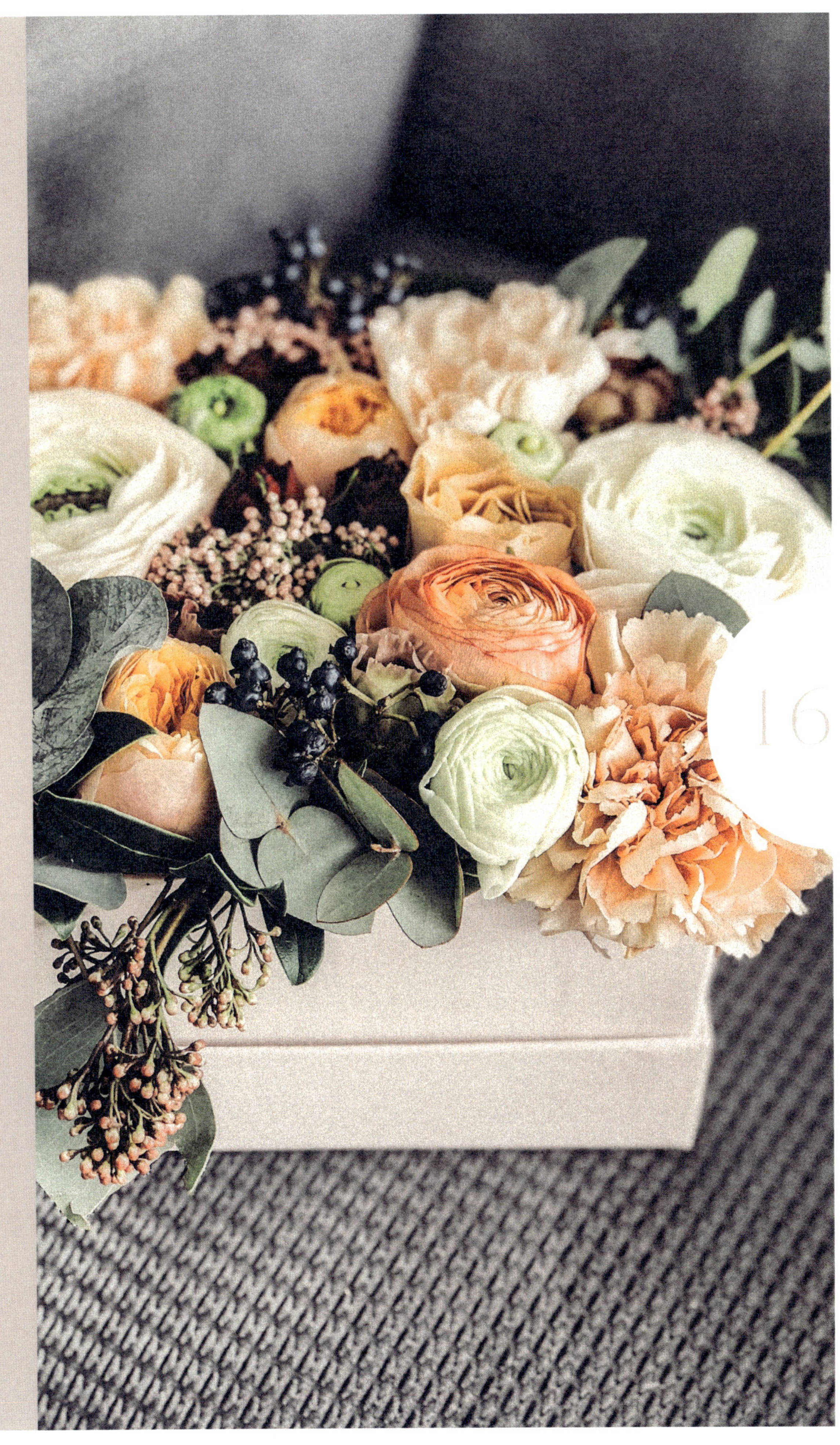

16

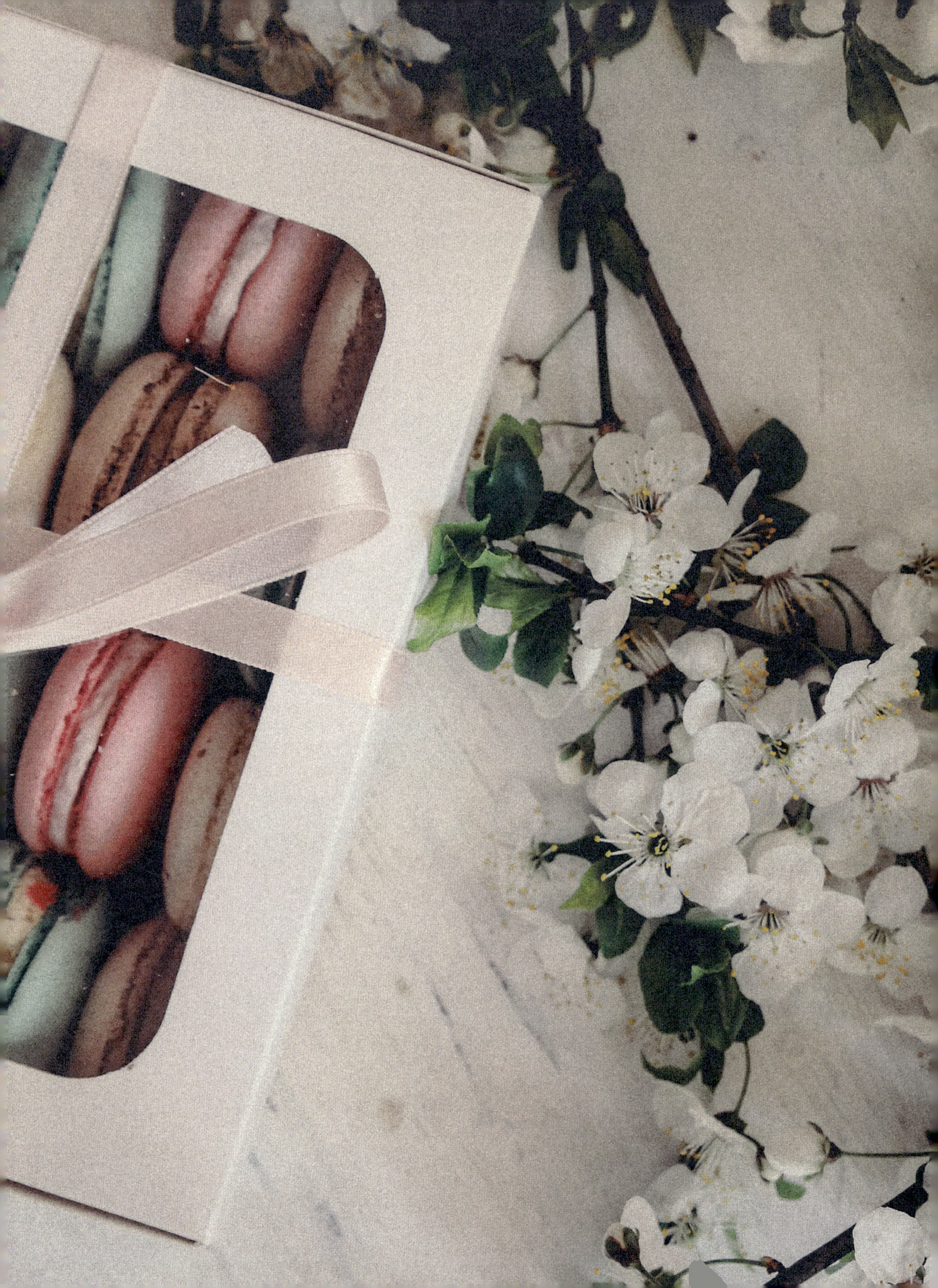

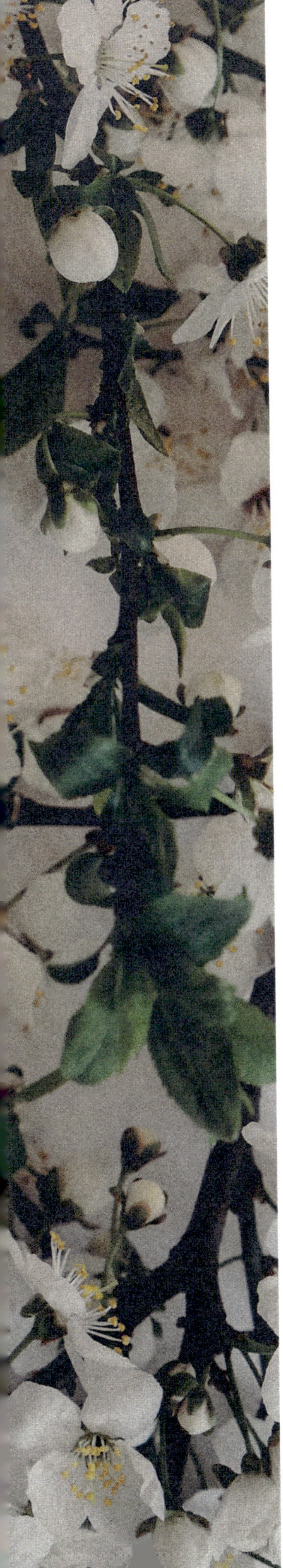

"How *are you doing over there on the couch? Can I get you anything?"* I call effortlessly from the kitchen. By the way your legs are curled up against you, it looks as if you are quite at home. I had gotten up to stretch my legs for a bit and put a fresh pot of water on the stove in my new tea kettle. I love this kettle. Vintage creme color with muted gold metal accents. The perfect kettle to make me smile in the dimly lit morning light. A fabulous find on Amazon.

*"I'm perfectly cozy,"* you say nestling down as snug as a bug in a rug, *"but I will take a fresh cup of tea when the water is ready."* As if your voice was confirming its completion, the tea kettle begins to whistle loudly.

*"Done,"* I say authoritatively as I move the kettle to the other side of the stove. I decide to give you a different kind of tea this time. *"How about Wedding Tea?"* I ask as I continue to divulge its details. *"A Mutan White tea with lemon-vanilla to taste, with a touch of pink rosebuds and petals."*[52] I love the way this tea is described. Perfection. Makes me want to eat it straight out of the tin.

*"Sounds delicious,"* you add, smiling brightly. Harney and Sons tea certainly boasts of its delicious blends, and they are right to do so. I've never had such beautifully blended teas.

I bring over your tea cup carefully and set it on the coffee table. Its steam ascends to the heavens as if to signal our conversation to continue, freshly new aromas from heaven. I plop down on the other side of the couch as we begin to talk freely …

I'm usually wiped out on Sundays. Don't get me wrong, I LOVE Sundays. They are literally one of my favorite days of the week. It's the day that I get to go and serve, love on others and learn about God in church—all the while surrounded by those I cherish. What could be greater than that? So, I serve hard, then I rest hard. This past Sunday my two oldest daughters had a youth meeting in the evening. My amazing husband decided to drive them so I could stay home and finish some "laundry," which in reality meant I was finishing a Hallmark movie.

Now I don't know exactly what happened during the youth meeting, but Jesus must have come down in person for a visit. When the girls got home, my thirteen-year-old walked through the doors and beelined for me in the kitchen. She wrapped her arms around me, nestled her head in my shoulders and said, "Mom, I just want you to know that I love you, and I'm so thankful that you're my mom." SHUT THE FRONT DOOR. What just happened? I was so shocked that I started tearing up.

For those of you who have teenage girls, you know I'm not lying when I say there comes a stage where you have serious parental cooties. Gone are the days of snuggling and physical touch. In fact, sometimes when I want to hug them, I've gotta sneak up on them like a panther waiting for its prey. Then bam, I go in for the hug and I usually get a, "Mmmmoooommmm, stop that!" The days when I could kiss my little ones on their luscious little lips are now replaced with forehead kisses. What's up with that? So, when she came in that door and hugged me of her own free will and told me how much she loved me—the floodgates of my heart and soul were gushing all over the place. I brought that moment before the Lord in prayer the following morning and just wept and thanked Him for His goodness. I began thinking of ways that I could bless her. The love she poured out on me marked me in a way that compelled me to give back to her. That's what love does, it makes us want to give back not begrudgingly or in scarcity, but with a full-on life of generosity.

> "THE LOVE SHE POURED OUT ON ME MARKED ME IN A WAY THAT COMPELLED ME TO GIVE BACK TO HER."

John 3:16 says: *"for God so loved the world ... that He gave."*[53] Someday I am going to write a book on generosity in all its deliciously fabulous forms. I couldn't imagine a more generous God. Generous in love. Generous in mercy. Generous in forgiveness. It's at the core of who God is and who He created us all to be. In fact, when I receive the generosity of God, I can in turn be generous to others. I get the exquisite opportunity to pour out His lush goodness onto the world around me. It's as if my heart and spirit are swept away in a tidal wave of His presence and I can't help but want to live there with Him, rising and falling on the tide of generosity—forever—and honestly it's solely because of His rich love towards me. I don't think you can actually experience the love of God in a transforming way without it leading to generosity. They go hand in hand.

There's a secret treasure found in the pages of scripture when

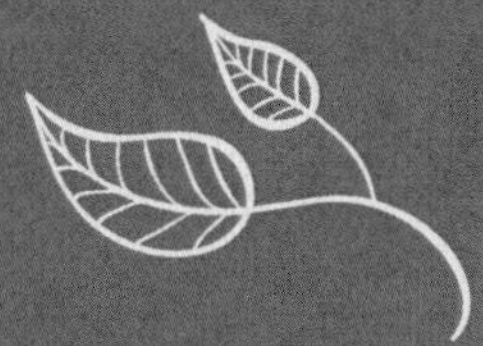

"BEYOND CHRIST, EVERYTHING ELSE IS JUST FROSTING."

-David Green

it comes to generosity. You must eagerly search for it or you may miss it. When you unearth it and embrace it, you can begin to crochet it into the fibers of your being. It will transform you, like the word of God always does. This precious, finer-than-gold fortune is found in Matthew 10:8, and it says this: *"Freely you have received; freely give."*[54] You see, friend, generosity is a three-fold cord. First and foremost, generosity is about receiving. It seems like an oxymoron to say that generosity, or giving, begins with receiving, but it is unquestionably the truth. Generosity begins with a willingness to receive

> GENEROSITY BEGINS WITH A WILLINGNESS TO RECEIVE AND THE KNOWLEDGE THAT EVERYTHING WE HAVE COMES FROM THE HAND OF AN ALL-TOO-GENEROUS GOD."

and the knowledge that everything we have comes from the hand of an all-too-generous God. The Bible says plainly, what we receive we can freely give to others. If we never learn to receive, we are missing a colossal piece of the puzzle. Can you remember being a child on Christmas morning? I don't know about you, but there was always one special gift I was eagerly awaiting to unwrap. I'm sure you experienced the same. It was that one thing you had been asking—no, begging—your parents to get you for months. On Christmas morning you woke up at 3 a.m. with excitement breakdancing through your innards. Waiting until dawn to open up presents seemed unthinkable, unimaginable, but somehow you managed to restrain yourself long enough to do it. With anticipation about to burst out of every buckle and seam, you finally reach the moment you had been waiting for. The time had come, the moment was there. When you opened the gift, you realized the gift was even greater than you expected. Instead of just a Cabbage Patch Doll, you got the doll and an entire wardrobe of clothes to go with it! Your heart was so delighted it could've exploded!

You may or may not have memories like this. If not, friend, I'm so sorry. But this is the way God gives to us. Now imagine, for a moment, that the minute you opened the gift, your inaccurate feelings of unworthiness trumped your need for the gift and you rejected it. Instead of reveling in the goodness surrounding you, you returned the gift. Even though you'd always wanted it, asked for it, and prayed for it, you never actually received it. What a tragedy that would be. The blessings that your parents intended for you would be left unwanted, unaccepted. Your decision to reject the beautifully precious gift would leave you without the blessing and leaves your parents hurt, knowing the good they intended for you would never be experienced by you. The same is true for us in relationship to God. We must learn to receive. Receiving isn't prideful in and of itself. Receiving when done with a humbly thankful, grateful heart is precious in the sight of God. When receiving this way, we can recognize that the gift wasn't given because of the goodness of its recipient, but rather the generosity of the Giver. Today, freely receive. Freely receive His extravagant love for you. Freely receive His exuberant joy. Freely receive His undeniable, unshaking peace. Freely receive the unwavering identity He has for you. Freely receive the gentle-nudging gestures of kindness He is placing in your everyday. Freely receive His superior provision for your life—above and beyond what you could do, earn or supply. Freely receive His unquenchable hope for this season. Freely receive delightful purpose and unwavering promises for you and your family.

The second aspect of a generous life is giving. We freely receive, then we freely give. The Bible says: *"The world of the generous gets larger and larger; the world of the stingy gets smaller and smaller. The one who blesses others is abundantly blessed; those who help others are helped."*[55] Generosity is giving what you have. In the Bible, Boaz left Ruth handfuls of grain so she wouldn't have to work so hard to collect food for herself and Naomi. It didn't seem like much, but he was sowing seeds of generosity—and Ruth was reaping those seeds with every step she took. Your life can sow seeds of generosity into the lives of others too. It doesn't always need to be a physical gift or something grand. Sometimes you sow peace, encouragement and joy. Sometimes you sow love through a warm hug or time spent with a cherished friend. I'd be ecstatic to say that I could share with you ways I've been generous in some luxurious sort of way. To say that I've given a beautiful home away, no strings attached, or a brand new car to the neighbor down the street who needs it—that would be wonderful. But in all honesty, I haven't given any of those things away. Now that doesn't mean I can't dream to give away some of those things in the future, but currently my giving is a little less glamorous than that. Note this: Your lack of resources doesn't excuse you from living a generous life. Give what you have when you can and when God asks.

YOUR LACK OF RESOURCES DOESN'T EXCUSE YOU FROM LIVING A GENEROUS LIFE. GIVE WHAT YOU HAVE WHEN YOU CAN AND WHEN GOD ASKS."

Generosity for me in this season looks more like giving away my favorite sweater to a sister who fell in love with it at first sight (she looks glorious in it, I might add). Or dropping fruity candy and Tylenol off on the doorstep of a sick friend. Giving my hard earned cash, meant as she-money, to a beautiful leader I admire. Dropping off gift baskets to my neighbors around the holidays. Taking my family to draw sidewalk chalk messages outside of the elderly home during the COVID crisis—that way they can look right out their windows and see encouraging love notes throughout the day. Telling the lady I just met at the pool she looks pretty.

I love what the Bible says in 2 Corinthians 9:8: *"And God will generously provide all you need. Then you will always have everything you need and plenty left over to share with others."*[56] God blesses you because He loves you, so receive it. He blesses you to bless others, so give generously. The fact is, no matter how much I give, I can never out-give God. Giving not only blesses the person you give to, but it has lasting effects on your heart and life as well. Maybe God is asking you to give, so that selfishness will release its hold on your life and generosity will open you up to something even greater God has in store. Maybe giving will help you trust God more because as you give, you see that God gives back to you beyond measure. It's receiving from God, then giving back to others with godly stewardship at its core.

> "THE FACT IS, NO MATTER HOW MUCH I GIVE, I CAN NEVER OUT-GIVE GOD."

The last aspect of generosity is found in the word "freely." Voluntarily. Willingly. When you receive, you receive with open hands. When you give, you give with open hands. Realize that God is the owner of every aspect of your life; you are simply a daughter who stewards. Someone who looks after and manages well that which has been given to her. Be thankful for what you have. Don't look to others wishing you had what they have, use freely what He has given you to bless others. When we have a right perspective on what we have, it helps us cultivate a "freely" mentality. Instead of God trying to pry our hands open to use what He's given us to bless others, we offer it freely, understanding it's His to begin with. I liken it to me just gifting my daughter with a giant pack of Skittles. She is so excited. I see her happiness beaming from her face, until I tell her to share a couple with her sisters. You'd think I'd just asked her to give her sister a kidney. She has an entire pack of Skittles that I blessed her with, but she can't share ten with her sisters. I literally have to go over to her and pry the bag from her hands, take the ten Skittles and distribute them to her sisters. Isn't this the way we act sometimes with God when He asks us to give to others? But how much more amazing would it be if when I asked my daughter to share with her sisters, she gave willingly, freely, with a great attitude because she just loved sharing what I gave to her? How much more apt would I be to give her more if that was the kind of attitude she displayed? I'd give her twenty packs of Skittles! If we freely give of what we have, God will be gracious to bless us with more.

God has a purpose woven into the miniscule fibers of a generous life. It ultimately makes room for the deeper work God wants to do in and through us. When you are called to sacrifice and be generous, make sure you're giving your best and not something you didn't want anyway. That's not true sacrifice. True sacrifice is giving the best of what you have with a great heart to those around you, even when it might hurt. Learn to freely receive. Remember, you cannot give what you do not have. Learn to freely give.

Just be generous today.

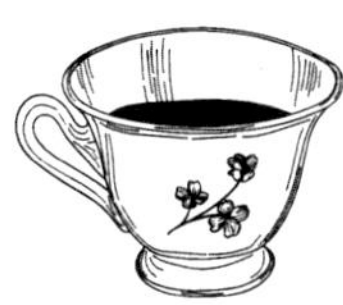

**BOOK RECOMMENDATION**

## The Blessed Life *by Robert Morris*

With principles focusing on the fact that you are blessed to be a blessing, this book focuses on tithing to God first—but the principles apply to every area of your life.

# Acts of Generosity

"I keep a calendar with the names of people that I want to bless. I write on the calendar things they like. Maybe it's something I've noticed in a conversation: a love for lemon bars, a love to write, a love of old things, Oreos or vintage records. I then try to come up with creative ways to bless them within my small budget. I ask questions like: How can I bless them and have that blessing encourage them to be who God created them to be? Don't forget to show love to those closest to you too. Give without expecting anything in return."

*-Jamie*

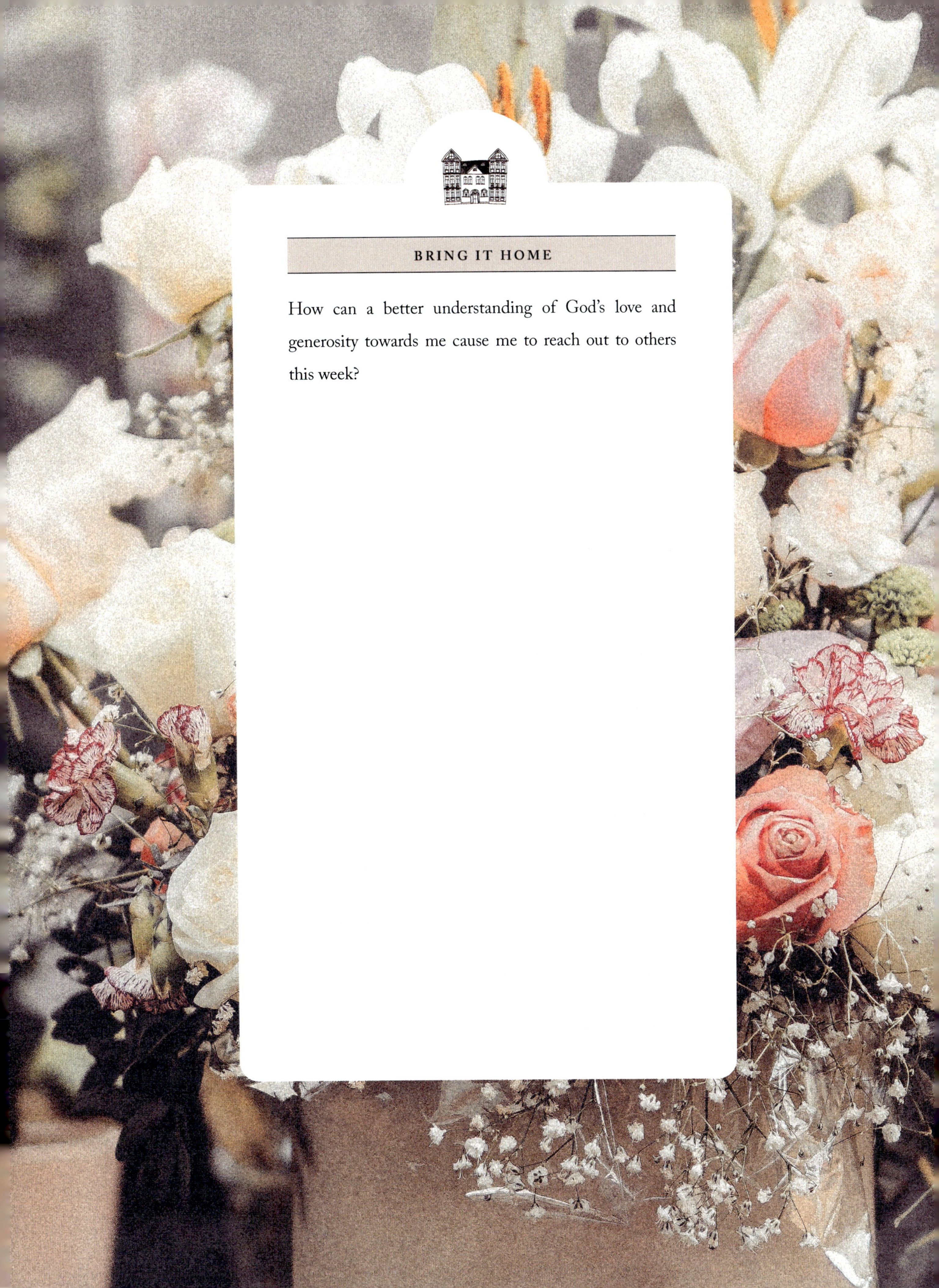

## BRING IT HOME

How can a better understanding of God's love and generosity towards me cause me to reach out to others this week?

CHAPTER SEVENTEEN

# JUST BE *A People-Valuer*

YOUR PROVISION LIES WITH PEOPLE

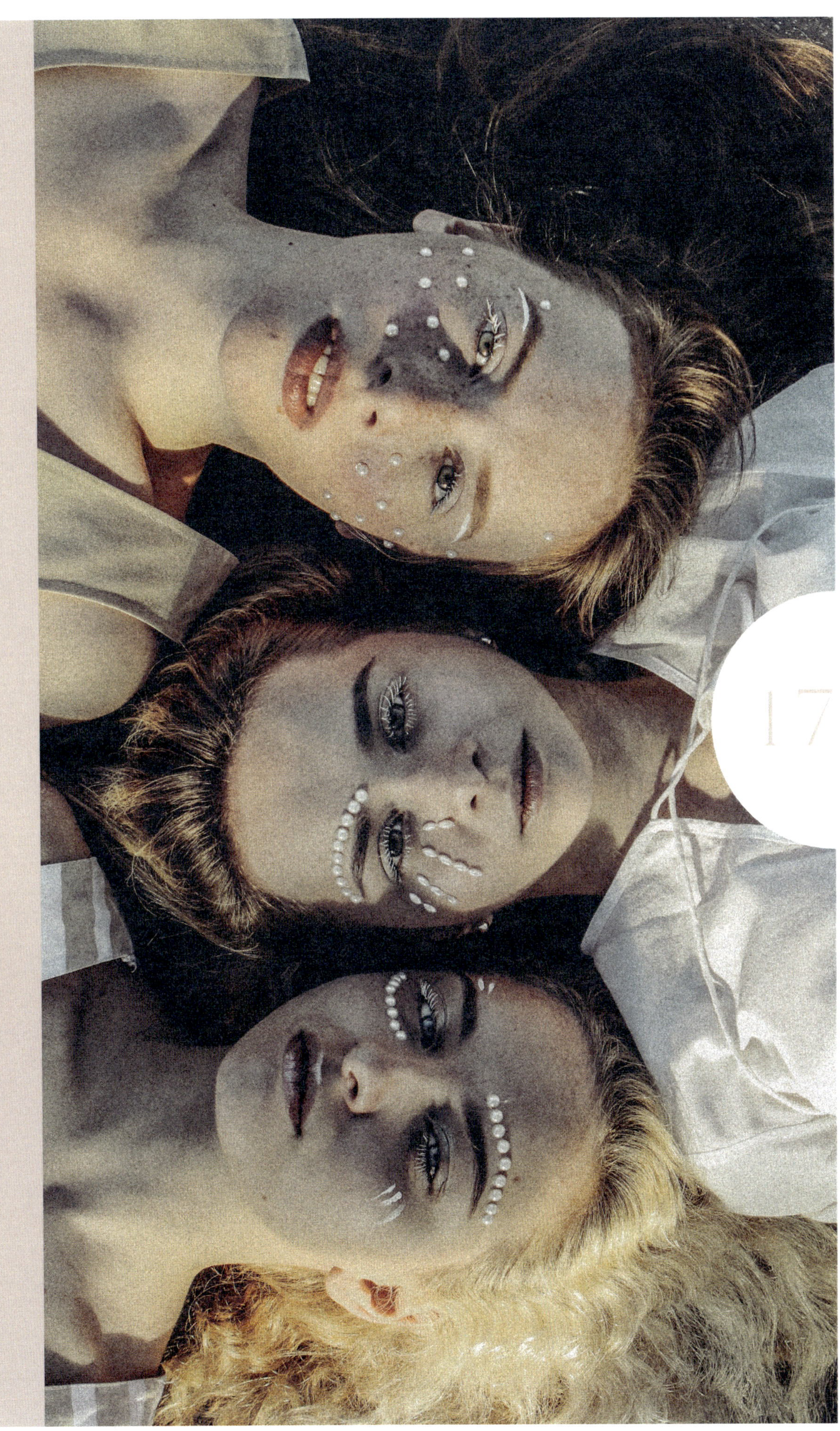

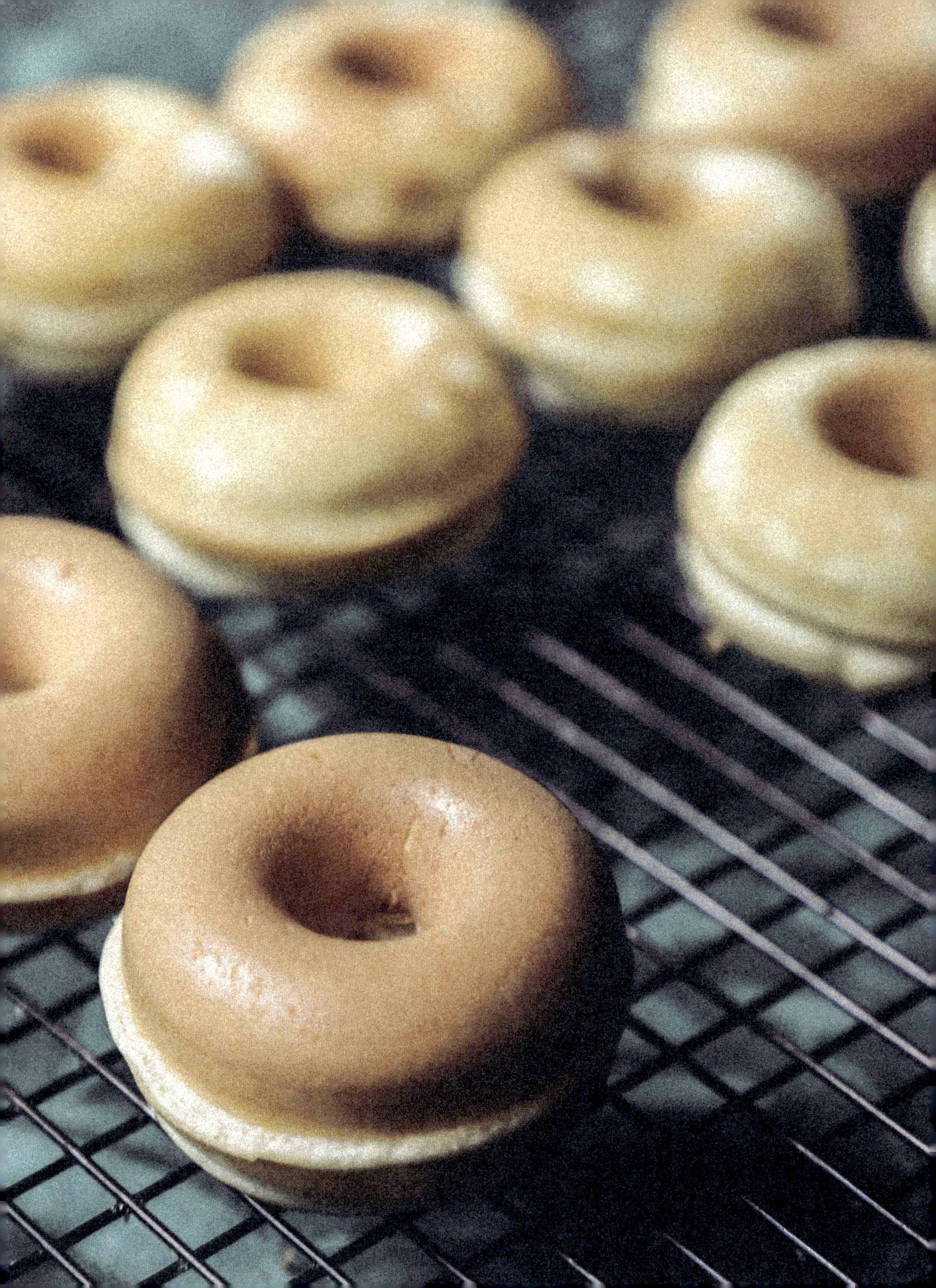

I'm not gonna lie, seeing manna fall from the sky would have been pretty cool. When the children of Israel wandered in the wilderness for forty years, God supernaturally provided this "bread from heaven" as provision for their hunger. The book of Numbers says that manna arrived on the ground with the dew of the morning. The book of Exodus says that raw manna tasted like wafers with honey.[57]

Call me crazy, but when I close my eyes I imagine manna looking and tasting like mini Krispy Kreme donuts, without the calories of course. Imagine waking up every morning to little mini donut-cakes scattered ever-so-sweetly across the ground outside your tent. My kids would freak out, reveling in the fresh smell of Krispy Kremes as we woke up with the dawn light. Sure, it was in wafer form, but a sweet honey wafer, how much better could it get? Krispy Kremes for breakfast, lunch and dinner. Krispy Kremes dried and ground up to make Krispy Kreme bread with melted butter on top. Krispy Kremes with milk. Krispy Kremes with meat. Krispy Kreme sandwiches. My mouth is watering just writing about it. If you've never had a Krispy Kreme donut you need to go out and get one, right this minute.

Now, I doubt that manna tasted like a donut, but it's fun to imagine. I can, however, come to one conclusion from this extraordinary act: God has some pretty creative ways to provide for His people. Whether it's parting the Red Sea, raining manna from heaven, or sending His only Son to die on the cross for our sins, God does not lack creativity or ingenuity. Neither does He lack resources or capability. God can do in an instant what it would take man a lifetime to accomplish. His provision can come in a plethora of ways.

Most times, whether in the process or the act itself, God uses people. People to provide. People to protect. People to help carry you into the promise He has for you. People as vessels to flow His miraculous power through to touch others on His behalf. He used Moses as a voice for His voice and to perform miracles that would usher God's people out of the land of slavery. He used Joseph to save his brothers and many nations from famine. He used David to slay Goliath. He used Mary to birth Jesus. He used Jesus to restore our relationship with the Father. We must understand something: our provision comes from God, but is often brought to us in the ever-so-beautiful vessels of people.

Sure, God could open up the heavens right now and drop that new car in your driveway. You could wake up, look out your front window with your morning breath and foggy eyes only to notice that shiny black new truck you've always wanted in your driveway. God could do it. Of course He could. But more than likely, He'll use someone to make it happen. He laid a desire on your heart, someone else saw the need you had and knew of that desire. That person, out of the selflessness of their heart, and the overflow of blessings from God, decided to drive a donated truck to your house. They parked it in your driveway. They left the keys there to bless you with a note attached about how God wanted to bless you. A little bit of love from the best Dad ever, God, given to you through a person.

side note

*I can't help myself right now, but I'm writing as I fly across the Atlantic and as I look out and see the breathtakingly gorgeous sun casting its rays over each fluffy cloud, it looks like I'm lost in a world of peach fuzz. Orangish-pink-golden yumminess surrounds me. I think to myself, who are we to be able to fly across God's creation like this? We are so small, so insignificant, but we grab the attention of the Creator of the universe, the One who calls us His children and raptures us in His love daily. This is crazy.*

Don't take people for granted. Relationships are so valuable. On your deathbed you won't be thinking about your achievements, you'll be longing for people. People to tenderly squeeze your hand and warmly embrace you. People who will tell you they love you and will not under any circumstances leave your side. The same people who believed in you, walked with you, loved you unconditionally, helped carry you through the hardest times of your life, laughed with you in good times and cried with you in bad and saw your potential when there's no way in God's green earth you ever thought He could use your meager life. People. Life is about people. So, love people. Value people. Open your heart up to people.

It's hard when people leave your life. The friends you thought would be there forever just moved fifty states away and you are left in the stinky-swirling-dust of their departure. Those retirement plans of living in a senior home together, you know like an old-person camp, are blowing away like chaff in the wind. You started wondering if it was worth it. Was the friendship worth opening your life up, fully to someone who may leave in the future? And who else might leave in the next five years? Unknowingly, a shift can happen in your spirit. You began to close your life off to those who are still surrounding you in attempts to guard yourself from any future pain. But the very wall you put up to protect yourself is isolating you from one of the very things that brings joy to your life—deep friendships, people.

> "OUR PROVISION COMES FROM GOD, BUT IS OFTEN BROUGHT TO US IN THE EVER-SO-BEAUTIFUL VESSELS OF PEOPLE."

I've had moments like this. Moments where I had unintentionally been hurt by people. After months of me stewing over it, with tear-stained cheeks and puffy-eyes, I finally had to make a decision before God to stop mourning. I would rather love people in a crazy-deep, vulnerable, giving-all-of-myself, God-breathed way for the time I have with them than close myself off, never to have loved at all. The truth is, knowing what I do today, I wouldn't trade one moment of our friendship for anything else. The years of openness, joy, life and giving were worth the pain I experienced when our paths parted (and you can still stay connected via texts and FaceTime, even when you are miles apart). As Alfred Lord Tennyson stated so eloquently, *"Tis better to have loved and lost than never to have loved at all."*[58]

I want to value the people God has placed in my life today. I want to love them like all get out. I want them to enter into their next season of life better, closer to God, because of the friendship they have had with me. I want to pull the God-treasures out of them. The truth is, many times, when you truly desire what's best for a person's life that may mean God has only placed them in your life for a season. Love that season. Cherish that season. But don't live for that season, clinging to it as if your identity is wrapped up in one tight knit ball and connected directly to a person. People are a gift from God, created to bring out God's best in you. Hold them with open hands. People can, and will, leave your life. If you value them beyond what they can do for you, then you'll welcome God's best for their life, even if their placement is beyond your sphere of influence. If it's true that God uses people to help usher in His promise for your life, then make a decision now to live open and vulnerable, full of love for the people He has placed in your life. Don't let hurt sidestep your purpose. Love others well, my friend.

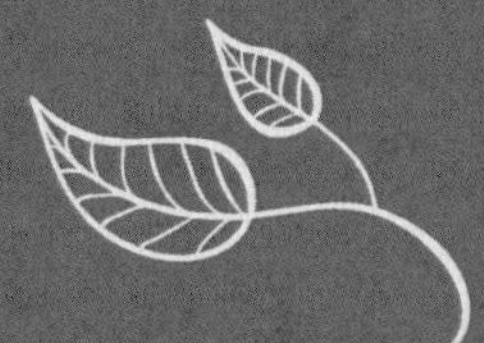

"WE ARE NOT JUST PRODUCTS OF OUR PAST, PEOPLE IN OUR PRESENT ALSO INFLUENCE US AND HELP MOLD OUR CHARACTER."

-David Packer

*The sun now looks like a fireball after having been sloshed around in your mouth for a good two minutes. It's not that dark red color, but more of that hot pink color. Fascinating.*

side note

## I'll have an eggwhite frittata, please

The other day I met a friend and her mother for breakfast. We have this restaurant chain in Colorado called Snooze, and they have the best breakfast food. I had been anticipating this meeting for two reasons. One, I got to connect with some dear friends in my life, and two, they sell a killer eggwhite frittata. I've never been a huge breakfast fan, but when I think about this meal my mouth waters incessantly like a dripping faucet. I had a feeling that this breakfast would be divine in my life on many levels, but I didn't realize how much until afterward. After meeting with these two beautiful women, I left encouraged in the depths of my spirit and just ... alive. It was as if God took a barrel-full of kerosene and dumped it on top of the dimly lit flame that was burning in my life and my passion suddenly exploded. I reluctantly got in my car after practically licking my plate clean. Having successfully held back the monsoon of tears that were threatening to burst out during breakfast, I sat in my car, shut the door and the dam broke. I just cried. I cried because God is so good and He knew exactly what I needed that day to put one foot in front of the other and just keep pressing on. He knew that I needed Him to confirm and reconfirm over the years what He was speaking and placing in my heart. He put the right people in my path to do just that.

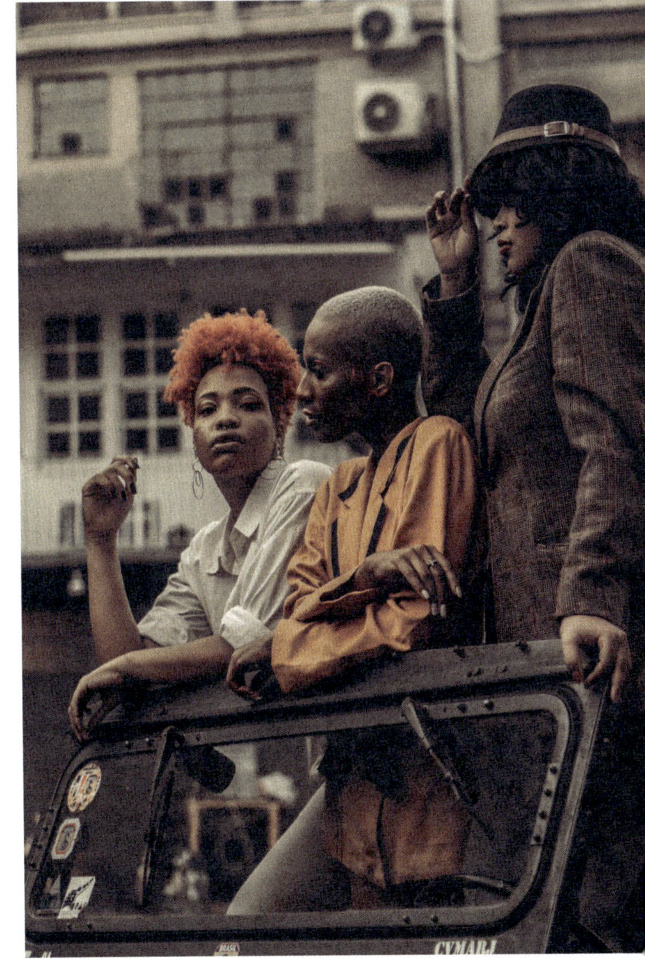

At every given moment, God has the exact right people in your path to help you accomplish the purpose He's placed in your heart. As you love well, God will open divine doors with people. So who has

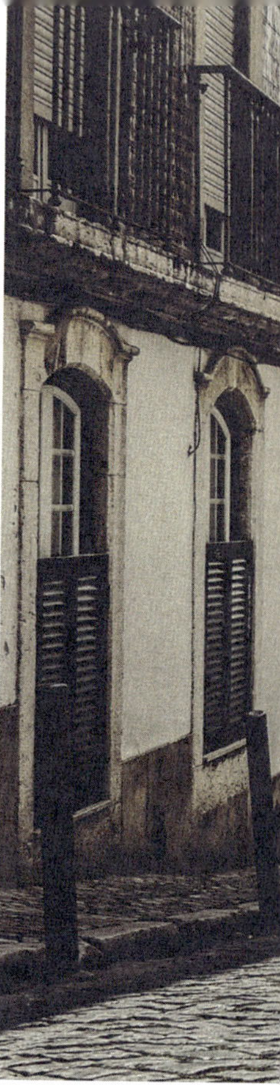

God placed in your life that can help provide for the purpose He's put within you? I'm not looking to use or abuse people. This isn't just you getting what you want out of others. But if you can genuinely love others well, I believe that God will provide above and beyond what you need in this current season through people.

Naomi, in the Bible, thought her life was coming to an end. She thought the good old days were over, but God had a different plan in mind. God wanted her later years to be better than her former. God wanted to bless her beyond what she had ever experienced. God blessed her and provided for her through a person. A person that she tried to abandon, I might add. But Ruth would not let Naomi go. In the end the Bible says that Ruth had been better to Naomi than seven sons![59] Ruth was better to Naomi than anything she had lost in the past and was setting her up for a beautifully bright future. God's above and beyond provision had come through a person.

What is one thing in your life right now that you are believing God for? Who is one person you could ask to help you with that thing? Is it a creative need? A financial need? A friendship need? Whatever it is, God has an answer waiting for you and many times that answer is found in a person. Don't get so busy that you forget to look around you and see the potential in the people God has placed in your life. Your miracle could be staring you in the face, just ask God to help you see it. Look at who God has placed in your life.

## A leather keychain

I never knew what kind of impact it would have on those around me. I just knew that if someone did it for me, I would have loved it. I had decided that I was going to pray for some of my closest friends and make a leather keychain for them with a single word on it. Now this word would be something specific to them based on what God was speaking to my heart about them. It was an encouragement from a verse, something scripture based. I wanted them to know that they were not alone, but surrounded by others who cared for them and believed God's promise for their lives. It took me months to complete this task. I prayed. I read the Bible. I asked God to speak. I researched how to make leather keychains of my own. I bought raw leather from my allowance (thank you, Milan) and a leather stamping kit from Hobby Lobby (I love you). The precious thank you texts and heartfelt hugs I received in the weeks to come said it all. God used this simple act to stir faith in those I loved.

Now for those of you wondering what all this entailed, let me be a little specific. To make these keychains I had to first cut the thick raw leather strip down to size. I then had to individually stamp

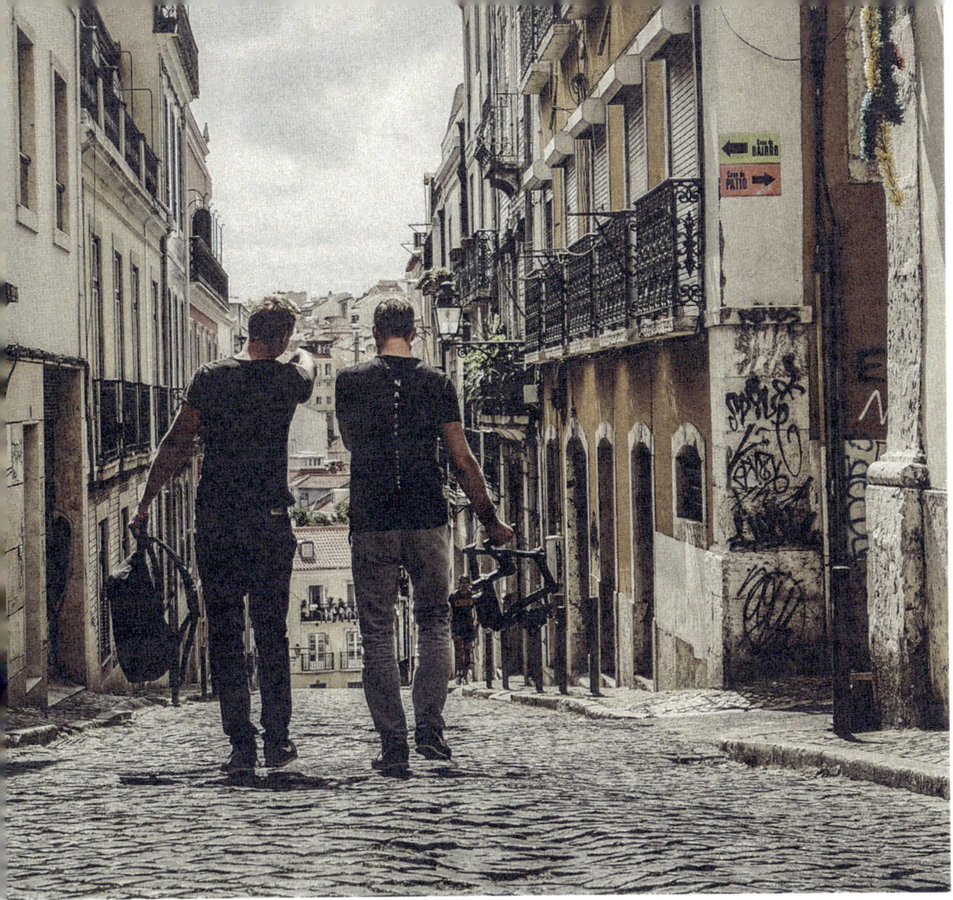

each letter to the hide with a hammer and leather kit. I proceeded to wipe each leather strip down with a wet cloth and used an ear-cleaning swab dabbed in leather stain to stain each one. I had to be careful with the last step because if I used too much stain on the swab it would seep into the letter itself and I wanted the letters a distinctly different color than the rest of the leather. I would start pounding upstairs, and there was no denying Mommy was up to something. At first, the family was excited to join. Then they were like, "When is this ever going to end?" Now they are like, "Oh there Mom goes, she must be making more keychains."

I was hoping it would mean a lot to my friends. My prayer was that it would strengthen their faith every time they saw it, reminding them God was working for their good. I believe it did just that.

The truth is, just as God uses people as provision for our lives, God wants to use you to provide a miracle in the life of another. It doesn't have to be something big or monumental. Sometimes it is, but sometimes it's just an encouraging word at coffee, or a voice text to that friend who always brings out the best in you, or a leather keychain. It's simple, but has a profound impact on those around you. You can be someone else's miracle through prayer and seeking God's face on behalf of them. How cool is it that we don't need to spend our days constantly asking God about our own needs, wants and desires, but we can actually seek God on behalf of others? Notice the miracles coming to you through the people around you, then take a step to be a miracle in someone else's life today.

## Bonus section: a note on people skills

In our walk with God, we've got to learn when to lay aside our preferences, thoughts and ideas, and take the high road with people (choosing to imagine the best about them, giving them the benefit of the doubt). It's one thing that I try to consistently make a part of my day-to-day life. I'm asking God not to just make it a one-time event, but a matter of character in who I am.

This is just relational advice. From one person to another, walking well with others over the long-haul can be a bit tricky, but I've found a couple of things that have helped me. First, remember, real people aren't perfect, only Jesus is. People make mistakes. People have tempers. People have a limited understanding. People get tired and cranky. And even when people don't want to let their own pressures in life contaminate their response to you, it often does. Meaning, many times when that person gets mad at you, it's not because they don't like you, but something else may be weighing on them that is far greater than what you know about. As soon as we start thinking that God's people will always act, think, talk and respond like Jesus, we will always be let down. Yes, we should strive to be like Jesus, but the reality is that we never will be like Him. Just this knowledge alone helps me have a little more grace to those around me.

Secondly, with this in mind, always take the high road with others. Taking the high road to me means doing the right thing when it's hard and no one is watching. It's choosing to forgive quickly, even when you've been wronged and that person hasn't approached you for forgiveness. It's turning the other cheek and not seeking revenge. The high road is letting go of bitterness quickly. It's the road less traveled, especially when we have this innate desire to defend ourselves. But in the long-run, the high road is faster and has less obstacles. When someone snaps at you or you get wrongly accused of things, remember there's more going on than what meets the eye. Maybe that person is going through things at home you don't know about. Maybe they had a really rough day at work. Maybe they just got fired, or they are under so much financial stress that they haven't been sleeping at night. I don't know about you, but with a couple of sleepless nights and high pressure days, I turn into Oscar the Grouch on all fronts! Maybe they ate too much cake that day and now they are feeling guilty that they've ruined their month-long bout of eating healthy. And maybe, just maybe, what you did was just fine, but they are responding out of other issues that are encompassing their life. Maybe, instead of blowing up, defending yourself and getting angry in return, you could be a bucket-filler of life for them and meet some needs behind the scenes. Take the high road. Go the extra mile. Burn off that extra piece of cake with them. This will go a long way in helping you love others.

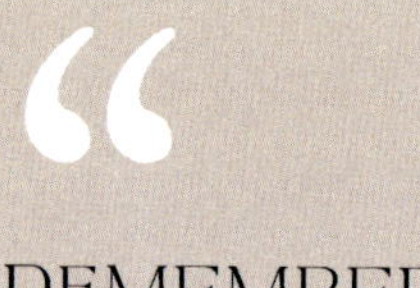

REMEMBER, REAL PEOPLE AREN'T PERFECT, ONLY JESUS IS."

*The sun is about to set and now it looks like a hot pink 80's t-shirt with a thousand-watt bulb shining from within it. The fireball has intensified and within seconds it's gone, sleeping peacefully underneath the skyline. It has left its array of color scattered across the horizon as far as the eye can see. Though the sun is gone its effects live on, ever pointing to the fact that it most certainly was here. I pray my life is like that. Though it is here for only a breath compared to eternity, may the ramifications of the love and faith I carry be stamped on the horizon of history long after I am gone. I pray the same for you.*

Side note

The last thing I try to do is imagine the best in others. You know how it feels when your best friend hasn't called or texted you for weeks. You pass them in the hall at work and they don't even acknowledge you. Your brain starts working overtime at this point. What did I do wrong, you wonder. Is she or he mad at me? Do they still want to be my friend? Maybe they've moved on to a better friendship. You are now in imagination-high-gear, analyzing every possible explanation as to why you haven't heard from them in weeks. It's at this point, you must stop and realize you have a choice. Instead of imagining the worst, decide to imagine the best in them. More than likely, they've just had a really busy couple weeks and maybe, just maybe, they need an amazingly beautiful text from you to encourage their heart. Great relationships aren't just built on the time we spend together; they are nurtured in the time we spend apart. Imagine the best in others. Fight for them, not against them—even when no one is watching.

Provision often lies in people, so be a connector of people, a lover of people and an investor in the lives of those that surround you.

BOOK RECOMMENDATION

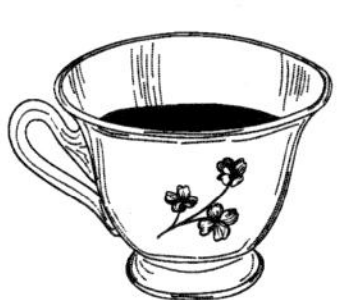

## How to Win Friends and Influence People *by Dale Carnegie*

Oh my goodness, this book. A book about valuing people beyond what they can do for you. Whether you're running a Fortune 500 company or wanting to cultivate deeper friendships, this book is for you.

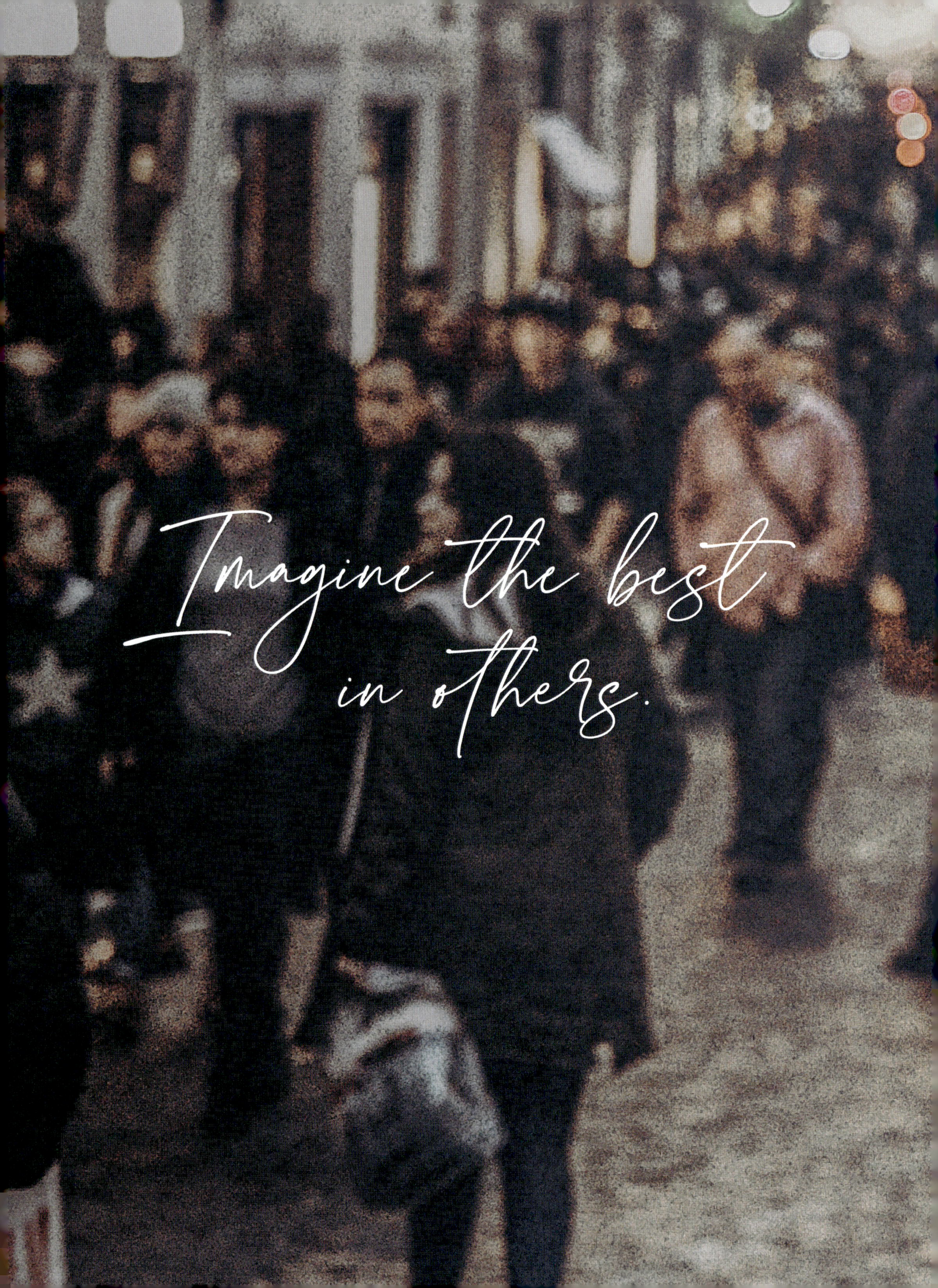

Imagine the best in others.

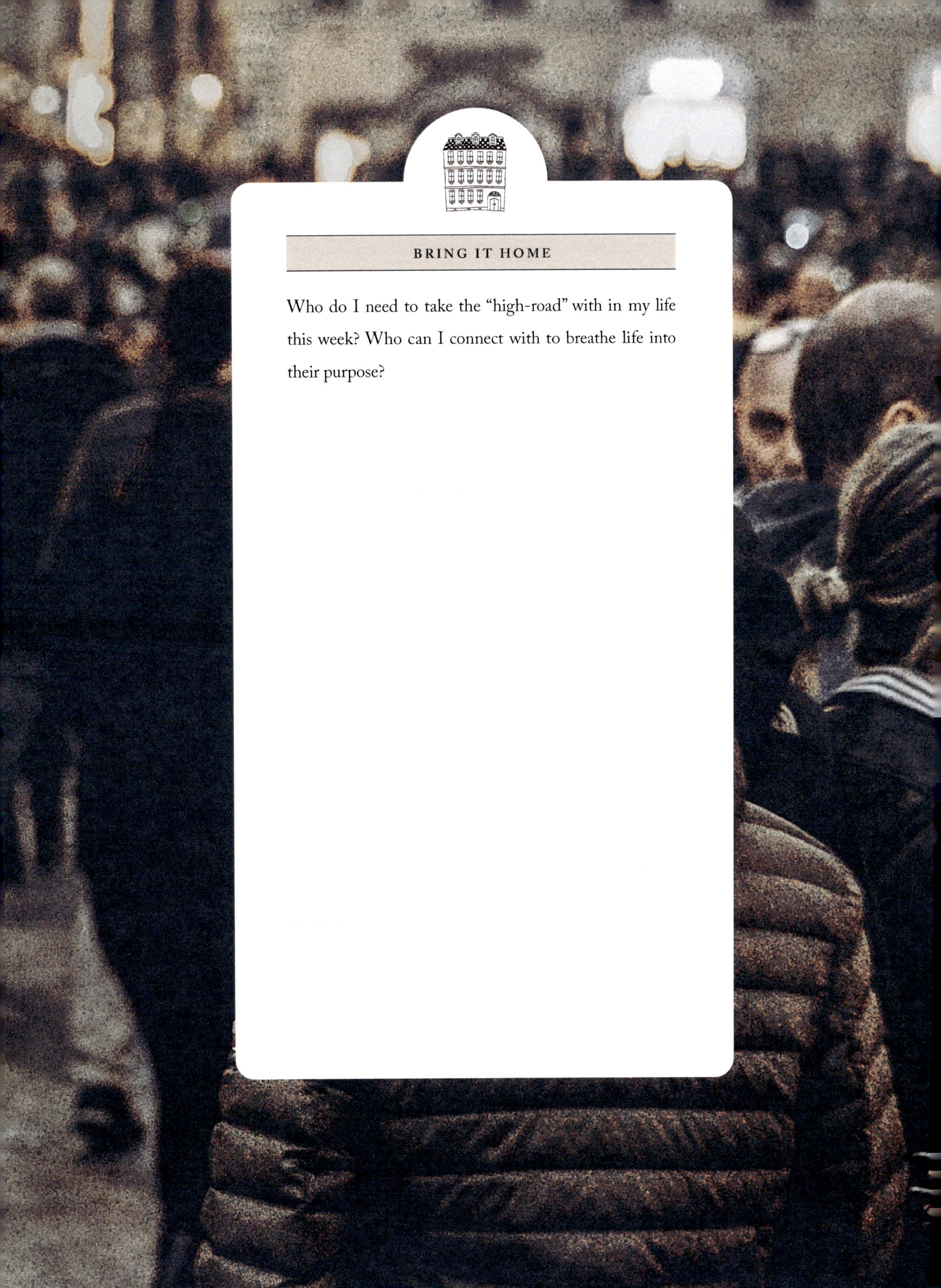

BRING IT HOME

Who do I need to take the "high-road" with in my life this week? Who can I connect with to breathe life into their purpose?

CHAPTER EIGHTEEN

# JUST BE *Courageous*

BOOT-SHAKING COURAGE

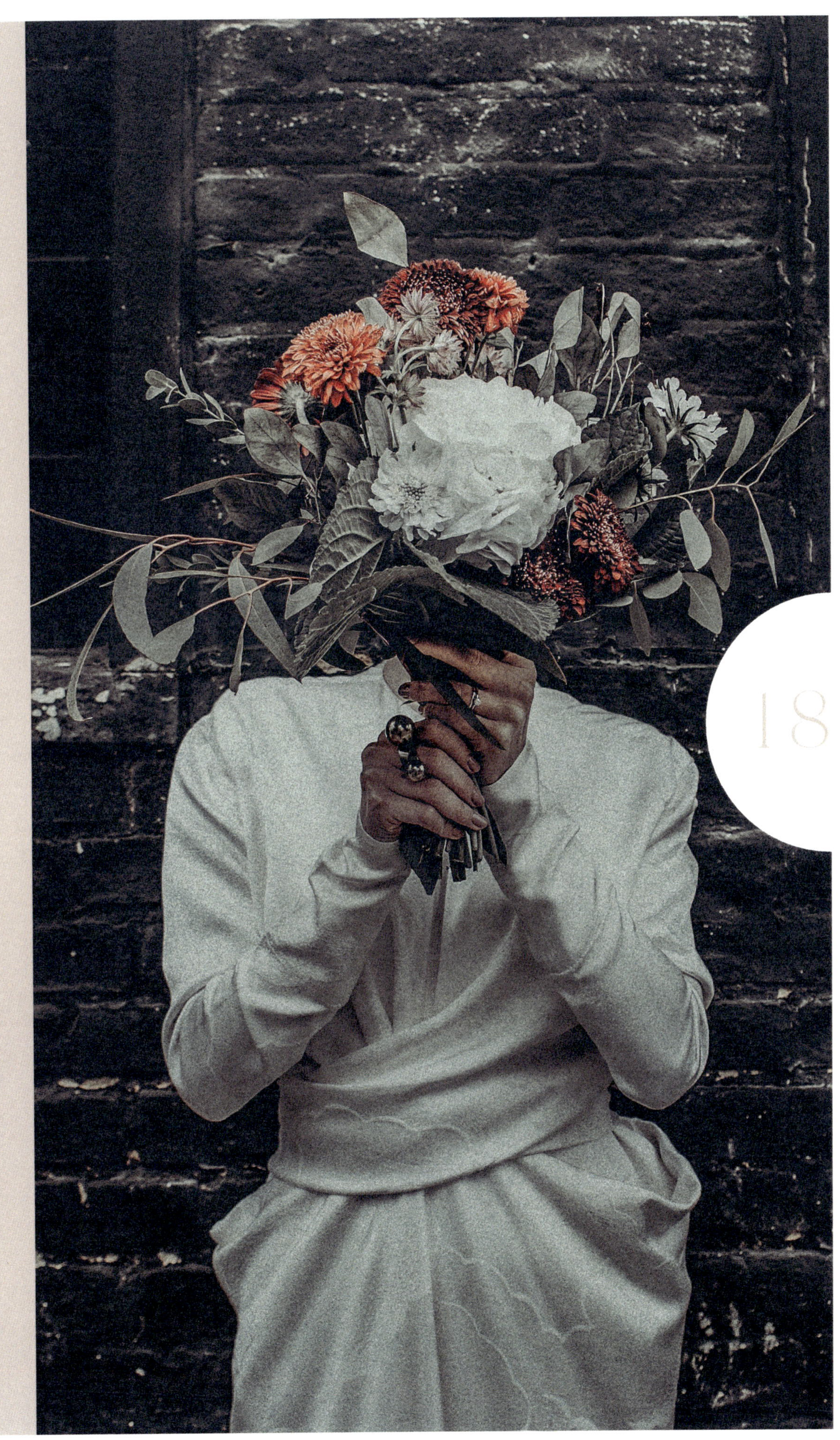

18

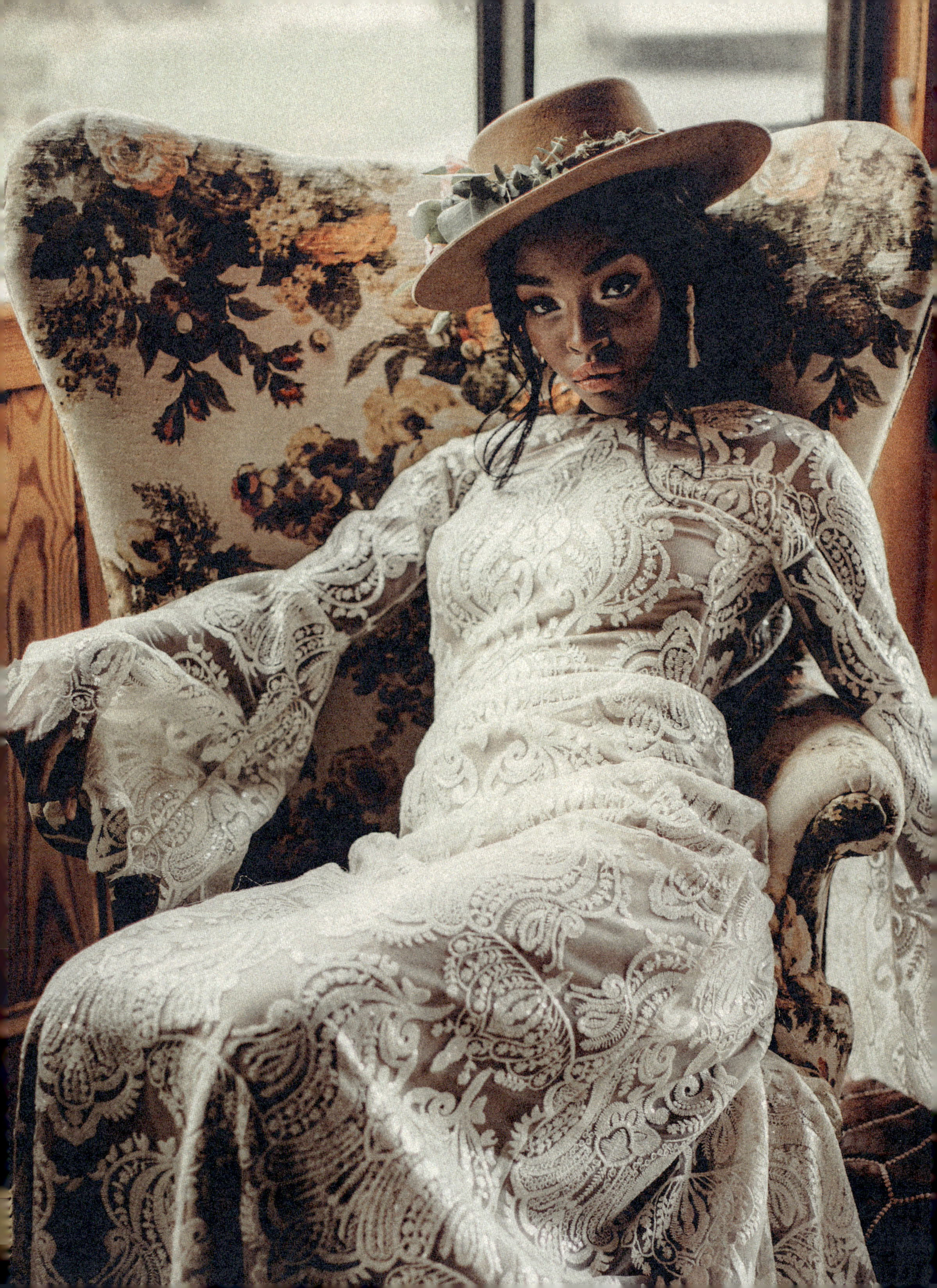

"Ruth's *mother-in-law Naomi said to her, 'My daughter, shouldn't I find rest for you, so that you will be taken care of? Now isn't Boaz our relative? Haven't you been working with his female servants? This evening he will be winnowing barley on the threshing floor. Wash, put on perfumed oil, and wear your best clothes. Go down to the threshing floor, but don't let the man know you are there until he has finished eating and drinking. When he lies down, notice the place where he's lying, go in and uncover his feet, and lie down. Then he will explain to you what you should do.'"*[60] *-Ruth 3:1-4*

The night had come. The atmosphere was electric, but now a peaceful lull descended upon the field. The months of labor proved worth the effort. The barns were overflowing. Her stomach was in knots as she approached the threshing floor, praying to God that she would go unnoticed by all except Boaz. She hoped that her hours of preparation would pay off. Would he notice her efforts? She wore her best dress, freshly washed and pressed. Her hair—simple, partly-braided, beautiful—was exceptional, especially for this occasion. Her perfume smelled like fresh lilies on a summer morning. The night air caressed her face and she felt her cheeks flush as she tiptoed her way to the open barn. And there he was. Asleep, just like Naomi had predicted. She quietly made her way to where he lay, uncovered his feet, knelt down beside him, and just stared. Before her lay a man so strong and handsome, with a heart so kind it touched all those he met. She gently laid herself down, offering herself willingly to him. She arranged her hair and dress in meticulous order so that when he woke she would look her best. Any moment now. Any moment he would awake. But it wasn't any moment; Boaz was in deep sleep, and as much as she wanted to remain awake to see his reaction to her there, she began to succumb to sleep herself. For here is where she belonged. Here she felt safe, secure and loved. So she slept, dreaming that when she woke she would have the courage to complete what she came there for and ask for his hand in marriage.

Rewind to earlier that week. It had been months since her first encounter with Boaz, a kind, generous man of character and integrity. Everything a woman could have wanted in a man, and more. The passing of time, of course, had only intensified these qualities in him. He had proven himself above and beyond generous to both Ruth and Naomi, and now it was time for Ruth to make her move. One day, having returned from the field, Naomi came up with a plan. *Go to Boaz after he is done eating, drinking and celebrating the harvest, and go lay yourself at his feet on the threshing floor. Oh yeah, and then ask him to marry you!* That's basically what she was asking Ruth to do.[61] Can you imagine? After all those months of serving alongside him and his servants, could she risk that relationship and agree to this plan which was so far outside her comfort zone? What if he said no? What if the respect he had for her faded with this one act of vulnerability? What if, what if, what if? Yet she agreed to it, even though it was socially unacceptable and there was risk involved. Even though she had to step into a position she wasn't comfortable with, she still did it. Ruth was courageous.

Isn't this what life is all about? Having the foresight to know what to do when those big moments come—the moments where we need to decide if we will take the leap, trust God, and just go for it, despite what we feel. Our inadequacies, evident. Our fear, present. Yet, we push past our feelings and do it anyway. Of course, we take time to pray and seek wise counsel before we make the leap, but when we know deep down in our hearts it's a God move, we have to take it. And that takes courage. Courage to believe. Courage to move forward. Courage that even if you fail, you will learn through it. We all have moments like Ruth's moment of courage. I would rather walk obediently toward these moments than live a life of regret having never made my move.

Of course, God doesn't promise a 100% success rate—at least not the way we view success. In fact, I think sometimes failure is a part of His big plan. He works more in me through my perceived failure than success at times. Either way, we've got to have courage to follow Him. The only alternative to Ruth not moving forward with courage was living a life of regret. Regret comes when you don't say yes to the things God is calling and asking you to do. Don't trade obedience to God for anything else in life. If Ruth would have thought more about what people thought of her, she never would have made her courageous leap of faith.

## Just write it

People pleasing has always been a habit that has come incredibly natural for me. The price of it, however, is no longer a price I want to pay. It robs you of the peace and joy of obedience and leaves you feeling empty, regretful and bitter towards others (who in no way have demanded that you choose them above God, I might add). Courage is given in quiet consistency with God. Every step of boot-shaking obedience only breeds more trust in a Heavenly Father who will never let you down. Putting God in His rightful place helps us walk bold lives and gives the courage we need to follow God at all costs.

> "EVERY STEP OF BOOT-SHAKING OBEDIENCE ONLY BREEDS MORE TRUST IN A HEAVENLY FATHER WHO WILL NEVER LET YOU DOWN."

For years I put off writing. I simply thought I didn't have time for it. We were helping launch a fully portable church—and if any of you have experienced it, you know that start-up churches take a lot of work. It was also a parachute church, meaning we just dropped in to our location and knew no one ahead of time. Flying through the sky, fearful, yet courageous. Trusting in the Pilot who told us to go, but still feeling the effects of the wind in our chute, hoping we landed in a safe place. Set up and tear down were a part of my every week. Building teams from scratch and relationships with people that you hoped would be lifelong friends—all of which took time. Not that it wasn't what we were called to do, but after a few years I realized it wasn't all we were called to do.

With four kids, homeschooling, and a husband working a few jobs to keep us afloat, my life was just too busy to pursue this part of who I was. Writing songs and writing books just had to go on hold. But as each year passed the excuses never dwindled, they only increased. The demands were ever present. The church and our family were constantly growing and needing more attention than ever. It seemed as if there would never be a time for me to jump in and start writing again.

Every time a friend would publish, I would feel this aching longing in my heart with a twinge of jealousy. It wasn't because that person was succeeding. Heaven knows I would have never felt that way if they had just won the world pole-vaulting championship. In fact, flailing my body into the air from a ginormous metal pole would only lead to a disastrous end, I'm afraid—likely leaving me with multiple broken bones and the deepest sympathy from those who had witnessed the event! It wasn't the same with writing. Writing I loved. I feel some odd sort of fulfillment from it, like I'm stepping into ... me. Writing just pours out of me. It's work, don't get me wrong. But it is "just because" work, not "I need to" work. Worship pours out of me, too, which is why I thought putting writing on hold and just focusing on church would be the right thing to do. Perhaps it was for that season. Perhaps God needed to teach

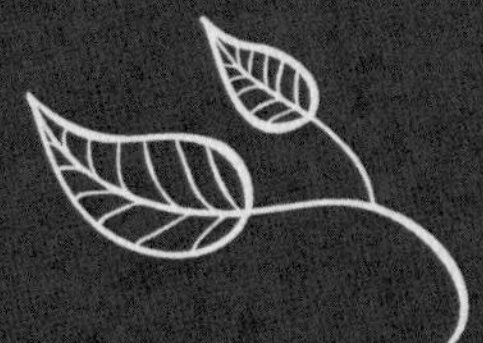

"MOVE FORWARD – FLAILING ARMS AND ALL – KNOWING THAT FLEDGLING, UNSTEADY STRIDES BECOME STRONG, SECURE ONES OVER TIME."

-Priscilla Shirer

me some things those first five years of church planting that I never would have learned otherwise. Hard lessons. Painfully beautiful. You know, those kinds of things that you secretly hoped you wouldn't need to go through to learn what you did? Yeah, those kinds of lessons.

It was on my 39th birthday, as a friend was praying over my life, that the word "release" came to my heart. It was in that moment that I knew God was releasing me to write. I had all these preconceived ideas as to why I couldn't write. I didn't want to attract attention to myself. I didn't want it to seem like I was promoting myself—with social media these days it seems like anyone with enough time, sweat and tears can make a name for themselves. They can become a one-hit-wonder with no character behind who they are. And many times, it seems their lives just revolve around themselves, you know? I also didn't want to take away from our church and what God was building. If I'm being brutally honest, I thought if I started writing again it would take away attention from God's church and focus it on one person. You name it, I imagined about every circumstance as to why I couldn't and shouldn't write. I wouldn't have enough time. I would never get published. Other areas of my life would suffer. My friends would think I'd lost it. I wouldn't be able to love others the way I wanted to. I'd miss God's ultimate plan for my life. I wouldn't be able to handle the pressure. But the ultimate reason why I wasn't writing didn't lie with a person or a season in life. The ultimate reason was because I wasn't being obedient to God's gentle nudging. He was nudging me toward writing, but I didn't trust Him enough to come through with that dream. Excuses always paralyze, but courageous obedience releases.

I'd like to say I was a wonder woman of courage. The ultimate example of charging forward and believing God's voice above all others, but I wasn't. It took me five years to say yes—no, longer than that, a good ten years—but I did. I figured, if I truly value God the way I say I do, then I can trust Him with my dreams. All the details and all the what-if's left in His hands. I'm not meant to do the impossible, I'll leave that to God. I am meant to walk in obedience and hand the rest over to Him.

*"Trust in the Lord with all your heart and lean not on your own understanding. In all your ways acknowledge Him and He will direct your path."*[62] *-Proverbs 3:5-6*

When I finally took that step to seriously place Him first, even if it meant I didn't understand everything, the most amazing thing happened. Instead of less energy, I had more. Instead of becoming selfish and all about me, I had a newfound joy in helping others with the dreams God had put in their hearts. Because I was being obedient behind the scenes, I no longer felt torn in helping others with their dreams. Placing people above God only leads to bitterness toward those you have sacrificed your dreams for. In my instance, I was the person—my voice and my reasoning—that had to fall into second place. The courage was found in obedience and trust—placing God's will first and trusting Him with the details.

What is true courage? I am convinced that you and I, walking fully in courageous obedience, regardless of what others perceive is best, will lead to our best selves. And we, living as our best selves in all God created us to be, will build God's kingdom at a rate we never thought possible.

So just be a little courageous.

BOOK RECOMMENDATION

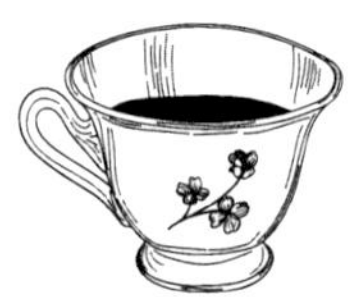

## 100 Days of Brave *by Annie F. Downs*

This is a great one for younger and older readers. It's a day by day thoughtful journey that will challenge you to add a bit of courage to your life. Easy, relational read.

"FORGET ABOUT BEING AN EXPERT OR A PROFESSIONAL, AND WEAR YOUR AMATEURISM (YOUR HEART, YOUR LOVE) ON YOUR SLEEVE. SHARE WHAT YOU LOVE, AND THE PEOPLE WHO LOVE THE SAME THINGS WILL FIND YOU."

—Austin Kleon

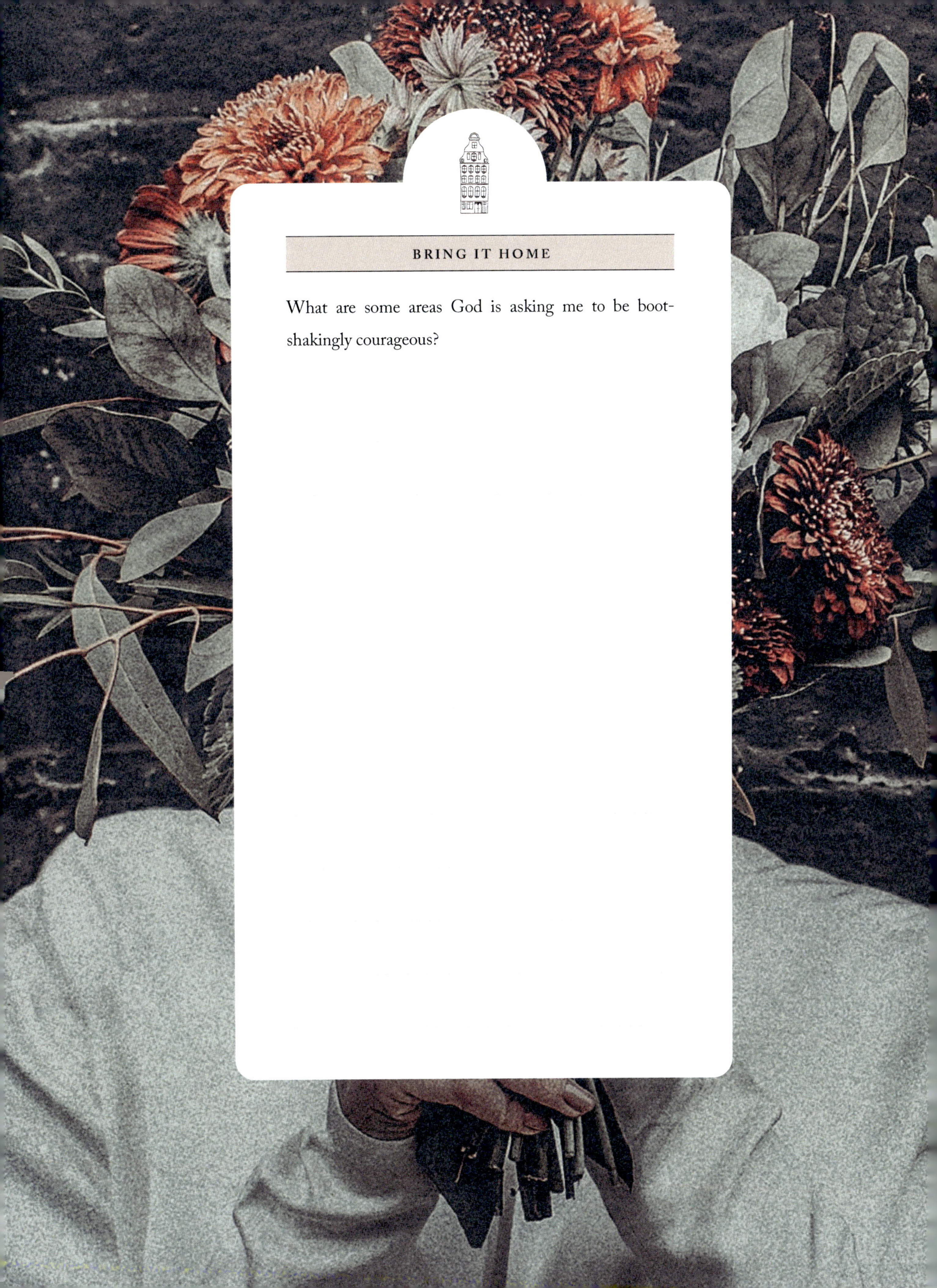

BRING IT HOME

What are some areas God is asking me to be boot-shakingly courageous?

CHAPTER NINETEEN

# JUST BE *A Discoverer*

A GOLD-FRAMED PAINTING FROM THE MASTER ARTIST

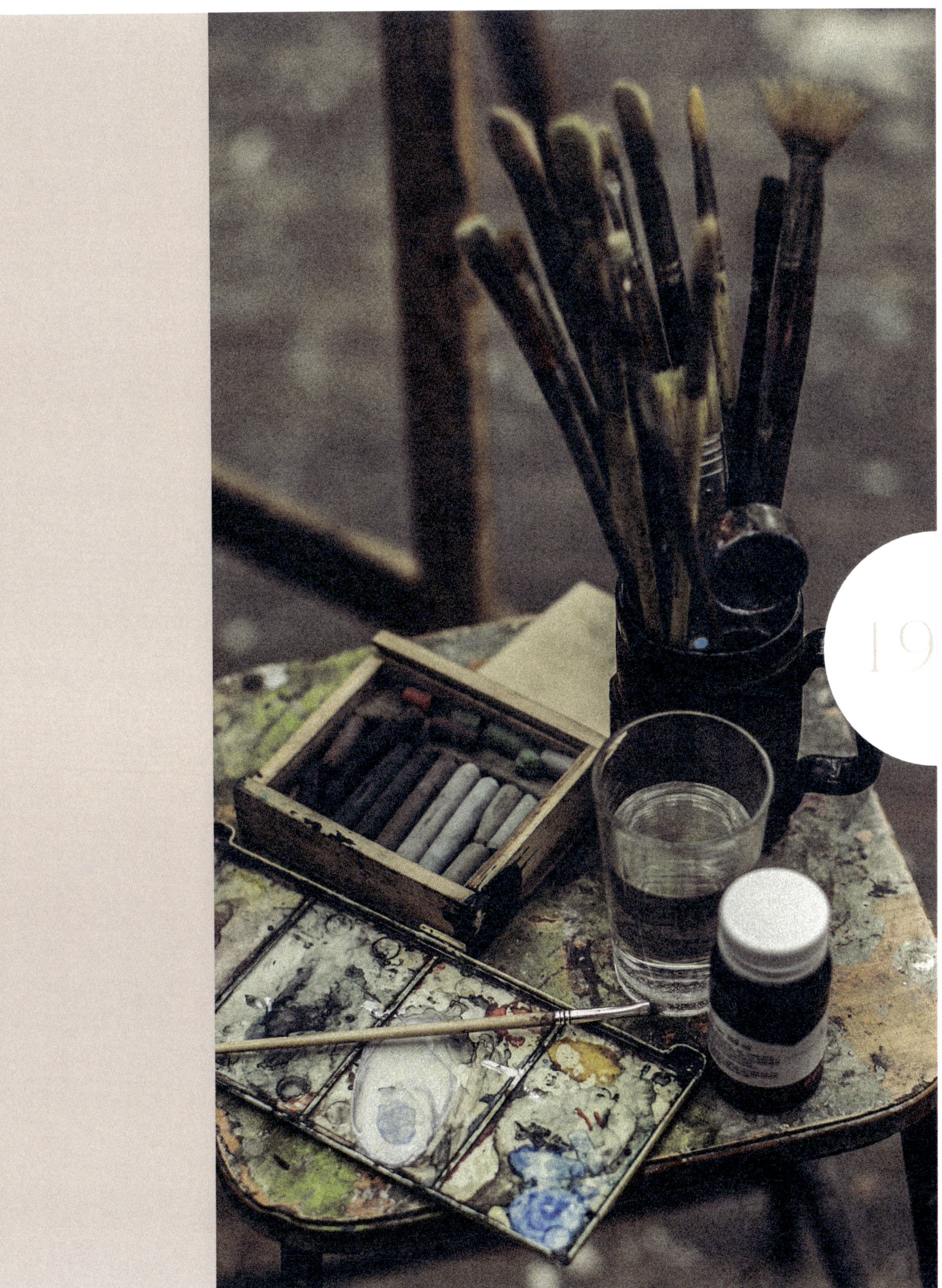

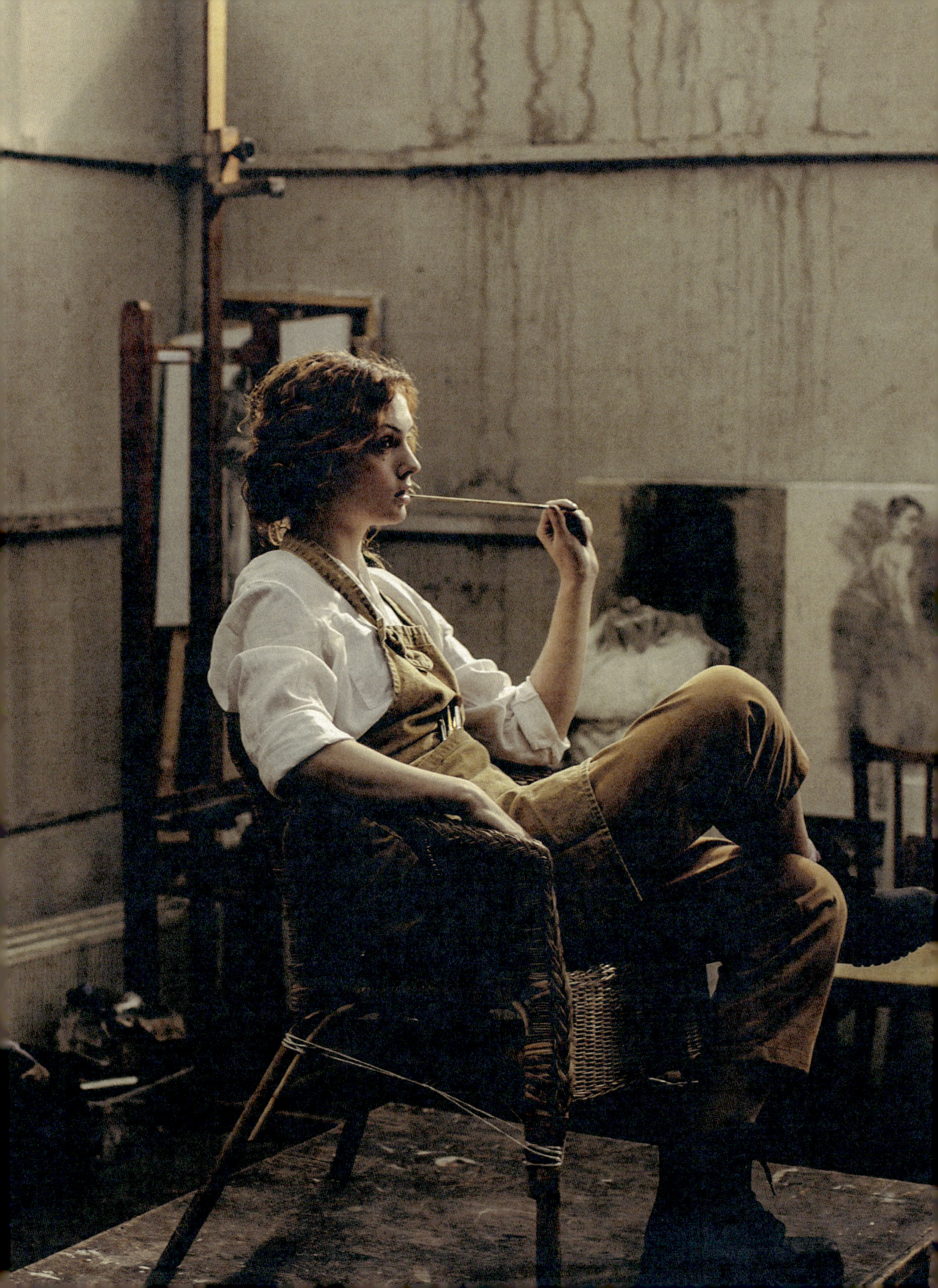

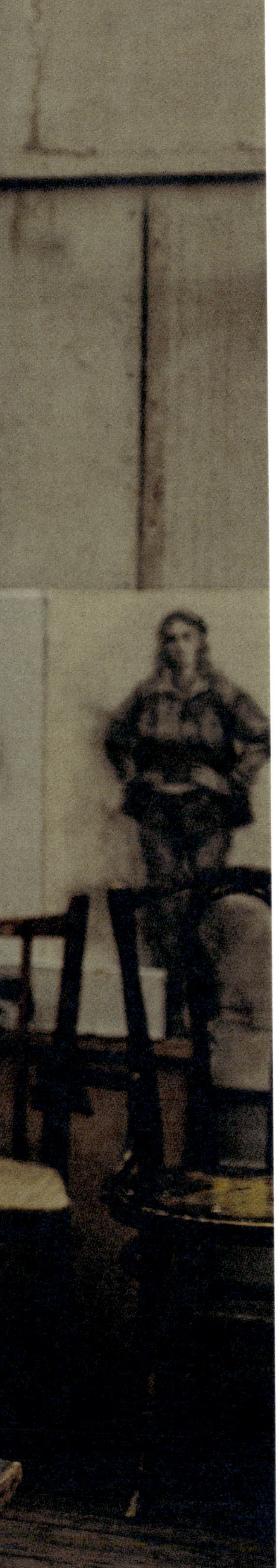

"Tell *me a little more about yourself,"* I ask, smiling nonchalantly.

*"What do you want to know about me?"* you ask inquisitively. You set your teacup down gently on the weather-worn-wood coffee table in front of you. You look at me, eyes searching.

*"Well, if I am a person God has brought into your life for this season, then I want to know about YOU. What are your hopes and your dreams? What do you love to do? What brings you life?"* I ask, trying to keep the conversation beautifully present with hopeful sights on the future.

*"I know it sounds strange,"* you begin, *"but I haven't really thought about that lately. With all the things I need to do, I honestly haven't put any thought into discovering what I love to do."* You shrug your shoulders ever so slightly. *"Does it really even matter?"* you say, not fully expecting the answer I am about to give.

*"Yes, it matters, of course it matters! Your life is a perpetual adventure, filled with discovery-laiden-paths ascending towards who and what God has destined you to be,"* I say with enthusiasm. A newfound faith fills the room as we continue our discussion.

Have you ever been to an art museum? I haven't been for a while, but I can remember going to visit the Detroit Institute of Arts as a child. I found art fascinating, while simultaneously confusing. In fact, many of the art pieces on display were hard to figure out. My friends and I would stand staring at a piece in complete perplexity. After much speculation and deliberation, we would walk away none-the-wiser for the art we had just seen. I always appreciated artists who painted a clear picture, a landscape and such that I didn't have to hypothesize about. For those extremely unique pieces, however, how nice it would have been to have the artist standing next to me. If the artist were there, I would have had no doubt what the piece was meant to be. Only the artist could truly tell us the meaning of the piece.

The same is true for our lives. The first step of discovery, as with so many other things, is asking the Creator what you were made for. We've

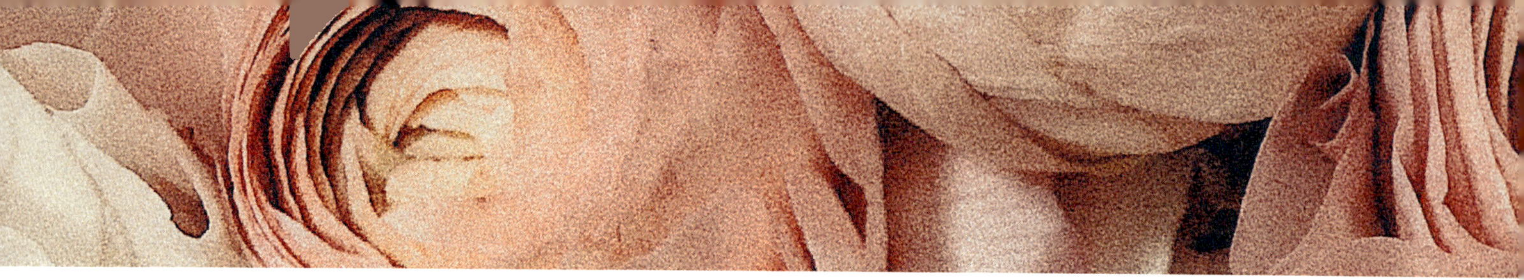

talked about this in an earlier chapter, but I can't drive home this point enough. Study His word. Spend time getting to know Him and embed in your heart who He says you are. Basing our identity on what others think is equivalent to asking a five-year-old what the purpose of a beautifully designed painting would be. He or she could give various answers, but if you want to know what the purpose of that painting is, you would need to go straight to the artist. God is the artist of our lives. He sees the beauty in every seemingly meaningless brushstroke.

The second step of discovery is tearing back the layers of the unspoken, unseen uniqueness of who you are. It's discovering the unique DNA He's placed inside of you. Discovery is not as hard as it looks, trust me, but it is a lifetime commitment. Look at the way He uniquely created you and embrace it. I love peony flowers. They are my absolute favorite. Every time I think about the process of discovery, I think of peonies. They start out as a smooth ball of potential. As they are exposed to the sunlight, however, they slowly begin to bloom, until finally they transform into one of the most beautiful creations God has made. As we angle our faces towards Jesus, petal after petal of potential begins to unwrap, each facet contributing to the unique creation He has called us to be in our journey of discovery. You begin to take strides towards the things you love. Is it cooking? It is painting? Is it a weird over-the-top love for old movies? Gardening? Or just helping others? As you begin your journey with God towards those things, you'll see Him open up a wonderful myriad of possibilities for your season. Each stride towards these passions God has placed in your heart opens up a new petal of your beauty.

> "STUDY HIS WORD. SPEND TIME GETTING TO KNOW HIM AND EMBED IN YOUR HEART WHO HE SAYS YOU ARE."

So many people I know are searching for their purpose. Who am I? Who has God created me to be? Besides being the man or woman of character He's called you to be, enjoying an intimately fulfilling relationship with Him and fulfilling the great commission, the sky is the limit—but you've got to develop a discovery mindset. Now, I'm sure your skin is covered with goose-bumped anticipation at the thought of learning how to discover some of your unique talents and gifting—so don't let me hold you back. Here are four tools that have helped me in self-discovery.

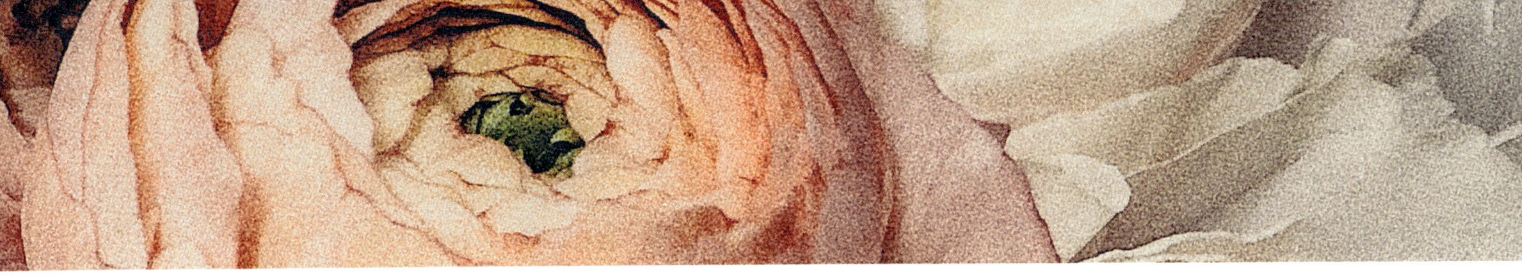

## Tool #1: The answer may be found with a friend

*"You're a great connector,"* my life-giving friend told me in passing.

*"I am?"* I replied. *"What do you mean by connector?"* I asked.

*"Well, you connect people to other people who help them in their calling from God,"* she said.

*"Really? I do that?"* I asked in astonishment.

*"Yes, you do,"* she said, beaming from ear to ear.

*"I never knew that about myself,"* I said, hugging her tightly. *"Thank you so much for sharing."*

The concept of being a connector had never really entered my mind before that moment. Maybe I am more of a connector than I realized. I walked away learning something new about myself from a trusted friend.[63]

Asking others what they perceive you're gifted at can be scary and rewarding all at the same time. Are you kind and selfless? A great leader? Faithful? Amazing at organizational skills? An excellent communicator? Maybe generosity is at your core? Perhaps you are musically skilled? It could really be anything. Asking a trusted friend for input is a great way to discover another facet of who you are. Many times, others see things in us more clearly than we see ourselves. Ask people what your strengths and weaknesses are. God's Word sheds light on our inner selves, but many times God has gifted us with talents that others notice. Trusted people can help develop the God-given talents in your life. Remember, it's more than okay to not be good at everything. I often don't like the feelings that criticism evokes in the moment, but the benefits FAR outweigh any discomfort. In retrospect, healthy criticism can bring about good fruit that may last for years to come. Hearing both the positive and negative from others can help you lean into what gives you life, rather than what drains you.

As you grow older and people or opportunities vie for your attention, knowing your strengths and weaknesses becomes invaluable. The more you discover you, the easier it is to say yes and no. Say yes to what you were created to do, and no to all the other "good things" that may come your way. Sometimes you need to let go of the "good" to pursue God's "best" in your life.

Don't go around asking every person you come in contact with to give you a positive and negative list based on who you are as a person. Instead, talk to a few trusted friends and leaders. Take five people such as your spouse, close friends or mentors in your life and ask them for their honest feedback. Make sure these are people who know you well. Their character is stellar. They've seen you in good times and bad and love you just the same. Ask them for two to three strengths they see in your life and then one weakness they feel you could work on. Take their advice to heart. After all, amidst a multitude of counselors there is safety. "Where no counsel is, the people fall: but in the multitude of counselors there is safety."[64] Add their responses to your journal. See if any of their thoughts align with the things you love and what God says about you. This can help you learn what your strengths are.

Who are you going to ask today?

## Tool #2: Take some personality tests

*"The unexamined life is not worth living."[65] -Socrates*

One friend got me intrigued, while another pushed me over the edge. I had never heard of the Enneagram Test before I met her. Perhaps maybe I heard it in passing, but that was it. Little did I know I was about to uncover a raving fan. I remember picking my friend up from the airport and welcoming her with a gigantic, full body, death-gripping hug accompanied by an onslaught of questions. That's the way friends greet each other when they only see each other once a year. Don't get me wrong. I love texting, voice texting, Marco Polo, Instagram and messages, but nothing can replace physically being with a person face to face. Isn't that how meaningful memories are created? And isn't life just a sum total of these kinds of moments that define us and create the reality we live in? As I began to pick her brain on how she had been, she managed to sneak one question in while I was mid-breath. She asked me if I had ever taken the Enneagram Test. I had taken the Myers-Briggs and classic spiritual giftings tests, but hadn't heard of this personality profile yet—and was I about to get a download. (Side note: I highly recommend the Myers-Briggs test. If you haven't taken it yet, get online and take it for free. I'm an ENFJ for anyone who is wondering.)[66]

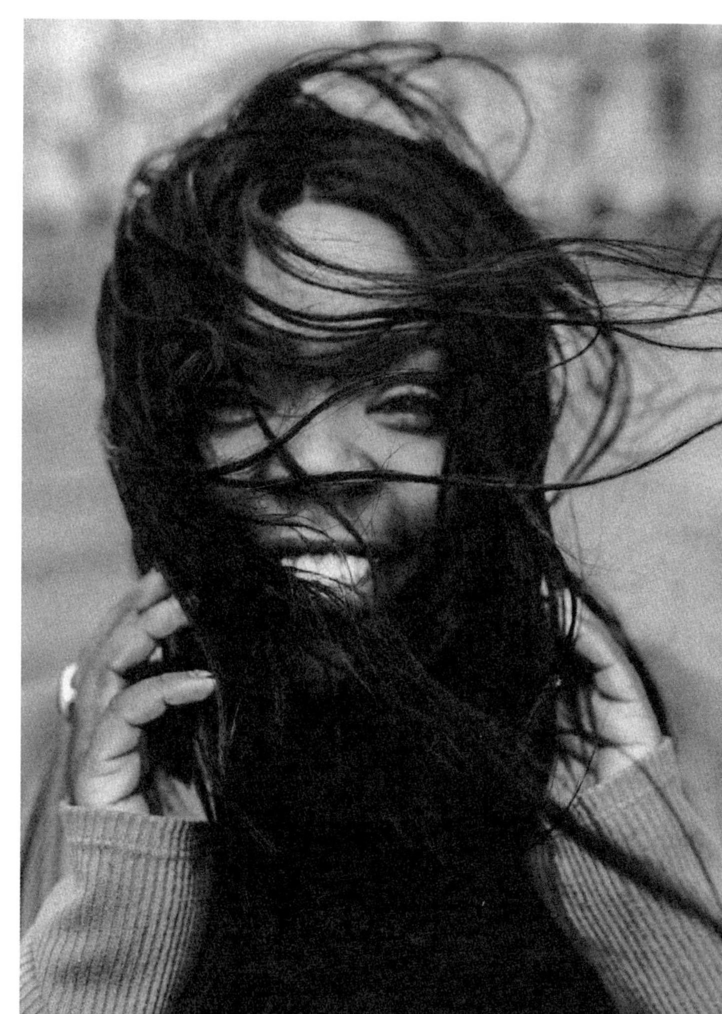

She explained to me how telling the test was of who she was as a person. As she began to speak, I could see her eyes light up and her entire countenance changed. She had discovered something that made her better. It wasn't just a test, it was a moment of self-discovery rooted in God. It piqued my interest, momentarily at least. I have to admit it wasn't until weeks later that I even took the test, only after another dear friend told me I had to take it. Part of me didn't want to take another personality test. God can change your character, after all, and all I wanted to do was love Him and love others and not let some test define who I was.

The test proved to be quite easy to take, and much more revealing than I thought. God's word is ultimately the reflection of who I am, but these tests were another facet of Him revealing to me part of what I was created to be. They helped me watch for pitfalls in my personality and helped me lean into what I was good at, so I could let the rest go.

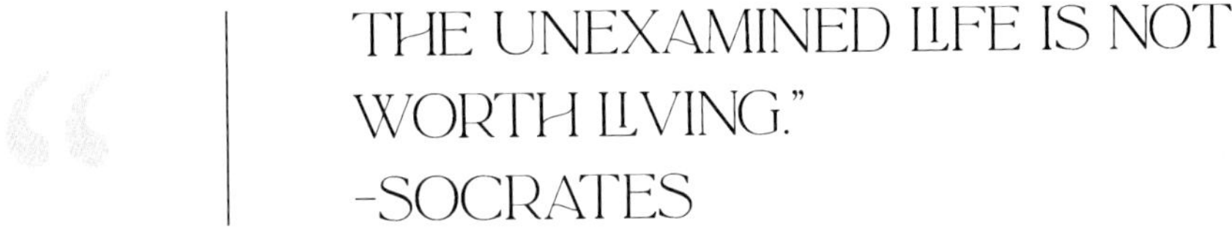


I find the people I'm most comfortable with are those who have personalities similar to me. I think that is partially due to the fact that they understand me on a different level, because they are wired much the same way as I am. But I challenge myself to surround myself with people who are unlike me. They, in turn, push me to see things in a way that I naturally am not bent toward and often make very rewarding friendships. They make me stronger. They encourage me in the areas God has called and gifted me to be in, and I see and support them in the areas they are gifted in. Run in your lane, but don't be afraid to switch lanes as life seasons change and as God's calling is revealed.

Another benefit to personality tests is a new level of compassion and understanding. The more I began to understand the different temperaments of people, the more I understood the "why" behind the way they acted. This enlarged my heart in ways I did not expect. I realized we all are different in how we respond and process things. Just because someone did not respond the way I thought they should did not mean it was bad, it was just different. Compassion replaced confusion in my heart. I am learning not to take things personally, instead I ask God to enlarge my heart to love more deeply.

At our core, there are similarities in all of us. We are not all that unalike. We all have basic needs, wants and the desire to be loved, though our personalities may be different. A book I'd recommend along with your tests is *The Road Back to You* by Ian Morgan Cron and Suzanne Stabile. This is a great book that dives deep into each personality type. Warning: it's not for the faint of heart. The author explains in his introduction how you, as the reader, will probably be angry at him by the end of the book. He focuses mostly on the weaknesses of each Enneagram trait, and no one really wants to read an entire chapter on their personal weaknesses, do they? Still, weaknesses can be eye-opening. It's a great read. Yet another step in discovery.

## Tool #3: Discover what you love, try eating a brownie

Trying something new can help direct you into areas that bring fulfillment to your life. Can you remember as a kid when your parents would ask you to try new food? Very rarely did I want to open my mouth. I never volunteered willingly, unless it was dessert. I loved dessert. I was quite fine living on a steady diet of hot dogs and macaroni and cheese with sweets as a distinctive end to every meal. I had no desire to try anything new, especially in the food department. Now, older and wiser, I enjoy trying new things. My pallet has changed and so have my cravings. As I broaden my food intake, I am learning what I love and what I don't. I am also learning that even if I love something, when I consume too much of it, it leaves me feeling yucky on the inside. The same rings true for what you pursue. Sometimes you won't know if you love or hate something until you're actually in it.

When I was in college, I desperately longed to be a librarian. I knew it would be the perfect job for me. I was reeling with excitement the day I discovered that out of all the applicants, I was accepted for the position. I walked confidently into the library my first day on the job. The doors opened and it was as if I had walked into heaven. An angelic glow surrounded each bookshelf beckoning me onwards. Reality abruptly set in, however, as the true librarian interrupted my dream and escorted me to the back office where she began her lengthy explanation of what I would be doing in this position. I was handed a giant stack of index cards and made aware that I would be the new catalogue employee. Now, cataloguing books may be an easy experience these days, but back then, it was archaic. Literally.

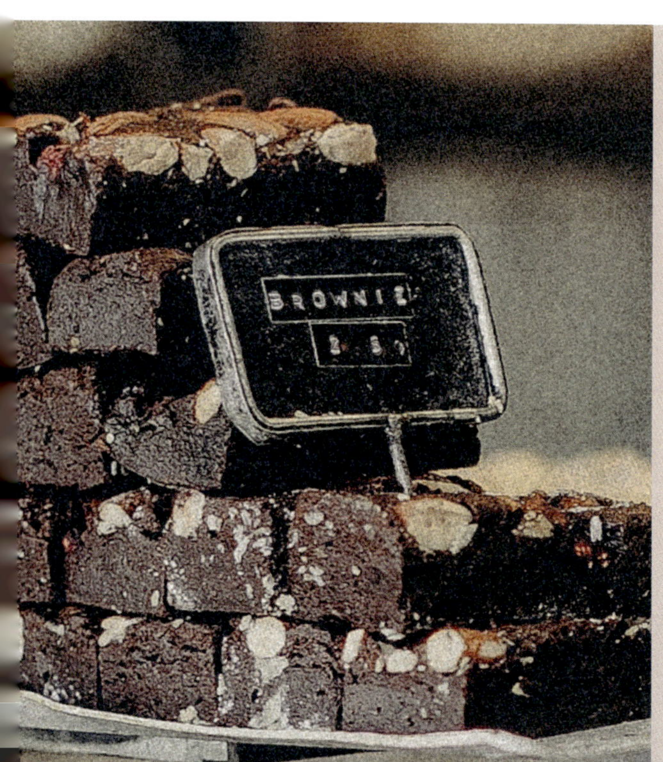


### *My Favorite Brownie Recipe*

Purchase a Betty Crocker Low-Fat Brownie Mix
Prepare as directed
Add one cup of chocolate chips
Bake as directed in a 9x13 pan
Allow to cool
Cut off all the edges for yourself
Save the rest for the kids

I was escorted to my desk where I came face to face with a 1950's typewriter. Yes, a typewriter. Not a computer. Not an iPad with a Bluetooth keyboard. A typewriter. I had never used a typewriter before in my life. I would soon discover that the entire process was tedious. If I did not place the card just right on the typewriter, each line and letter became horribly crooked. White-out would become my

> "IF I HAD PLANNED MY LIFE, IT NEVER WOULD HAVE ENDED UP LIKE THIS. SO MAYBE IT'S KIND OF FUN NOT TO PLAN. MAYBE IT'S MORE FUN JUST TO SEE WHERE LIFE TAKES YOU."
> -JOANNA GAINES

secret BFF, and it seemed as if the index cards in and of themselves held a magical quality because the pile never seemed to diminish. Stacks of books would engulf me daily. As I entered the library each day, I began to feel claustrophobic. What had I gotten myself into?

That semester I realized that the reality of working in a library did not line up with the dream I had in my mind. It took me a while to figure it out, but I was in love with a dream. I loved the way books looked, but didn't necessarily like to read them. It was what they represented that I admired. Someone's life and story held within the beautiful pages of time. A room filled with knowledge and creativity. Dreams. Hopes. People. I loved the people. They inspired me, but I never got to see them while sitting behind a desk. I realized that although I loved the library in theory, working there drained me and would not make it on my list of career dreams. If I had never tried working there, I would never have experienced what would be a good fit for me in the future.

Early on in life, I discovered I had an undeniable love for brownies. There's just something about a warm, chewy brownie melting in my mouth that gives me shivers of delight. I have used the years of my life wisely, attempting to master the art of making the perfect brownie. Here's what I have discovered can make the perfect batch: Ghirardelli brownie mix, with added semi-sweet chocolate chips. Cook until the edges are nice and firm. If I'm on a budget, Betty Crocker brownie mix works great too. And if you're wanting to reduce the fat, the reduced fat brownie mix works wonderfully. When I'm in high altitude, I add an extra tablespoon of flour to the mix. Once the brownies are done I set the pan on the counter. Key point: I make sure to bake the brownies during the day when the kids aren't home. I set them on the counter to cool with a butter knife lying peacefully by the pan's side. As they cool, every time I walk by I cut a piece of the crust off. Usually, by the time the kids are home the edges of the brownie are entirely gone. I have this weird misconception going on in my brain that tells me if I eat small portions here and there, it's like I am not really eating that many calories—when truly I probably have eaten three full brownies in edges. I don't like the brownies too mushy, but neither do I like them too hard. I had to discover the perfect mix. Just like mastering my brownie-making skills, discovering what you love takes time. As you try new things, you will discover what brings you life and what doesn't. Try serving in different departments at church. Try volunteering to help out different businesses. Discover what makes you "you" and what you love to do.

As life moves on, it may feel difficult to drop what you are currently carrying and start pursuing things that you love. In order to live a life fully on purpose, sometimes you have to do just that. Maybe it's putting your hand to a specific desire in your free time. Perhaps you can take a weekday night, and instead of watching TV, you devote an hour of time to that one thing you love. Writing. Studying. Learning a skill you've always wanted to learn. Playing the piano. Editing videos. Writing that cookbook you've always wanted to publish. Trying new meals. Investing in your marriage. Whatever it is, start your pursuit. Life is too short to waste time on things you don't love. Try something new, discover what you love, and do it!

Now go eat a brownie, you deserve it!

## Tool #4: But then, God

In Exodus chapter two, Moses was born of a slave yet raised in a palace. A prince. A murderer. A shepherd. Yet, one day he encounters God. At this point, many believe Moses was approaching the ripe age of eighty! Yes, you read that correctly, Moses was eighty years old. By this time in his life, he knew who he was. He knew what he wanted to do and what he wasn't gifted at. He was a father and a shepherd. He lived a quiet, uneventful life. I can imagine him relishing the life he had been given. The peaceful morning walks with his sheep. The cooling breeze by the streams of water where his flock would drink. The mountain journeys where he would gain fresh perspective over the vast hills and valleys. I imagine he was quite content. But his life dramatically changed when he came face to face with God.

In Exodus three, God tells Moses that He has chosen him to deliver the people of Israel from the hands of their oppressors, the Egyptians. Moses is to be God's mouthpiece to Pharaoh. Moses, in all the humility he can muster, responds, *"Please, Lord, I have never been eloquent—either in the past or recently or since you have been speaking to your servant—because my mouth and tongue are sluggish."*[67] Moses comes straight out and basically tells God: I'm not a good speaker. Don't use me in that way. Find someone else. I took all the personality tests. I've tried new things. I've asked people what I'm good at, and trust me, I can't do this. In essence, God is calling Moses a speaker, a representative on God's behalf to a nation. Why would God call Moses to do something that wasn't in his strength zone, something he didn't love to do? No one recognized this specific gift in his life. Not only that, but God is calling him back to the place he had fled from forty years earlier. Egypt was a place of personal failure. Moses had tried to be a deliverer in his own strength and had killed a man while defending his people 40 years earlier. Why would it be any different now? Egypt was a place of fear. Fear for his life, his future and his family. Doesn't God know how uncomfortable it would be for him to go back? It's almost as if Moses is saying, "Yeah, God, I had the dream of becoming a deliverer 40 years ago and You saw how that worked out. There's no way I'm going back there."

"JUST BECAUSE SOMETHING IS NOT IN OUR AREA OF STRENGTH OR COMFORT DOES NOT MEAN WE ARE EXCUSED FROM COMPLETE OBEDIENCE."

God responds, *"Who placed a mouth on humans? Who makes a person mute or deaf, seeing or blind? Is it not I, the Lord? Now go! I will help you speak and I will teach you what to say."*[68]

The point is, sometimes God will call us to do things that are out of our strength zone, comfort zone, peace zone, passion zone and every other kind of zone we can imagine. We feel as if we are fighting tooth and nail against what He is calling us to do. At this point, God has to be the One to take over. Just because something is not in our area of strength or comfort does not mean we are excused from complete obedience. God asks for obedience and trust in every season of life, even when we don't understand. We may plead and beg Him to ask another—*send anyone else but me.* In those moments, remember that we serve a faithful, good, loving Father who only wants what is best for all His children. Choose to trust instead of fear.

God sent Aaron, Moses's slave brother, to help him. God used Moses's upbringing in the palace as a foundation of wisdom for the journey ahead. God used Moses's staff as a shepherd to work miracles. God used his past failures to remind Moses of his need for utter dependence on God. And later, God used Jethro, Moses's father-in-law, to help him become a better leader to the children of Israel. You know what that tells me? No season is wasted. God pulled from every aspect of Moses's past and present to bring him successfully into his future. God will do the same for you. If you learn to trust Him and cultivate obedience to pursue what's in your path for this season, He will bring those other God-desires to pass in His perfect timing. Simply trust.

In the end, doing what God is calling you to do is the most fulfilling thing you will ever experience. Even if it seems like the last thing in the world you would ever want to do, God knows you much better than you know yourself. What God calls you, you are, even when you don't think it so. Now is the time to discover who you truly are.

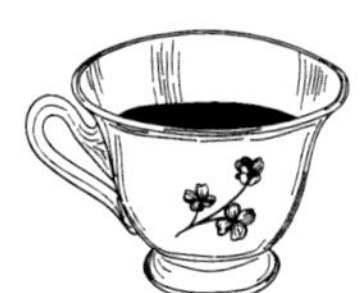

BOOK RECOMMENDATION

## The Wright Brothers

*by David McCullough*

I like reading about the lives of other innovators, the challenges they faced and the perseverance it took to introduce something new into a culture of disbelief and opposition. Great textbook read on the gift of flight, with added interpretation by the author.

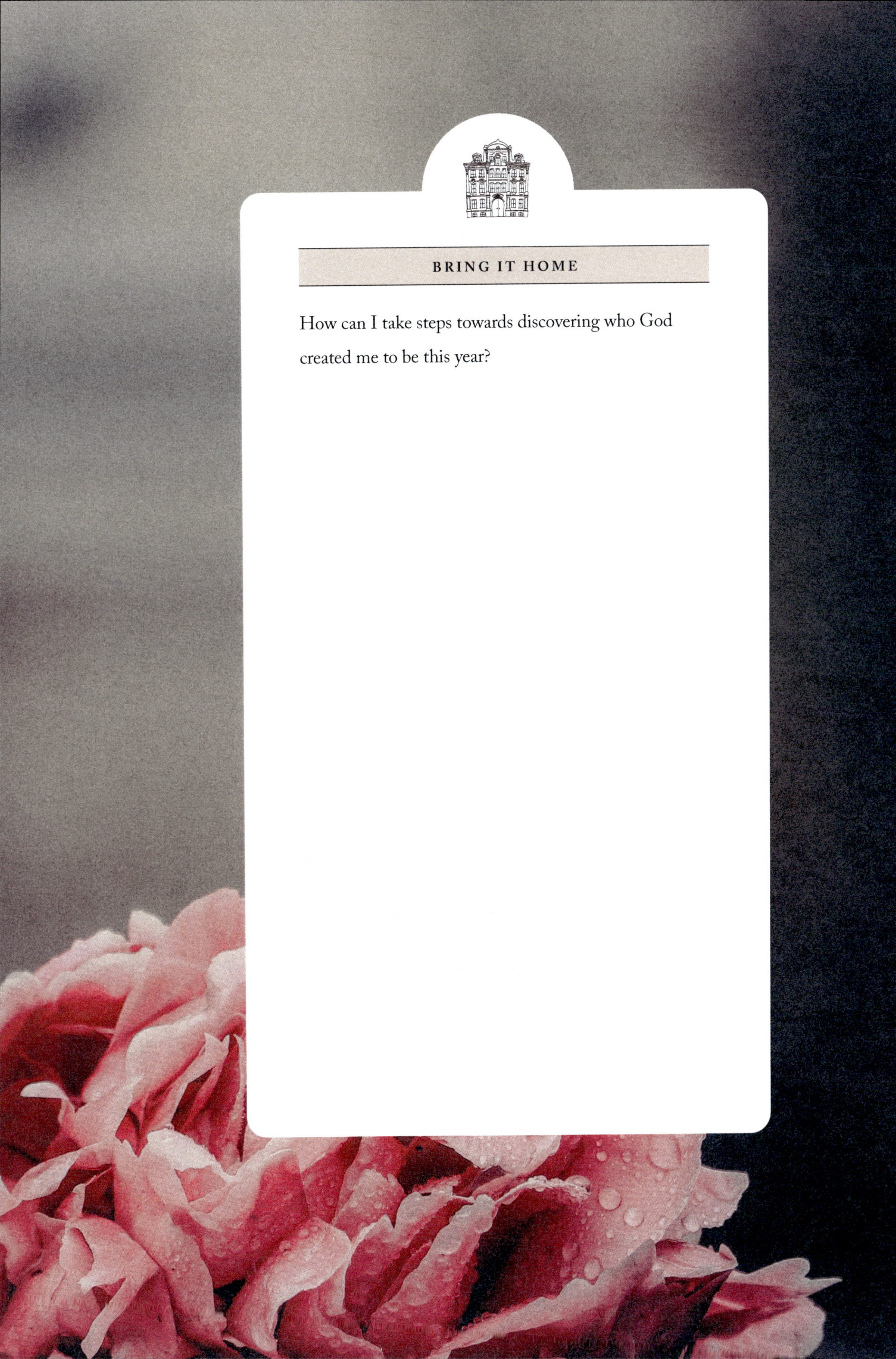

BRING IT HOME

How can I take steps towards discovering who God created me to be this year?

CHAPTER TWENTY

# JUST BE *Childlike*

THINKING LIKE A KID ON CHRISTMAS

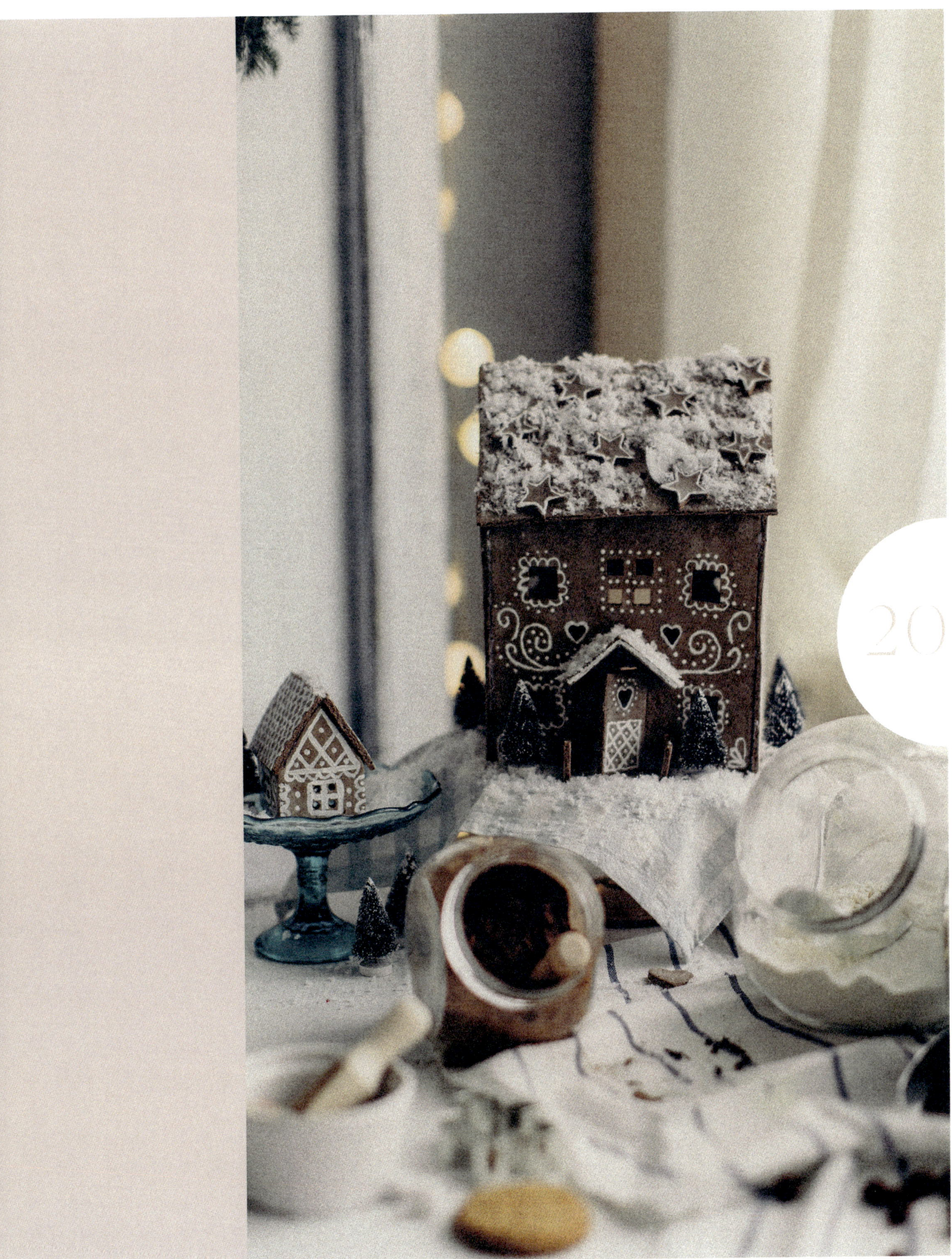
20

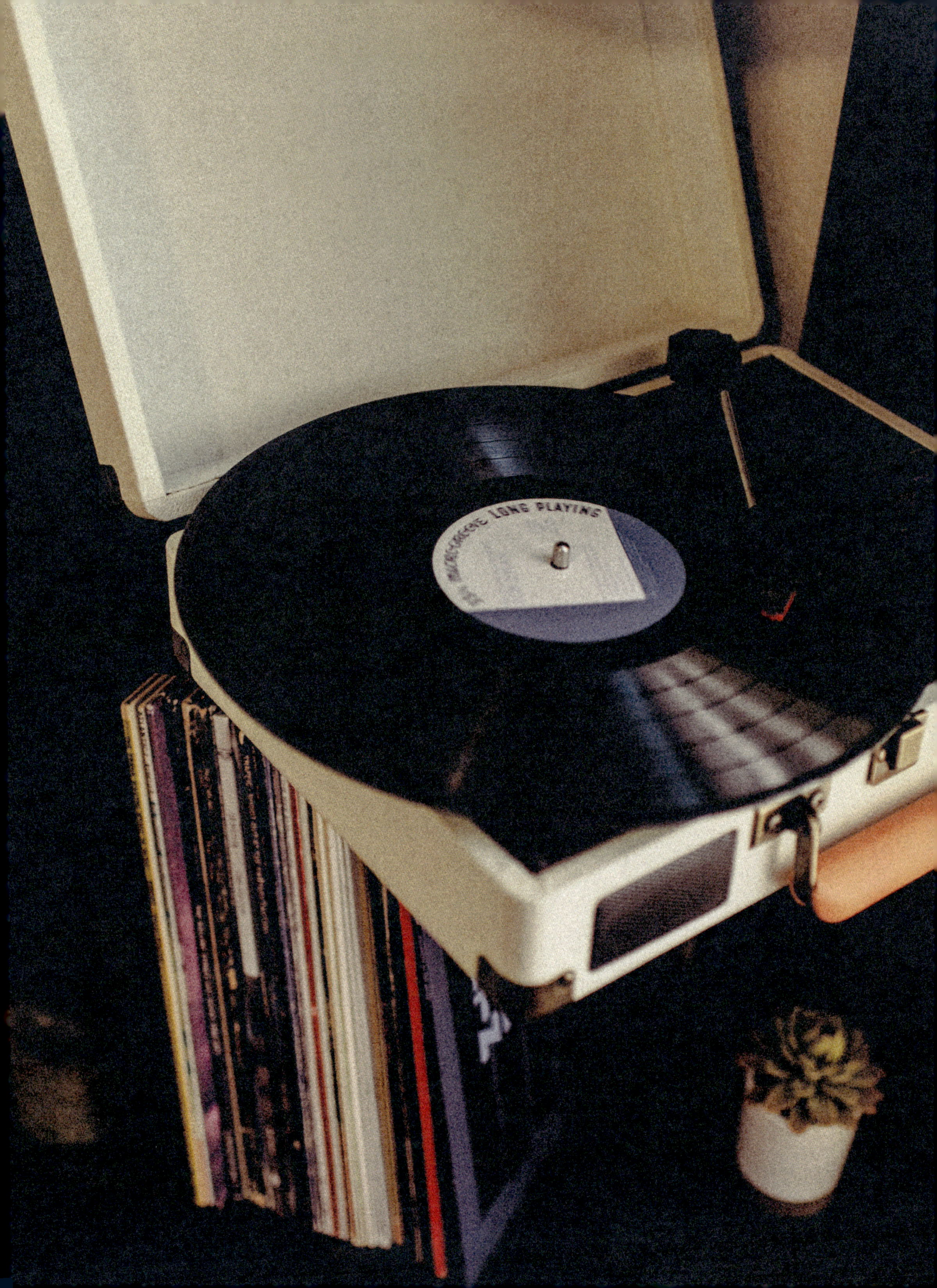
LONG PLAYING

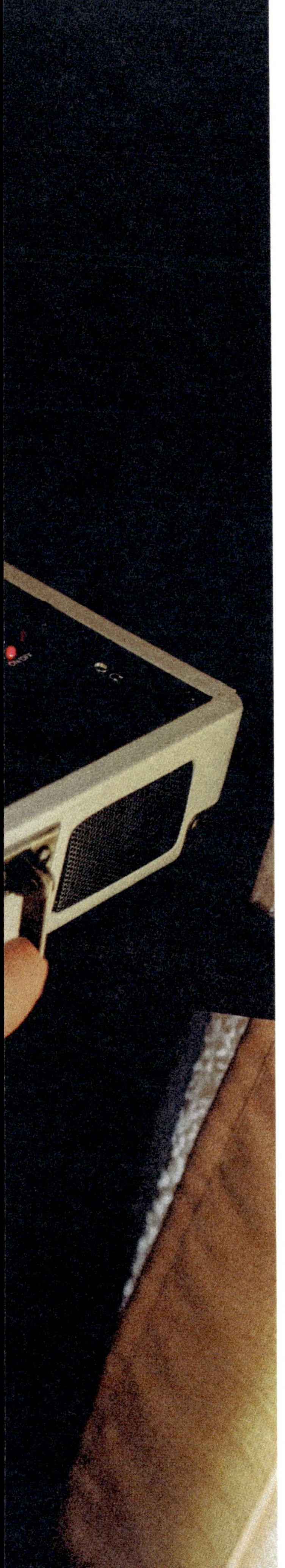

*"Naomi took the child, placed him on her lap, and became his nanny. The neighbor women said, 'A son has been born to Naomi,' and they named him Obed. He was the father of Jesse, the father of David."*[69] *-Ruth 4:16-17*

I think Naomi had to have brain surgery. Not literal brain surgery, of course, but spiritual surgery. She had to go back to the place internally where she once again trusted God. A place where she truly believed that God was working for her good, no matter what she saw with her eyes. A place where she not only saw glimmers of hope, but where she was basking in the overwhelming goodness of God. Sunlit warmth of promises surrounding her. The miraculous within her. She had to become like a child once again. Embracing that childlike faith in a God who would always take care of her. Climbing under the covers and snuggling with a Father who would keep her wrapped in the warmth of His arms—driving away every fear, every worry, and replacing it with His peace. She needed to become childlike again.

If anyone knows me for even a fraction of a millisecond, they will know that I have a deep, unending love for Christmas. I'm sure it stems from my childhood. Coming from a family that didn't have a plethora of material things growing up, Christmastime was the one day I could open presents! Not just one present, either. Many times I got three to five presents all in the same day! Consider my mind blown.

As a kid, I couldn't help curb my longing for Christmas to arrive. It was like Christmas was calling on a private phone line to my soul, beckoning me to come, and the sooner the better. I'm not admitting to this, but I may have started my Christmas paper ring countdown 100 days out. Now, for any of you that hold this same tradition, you know cutting 100 strips of paper, taping them together and then finding a place to hang your amazing Christmas countdown garland is a challenge—but not insurmountable for me. Nothing made me more excited than that big day. It wasn't just the presents, though, it was everything about the season that I loved. The lights that twinkled and glowed on each home late at night, dangling in the bitter breeze of winter as if to say "there is hope" and "spring is coming." Then there are the Christmas songs. Does anyone else find Nat King Cole and Bing Crosby some of the best, most relaxing artists of all time? If my heart could smile, it would beam ear to ear when White Christmas plays on Spotify. Throw Harry Connick Jr. and Michael Bublé in there and you've got enough classical Christmas hits to last you months—not to mention their voices feel like melted butter on a hot piece of sourdough bread freshly baked in the oven.  And who doesn't love tossing in a little Justin Bieber on their playlists here and there?

The eggnog and nightly readings of the Christmas Story were always memorable times for me. Did I mention that we had special cups to put our eggnog in? Or the fact that we would wake up at 3 a.m. and sneak downstairs to play board games, awaiting with anticipation the moments our parents would wake up? And still that didn't even touch the surface of all the good surrounding Christmas. It was the one time a year that people made room for family. No matter how busy they were with life, it was the one time where everyone would come together. And when we were together, magic happened. Memories of sliding down the stairs in our sleeping bags or sneaking into our stockings are etched in my mind. The generous heart and spirit that envelops you everywhere you turn. It's one time of year where people lift up their eyes from an inward focus to the world and needs surrounding them. I think every day should be Christmas in this sense.

## Your official Christmas list

Speaking of Christmas, do you remember making a Christmas list? You know that time in October or November when you could write down a list of all the things you were hoping to receive for Christmas? It was almost like a magical piece of paper, where no request seemed too big. The sky was the limit. No boundaries. One requirement: just dream. As a kid, puppies and ponies were frequently found on my list. Every year that list changed. As I grew older, I had different desires in my heart; my priorities and needs changed, but that list was a place of hope that maybe, just maybe, this would be the year that I received those gifts—no matter how big or outlandish the request. It was my opportunity to dream big.

As a kid, and even a teenager, it was easy and exciting to make my list. But as an adult, a Christmas list didn't seem all that important anymore. Be real, when's the last time you made a Christmas list? We've got bills to pay, problems to solve, and too much stress to take time to think about our wants and desires. Even when we do have time to make a list, we know something is terribly wrong when towels and washcloths make it as our number one request. Those thoughts of the impossible that we once relished as children, gone. And many times, they are replaced with doubts and determination to live within our means, and within reason. But it doesn't stop there. We begin to believe that what we see with our eyes is our lot in life, and we bring that same attitude into our walk with God. Now don't get me wrong, contentment is a beautiful thing, but that's not what I'm talking about. I'm talking about how we often lose that childlike faith in our Father by simply accepting our norm. I believe that this chapter is going to serve as a catalyst for divine reversal in your thinking. God wants to shift the way you've been doing things, to grab ahold of you, sit you down, transport you back in time, and rekindle that desire for the impossible. Oh, and your Father, He's asking for a list.

You see, I believe God takes into consideration the desires of our heart. God says in His word, *"Delight yourself in the Lord and He shall give you the desires of your heart."*[70] The key to this verse is to first delight in God. Delight means to have *"a high degree of pleasure, enjoyment; joy; rapture."*[71] Delighting is like taking a bite of your favorite ice cream sundae. Let's just say this sundae is gluten-free, carb-free, fat-free, calorie-free and vegan, but with all the real flavor. Let's go a step further and say if you eat this sundae, you will actually lose weight instead of gaining it! A dream comes true! Vanilla ice cream, warm brownie, peanut butter cups and cookie dough all in one blissfully blessed spoonful. Now take a bite and just savor it. Now multiply that by 100 and maybe it will scratch the surface of delighting in God. It's not a chore. It's not a duty. It's what you love to do and Who you love to be with. It's the joy of your heart. In food terms, it's what you drool over! With delight in place, God then puts desires in your heart. Things you long for. Hopes and dreams. Have you ever thought that God placed those specific dreams and desires in your heart for a purpose? But how good are they if you never ask Him for it? Is a Christmas list of any value if you never make it?

Think about it in the context of your family. Step one for my kids is expressing what they want or need from me on the Christmas list. The worst is when they say, "I don't care what you get me, Mom" or "I don't know what I want." Okay, so that's never really happened with my kids, but if it did I would know my kids well enough to be able to get them something that would bless their hearts. How much

"YOUR JOB IS NOT TO MAKE THE PURPOSE HAPPEN, IT'S TO HOLD THE PURPOSE AND DEVELOP IT UNTIL IT'S TIME TO BE BORN."

-T.D. Jakes

better is it when you know exactly what your kids are wanting? They make it clear and they write it down. Sometimes they even list it in level of importance, how great is that? Now, in the end it's up to my husband and I to decide what's best for them in this season, but at this point they just need to do the work of making that list.

In the same way, each season, every year, God is asking us to make a miraculous, faith-filled list. Except in this instance it's not a Christmas list, it's a God list. It's a list of what's in your heart. It's a list of the impossible and insurmountable things that, if there were no limits, you would like to see God do in and through your life. Make a list of your hopes and your dreams. Make a list of your wants and desires. Make a list of things that have to do with God, label it as spiritual, then make a list of the things that are so far out there you aren't even sure if God cares about them! God's not asking for us to determine what He will or won't do for us, all He is asking for is to take the first step and have faith in a good Father and make a list. In all honesty, I think we need that list more than He does. As we present our list before Him, He will decide, as our Father, what's best for us in this season of our lives.

## Parental rights

My daughter has been asking my husband and I relentlessly for an iPhone. She has put that thing on her Christmas list for what feels like the past decade. The thing is, we, as parents, don't feel like a phone is the best thing for her in this season of her life, nor does she need it. Aren't you glad that you, as parents, reserve the right to decide whether or not your children receive those things they ask for on their lists? We have seriously considered it. She has begged and pleaded, but we feel that the negative influence of the phone far outweighs the benefits at her age. As she matures and grows, a phone may be exactly what she needs, but for this season, it's a no. That doesn't mean it will always be a no, but right now, it's a request that is left unanswered. Our desire is for her to become the woman that God has destined her to be. This purpose is at the core of every decision we make for her. And we won't allow it to be compromised by passing desires that are not needs in the here and now. We love her too much. Still to this day, a phone is on her list; our no doesn't stop her childlike faith.

Make your list, then allow God the freedom to fulfill the things in your heart in His time. We may not understand why He doesn't grant a request or prayer when we want Him to, but He's got a greater purpose in His mind. He won't compromise our destiny in order to fulfill our passing desires. He loves us far too much for that. We may not get our desire this year because we aren't ready for it, but it doesn't mean we will never get it. As we grow and mature in God, He knows the exact time and placement of that dream and when it will be in our best interest to fulfill it. Ask, and ask again. Make your list and place it trustingly in His loving hands.

## A bird's-eye view

Three things happen when you make this list. First, it causes you not to forget. In a society with so many distractions spinning around us at any and every given point in the day, it's easy to forget things that you like or ideas that God has put in your heart. Ideas to create or invent or even bless others. Something happens when you write those desires and ideas down. They go from your imagination to something permanent when they are on paper. That paper will remind you that nothing is impossible with God.

The second thing that happens is it causes you to ask some tough internal questions. Am I on the right road for my life to get me to the destination I want? For example, if I want to run a marathon this year, am I putting in enough training to do that? If I want my kids to learn to play the piano, maybe I need to get them in a regular rotation of practices. If I want to own a multimillion-dollar corporation, am I on the right road to get me there? We need to sit down and ask ourselves, am I willing to pay the cost of what it will take for me to walk toward these things? *Principle of the Path* by Andy Stanley is one of the best books I've ever read. The book can basically be summed into one simple statement: *Direction, not intention, determines your destination.*[72] It's a must-read for high school and college graduates. I often have desires to do things, but unless I put action behind those desires, they never come into existence. The same is true for all of us. *Manage Your Day to Day* by 99U is a superb book for creatives, written by creatives. Its short chapters leave me with a sense of accomplishment, while its principles have changed my life. Consistency, time management and discipline are heralded in this book. For any of you looking for a great read, pick up these books this year and they will be game-changers in your life.

> "HE WON'T COMPROMISE OUR DESTINY IN ORDER TO FULFILL OUR PASSING DESIRES. HE LOVES US FAR TOO MUCH FOR THAT."

Finally, a list causes us to ask, are these really the values I want to have? Sometimes I write things down and I decide the cost is really too great to start walking down that road in that season of my life. Maybe in the future, God will open doors to it. But in that moment, based on my other values and desires, it needs to sit on the shelf for a while—and that's okay. Add and take away if you want to. It's from the list and nothing is permanent.

You know what the best part of making a list is? It cultivates a thankful heart and a catalogue of miracles, written on paper that you will never forget. You actually have documentation of the things you are hoping for so that when it does come to pass, you can look back and say, "Thank You, God, for Your miracles in my life." You can look back and realize, "I asked God for this and there is NO WAY I could have ever made it happen, and now, look what God did." Isn't that amazing? You get to thank God for the things that you've written down in secret. You become more aware of the goodness of your Heavenly Father. With each new faith-miracle fulfilled, you develop more faith to believe Him for the impossible.

I wonder what would have been on Naomi's list in the beginning of her life. Or what would have been crossed off her list in the season where she lost her husband and sons. I would have loved to see the divine reversal of her faith when she saw God come through for her, working miracles on her behalf. Maybe some of those old hopes would have reappeared on her list of faith before God. I wonder what was on Ruth's list after she lost her husband. Childless, destitute and grieving. I'm sure a husband and children would have been crossed off her list, miracles too big and painful for her to even hope for. I know becoming great grandmother to the most loved and anointed king of all time was not on that list. After all, she was a Moabite. Little did both women know that God is in the business of faith-restoring miracles.

You, my friend, are marked for miracles. May God restore your childlike faith in Him.

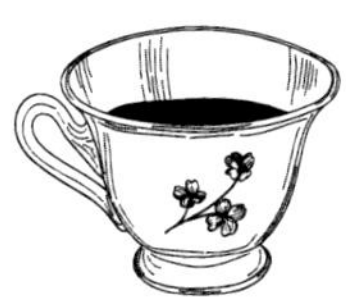

BOOK RECOMMENDATION

## Follow the Star *by T.D. Jakes*

I have returned to this book multiple times since I read it. It's all about Christmas and life lessons the author has learned throughout the holiday season. The section on dreams is beautifully written—nurturing, loving and setting boundaries around the season you are currently in while cultivating purpose at the same time.

# *My favorite part of Christmas*

Making our thank-you cards to Jesus has got to be the highlight of my Christmas. We each write a personal letter to Jesus and then place it on the tree prior to the big day. Christmas morning, we open up our cards and read them out loud as a family. It is one of the most memorable moments of the season. One of us always ends up crying and it refocuses our hearts on the true meaning of Christmas.

*-Jamie*

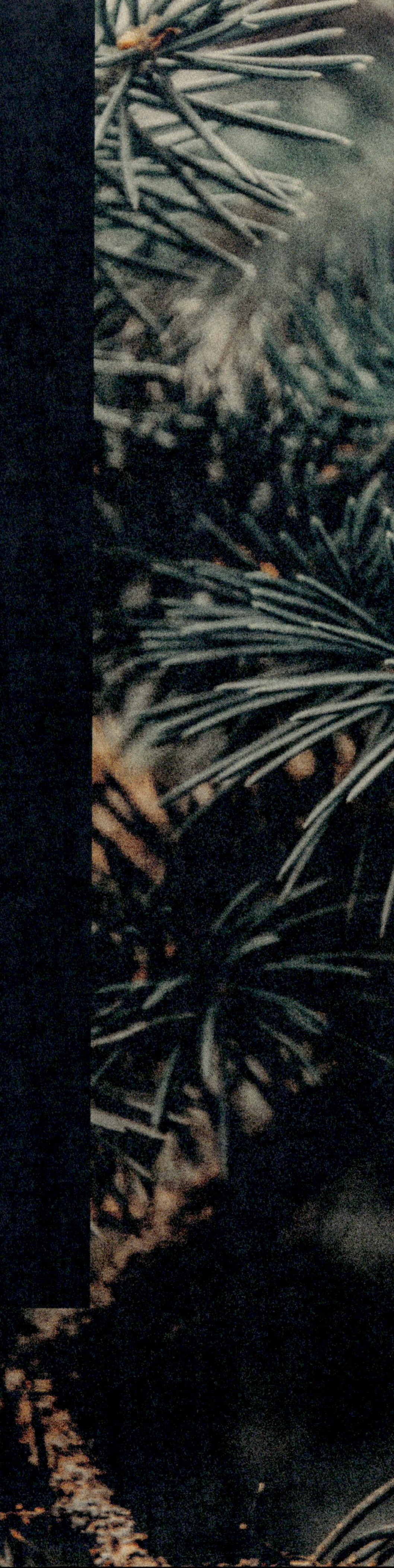

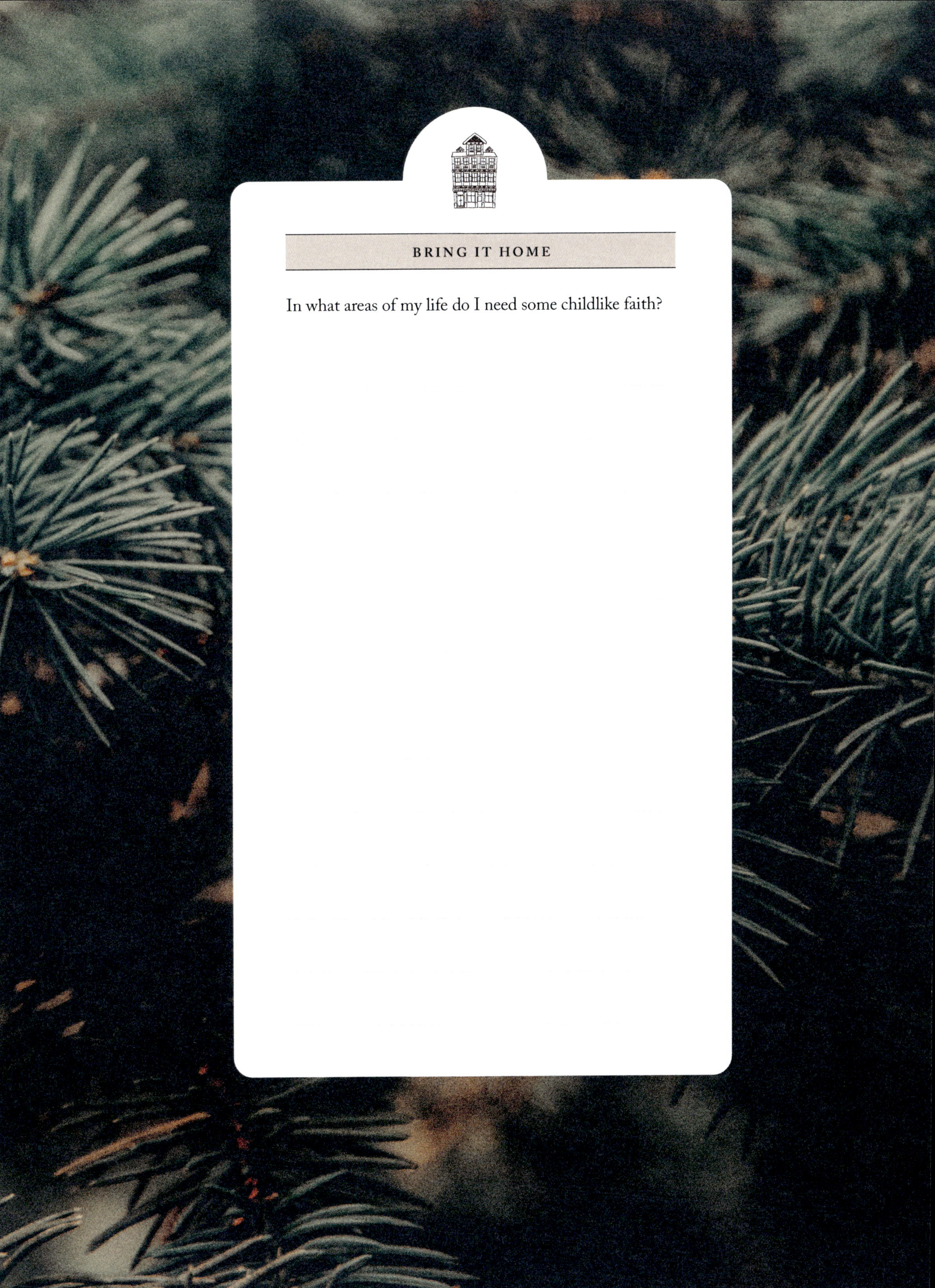

BRING IT HOME

In what areas of my life do I need some childlike faith?

CHAPTER TWENTY-ONE

# JUST BE *A Dreamer*

---

NOW IT'S TIME TO MAKE YOUR LIST

---

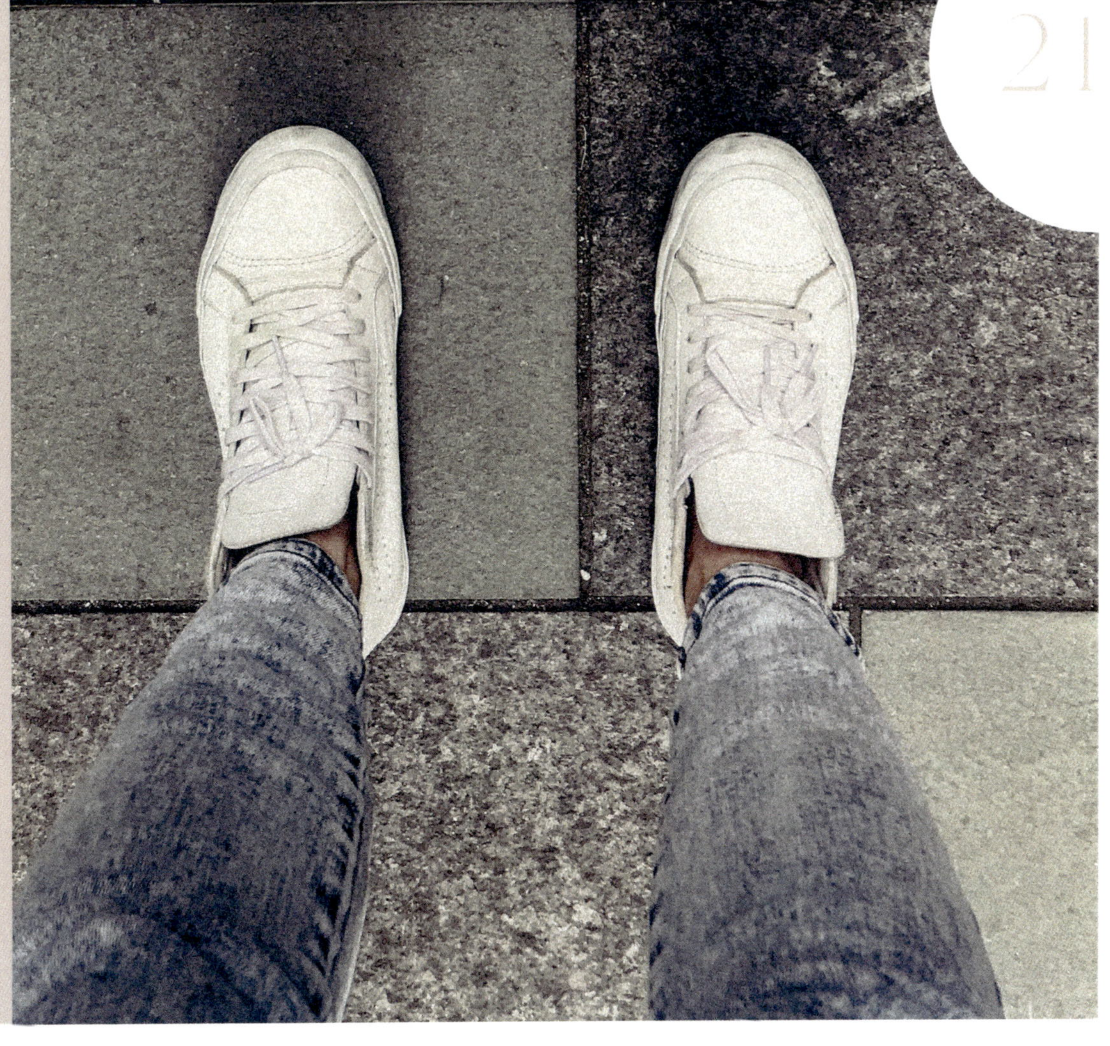


21

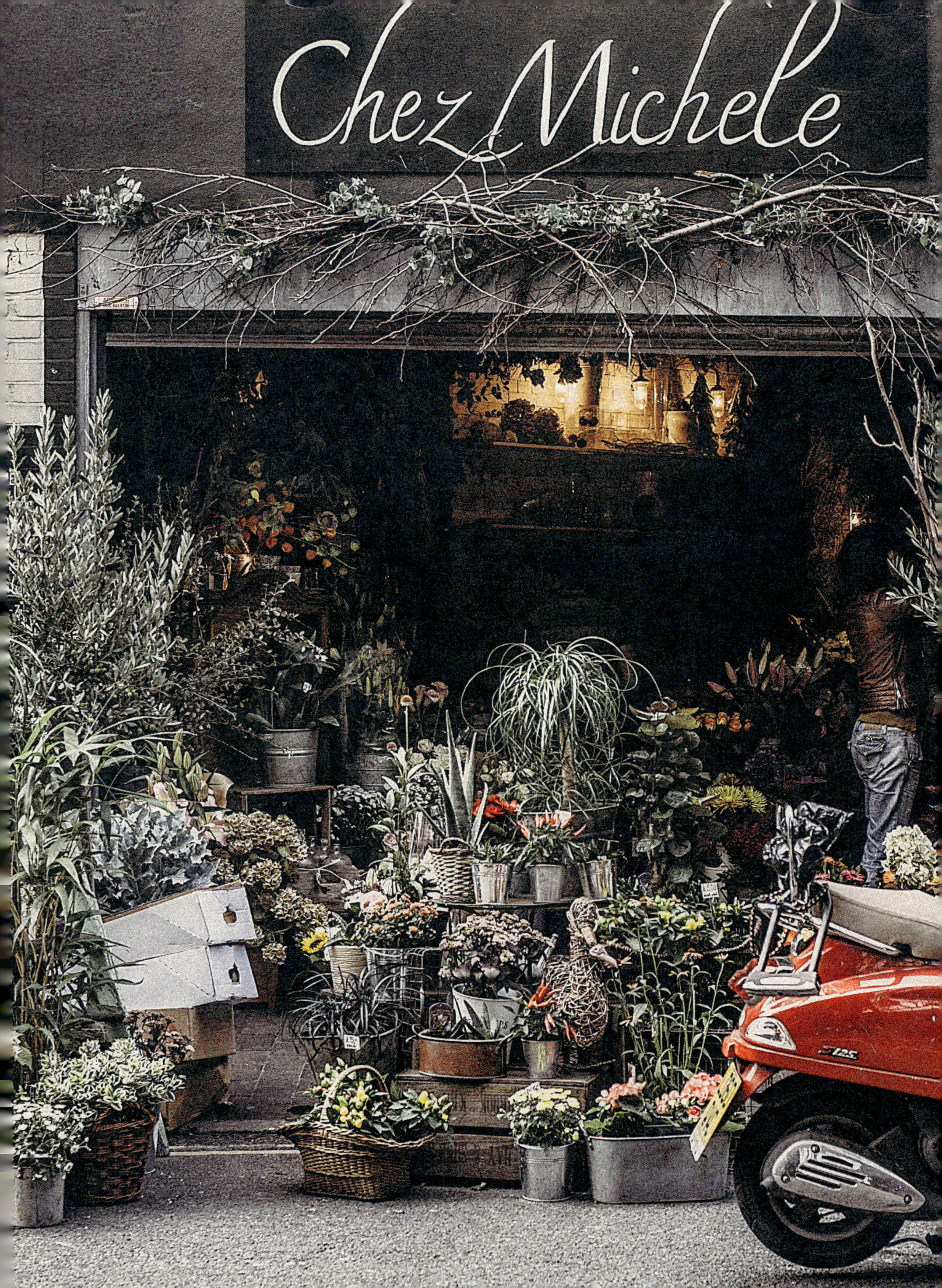
Chez Michele

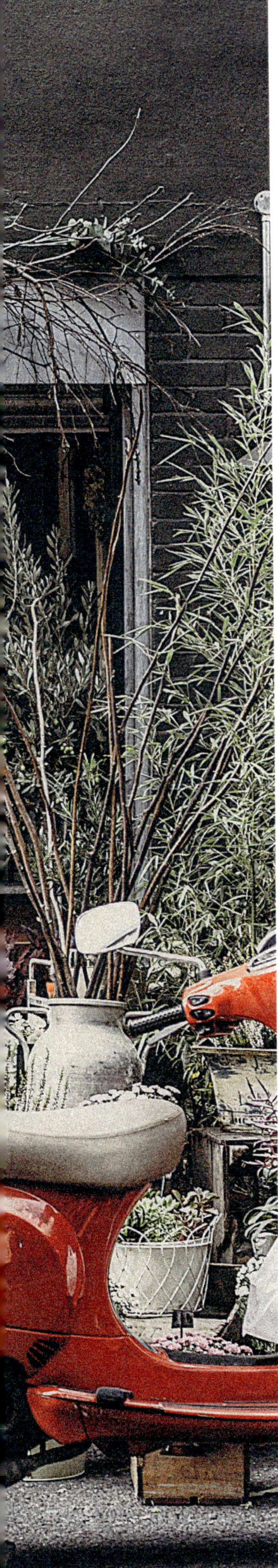

I got started with my dream list by asking myself some questions. Though every season is different and not every dream may come to pass now, I do know that God tends to use your desires, in addition to how He has wired you, in unexpected ways to fulfill your purpose. If we can write down on paper what He loves and what we love, we will look back on life and see how God has taken those seemingly small desires and woven them into our purpose. I've seen this truth in my own life. God takes who He's created me to be, and weaves my uniquely beautiful quirkiness within my purpose. Though God seldom fulfills all my desires the way I plan, He often fulfills them in ways far greater than I could ever imagine.

Now we are going to put into practice some of the things we've talked about in the last few chapters. No more reading, no more absorbing—it's time for action. So what makes your heart skip a beat? Do you know what that thing is? The thing that, when you step toward it, it's as if you become breathless with anticipation of what could happen. What could be. You wake up bubbling with excitement to put your feet on the ground and start running. You get butterflies in your stomach because you can't wait to put your hand to it. You fear it, too, because you sense a deep love for it, as if something is drawing you to it. A sober fear is more like an urgency to keep that thing in its right place and God in His. A humility washes over you, realizing that with this "thing," it's got to be all about God and not about you. What is that thing that makes you come alive?

As a high school student, I loved working with kids. I would spend my summers working in a latchkey program for kids whose parents worked full-time. I loved those kids, especially the two and three-year-olds. They were always loving, and came alive seeing someone consistent in their lives over the summer. For me, in that season, that latchkey program filled my bucket. I was discovering what I loved.

So what does your heart beat for in this season? For some it could be simply being a mother or father. Side note: I'm going to assume that

"THOUGH GOD SELDOM FULFILLS ALL MY DESIRES THE WAY I PLAN, HE OFTEN FULFILLS THEM IN WAYS FAR GREATER THAN I COULD EVER IMAGINE."

some men are reading this book. Though what is in your hands may not be the most testosterone-filled pages, I know valuable treasures are held inside that all genders can learn from. In fact, some of my favorite authors, teachers, mentors and parents in the faith have been of the opposite sex. So, here's to the courageous men willing to pick up these pages! Parenting could be many people's calling for a season. Adoption. Owning a business. Being a part of a certain business. Working with your hands. Serving at church. Helping others. Knitting. Writing. Creating. Leading. Following. Loving. Caring. Whether a nursery worker or owner of a Fortune 500 company, there's no set rules for what you can and cannot be, and no one thing is better than the other. We are all part of a bigger plan. His story is unfolding in each and every aspect of our lives.

Maybe you've never taken time out to discover what you love. You know what God loves. You've studied His heart. You know who you are through His Word, but how has He wired you personally? There's no better day than today to start the discovery. Actually, get a pen and paper out right now and start with these questions:

- What do I love?
- If I were guaranteed not to fail, what would I venture out to do?
- When I was a kid, what did I dream of becoming?
- What makes my heart skip a beat?
- If money weren't an issue, what would I love to do for the next decade?
- In the secret places of my own home, what's one thing I wish I could learn to do?

**Write your answers down.** Hopefully, in all these answers you'll see a common thread. Now take time to pray over these things. Bring them before the Lord. Remember too, pursuing God-given desires does not mean that you neglect other areas of responsibility. Sure, I've always wanted to write on the beaches of Hawaii, but I know my children would have major objections to me up and leaving them for a month. Find a healthy balance between what you need to do and what you would love to do. Come up with a plan to start actively pursuing a dream or two for a season. Don't go overboard. Make them doable within your time constraints. Place them in God's hands and see what doors open. If you fail, you fail, but at least you'll fail trying.

**Make sure you dream big.** I love the quote below by Theodore Roosevelt. In fact, I have it hanging over my desk where I write, create and worship God. It's a constant reminder that I would rather try and fail than not try at all. I hope it encourages your heart.

*"It is not the critic who counts; not the man who points out how the strong man stumbles, or where the doer of deeds could have done them better. The credit belongs to the man who is actually in the arena, whose face is marred by dust and sweat and blood; who strives valiantly; who errs, who comes short again and again, because there is no effort without error and shortcoming; but who does actually strive to do the deeds; who knows great enthusiasm, the great devotions; who spends himself in a worthy cause; who at the best knows in the end the triumph of high achievement, and who at the worst, if he fails, at least fails while daring greatly, so that his place shall never be with those cold and timid souls who neither know victory nor defeat."*[73]

**Make a list of desires and wants.** If you don't know what's in your heart, just start writing things down. Starting small can be helpful. Many times, purpose is birthed from desires. The word "purpose" in and of itself can be intimidating, but if you sit down long enough, most of us could write a list of what we want. When I say "make a list," that is all I am asking you to do. Personally, when I write this list I reserve the right to cross things off the list. For instance, I may have wanted to skydive at eighteen years of age, but now at forty I don't necessarily have a driving determination to throw my flailing body out of an airplane going 120 miles per hour in hopes that my parachute works. All that is to say, you can add to your list and you can take away—it's as simple as that.

**Look at your schedule.** Write down things you like to do in your free time. If you don't have any free time (like many of us), what would you do if you *did* have free time? If you like to play volleyball, maybe participating in a weekly tournament would be a great dream for this season of life. If you like to decorate, work on a decorating sketchbook or dreamboard where you can design dream rooms in your home. If you want to get into shape, maybe going to the gym three times a week could be on your list. Maybe you're like me and you love Hobby Lobby. A simple visit once a week can do wonders for my heart. I walk through the aisles, read the inspirational quotes, listen to the old school hymns like a melodic anthem in the overhead speakers, and just dream. It's just something I love to do, as my husband can attest, as long as I have the budget to do it! Include small things on your list. Like family vacations. Kissing your spouse on top of the Eiffel Tower. Making a goal to tithe 10% each year to your church. Doing family nights once a week. Reading one book a week. Using Fridays to take two hours of alone time to replenish. Ask yourself: If my life could look any way I wanted it to, how would it look?

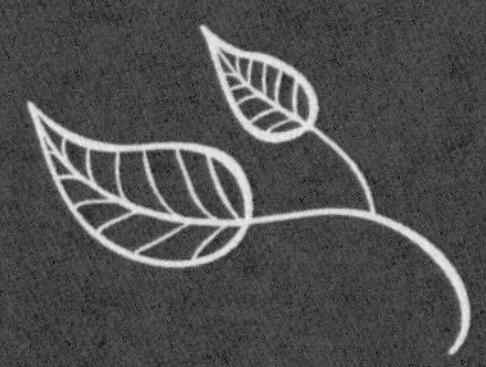

"WE START DYING THE DAY WE STOP DREAMING. AND IRONICALLY, WE START LIVING THE DAY WE DISCOVER A DREAM WORTH DYING FOR."

-Mark Batterson

I also like to include some financial dreams. These types of dreams include saving for retirement, home projects, tithing and giving, generosity to others and so much more. I like to think if I dream hard enough, by age fifty we could be out of debt, with our house paid off and living off 50% of our income. That would be amazing. I would also like to give away a car or home one day. It may seem ridiculous, but God could make a way. With hard work, sacrifice, and a miracle-working God, anything is possible. I also include dreams for my family, my children and my relatives. I even dream about my friends' lives, what they could be and what we could be doing together. I include work and ministry too! The sky's the limit, just begin to dream!

**The reality and final thoughts.** Before you begin creating your list, I want to address those of us who have gone through such deep, soul-rocking hardship that we no longer want to dream. The reality is that our circumstances do not change the character of God. I believe in this next season that God has things He wants to fulfill in your life. Although life can be hard, God is good. I'm praying that as you step out in faith, this next season is not marked by disappointment, but a deep dependence on God and that He reveals His goodness over and over again to you.

Here's a sample of my dream list to help you get started on yours.

## Jamie's dream list

Please note: these are "anything goes" types of dreams. Meaning, if there were no limits and anything was possible, this is what I would ask God for.

**Financial**

1. Give 15% in tithe this year, increase yearly by one percent
2. Live off 50% of our income by age 50
3. Start a charity
4. Pay for our children's education
5. Be debt-free by the age of 50
6. Give all our savings in an offering
7. Give the increase of our first paychecks and raises
8. Set aside 1% of our income just to bless others, increase that amount yearly by one percent
9. Give away a car or a house, or both
10. Start an organization that helps fulfill other's dreams
11. Give 51% of all creative publications to God (after all, He owns the company)

**Personal/Purpose**

1. Teach, love, give, bless and mine out greatness in other people and teams
2. Write songs that globally connect people to the heart of God
3. Travel to Nashville to record and write consistently, 2x per year
4. Lead and serve thousands of multicultural and multigenerational people in worship
5. Create river-to-the-nations resources
6. Write at least ten books in my lifetime—have a book sell over 10,000 copies and make it to the NY times bestseller list. Write one book a year in my 40s.
7. Farmhouse Dream—to live on more land and maybe even rent our house out
8. Own an extra smaller, beautiful home to send people to, to relax, recover and write music and books
9. Sing in the Brooklyn Tabernacle Choir for one service
10. Speak at some conferences—maybe speak with friends at the Hillsong Color Conference one day
11. Write songs with other worship writers I admire, such as Jane Williams, Kari Jobe, Joel Houston, Jaimie J., Jared Anderson, Jon Eagan, Dante Bowe, Aaron Wagner and the team at our church
12. Serve with/on a team that will impact this nation and world for God
13. Go to the Albion Fitness Retreat (first one to make a million buys the tickets, my friend)
14. Run a half marathon in my 40s
15. Run a marathon in my 30s
16. Learn to ride a motorcycle
17. Learn to fence
18. Make it to the top of Pikes Peak
19. Build an orphanage for a hundred girls
20. Meet Ron and Katie Luce
21. Sing Ave Maria with Harry Connick Jr.—just harmonize with him

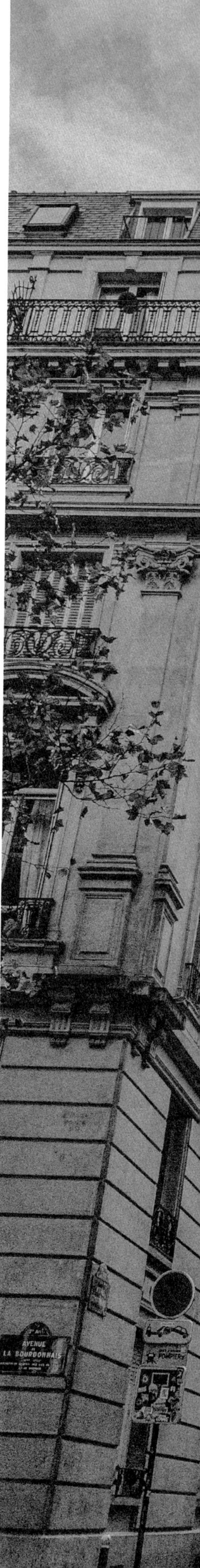

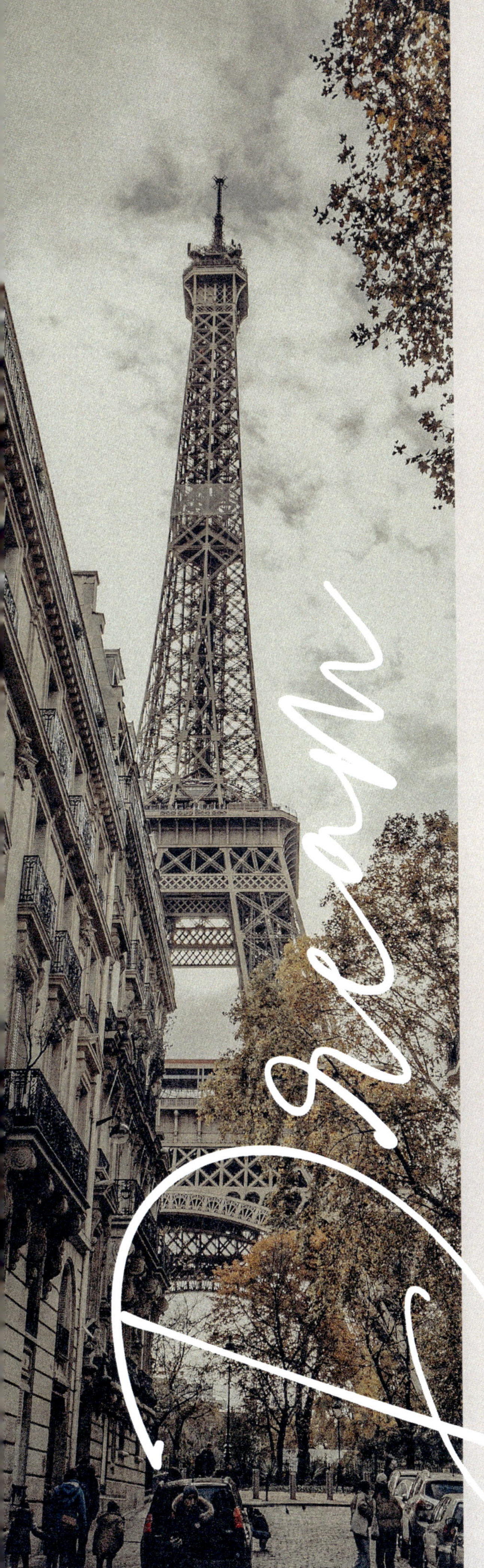


**Family/Friendships**

1. Raise children who know and love God first, and develop a love for learning, God's church, music and people. Children who are grounded in truth, love others, and are courageous women of integrity
2. Have each child marry a man that loves God with all his heart and loves them as well
3. Take each child on a 12-year-old mommy-daughter trip
4. Personally, have lifelong, God-bound friendships and always remain open to new friendships. Asking the same for our girls
5. Help push my friends towards God's best and stay rooted where God has placed us
6. Travel to Europe with Milan and the girls, allowing his history to become a part of who we are
7. Actually do the mountain home lake thing described in my first chapter, which includes jumping nude in the lake with a group of girlfriends. No phones, no cameras, no people around other than us! Maybe in each book I'll have one outlandish goal like this with no real purpose but fun and memories
8. Attend Hillsong Conference with Milan again
9. Celebrate 50 years of marriage together with Milan
10. Take each child on a mission trip
11. Kiss Milan on top of the Eiffel Tower
12. Travel down the Amazon
13. Visit the Great Wall of China
14. Create a family vision board
15. Be surrounded by great mentors in life, writing, marriage and ministry
16. Meet and rub shoulders with Joanna Gaines

These are not all of my dreams, but some of them. Some are wild and crazy, others are more goal oriented. Either way, God sees them there. My list is made, now all I need to do is trust Him. Trust is saying, "God, here is my list. Here are my hopes and dreams. Here's my life and my family. God, in this moment, in this season, I trust You."

God has got your list. He knows your season, your rhythms, and the purpose that is best for your life. Not only that, but He can and will perform divine miracles to provide for some of those things that you never thought possible. He's done many of these things on my list already. I know He will do the same for you.

Dream on, my sweet friend!

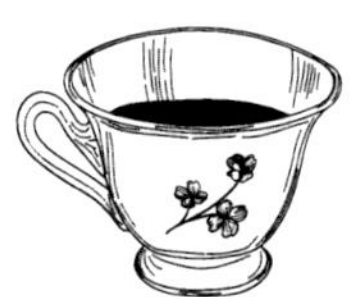

**BOOK RECOMMENDATION**

## Sun Stand Still *by Steven Furtick*

I had to include a book by Steven Furtick. He's an amazing communicator. He brings the Bible to life. This is one of his earlier published books focusing on dreaming big and asking God for the impossible.

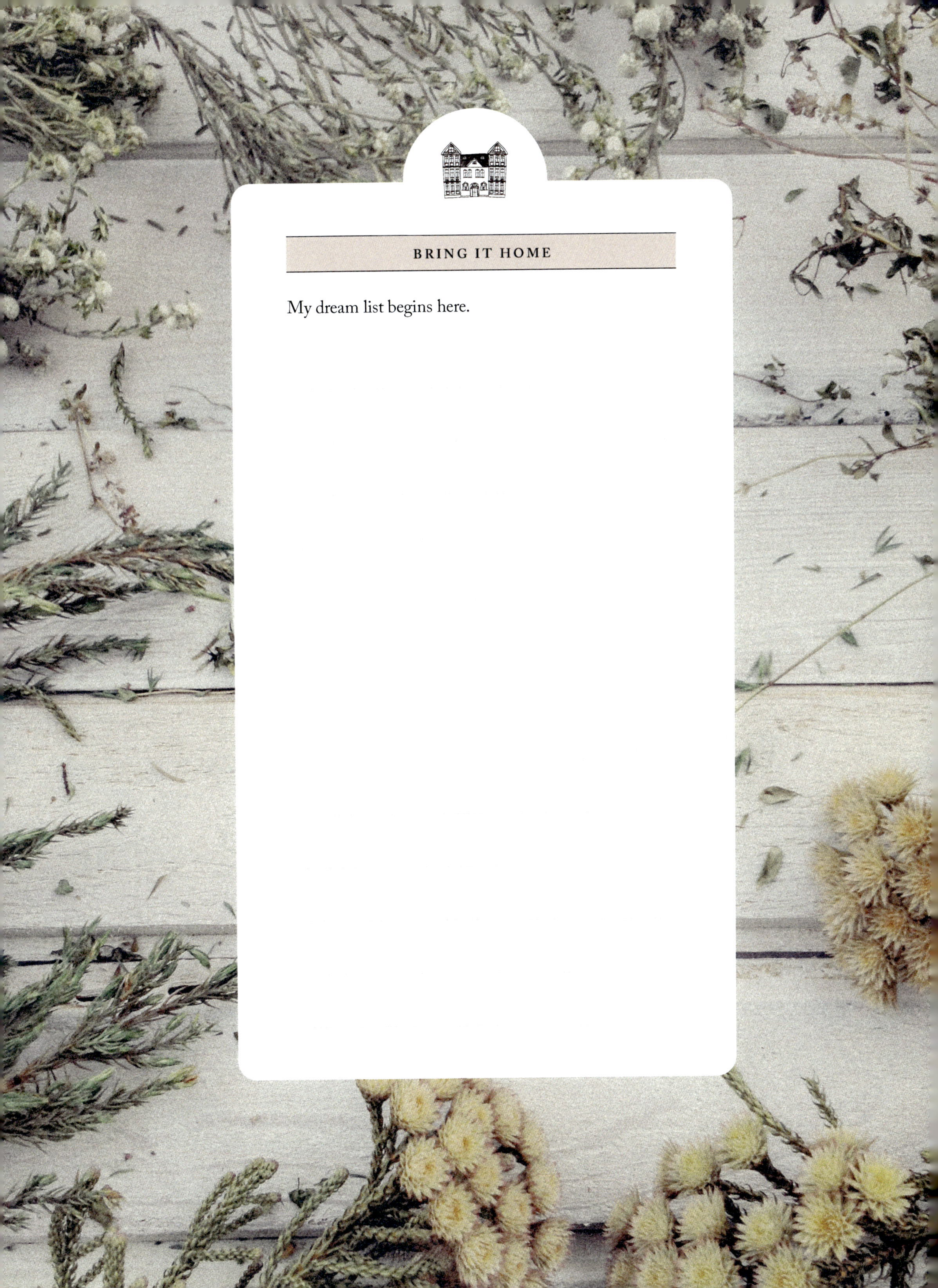

## BRING IT HOME

My dream list begins here.

CHAPTER TWENTY-TWO

# JUST BE *Hopeful*

WHEN THE DREAM DIES AND YOU DON'T WANT IT TO

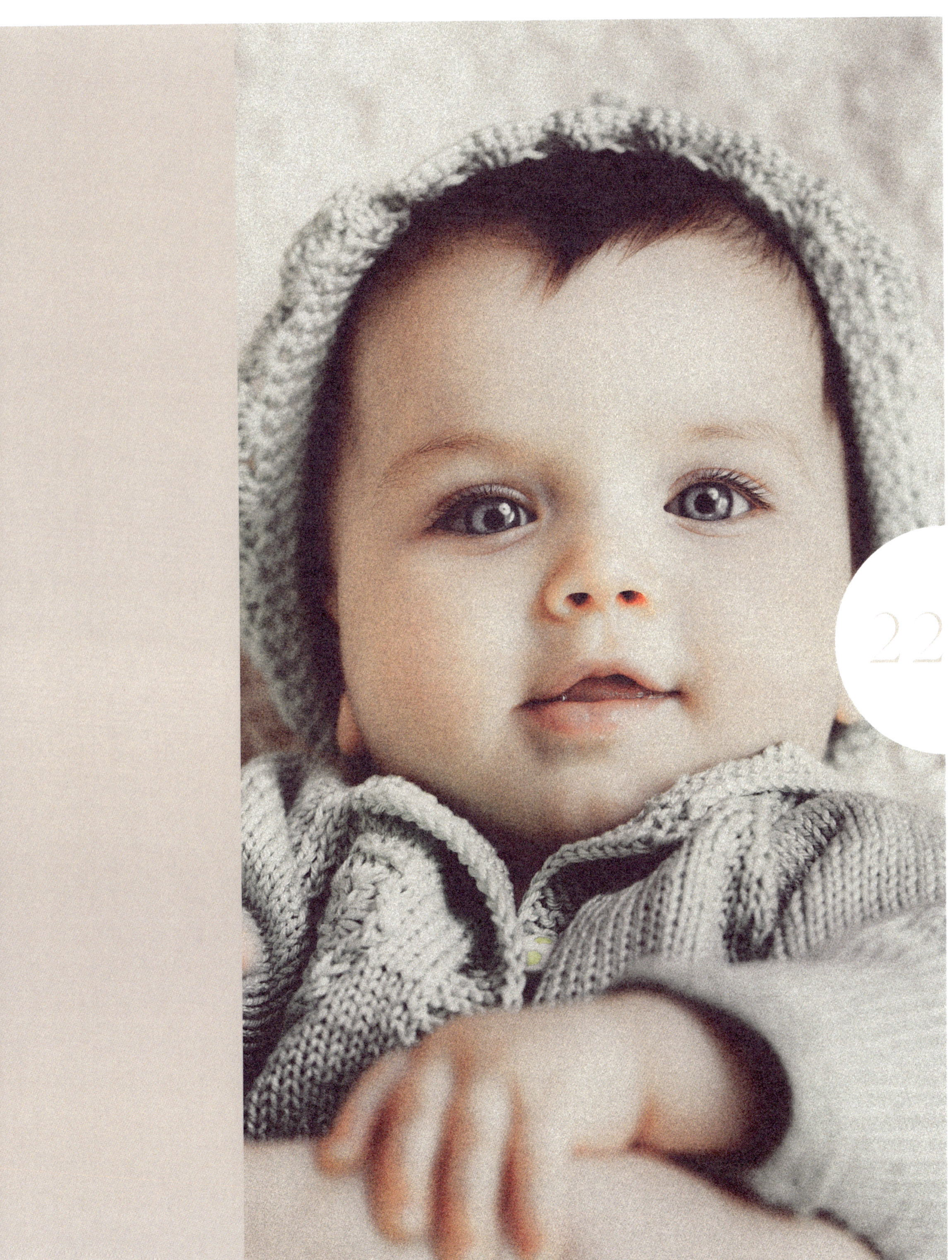

22

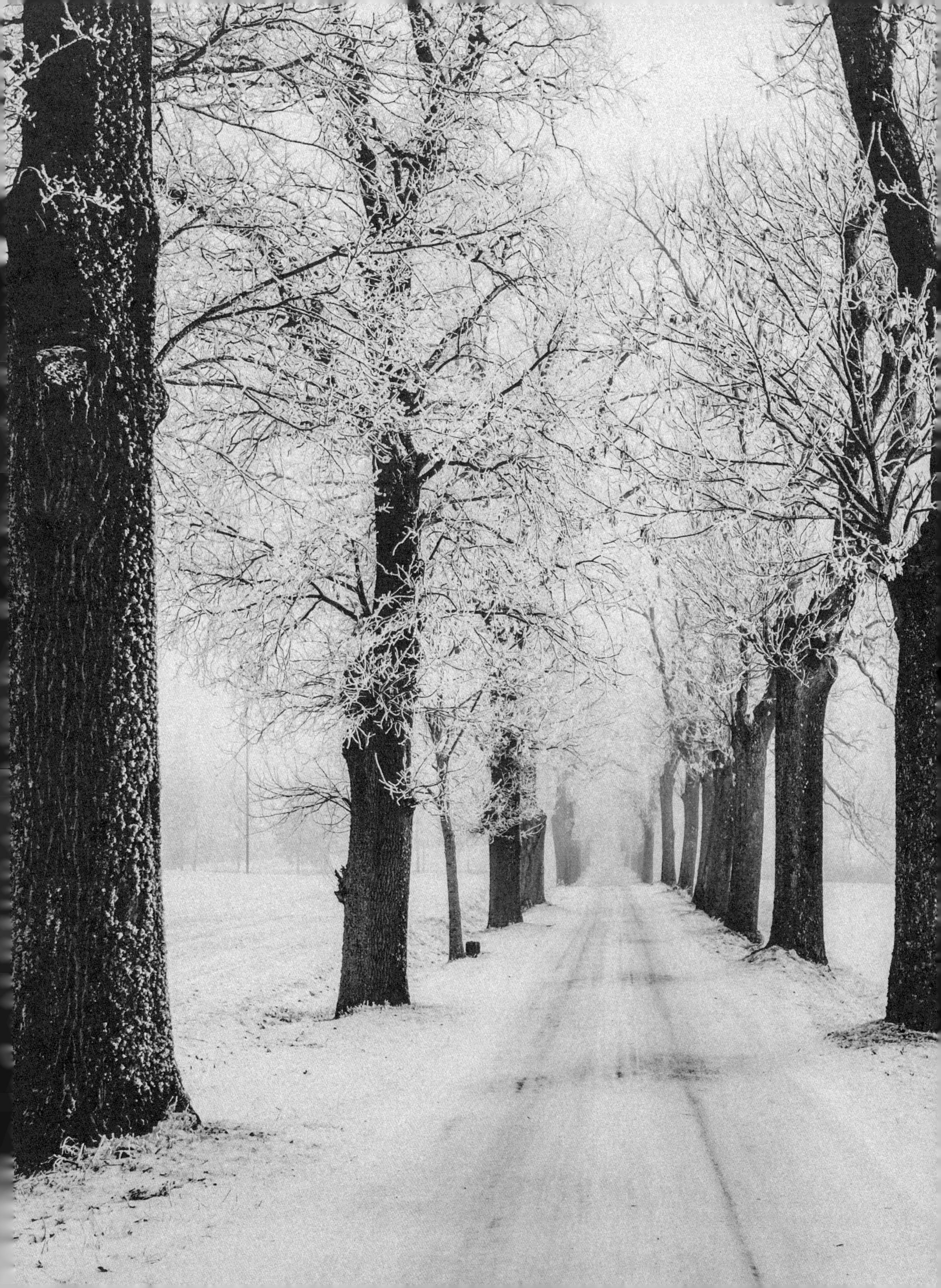

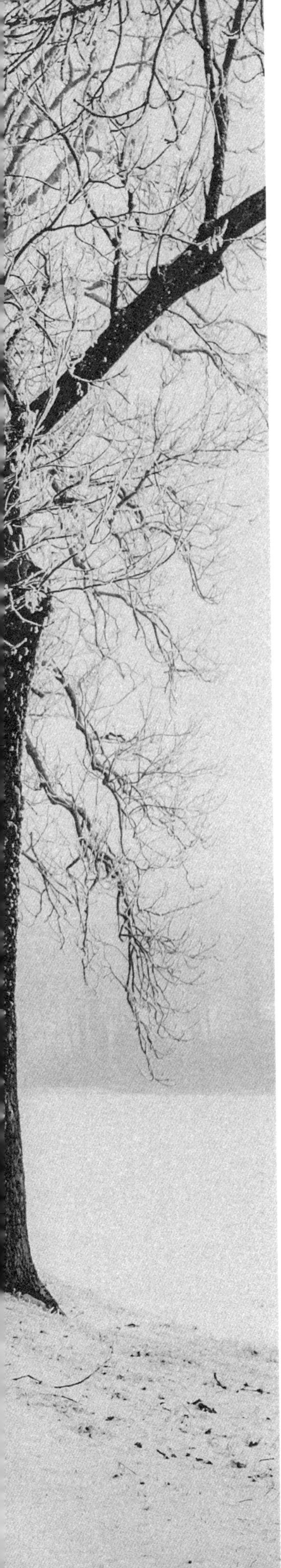

I had been praying and believing God for a miracle—you know, the kind that can divinely reverse your situation in an instant. It was the week of June 8 in 2009 when I started spotting. I was almost thirteen weeks pregnant. I hadn't heard a heartbeat yet, but they assumed it was because my uterus was tilted backward. A similar situation happened with my first two girls, but not this late in the game. When I went in for my doctor's visit that week they said I had nothing to worry about. Even though I was spotting a bit, my hormones were good and the following week, they would try again and were sure they would hear a heartbeat. By Friday June 12, the bleeding hadn't stopped, and despite all efforts to be hopeful, my heart was worried. I remember exactly where I was when I dropped on my knees to ask God to intercede. I had snuck away from the cheer and festivities of our dear friend and pastor's thirtieth birthday party for just a moment. Amidst the laughs and excitement, I knew I needed some alone time with Jesus. So I escaped to the only place I knew no one would find me—the church office bathroom. It was a single room with a toilet and sink and some pictures on the wall of memories throughout the years. The minute I pressed that little lock button on the door I began to weep. Alone with Jesus at last, I knelt to the floor, sobbingly clung to the toilet and did the only thing I could do: plead with Jesus to save my baby. A black shaggy rug lay on the floor, leaving little imprints on my shins and knees where the fabric bulged out. After some time, I knew I needed to return. My face was blotchy, my eyes looked like baby marshmallows and I felt like I had just used an entire roll of toilet paper as Kleenex. I rose to my feet, straightened up my brand new shirt from Forever21—the black silky one, with tiny jeweled flowers sewn delicately to the top—and made my way back to the party. Still praying for a miracle. In those desperate moments, you don't really care about where you are or what you're touching. I doubt I would have been using the toilet seat as an elbow rest to hold my praying hands upward in my normal frame of mind, but I was desperate. It's amazing how you can love someone so much that you haven't even met. I was, after all, a good six weeks into my dreaming for this new little Klusacek baby and I wasn't about to accept the possibility of losing it.

Sunday, June 14 rolled around. It was Father's Day. We decided to make the drive up to my dad's to spend the holiday with him. I was sitting on his light cream sofa when I got up to notice a spot of blood on the sofa. I quickly covered it up with a blanket and walked calmly to the bathroom. As soon as I sat down the intense bleeding began. I started sobbing and called for my dad—who, being the amazing, compassionate, level-headed doctor he had been for over thirty years, proceeded to stick his hand in the toilet and search through the heavy clotting for a baby. Now that's fatherly love! He told me to get in the car and drive to the ER. I cried the entire way. I cried while calling my dear friends and asking each of them to pray. I cried filling out the ER paperwork. I cried when they did the ultrasound. I cried when they told me my baby had no heartbeat and I cried when they had me schedule my first D&C procedure for the following week. I cried on the way to the D&C. I wept like a baby when I woke up from the surgery, realizing that the life I once had within me was gone, never to return. Little did I know in that moment, it wouldn't be the last time I would experience this situation.

With your permission, I'd like to tenderly transition this chapter over to the loss of a dream. I'm not blind to the fact that some of you reading this chapter have suffered painful physical loss. Loss of a loved one or perhaps more than one loved one. Maybe your loss was attached to a mother or father abandoning you or a spouse deserting you. For that, from the depths of my heart, I am truly sorry. I pray that as time progresses, God mends your heart, soul and spirit. I've had my own personal losses throughout the years. If you allow me, as lovingly as I know how, let me share with you some of the things God has tried to teach me through them—in ways that only He can. So let me share some parallels from my personal loss and the loss of a dream and how they relate.

**Release your need to understand it all.** Losing two children through miscarriages was a huge personal loss for me. I was left asking God, why? Why did He allow this to happen? Was it something I had done? Was it something I hadn't done? Did I not pray hard enough? Did I not have enough faith? What was wrong with me? If an all-powerful God who created heaven and earth could raise the dead and heal the sick, why was I not precious enough in His sight to intervene? All these "why" questions consumed my prayers. In the days after the surgery I can remember getting up and making the slow descent to my basement every morning to spend time with Jesus. The first month I think I cried every day and asked Him why. I was completely open with Him, baring all my feelings, and He was just there to listen. It was a sweet, precious time that I wouldn't trade for the world. Not once did I feel Him reprimanding me or telling me to suck it up and be strong. Instead, I would imagine Him simply holding me in His arms and whispering to my heart that everything was going to be alright. Through time, He moved me past the hurt and heartache and renewed my trust in Him once again. I had to be honest with Him in order for Him to bring healing. I released my need to understand why it had happened, because in all honesty it was out of my control.

It is the same with our dreams. Sometimes there are reasons why the dream is not happening that we can control. Maybe as we ask God, He will reveal that we need to be more diligent in pursuing it. Maybe we need to slow down and release it to Him. Maybe we need to change our lifestyle a bit to accommodate it. But when it comes to things that are beyond our control, we must release our need to understand why it's not happening back to God. You don't understand all of God's ways? You find yourself asking why? Welcome to the club. The bottom line is that we need to learn to trust God past our present pain. He taught me this through my physical loss and He's showing me this through the delay and sometimes denial of things I thought were from Him. Release your need to understand it all and simply trust.

**Don't let past pain project itself into your present and future.** Just because you've experienced the death of a dream does not mean your future is lifeless. As soon as I lost one child, I began seeing my future childless. I wondered if I would ever have another child again. My future, which once looked full of promise, now seemed bleak and daunting. My present pain was clouding my thoughts. Here's a thought, if our past pain isn't released to God, it often projects itself into our present and future. When I was pregnant with my sixth child, having lost two of the six, I was worried the entire first trimester. My past pain had me tied in knots over my present. It was robbing me of the joy I had once found in being a pregnant mama. What should have been an exciting season held with it shadows of worry and what ifs. There came a point in time when I had to make up my mind that I wouldn't let my past pain rob me of my present blessings. Every time I had a thought of worry, I would quote the scripture found in Hebrews 11:6: *"Without faith it is impossible to please God … He rewards those who earnestly seek Him."*[74] I would remind myself to have faith and to trust God. Friend, believe today that your future is full of hope, rich life and dreams being fulfilled. Don't let past pain project itself into your future. God is a healing, restoring, rebuilding type of God. The future is limitless.

**Remember who you are.** The death of Naomi's sons and husband heartlessly gouged out part of her soul. It left a huge festering wound of pain, disillusionment and disappointment. Disappointment for Naomi led to discouragement, which led to a distorted identity of herself. Instead of being called blessed, she asks her friends to rename her Mara, meaning bitter. Naomi tried to give herself a new name as she walked through the literal death of loved ones. Never rename yourself in the midst of

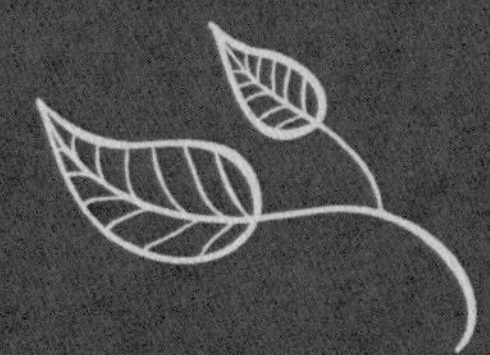

"CHARACTER CANNOT BE DEVELOPED IN EASE AND QUIET. ONLY THROUGH EXPERIENCE OF TRIAL AND SUFFERING CAN THE SOUL BE STRENGTHENED, AMBITION INSPIRED, AND SUCCESS ACHIEVED."

-Helen Keller

heartache. Remember who you are past your pain. You are not a failure. You are not a nobody. You are not meaningless and purposeless. You are a child of the most high God. He has marked you with purpose. The apparent death of this dream was allowed to do something in you. You will come out stronger. God will open up doors of favor and opportunity ahead of you. You are more than, in His eyes. In our lowest moments when it seems as if God has taken up residence in Antarctica, as far away from us as possible, remind yourself of who He is and make decisions based on that. Remember who He has called you to be and dare to move forward, choosing faith over fear. Don't let fear of the future paralyze you because of what has taken place in the past. Move now. Stay true to who God has created you to be. The feelings will come later.

> "DON'T LET PAST PAIN PROJECT ITSELF INTO YOUR FUTURE. GOD IS A HEALING, RESTORING, REBUILDING TYPE OF GOD."

**Trust in the God of the miraculous.** Regardless of our experiences, God is still a good God. He's your God. Faith doesn't take away our feelings of loss, but it gives us a greater reason to hope, to move, and to live beyond what we see. If one dream has died, God will have a purpose in it as well as a different dream in front of you that will fit you perfectly. And what if that dream really isn't dead? What if God wants to breathe life into it once again like He did for the widow in 2 Kings 4? What if Jesus came along today and told you that dream was only sleeping? Awaiting its time for God to touch it and a miracle to break out. Sometimes our dream isn't dead at all. Sometimes it's just the wrong timing. Sometimes we aren't ready for that dream. Sometimes God looks at us and decides our character isn't what it should be and we couldn't even handle that dream. I don't know how long you've been asking, searching, praying and pursuing, but I do know that if you know deep down that thing is of God, don't stop. Don't give up. Keep believing. Keep hoping. Keep taking steps toward it and surround yourself with people who believe God's best with you.

**Receive fresh hope.** The future is not to be feared. There's a verse I love about this in Proverbs 31 describing a woman who loves and trusts God. It says, *"She is clothed with dignity and honor, she laughs without fear of the future."*[75] I'll be honest, there are seasons in life where I will literally look up to the sky and wail out a gigantic guttural laugh! I turn my face toward heaven and laugh to remind myself that I will not fear what's ahead but that God's got me. I want to be like that Proverbs 31 woman, but I know I've got to learn to trust and live in hope. Hebrews 6:19 talks about how Jesus is like an anchor of hope for our souls. Living in a life-giving relationship with God always, always, always leaves room for hope. Hope for our present. Hope for our future. Hope for the miraculous. Hope for healing. God has everything worked out already to bring you to the place He's called you to be. He takes the past and present into account for His plan for your life. Regardless of what you've experienced thus far, God has great, awe-inspiring, beautifully crafted, wonderful plans for you and those you love.

Choose to believe again. May God breathe into you fresh hope for your past, present and future.

*Just Be* hopeful.

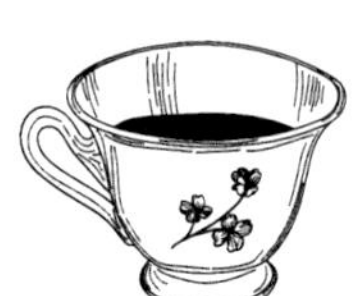

BOOK RECOMMENDATION

## Through the Eyes of a Lion

*by Levi Lusko*

This book is for anyone who has experienced loss. Levi tells the story of his daughter's death from an asthma attack and the months and years of difficulty that followed. Emotionally touching read on finding strength to move past your pain.

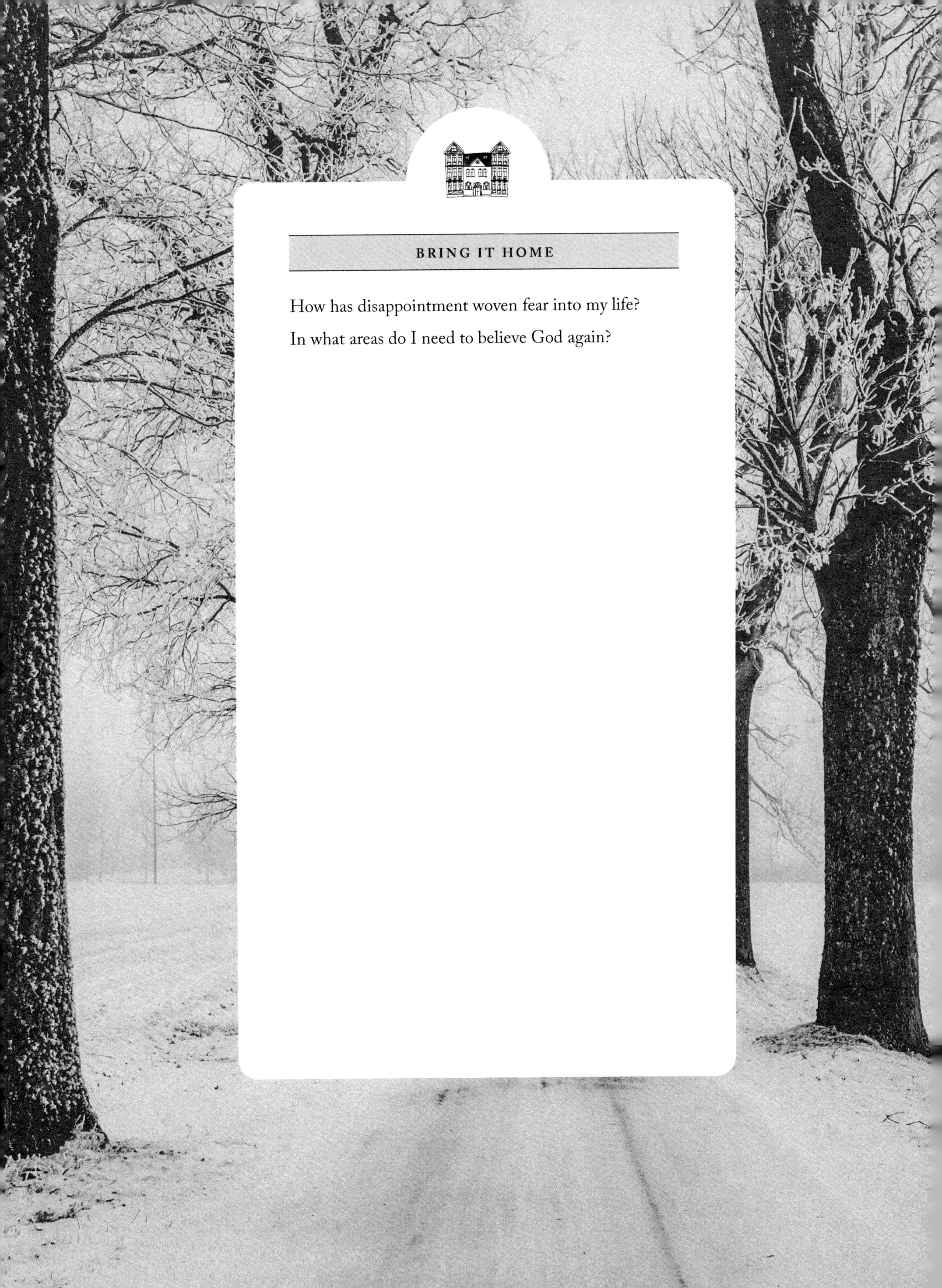

## BRING IT HOME

How has disappointment woven fear into my life?

In what areas do I need to believe God again?

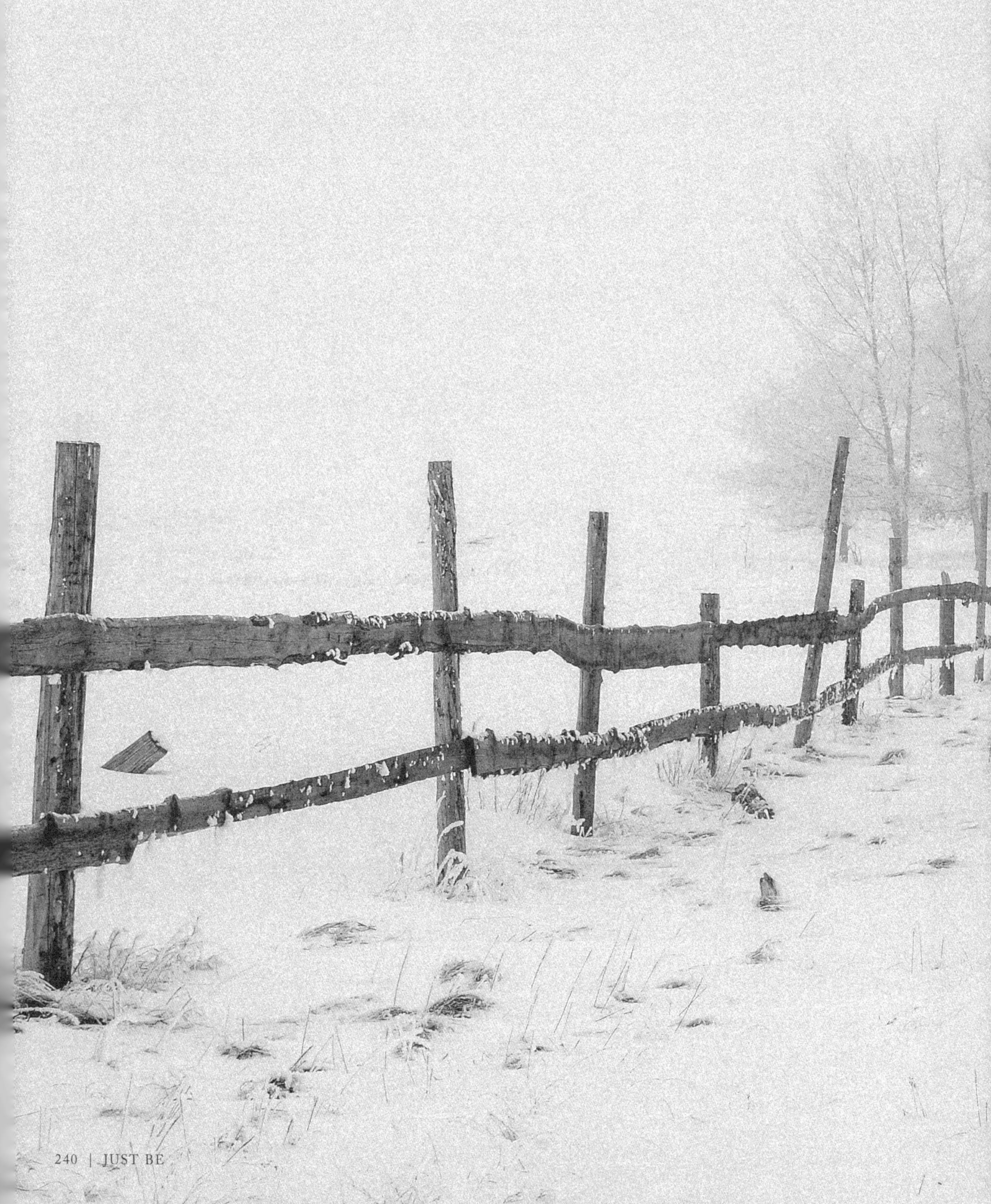

## There's beauty in the dawn

When the morning light casts its first shadows and the air is crisp and clean and wet. With sleepy-eyed, hopeful hearts of what is to come.

## There's beauty in the day

When I can see everything clearly in a fresh perspective. When there is nothing hidden, no secrets, no ulterior motives. Light. Bright. Beautiful.

## There's beauty in the darkness

When I can't see a thing and the scary imaginations of my thoughts act as if they are reality. When I don't know up from down and all I can see is the one step in front of me. There's beauty in this too.

CHAPTER TWENTY-THREE

# JUST BE *Moving Forward*

YOUR FUTURE IS BRIGHT AND BEAUTIFUL

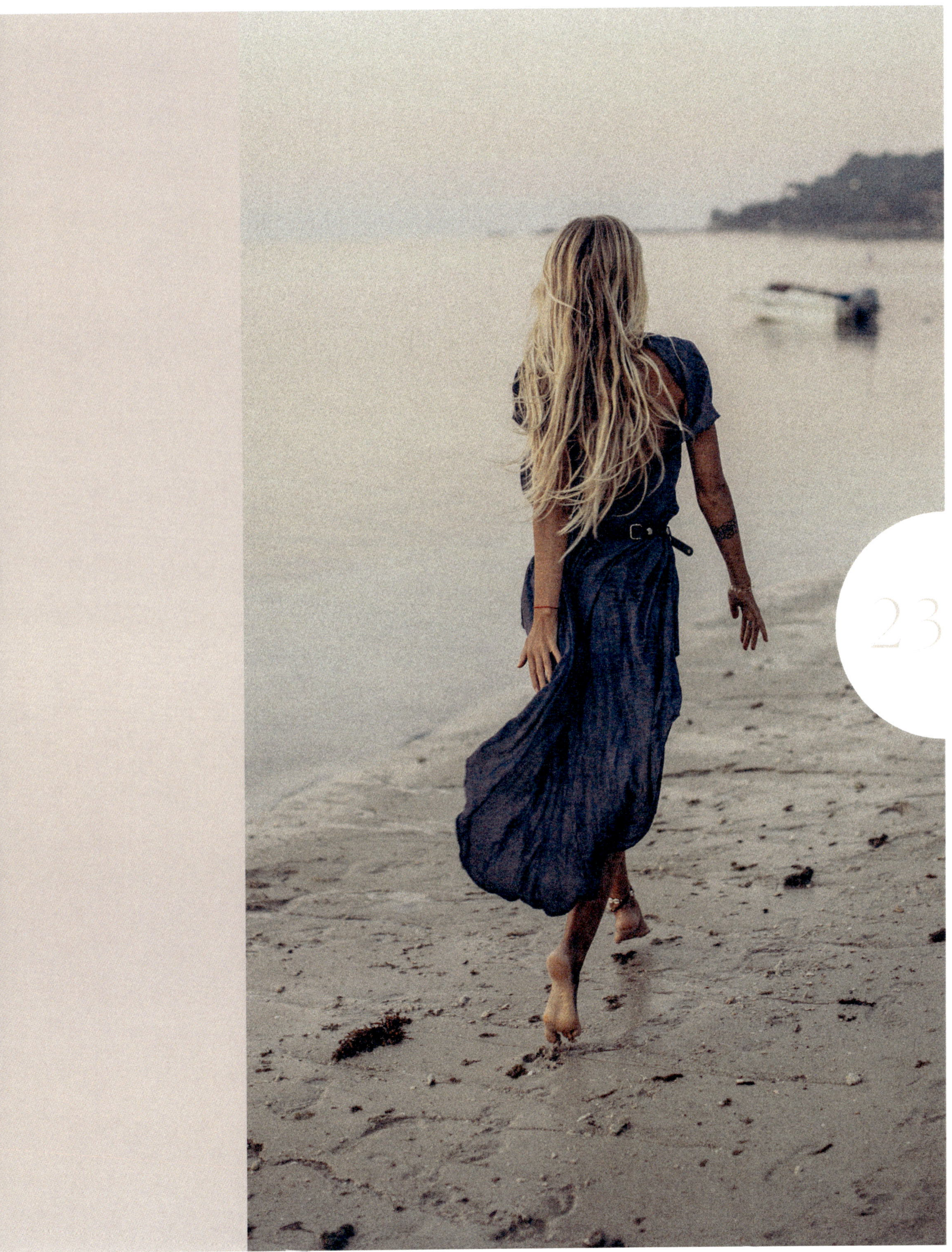

# 23

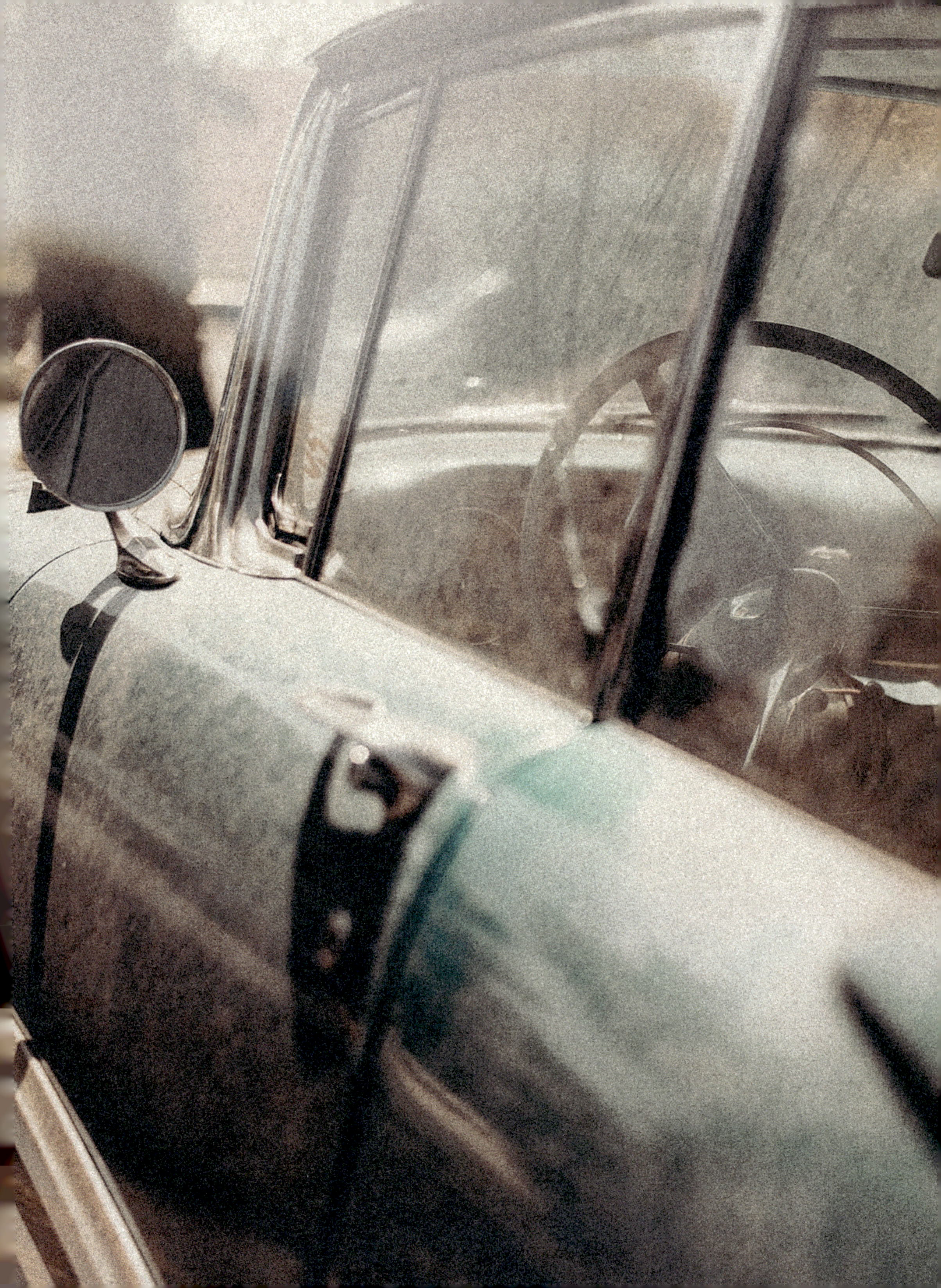

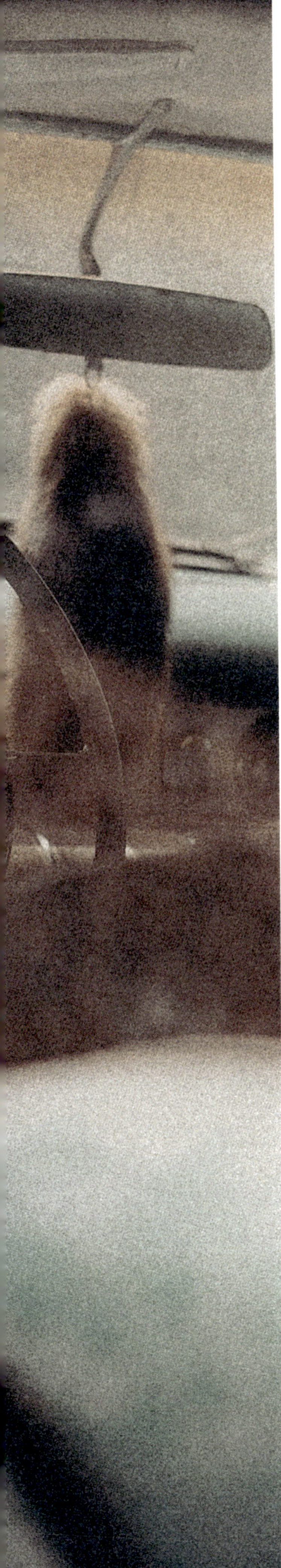

"I *can't believe our time together has come to an end,"* I say mournfully. We begin to fold our blankets and place them back in the white blanket bin to the left of my couch. We grasp our teacups and crumb-covered plates with remnants of banana bread and place them gently in the sink. *"Don't worry, I'll take care of it later,"* I say as I angle my head towards what's left to clean up. We stare briefly at each other as if mustering up the courage to part ways.

*"I guess I could stay five more minutes,"* you say smiling my way.

*"I'll take it! You can stay five-thousand more minutes if you like! You know I've got a guest bedroom downstairs with your name on it."* We laugh and hug each other then and there as if to remind ourselves that we are surrounded by those who love us. I release you and continue. *"If that's the case, I have one more thing to share with you,"* I say, grinning.

*"What's that?"* you ask.

*"Just keep going. You got this. Keep moving forward."* The words from my lips rest with conviction in my soul.

I love the movie *Meet the Robinsons*. It's the story of a young orphan boy with crazy blond hair who determines if he could only turn back time and meet his mother, all his problems would fade away. He sets his mind to building a time machine that will take him back to the past where he can meet his mom and for the first time and find her in the future. Unfortunately, his plans unravel and, long story short, in the end he discovers that changing his past doesn't matter as much as living in his present. If he just keeps moving forward, despite the difficulties and failures and triumphs, everything will turn out all right. What a great message for my kids. What a great message for me.

There are moments when I'm tempted to turn around, leave it all behind and switch into freak out mode. You know, that moment where you can sense your emotions rising up and you feel like you can't handle one more ounce of bad news, things not going as expected, or even one more comment from that person who loves to give their opinion at any and every moment they can in your life. You feel as if you are getting

"LIFE CAN ONLY BE LIVED FORWARD AND UNDERSTOOD BACKWARD."

-Jeff Godin

swept away in the endless amount of to-do's from work, family and kids, whacked in the face by flying debris everywhere. These times in my life usually occur right before God is about to do something great. Many times, I need to release some things in order to step into the greater calling God has for my life and the lives of others around me. Release is not retreat. Moving forward often means honing into the voice of God for your life and releasing some things that are keeping you from the peace, rest and purpose God wants to give freely. Release for me is never pleasant, but in order to go higher, letting go is a must. Don't just keep pressing on in those moments, but allow God to search your life and speak to you, adjusting your path. I need this book as much as you! I come to you from a place of not having arrived, but rather a place of humble asking. Humble seeking. Humble release. Allowing God to strengthen me to take step after step of courageous obedience. I'm not what I was ten or even five years ago, but I still have a lifetime of learning ahead. So I keep moving forward.

Now let me say that moving forward does not mean sprinting ahead at a breakneck pace. Sometimes moving forward means resting. Sometimes it means walking. Sometimes, yes, it does mean running. Moving forward simply means staying in tune with God and walking in the direction He has for you. God is building a name for Himself, and He wants to do that personally in your life. He is building a reputation in you so that the faith in your life is not a faith built off of someone else's divine moments. Your faith is built off of moments that God has designed to show and prove Himself, His promises and His character to you. Each yes to God is a step towards God's best for your life and a greater discovery of who He is.

MOVING FORWARD DOES NOT MEAN SPRINTING AHEAD AT A BREAKNECK PACE. SOMETIMES MOVING FORWARD MEANS RESTING."

Yes, it's true that when we don't trust God completely, life may appear to be easy and comfortable—but that's just a mirage. The only truly safe place to be is in the arms of God. When we choose to trust God, the obstacles that come our way are opportunities for miracles. Miracles that shape our faith and future. A chance for God to do something so divine in your life that no one could explain it but through the hand of God. These are moments I don't want to miss. This is where I want to live, so I keep moving forward. I've tried doing it on my own and I make a mess 100% of the time. But the minute I say yes to trusting God, no matter what my eyes see, my ears hear, or my heart experiences, I step forward into the miraculous.

With only One person in all of creation who knows your beginning from your end and created you with a specific purpose in mind, why not trust Him to carry out the plan for you? In His timing and in His way, just keep moving forward. If you make a mistake, that's okay. God's grace and power is enough to cover that. If you choose the wrong path, God will have another way to get you to your destiny, just keep moving forward. If you have to say yes to something scary, trust that He will be with you. If you need to say no to something you've done your entire life, have the courage to do it, just keep moving forward. Trust and believe God.

Your life is a blank page in the hands of the greatest Author of all time. *Just Be* the character He's created you to be. Full-out, all-in, completely surrendered to Him and recklessly accepting and embracing who you are.

*"I look forward to seeing all that God does in and through you in the weeks, months and years to come,"* I say as we walk towards the front door. There's a lightly falling snow descending from the heavens.

YOUR LIFE IS A BLANK PAGE IN THE HANDS OF THE GREATEST AUTHOR OF ALL TIME. JUST BE THE CHARACTER HE'S CREATED YOU TO BE."

It's covering the earth with shimmering beauty. Each tree swaying in a blanket of white diamonds. It reminds me of the fresh work God is doing in our hearts and lives. New. Pure. Washed as white as snow.

*"I can't wait to see what God does in me and in you,"* you whisper with faith-like confidence. I'm reminded once again how precious and beautiful you are.

*"Thank you,"* I say as a tear trickles down my cheek. I smile and touch you gently on your shoulder.

*"For what?"* you ask as you wrinkle your brow. *"What did I do?"*

*"Thank you for allowing me into your life. Thank you for letting me love on you these past few hours. Thank you for allowing me to stand in faith with you for God's best to come to pass in you. Thank you for allowing me to breathe seeds of purpose in you from God's Word,"* I say as I open the door.

Your shoes are on, your coat looks wonderfully warm and cozy. We embrace one last time before you step onto the porch. It's not a goodbye, per se, but rather, until we meet again. From this moment forward our lives will be intertwined in a heavenly, God-altering way. We are now a part of each other's story. Cheering from the sidelines of life, strengthening each other on this faith-filled journey.

I watch your car pull away and wave goodbye one last time. With a smile on my face I walk back inside, close the door and whisper to myself ... *Just Be.*

Keep moving forward and journey well, my friend.

*Xoxo, Jamie*

BOOK RECOMMENDATION

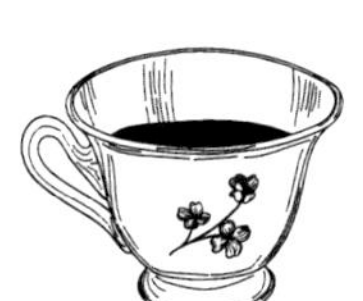

## Manage Your Day-to-Day

*by Jocelyn K. Glei*

I read this book years ago and find myself coming back to it frequently. It's a compilation made by creatives and tools they personally use to promote consistency in their work. I love the layout, it's not masses of text. It breathes and has color. Short. Sweet. Practical.

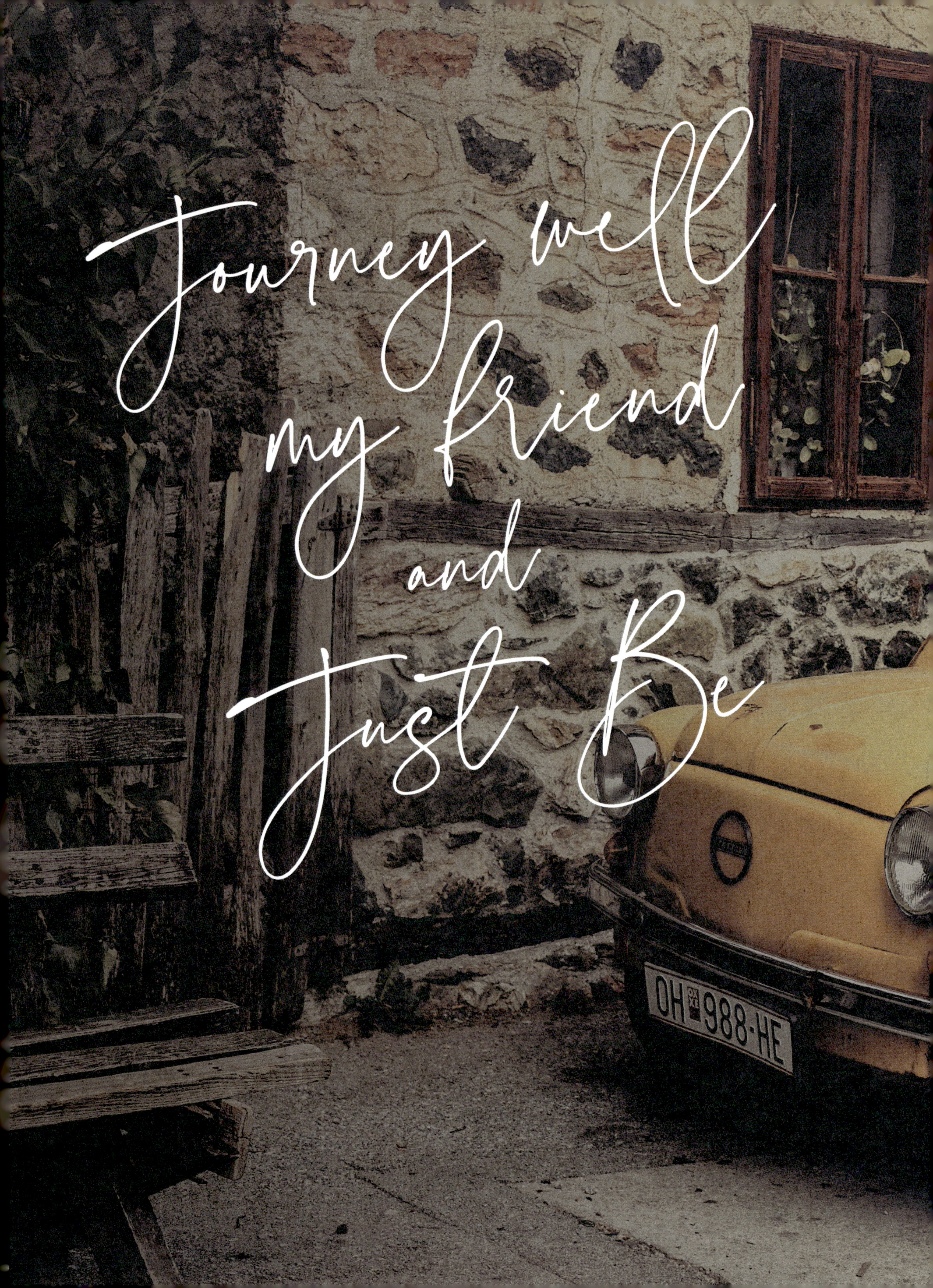
Journey well
my friend
and
Just Be
OH 988-HE

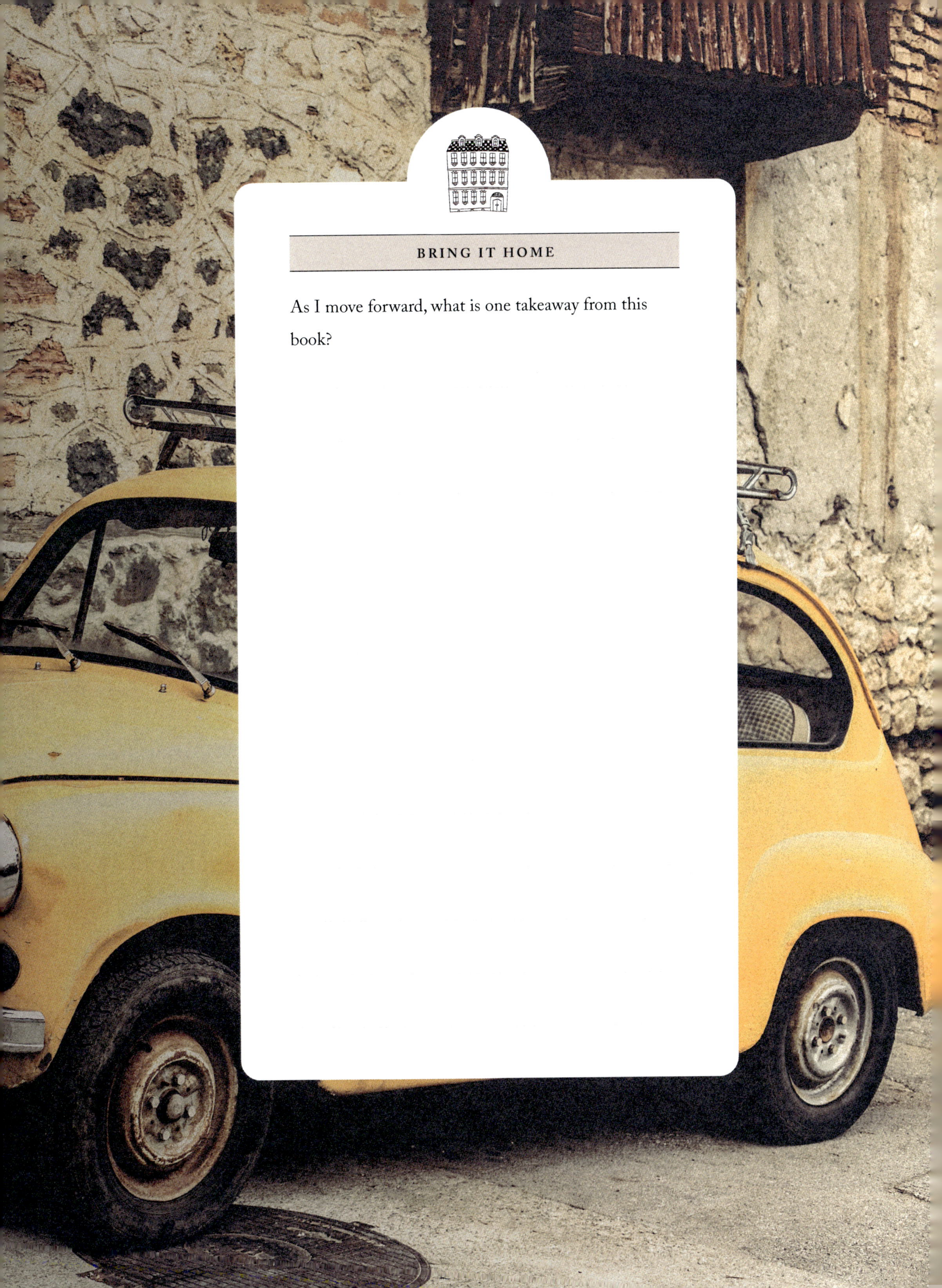

## BRING IT HOME

As I move forward, what is one takeaway from this book?

# Salvation Prayer

I couldn't end this book without giving you the opportunity to pray and commit your life to Jesus. My prayer is that you have seen His love for you woven intricately throughout these pages and that you have felt His desire for you specifically in every chapter. Having a relationship with Jesus is the only thing that can fulfill the gaping hole in your heart and life. It is also the best decision you could ever make. The Bible says in Romans 10: 9-10 that if we confess with our mouth that Jesus is Lord and believe in our heart God raised Him from the dead, we will be saved. Join me in the following prayer of asking Jesus to be Lord of our lives. Make it personal.

*Jesus, I admit my need for You. You are the only One who can satisfy the deep longings in my soul. I believe that You are God, that You died on the cross for my sins and rose again. I invite you in to be Lord of my life. You created me, therefore, You have the best plan for my life. I surrender to you my hopes, my dreams, my hurts and wounds. All that I am I lay at Your feet. Take control of my life and make something beautiful. Come into my life and bring the salvation that only You can give. In Jesus name, amen.*

If you have prayed that prayer for the first time, or your tenth time, I am celebrating with you today. Start reading your Bible and praying daily. Get to know God, approach Him like you would any other friendship in your life. Get to know Him by spending time with Him. Start going to church and surround yourself with other people that can bring out God's best in you. The journey has just begun ...

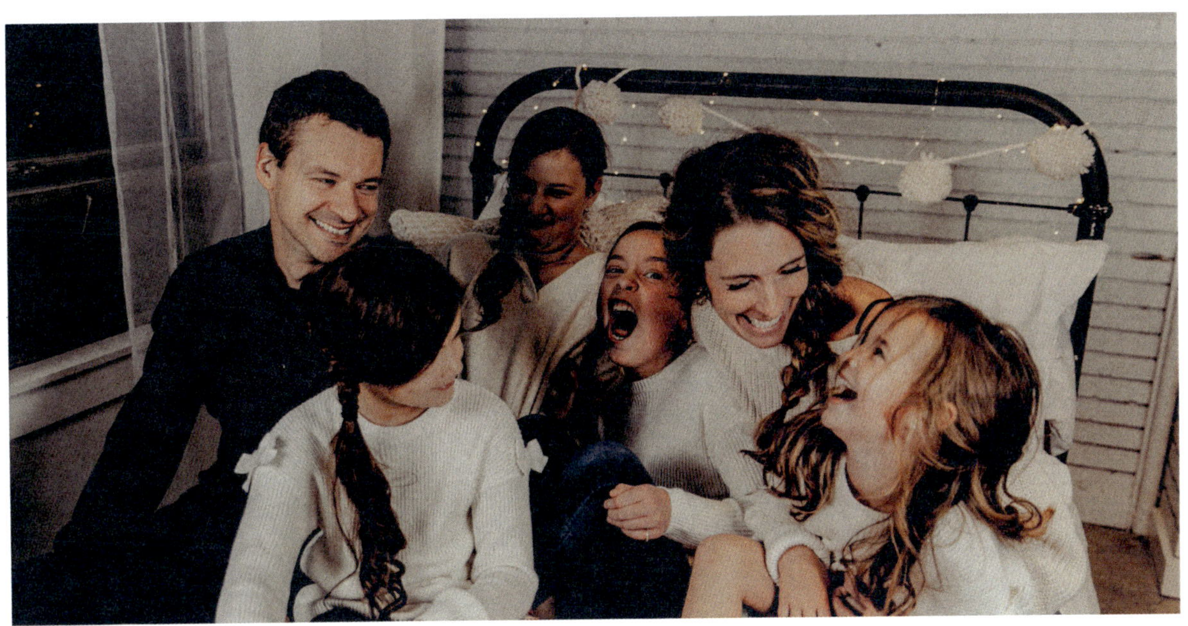

# Connect with Jamie

Jamie Klusacek lives in Colorado with her amazing Czech-born husband, Milan, and four preciously gorgeous daughters, Grace, Anna, Selah and Noella. Her passion is to know and love God and others well. Her desire is to walk courageously obedient with Jesus and to see others do the same no matter what season they are in. She believes that God is near and stills speaks personally to us today—and that each of our lives are marked for miracles as we join in this adventure to make His name known throughout the earth. Whether serving in her part-time role at church, drinking steaming hot tea and writing books, speaking, singing bedtime lullabies to her children, or baking chocolate chip cookies to simply eat with friends—each day is a gift to be cherished, holding opportunities for us to share the genuineness of God with those around us.


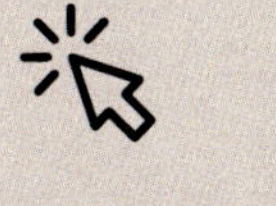

jamieklusacek.com

hello@jamieklusacek.com

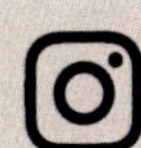

@jamieklusacek

# Acknowledgments

I've heard it said that we weren't made to hold glory, we were made to deflect it to the only One who deserves it. So to that end, thank You Jesus. Thank You for the gift to write. Thank you for sustaining me and being more than enough throughout my lifetime. Thank You for breath and life and for lessons taught throughout the years. Thank You for using imperfect vessels to shine the light of Jesus to an imperfect world. You deserve the glory and the credit for these pages, not me. You give so that we can give back to others. I remain an open vessel for You to use.

Milan Klusacek, you are my one true love. You give me strength. You remind me of God's promises, even when I doubt. You push me towards all that God has purposed for our family. You are a leader, world-class creator, encourager and my best friend. I'm honored to be your wife. You designed a beautiful book.

Grace, Anna, Selah and Noella the greatest gift I hold is being your mother. You are so precious to me. You will change this world for Jesus.

Mom, Dad and Terri you've helped me learn, grow and have loved me deeply in every season. You are a gift to me. I thank God that He made you my parents.

Pastors Jake and Hannah Ouellette, you are treasured friends who have been walking this faith journey with us for over thirty years—we love you deeply. All the friends who have encouraged me to write, dream and believe God for the impossible—you know who you are. Cheetah Boss Creatives, for pushing me to create. Lauren Atherton, for design input. Mark McGuinness, for your mentorship. Katie Samuels, as an early reader your enthusiastic texts fueled me. Anne Evans, you mentored me in a critical part of my journey. Jacey Carroll, *Just Be* inspiration.

Suzanne Strobel, Terri Dunham and Shannon Ackerman, thank you for the edits. The time and effort you spent combing through each page is a blessing to my heart.

To our church. We love serving alongside you weekly seeing God's kingdom come to earth, breathing hope and life to those in our city. Being rooted in the local church is a gift. We live to make God famous.

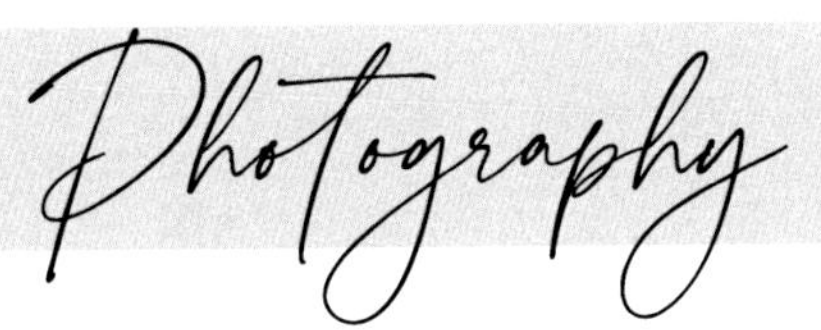

All photos provided by *pexels.com* unless otherwise noted.
Big props to the many amazing photographers below.

**Intro Pages**
Dedication flowers by Secret Garden
Table of Contents tea jars by freestocks.org
Before you read this book by Taryn Elliot

**Chapter 01**
House by Eberhard Grossgasteiger
Mountain lake by Eberhard Grossgasteiger

**Chapter 02**
Open book with flower by Ylanite Koppens
Library by Janko Ferlic

**Chapter 03**
Cup of tea with flower by Olenka Sergienko
White Kettle by Lina Kivaka

**Chapter 04**
Man on long road by Max Ravier
Sheep by Janko Ferlic
Banana bread by Marta Dzedyshko

**Chapter 05**
Swan by Michael Block
Woman feeding swans by George Desipris

**Chapter 06**
Homes on water by Avonne Stalling
Blueprint by Jimmy Chan

**Chapter 07**
Freckled girl by Matheus Bertelli
Crowded pool by Sergio Souza

**Chapter 08**
Wheat by Julia Kuzenkov
Chair in wheat by Ekrulila

**Chapter 09**
Chair by Eberhard Grossgasteiger
Camera by Jan Kopriva
Field by Eberhard Grossgasteiger

**Chapter 10**
Bacon wraps by Pixabay
Stone path by Avonne Stalling

**Chapter 11**
Mozambique children by Gabriele Mango
Man with pottery by Raman Deep

**Chapter 12**
Planner with flowers by kaboompics.com
Cul-de-sac by Michael Tuszynski

**Chapter 13**
Old woman by Wildan Zainul Faki
Woman and grain by Click'r Sharad Patil
sp-dv
Flowers with the chair by Secret Garden

**Chapter 14**
Green coffee house by Lisa Fotios
Coffee house indoors by Lisa Fotios
Navy man by Mael Balland
Coffee and journal by Spencer Selover

**Chapter 15**
Swings by Todd Trapani
Flower in hands by Flora Westbrook
Tea kettle by Todd Trapani (unsplash.com)
Wood by Dominika Roseclay

**Chapter 16**
Flowers on the chair by Secret Garden
Flower gift by Brigitte Tohm
Flowers in pink vase by Hassan Ouajbir

**Chapter 17**
Three women by Anfisa Eremina
Donuts by Buenosia Carol
Friends in Jeep by Vitoria Santos
Friends walking by Bas Masseus
Crowd of people by Davi Pimentel

**Chapter 18**
Woman with bouquet by Flora Westbrook
Wedding dress by Avonne Stalling

**Chapter 19**
Paint brushes by Cottonbro
Woman artist by Cottonbro
Peonies by Secret Garden
Beautiful girl Avonne Stalling
Brownies by Lina Kivaka
Pink peony by t4hill

**Chapter 20**
Christmas décor by Lina Kivaka
Record player by Spencer Sealover
Pine tree by Irina Iriser

**Chapter 21**
Christmas bike by Daria Shevtsova
Eiffel Tower by Elina Sazonova
Dry flowers by Daria Shevtsova

**Chapter 22**
Baby by Pixabay
Trees by Freestocks.org
Fence by Pixabay

**Chapter 23**
Girl on the beach by Elina Sazonova
Teal car by Spencer Sealover
Yellow car by Matthias Zomer

**Ending Pages**
Prayer and Connect by Aslak Sonderland
Footnotes by Emre Can

# Footnotes

**Chapter 2**

[1] Here are some authors I like for fictional writing: Melanie Dickerson's Young Adult Fairy Tale Retelling series. Elizabeth Camden's series are more historical and I love them too!

[2] This sort of reminds me of that movie, How to Lose a Guy in 10 Days. Remember how she made that scrapbook of their wedding and their children … LOL - that would be me with Jesus.

[3] Reference from Romans 8:28

**Chapter 3**

[4] You can still buy this DVD on Amazon starring Elanor Bron, Liam Cunningham and Liesel Matthews.

[5] Reference from Romans 8:28

[6] Loving the book of Ruth. She was the inspiration for most of this book.

[7] Romans 12:2

[8] Check out Psalm 45

[9] Study Jeremiah 33 and Psalm 18

[10] Philippians 4:19

[11] Matthew 5:14

**Chapter 4**

[12] My mom got this recipe in Grenada, where my dad was studying to be a doctor. While she was there, some American Missionaries told her about Jesus and she gave her heart to God then and there.

[13] Shannon, my friend who edited this book, is fairly certain David had RED HAIR! In fact she took twenty minutes researching this very fact. Though when I picture him, I still see him with dark hair.

**Chapter 5**

[14] Hans Christian Andersen, The Ugly Duckling, http://hca.gilead.org.il, published in 1844

[15] Hans Christian Andersen, The Ugly Duckling, http://hca.gilead.org.il, published in 1844

**Chapter 6**

[16] Christian Standard Bible, Jeremiah 29:11, Holman, 2018

[17] Eugene H. Peterson, The Message Canvas Bible, Jeremiah 32:37-40, NavPress, 2016

[18] Buy Calamity Jane on Amazon, directed by David Bulter

[19] A Christmas Tale, produced by Cornerstone Church in Highland Michigan was the first musical score and script I took part in writing. It was a musical centered on God's redemption, based off of Charles Dickens classic novel A Christmas Carol, Chapman & Hall, 1843

[20] Eugene H. Peterson, The Message Canvas Bible, Jeremiah 31:9, NavPress, 2016

[21] Eugene H. Peterson, The Message Canvas Bible, Jeremiah 33:3, NavPress, 2016

**Chapter 7**

[22] Christian Standard Bible, Isaiah 49:15-16, Holman Bible Publishers, 2017

[23] Christian Standard Bible, Jeremiah 31:3, Holman Bible Publishers, 2017

[24] For the record, I love my freckles. I think they are kisses from heaven. I love being tall. I love NOT wearing makeup too. Wearing makeup makes me feel like I have a mask suffocating my face.

**Chapter 8**

[25] Christian Standard Bible, Ruth 2:11-12, Holman Bible Publishers, 2017

[26] Personal paraphrase of Psalm 5:12

[27] Christian Standard Bible, Ruth 1:17, Holman Bible Publishers, 2017

[28] Christian Standard Bible, 1 Timothy 6:6-7, Holman Bible Publishers, 2017

[29] Ruth facts at Jewish Women's Archive: jwa.org

**Chapter 9**

[30] New Living Translation Ruth 2:15-16

**Chapter 10**

[31] Christian Standard Bible, Psalm 119:31-32, Holman Bible Publishers, 2017

[32] Christian Standard Bible, Act 10, Holman Bible Publishers, 2017

[33] Christian Standard Bible, Act 10:15, Holman Bible Publishers, 2017

**Chapter 11**

[34] Christian Standard Bible, Ruth 2:2-3, Holman Bible Publishers, 2017

[35] Christian Standard Bible, 2 Kings 4:1-7, Holman Bible Publishers, 2017; bold added.

[36] Christian Standard Bible, John 6:5-9, Holman Bible Publishers, 2017

**Chapter 12**

[37] Christian Standard Bible, Ruth 2:23, Holman Bible Publishers, 2017

[38] Biblegateway.com, Ephesians 4:1-3, MSG; Bold font added by me

**Chapter 13**

[39] New Living Translation, Ruth 1: 1-2

[40] Christian Standard Bible, Exodus 12:36, Holman Bible Publishers, 2017

[41] Climatestotravel.com, The climate of Israel

[42] Christian Standard Bible, Ruth 4:14-15, Holman Bible Publishers, 2017
[43] Romans 8:28
[44] Merriam-webster.com, renew defined

**Chapter 14**
[45] New Living Translation, Ruth 2:13-19, Biblehub.com
[46] "The prince of the people," Boaz search on Wikipedia.org
[47] Visit Jamie Klusacek's Spotify playlist
[48] Ephesians 3:20 paraphrase

**Chapter 15**
[49] Christian Standard Bible, John 3:16, Holman Bible Publishers, 2017
[50] Matthew 22:36-40 paraphrase
[51] Matthew 22:36-40 paraphrase, again

**Chapter 16**
[52] Wedding Tea, harney.com/products
[53] John 3:16 paraphrase
[54] Biblegateway.com, Matthew 10:8, NIV
[55] Proverbs 11:24-25, MSG, Biblegateway.com
[56] Biblegateway.com, 2 Corinthians 9:8, New Living Translation

**Chapter 17**
[57] Numbers Chapter 11 and Exodus Chapter 16
[58] Alred, Lord Tennyson, from the poem: In Memoriam A.H.H., knowledgenuts.com
[59] The Bible, NIV, Ruth 4:15

**Chapter 18**
[60] Christian Standard Bible, Ruth 3:1-4, Holman Bible Publishers, 2017
[61] Ruth Chapter 3 content
[62] Biblegateway.com, Proverbs 3:5-6, NKJV

**Chapter 19**
[63] Great book recommendation from this friend is Own Your Brush by Rebeca Flott.
[64] Biblegateway.com, Proverbs 11:14, KJV
[65] The-philosophy.com, Socrates Quotes
[66] You can google free Myers-Briggs tests online and multiple websites offer a free version. It's the same with the Enneagram, though I recommend taking the full 45 minute paid version of that at enneagraminstitute.com for $12
[67] Christian Standard Bible, Exodus 4:10, Holman Bible Publishers, 2017
[68] Christian Standard Bible, Exodus 4:11-12, Holman Bible Publishers, 2017

**Chapter 20**
[69] Christian Standard Bible, Ruth 4:16-17, Holman Bible Publishers, 2017
[70] Biblehub.com, Psalm 37:4, English Standard Version
[71] Dictionary.com, delight defined
[72] Goodreads.com, Andy Stanley Quotes, Principle of the Path

**Chapter 21**
[73] Roosevelt, Theodore, Citizenship in a Republic, speech given at the Sorbonne in Paris, France on April 23, 1910. Page 7 of the 35 page speech.

**Chapter 22**
[74] Biblegateway.com, Hebrews 11:6, NIV
[75] Biblegateway.com, Proverbs 31:25, New Living Translation

**Full Page Quotes**
Goodreads.com, T.D. Jakes quote, pg. 16
Goodreads.com, Mother Teresa Quotes, pg. 25
Brainyquote.com, Saint Augustine Quotes, pg. 35
Sermonquotes.com, Martin Luther, pg. 53
Ruth Chou Simmons, Beholding and Becoming, Harvest House Publishers, 2019, pg. 66
Lysa TerKeurst, Embraced, Thomas Nelson, 2018, pg. 77
Quotes.net, Johann Wolfgang Von Goethe, pg. 86
Goodreads.com, Joanna Gaines, pg. 94
Goodreads.com, Erwin McManus Quotes, pg. 103
Goodreads.com, Erwin McManus Quotes, pg. 112
Instagram.com, @joelosteen, Quote, pg. 122
Goodreads.com, Margaret Feinberg Quotes, pg. 132
Goodgreads.com, Mother Teresa, pg. 142
Goodreads.com, Mother Teresa, A Simple Path, pg. 152
David Green, A Generous Life: 10 Steps to Living a Life Money Can't Buy, pg. 161
Wow4u.com, David Packer quotes, pg. 174
Priscilla Shirer, Awaken: 90 Days with the God who Speaks, pg. 188
Austin Kleon, Show Your Work! Goodreads.com quotes, pg. 190
T.D. Jakes, Follow the Star, Chapter on dreams, pg. 212
Goodreads.com, Mark Batterson, Chasing the Lion, pg. 224
Positivityblog.com, Helen Keller quotes, pg. 236
Jeff Goins, podcast, pg. 246

Made in the USA
Columbia, SC
27 January 2022